The Mid 1950's

FORGOTTEN GLORY

THE STORY OF
CLEVELAND BARONS HOCKEY

WRITTEN BY
GENE KICZEK

DESIGNED & PRODUCED BY: ED CHUKAYNE
BLUE LINE PUBLICATIONS, INC.

Dedications

*This book is dedicated to all of the former Cleveland Barons players who gave so much of themselves to the game of hockey and to the City of Cleveland.
To my mother (Wanda), father (Stan), sister (Kathy), and brother (Steve).
To Lorraine Jenkins and to Becky Jenkins, Cleveland's #1 hockey fan.*

First published in 1994 by:

Blue Line Publications Inc.
22400 Euclid Avenue, Suite 104, Euclid, Ohio 44117
934 East 250th Street, Euclid, Ohio 44132

Copyright © 1994
FORGOTTEN GLORY
The Story of Cleveland Barons Hockey

Written by:
GENE KICZEK

Design & Produced by:
EDWARD CHUKAYNE

Text Document prepared by:
Polly Shilander

Composition Typography by:
TSI Typesetting Service, Inc./
Marty Goren, Franklin Kotnik, Bonita Albrecht

Book manufactured by:
Braun-Brumfield, Inc.
Ann Arbor, Michigan 48106

ISBN - 0-9641772-9-3

Library of Congress Catalog Card No. 94-071651

All rights reserved. No part of this publication may be reproduced, stored in retrieval systems or transmitted in any form by any means, electronic, mechanical, photocopying or otherwise, without first obtaining the written permission of the copyright owner.

Printed in the United States of America

Foreword

It was a proud Saturday night for this cub reporter in February, 1964, when he was dispatched to the Cleveland Arena to cover Cleveland's only winter sports team. There was a simple symmetry to the Cleveland Sports scene at the time. The major stories were the Indians, the Browns and the Barons and each had its season. Remember, Cleveland State University was still Fenn College, good for two paragraphs the morning after a basketball game. The Cavaliers did not come along until 1970. Indoor soccer did not arrive in Cleveland until 1978. For more than 30 years the Barons had the months of January and February all to themselves.

Your reporter was spiffed up in his only suit and his new camel's hair overcoat when he walked in the back door of the Arena, carrying his Hermes portable typewriter. The familiar aroma of the concession stands, a combination of hot dogs and popcorn, greeted his nostrils. Ah, the smells of our youth. But now we were entering a new stage in our life. Yes, we had arrived.

In retrospect, what the Barons enjoyed was a cult following. Members of the cult were geographically compacted into a 50-square-mile area bounded by the cities of Euclid on the east, Lakewood on the west, and Garfield Heights on the south. Within that triangle lived the 7,000 faithful fans who cheered on their winter team almost every Saturday night at the Arena. If you used those three cities as the points of a triangle, you would find that in 1950 most of the people in Greater Cleveland lived within that triangle.

In 1950 those of us at St. Clement's grade school in Lakewood were introduced to hockey by a mysterious benefactor. St. Clement was a wealthy parish in that the mortgage was paid and the roof did not leak, but the individual households did have mortgages, blue collar fathers and more children than bedrooms, so hockey games were extravagances that were not budgeted. By listening to the play-by-play voices of Ron Cook, Gail Egan or Stan Gee on WERE radio, whose 5,000-watt signal reached everyone within the triangle but not much farther, we learned to visualize the sights and sounds of the Arena, the chalk white ice and the dimmed house lights, the sudden roar of the crowd when the Barons made an attack on goal and the groan when it was rejected.

Understandably, it was a sparse mental image until one day tickets began turning up at St. Clement's. We did not know their source. We raised our hand and the nun handed them out. We asked not the reason. In groups of three or four we would take the No. 25 Madison streetcar downtown, where we transferred at Public Square to a Euclid Ave. bus to the Arena at 3701 Euclid. We were now able to fill in the picture, the nooks and crannies of the Arena, the colors and the smells.

Later I was led to believe that Jim Hendy, who ran the team for the investment group that bought it from Al Sutphin, provided free tickets for the children at St. Clement's and the other schools in Lakewood. It was a nice story, since Hendy lived on Clifton Blvd. in Lakewood, but now I am told by Hendy's son, James Peter Hendy, that we were not the chosen few. It was simply one facet of the Barons' marketing program. The theory was that a kid with a free ticket would have a father tagging along.

That's how it began for us. Later we listened to Bill McColgan and Gib Shanley paint the picture on WGAR radio and to Bob Neal when the games moved back to WERE. They tore up the trolley tracks on Madison Ave. and replaced the streetcars with buses, but we continued to ride downtown and make the switch at the Square.

We knew the players through the words of Geoffrey Fisher and Shel Fullerton in the Cleveland News and John Dietrich in The Plain Dealer. When the News folded in 1960 Fisher moved to San Francisco and Fullerton became the public relations director of the Barons. Dietrich retired in 1964.

And so it was that on February 1st I slipped into Dietrich's old folding chair in the Arena press box and began watching sports from a new perspective.

The Barons beat the Rochester Americans, 6-2, before 7,509 and afterward Gail Egan and I adjourned to the Lakewood Village, a bar along the No. 25 bus line on Madison Ave., to celebrate my first night as a hockey journalist. You will notice that we did not stray outside the "triangle".

In early May, 1964, when the Barons clinched the Calder Cup in nine straight playoff victories, we stood two deep at the bar of the Lakewood Village.

By now, Paul Bright owned the Barons and his wife, Sally, owned the Lakewood Village, which makes everything clear. Most of the team was there except for one notable absence. I never saw player-coach Fred Glover drinking with the boys at the Lakewood Village, which probably was a smart policy. It was a warm spring morning when the crowd thinned out at the Lakewood Village. We stumbled out into the light. Behind us players were slumped in booths against the wall and one was stretched out on the bowling machine. The Calder Cup itself was on the back bar, between the cash register and the pickle jar, where it remained until Paul Bright had to give it back the next year.

That was the Barons' last great moment. They were the seventh-best team in all of hockey, not a bad label for a minor league team.

In 1969 Nick Mileti, who had the best of intentions, bought the Barons and the Arena. He brought the "big leagues" to Cleveland but then he took it all away when he built the Coliseum and moved hockey to Richfield in 1974. It is an article of faith that hockey died here when it moved out of the "triangle". The No. 25 does not run to Summit County. The Lakewood Village is still there but nobody has seen a hockey player there for two decades.

By 1976 Mileti owned a big winner and a big loser and both developments surprised him. His Cavaliers basketball team was selling out the Coliseum during the playoffs, "The Miracle of Richfield." Meanwhile, his Crusaders of the World Hockey Association were dying. Late one night at the Theatrical Restaurant downtown on Short Vincent St., Mileti admitted that he guessed wrong.

"I thought hockey would be an instant success and I thought basketball would take much longer," he said.

The Cleveland Crusaders and the World Hockey Association should be mentioned only because they marked the end of pro hockey in the Cleveland market for a dozen years. When Mileti secured a WHA franchise in 1972, he believed that he was moving Cleveland up to the big time. Mileti's Crusaders were supposed to represent "major league" hockey but by the early 1970's nobody knew any longer what "major league" meant.

Because of the advent of the short-lived World Hockey Association, which lasted from 1972-79, and wild expansion by the National Hockey League, "major league" hockey went from six teams in 1967 to 30 teams in 1977. Who was kidding whom? Since most hockey players came from Canada, which had as many people as the state of California, it was ludicrous to pretend that Thunder Bay could suddenly increase its production of hockey players by 500 per cent at the snap of a finger. The public wouldn't buy it.

Let me summarize. In 1964 when the Barons were the seventh-best team in hockey, they were minor league; but it was a stigma Cleveland fans could live with. In 1974 the Crusaders were major league but they were the 20th best team in all of hockey and fans had to drive twice as far and pay twice as much to see them. This was very confusing. It became worse when the Crusaders moved and were replaced by a vagabond NHL team in 1977 – a very bad team which borrowed the name Barons. The story of that gypsy franchise is a compendium of bad memories in three time zones. It began in Oakland as the Golden Seals, came to Cleveland as the Barons in 1977, vamoosed to Minnesota as the North Stars in 1979 and then moved on to Dallas in 1993.

In 1994 hockey came back downtown after a 20-year absence and that completes the circle, or, more accurately, the triangle.

The fate of the sport is now in the hands of a new kid on the block. The future of owner Larry Gordon's International Hockey League Lumberjacks is bright. Entering the 1994-95 season, the 'Jacks will be playing in the brand new Gateway Arena. Interest in hockey is at its highest level in years and a winning team promises to bring fans back downtown where the sport belongs.

But to this reporter, memories will always drift back to the Barons. For 36 years the Aristocrats of Hockey ruled over Cleveland's icy winters. Now, you and I both can relive those magical years in "Forgotten Glory: The Story of Cleveland Barons Hockey". In author Gene Kiczek's new book, we have a rinkside seat to every season of this truly unique team.

So buckle up and travel back in time to a fascinating era in Cleveland's sports history. The ride will surely amaze you.

Dan Coughlin

WJW-TV, Cleveland, Ohio

Acknowledgments

*In the course of this project, a great number of people came into my life. I am fortunate in that many of them have become good friends.
Their assistance, whether direct or indirect, was invaluable.*

Employees at the Euclid Public Library probably thought of charging me rent since I spent so much time in front of their microform machines. It was here that I came to fully appreciate the vast talents of the many beat writers and feature columnists who covered the Barons. Their contributions to hockey in Cleveland cannot be overstated. It is through their written words that the Barons live on forever.

From the Cleveland Plain Dealer: John Dietrich, James E. Doyle, George Peters, Gordon Cobbledick, John Henahan, Bob Dolgan, Tom Place, Dan Coughlin, Russell Schneider, Rich Passan, Bill Nichols, Hal Lebovitz, Chuck Heaton, D'Arcy Egan, and Dennis Lustig.

From the Cleveland Press: Franklin Lewis, Carl Shatto, Isi Newborn, Bob August, Phil Hartman, Bill Scholl, Bob Sudyk, Regis McAuley, Jim Braham, Doug Clarke, Bob Schlesinger, Harry McClelland, and Chuck Day.

From the Cleveland News: Geoffrey Fischer, Shel Fullerton, and Ed Bang.

It is my pleasure to feature the work of four great artists in my book: Dick Dugan and Fred Reinert from the Plain Dealer; Lou Darvas and Bill Roberts from the Press. While my title "Forgotten Glory" refers to the exploits of the Barons, it could also be used for the portraits and caricatures of these rare talents.

Interviews with several former players, executives, and writers were essential in gathering information for this book. The hours they spent talking to me flew by as they shared many of their fond memories. Special thanks to:

Ed "Whitey" Prokop - Whitey, quite frankly, is an untapped Cleveland relic. He is a veritable treasure trove of hockey lore. When he called me his friend, he put an exclamation point on this project.

Bob and Betty Carse for their hospitality and great stories. They stayed in Cleveland after Bob retired from hockey and our city is all the better off to have them.

Tommy Burlington, for taking time out from his home in Owen Sound, Ontario, to take me back through his hockey past.

To writers Russell Schneider and D'Arcy Egan. They showed their appreciation for what I was doing and gave me their support.

Special thanks to Dan Coughlin. I am honored that he wrote the Foreword for this book. His special style is truly one of a kind and a joy to read.

It was through Dan that I met James Peter Hendy. Jim Jr. is the son of Jim Hendy, who ran the Barons from 1949 until his untimely death in 1960. James Peter shared many inside stories of hockey in Cleveland. He also contributed many great pictures and mementoes that appear in this book.

After finishing my text, the hunt for photos and memorabilia was on. To all of these collectors and fans I owe a special debt of gratitude. They trusted me with their prized possessions and helped me make this book what it is. Heartfelt thanks to:

Walt Voysey - Walt is Cleveland's #1 hockey memorabilia dealer and one of this city's great hockey boosters. He has been behind my efforts from the start and has been a great support. Any reader interested in getting a free catalogue of Walt's hockey memorabilia can contact him at: PNW Sports, P. O. Box 26351, Fairview Park, Ohio 44126.

Dennis Turchek - Dennis is one avid collector. He was gracious enough to lend his Barons programs that appear at the beginning of each seasonal chapter. He was always ready to help by offering his photos and mementoes.

Jim Leitch and the Al Sutphin Family - Thanks for the portrait of Al. He would be proud of you all for carrying on his legacy.

Larry Smith - On any given winter night Larry can be found watching hockey at Whitey Prokop's house. A former engineer at the Arena, Larry provided me with many great pictures and documents.

Dick Dugan - Once again, thanks to this great artist. In addition to his fine drawings, Dick provided many super photos. His imprint on this book is a true bonus.

Kay Horiba - Kay was a barber at the Belmont Hotel across from the Arena. He became close friends with many of the players - a true Superfan.

Bill Hudec - Bill is a unique individual. One of the more vocal fans during the 1950's as a youth, Bill bled Baron blue and white. He is now an accomplished poet in addition to being one of Bob Feller's greatest fans.

Once again, thanks to Whitey Prokop and Bobby Carse for the photos they supplied.

Photographs also appear from the collections of the Cleveland Public Library Main Branch and the Cleveland State University Archives.

I am especially grateful to Bill Becker, archivist at Cleveland State. He was instrumental in my receiving the best photos that C.S.U. had from their Cleveland Press collection.

Whenever possible, the name of the photographer is mentioned under each picture. However, not all original photos and copies listed the photographer's name; so my hands were sometimes tied. My apologies to anyone whose work was not acknowledged.

Marge and Nick Kekic and Dudley Humphrey supplied the wonderful photos of the Elysium.

Bud Pecnik for lists of Cleveland area ice rinks.

Jim Mileti of the Cleveland Lumberjacks supplied the team photo of the 1970-71 Barons as well as loads of enthusiasm.

Michelle Fuller of Morse Graphic Art Supply on Euclid Avenue was an immense help by photocopying numerous pictures and documents.

Terry Pluto of the Akron Beacon Journal, John Grabowski of the Western Reserve Historical Society, David Gray of David Gray and Co. Publishing, Bill Switaj Sr. and author James Toman supplied important leads in gathering information for this project.

Franklin Kotnik, Bonita Albrecht and Marty Goren of Typesetting Service, Inc. provided all of the superior typography seen in this book.

Carolyn Chukayne and Catherine Lehman supplied various hockey items and support in the areas of production, promotion, and merchandising.

Lorraine and Becky Jenkins, Robert Niccum, John and Laura Boris, Catherine Lehman Kirbish, and Charles and Shelly Lehman were also ready to lend a hand and help out whenever needed, which was often.

Special thanks to Editor David Hall of the Cleveland Plain Dealer for granting permission to use various quotes and artwork seen in this book.

Mort Tucker Photography, Inc. is always ready to produce yet another great Cleveland Sports memorabilia montage. Some of which grace the inside and back covers. Many thanks to Mort and Brian Misch.

No list of acknowledgments for this book would be complete without the names of two irreplaceable individuals - Ed Chukayne and Polly Shilander.

When storm clouds were rising and efforts to publish this book were in limbo, Ed Chukayne came to the forefront. He put his full backing into this project where it counted most. His artistic talents are second to none and I cannot thank him enough for his great designing of this book. His creative and merchandising efforts were instrumental to the success of this project. I was indeed fortunate that he came on board.

From the very beginning, Polly Shilander was a great pillar of support. She became interested in my efforts through her son, and my friend, Dave. Polly is a former teacher and was administrative assistant to Cuyahoga County Auditor Tim McCormack before her recent retirement. She helped make my version of the English language readable and put my manuscript on to computer disc.

Whenever I needed a favor or another bit of typing done, this extraordinary lady was always there to help. She spent countless hours helping me with this book and truly was my angel. I could go on, and every kudo would be deserved. Let me end by saying from the bottom of my heart, THANK YOU, POLLY!

While discussing hockey with me, Dennis Turchek stated that "...the Barons had such a great history, and now you are part of it." This gave me a special feeling.

To everyone who helped in the making of this book, you are now part of Cleveland Barons history. Consider yourselves special.

Gene Kiczek

Table of Contents

	Page
PROLOGUE	**8**
I. The Al Sutphin Era: Glory Years	
Before There Were Barons	**11**
Al Sutphin and The Cleveland Arena	**15**
1937-38 Season	23
1938-39 Season	34
1939-40 Season	42
1940-41 Season	47
1941-42 Season	58
1942-43 Season	64
1943-44 Season	71
1944-45 Season	78
1945-46 Season	85
1946-47 Season	93
1947-48 Season	100
1948-49 Season	111
Farewell to the Iceman – Hello, Jim Hendy	**118**
II. The Jim Hendy Era: Continued Success	
1949-50 Season	121
1950-51 Season	130
1951-52 Season	139
The NHL Strikes Back	**145**
1952-53 Season	148
1953-54 Season	157
1954-55 Season	162
1955-56 Season	168
1956-57 Season	173
1957-58 Season	180
1958-59 Season	187
1959-60 Season	196
1960-61 Season	202
III. Struggles of the 1960's	
1961-62 Season	208
1962-63 Season	216
1963-64 Season	225
1964-65 Season	234
1965-66 Season	239
1966-67 Season	250
1967-68 Season	259
IV. The Nick Mileti Era: Rocky Road and Revival	
1968-69 Season	267
1969-70 Season	273
1970-71 Season	275
1971-72 Season	286
1972-73 Season	293
EPILOGUE	**296**

Prologue

It was a cool, cloudy night in March of 1977 when I drove to downtown Cleveland to say goodbye to an old friend, The Cleveland Arena. The great Ice Palace at 3715 Euclid Avenue was being torn down, just shy of its 40th birthday.

The Arena was home to Cleveland's legendary hockey team, The Barons. From 1937 to 1973, the Aristocrats of Hockey thrilled millions of ice fans, and I was lucky enough to be one of them.

I saw my first hockey game on February 7, 1965, and it was love at first sight. It mattered not that Cleveland was beaten by Providence, 3-2. I was awed by the beauty of this fascinating game. The speed. The grace. The action. The violence. It was all there, rolled into one beautiful symphony on ice.

I was immediately hooked. This thirteen-year old took two C.T.S. buses to and from each Saturday night game for the rest of the season. I could not get enough hockey. Two years later, I got a job at the Arena as a popcorn vendor. I didn't make much money, but who cared. I was now able to see every game.

From that point on, I rarely missed a Barons' home game. I was a bonafide hockey nut and couldn't be happier. I probably spent more time at the Cleveland Arena than anywhere else. To me, the Arena was a magical place. Time seemed to stand still as the Barons' blades flashed across the frozen ice. Back then, everything seemed so right.

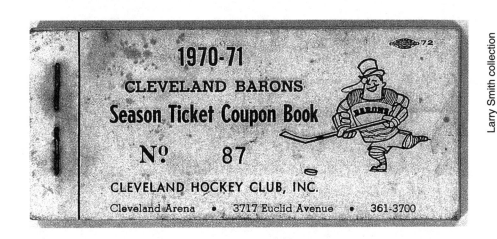

Larry Smith collection

But in March of 1977, my heart sank when I pulled into the Arena parking lot. Only half of Al Sutphin's great sports edifice remained standing — the South and West ends.

I waded through the fallen debris and climbed the stairs of Section 33. All of the seats had been taken out, so I took a seat on the steps. What a strange and eerie feeling came over me. It was as if I was suspended in time as I gazed around at what was left of my home away from home. What a great building it was. What memories it held.

As I looked out at the floor where once shined a shimmering coat of ice, I let my imagination run wild. I could feel, and almost see, the great Baron stars of the past skating where they once were kings — Moe Roberts, Les Cunningham, Phil Hergesheimer, Tommy Burlington, Bobby Carse, Johnny Bower, Eddie Olson, Fred Thurier, Fred Glover, and so many, many more.

But they were all forgotten now...buried in the dusty, cobweb memories of long ago. Heroes of another time. They deserved so much more than to be forgotten. Forgotten names...forgotten games...forgotten glory...Until now...

The Al Sutphin Era:

GLORY YEARS

BEFORE THERE WERE BARONS

The roots of organized hockey in Cleveland date back to November, 1907, when Harry Humphrey built the Elysium at East 107th and Euclid Avenue. This was the same Harry Humphrey who owned the famous Euclid Beach Amusement Park.

The Elysium was Cleveland's first indoor ice arena. Seating capacity was a little more than 2,000, although upwards of 4,000 were jammed in on occasion.

Hockey was played in Cleveland on a casual basis until 1920, with the formation of The Cleveland Blues. The Blues played in the United States Hockey League, which included teams in Minneapolis, Eveleth, Pittsburgh, Duluth, and St. Paul.

Colorful players, such as Joe Debernardi, Moose Jamieson, and Cody Winters, formed the backbone of the team along with the great Nels Stewart.

The Elysium was the first home to professional hockey in Cleveland.
Cleveland State University archives and Marge Kekic collections.

Humphrey needed a star, and Stewart was his man. He induced Nels to play in Cleveland by giving him not only a salary but also free rent and the cigarette, cigar, and tobacco concessions at Euclid Beach Park. It was said that Stewart made $10,000 a year in Cleveland, an astronomical amount for the time.

In 1925, Stewart joined the Montreal Maroons of the NHL. Other stars followed, and the Blues ceased operation.

There was no hockey in Cleveland until 1929. That is when Harry (Hap) Holmes came to town. Holmes arrived in Cleveland unknown and unannounced.

He literally walked into city newspaper offices, saying he was moving his Hamilton, Ontario franchise in the International League to Cleveland and could use some publicity.

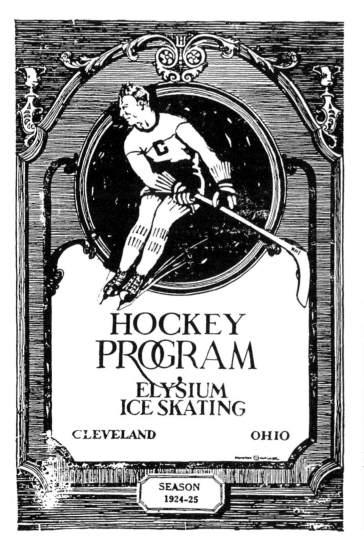

Marge Kekic collection.

A former goaltender himself, Hap Holmes lived for the game of hockey.

He was a straightforward and plain-spoken man filled with enthusiasm for the game he loved.

The Great Depression was raging, but Holmes honestly believed that hockey was the tonic to lift the town's spirit. Most people disagreed. They doubted that pro hockey could succeed in such poor economic times. But Holmes persevered with great determination and an effervescent smile.

He named the team the Indians, after the baseball club. On November 16, 1929, the Indians played the first professional hockey game in Cleveland against the London Tecumsehs. Holmes was the man of the hour.

Garbed in alternating red, white, and green-striped uniforms, the hockey Indians became the talk of the town.

Crowds jammed the Elysium and the team went on to win the International League championship in its first season.

The Indians made the playoffs the next season but were quickly defeated.

Marge Kekic collection.

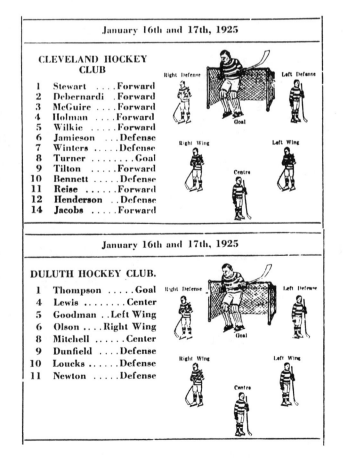

Then the Great Depression hit Hap Holmes with its true force. His top financial backer, Teddy Oke, went broke.

The bank that held the hockey Indians' money closed. Operating capital was lost.

People quit going to the Elysium because they couldn't afford hockey games and the team was finishing in last place for three consecutive seasons.

The players' enthusiasm was at a low ebb. Who could blame them? They never knew if or when they would be paid. Often they would line up after a game hoping to draw some pay from the night's game receipts. The team was operating on a game-to-game basis. Somehow, Hap Holmes called upon his great spirit to carry on. Creditors were closing in, but his love for the game of hockey never waned. He needed a savior. One was right around the corner.

International Hockey League

This is to Certify that the _Harry Holmes_ ~~Corporation~~ owning and operating a Professional Hockey Club in the City of _Cleveland_ in the ~~Province~~/State of _Ohio_ having duly complied with all the conditions pertaining to membership in the International Hockey League, this Certificate evidences the right of said _Harry Holmes_ to membership and franchise in said International Hockey League under the provision of its constitution, subject to all the terms, conditions and requirements of the constitution. This membership may be transferred and assigned in accordance with the terms and conditions of the constitution of the International Hockey League.

International Hockey League

Signed _Chas. F. King_, President.

James Peter Hendy collection.

Al Sutphin and The CLEVELAND ARENA

> For the consideration of Seventeen Hundred ($1700.00) Dollars, I herewith sell and assign to Al. Sutphin all my right, title and interest to the within franchise and represent said franchise as being the exclusive franchise for Professional Hockey in the City of Cleveland, including the franchise of the National, International Hockey leagues and all other leagues playing professional hockey. The within assignment carries with it whatever obligation by way of tax or assessment may be due thereon to the International Hockey League.
>
> Witness:
> *Ray [Miller]*
> *Earl F. [Pegans]*
>
> *Harry Holmes*
>
> Cleveland, Ohio – November 8, 1934.
>
> For a valuable consideration I hereby sell, assign all my right, title and interest to the within franchise to the Cleveland Hockey Club Inc. said assignment carries with it all obligations which may be due by way of tax or assessment of the International Hockey League.
>
> Witness:
> *Ray [Miller]*
> *Earl F. [Pegans]*
>
> *Albert C. Sutphin*
>
> 186856
>
> The assignment is accepted Nov 8 1934
> The Cleveland Hockey Club Inc.
> *Albert C. Sutphin* Pres.
> *Ray [Miller]* Secretary

James Peter Hendy collection.

Harry (Hap) Holmes went looking for a buyer. Through his many friends, in particular Franklin (Whitey) Lewis, Sports Editor of The Cleveland Press, Holmes was introduced to Albert C. Sutphin, Vice President of the Braden-Sutphin Ink Co.

After a series of lengthy negotiations, Al Sutphin purchased the Cleveland Indians hockey team from Hap Holmes on October 26, 1934. Sutphin became President and Treasurer, while Holmes was retained as Vice President and Coach.

Al Sutphin and Alex (Bud) Cook. Cook was the first player Al purchased as owner of the Falcons. Cleveland Public Library collection.

Al's first order of business was to change the name of the club to the Falcons in order to avoid conflict in names with the baseball club.

Al Sutphin was a self-made man. His rise to the top of the Braden-Sutphin Ink Co. was swift and sudden.

The story goes that on his way home, after being sent home from Central High School after a disagreement with the principal, Sutphin met up with James Braden. Braden was a good friend of Al's father and president of his own ink company.

Braden felt sorry for young Al and offered him a job in his ink shop at $5.00 per week. The rest is history. By the time he was twenty-five years old, Sutphin was in charge of the plant.

Braden was sold on the smooth-talking, hard-working young man. He later became a partner and made a fortune in the ink business.

Al Sutphin had always been a sports enthusiast. He played goalie on the Central High hockey team. Later he was appointed boxing commissioner of Cleveland in 1931-32 by his close friend and Mayor of Cleveland Ray T. Miller. He even promoted two fights in 1933.

Sutphin, a tireless worker, threw his entire being into making hockey a success in Cleveland.

Basically a wild-eyed sports nut, Al became an ardent student of the game. He worked tirelessly to become an astute judge of talent. But progress was slow.

His first two teams made the playoffs but were bounced out quickly in two straight games.

In 1936, four teams from the International League, including Cleveland, merged with four teams from the Canadian-American Hockey League. The league was called the International-American League. It operated under this name until the 1939-40 season when it officially became the American Hockey League.

After various player deals, Sutphin had high hopes for the 1936-37 season. But the Falcons started the season with 3 wins, 15 defeats, and 6 ties. They finished last by 13 points.

Al was greatly disappointed; but through all this mess, he never lost sight of his ultimate vision. He had dreams of a great new sports palace for the City of Cleveland.

People thought he was nuts. The country was in the aftermath of its worst depression, and this man thought he could build a huge new hockey arena. How could he possibly get the money?

Groundbreaking ceremonies for the Cleveland Arena on May 16, 1937.
L to R: Fred Potts (Team Secretary), Al Sutphin, Mrs. Helen Braden, Harry (Hap) Holmes.
The Arena became a showplace for Al Sutphin. He was forever visible and would mingle with the crowd and greet fans as they entered the Arena. Al was a promotional genius and came up with the bold idea of giving away a new automobile at every home game during the 1939-40 season.
Cleveland State University archives.

They didn't know Al Sutphin. To the man who always wore a bright red tie, no obstacle was insurmountable.

Sutphin made a vast number of influential friends through his ink company. Together with his great ally Carl F. Lezius, the two miracle-workers came up with the money to build a great new sports arena.

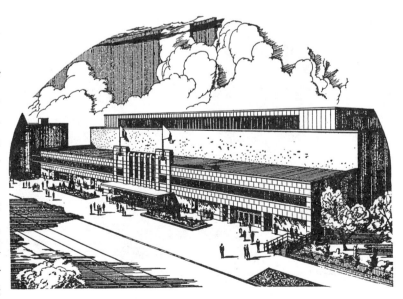

Patterned somewhat after the famous Maple Leaf Gardens in Toronto, ground was broken for the Cleveland Arena on May 16, 1937. Cost was estimated at approximately $1,500,000. To raise this much money during the Depression was unbelievable.

NUMBER A 447

AMOUNT $100

STATE OF OHIO

CLEVELAND HOCKEY CLUB, INC.

FIFTEEN YEAR FOUR PERCENT DEBENTURE BOND

CLEVELAND HOCKEY CLUB, INC., a corporation organized under the laws of the State of Ohio, hereinafter sometimes called the Company, for value received, hereby promises to pay to the registered holder of this bond

ONE HUNDRED DOLLARS

in lawful money of the United States on the first day of July, 1952, unless before that time this bond shall be redeemed, and until said ... 1937, at the rate of four percent per annum in lawful money of the ... January and the first day of July in each year. Such interest to ... day of June and the fifteenth day of December, respectively, of said ... check mailed to such holder at his most recent address appearing ... in the City of Cleveland, Ohio, upon surrender hereof.

...ded automatically to meet the provisions of the amendment to the ...ke tenor and effect, differing only as to the definitive numbers and bonds of said issue which may be outstanding at any time shall 00.00 are designated by the letter "A" and numbered consecutively y the letter "B" and numbered consecutively from 1 upward; those numbered consecutively from 1 upward; those of the denomination ely from 1 upward. All of the said debenture bonds shall be regis- rsed on the respective debenture bonds. Debenture bonds may be er with a written instrument of transfer in form approved by the bond shall be transferred upon the registry and such transfer shall t-nsfers may likewise be made The company agrees that until of all other ... nture bonds this issue, ... rovision ther - d delivered to the company, it will not pay in money or prope..y at any time hereafter constituted, but this agreement shall in no pon its capital stock as now constituted or upon any class of its ock either as now constituted or as may hereafter be constituted.

ncel all or any part of the debenture bonds at any time outstanding, nt of the principal and accrued interest. If at any time less than ed, they shall be chosen by the company by lot and the right of the shall not be deemed exhausted by one or more uses of such rights. s first give written notice to the registered holder thereof, or if less to the registered holders of the bonds chosen for redemption directed l registration books, which notice shall state that the company will r redemption at the price above specified, naming such price, upon ..., or such other place as may be designated in such notice. Such strument signed by the holder of any debenture bond so chosen for

manner aforesaid, if the holder or holders of any debenture bonds ne and place in said notice specified, such debenture bonds as may r redemption, but the company upon such date shall deposit in a so called for redemption, with interest to date specified for redemp- ayment of any such debenture bond upon subsequent presentation

ture bond or upon any agreement contained herein, and the holder right of action shall accrue upon this debenture bond or upon any bond, or second, when and if any installment of interest as pro- h latter event any right of action thereon, either in law or in equity, rears, and in no event before maturity hereof shall any right based nt for interest give rise to any other action in law or in equity, but im upon said debenture bond and for any interest due and unpaid required by law.

bond is limited by a provision in the amendment to the Articles ne that a certain mortgage note executed and delivered by the cor- until the establishment of a reserve of not less than $65,000.00, as any time that said reserve is impaired, and the payment of the amendment to the Articles of Incorporation, until said mortgage installment or of the principal amount of this debenture bond at r provisions, shall not constitute a default hereunder, but the time

interest on this debenture bond against any incorporator, share- r directly or through the company, by virtue of any statute or con- rwise whatsoever, any and all liability of any of such being hereby l have become authenticated by the execution by the treasurer of the

ub, Inc., has caused these presents to be signed by its President of July, 1937.

CLEVELAND HOCKEY CLUB, INC.

OFFICERS and EXECUTIVE BOARD
CLEVELAND HOCKEY, INC.

ELLIS RYAN
Vice President

AL SUTPHIN
President

CARL F. LEZIUS
General Manager

J. FRED POTTS
Secretary

T. J. CONWAY
Treasurer

O. M. GARBER
Ashland

J. A. GIDEON

THE ARENA
Home of
Cleveland Barons

General Offices
3700 EUCLID AVE.
ENdicott 3700

One of Al Sutphin's main means of financing the building of the Arena was the sale of debenture bonds shown at left and on opposite page. Larry Smith collection.

DIRECTORS—CLEVELAND HOCKEY, INC.

WILLIAM GUNDELFINGER

ELLWOOD FISHER

PAUL HOYNES

C. E. SUTPHIN

DON ROBINSON

FRANK CONAT

G. L. ERIKSON

FRANZ WARNER

FRED DANNER
Akron

A. M. MILLER
Columbus

CLIFFORD R. WRIGHT
Cincinnati

The people of Cleveland were captivated by the prospect of this great new edifice being built in their city. Hundreds of people lined the building site at 3715 Euclid Avenue to watch its progress.

The building that would hold 9,739 seats would have its official opening on November 11, 1937. The first attraction would be a performance of The Ice Follies.

It was a great night for Al Sutphin. The over 8,000 people in attendance were totally in awe. They beamed with pride in the red, white, and blue sports palace. In its time, the Arena was as great as it got.

Fans gave a standing ovation during opening ceremonies when Mayor Harold H. Burton praised the "fighting heart of Al Sutphin." Al then gave an emotional speech of his own. It was a night he would never forget.

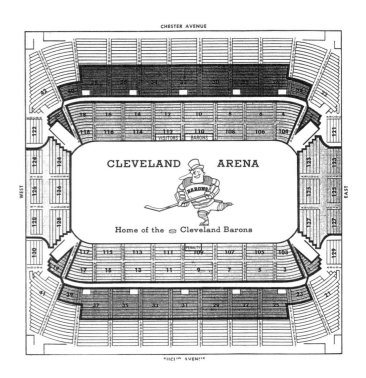

Cleveland Arena Seating Chart
Walt Voysey collection.

The Cleveland Arena
Cleveland Public Library collection.

THE ARENA

Facts and Figures

THE ARENA is regarded by many competent observers as one of the finest buildings of its type on the continent. It was designed by the architects' firm of Warner and Mitchell and constructed by Gillmore, Carmichael and Olson at a cost of more than $1,100,000.

The history of the building itself is a thrilling story of speed and efficiency. Ground was broken on May 8, 1937. The building was opened to the public exactly six months and two days later, Nov. 10, 1937.

The overall dimensions of the building are 265 by 329 feet. The north lobby in which the Pilsner Bavarian Village is situated is 128 by 46 feet. The south lobby which contains so many attractive advertising displays is 56 by 54 feet.

You will notice that the ice surface is somewhat below ground level. This was done to lessen construction costs; there is no other Arena in the country so constructed.

In order to achieve this bowl effect it was necessary to excavate no fewer than 35,000 cubic yards of soil.

Those four enormous roof trusses which give the greatest number of spectators an unobstructed view of the action each weigh 75 tons and are 204 feet long. Raising them into place was a delicate job since their tremendous weight placed a terrific strain on the cranes used to lift them. Heavy supporting cables were buried deep into the ground during the process, and it was necessary to keep close watch on each of the cables lest they snap under the tremendous pressure.

The trusses represent only a small fraction of the 1200 tons of structural steel used in the Arena.

The Arena walls contain 700,000 bricks—you are invited to count them if you wish—weighing 2,500 tons. The outer walls are insulated with 70,000 Haydite units weighing 500 tons.

Imbedded in the cement floor of the Arena are more than 50,000 feet, 9.7 miles of 1¼-inch pipe in addition to a four-inch layer of rock cork, a layer of asbestos paper and a layer of sheet zinc. The pipe of course is a part of the refrigeration unit installed by M. R. Carpenter.

With this system it is possible to lay a new sheet of ice half an inch thick in approximately 16 hours.

Altogether 14,000 barrels of cement were used in the building.

The ice surface is 84 by 195 feet.

The seating capacity of The Arena for hockey is 9,847. The seats are divided as follows: 2,007 red or box seats, 1,532 white seats, 3,720 blue seats, and 2,588 bleacher seats. For boxing an additional 2,812 seats will be placed on the floor, making a total of 12,659 seats.

Inside view of the Cleveland Arena. 1942-43 Program.

Cleveland State University archives.

An inside look at the Arena.
Cleveland State University archives.

During the summer of 1937, in anticipation of this new hockey home, a newspaper contest was held to rename the team. The name Barons was chosen. It symbolized the aristocrats of hockey.

So Al Sutphin had his Arena with a newly named hockey team that finished in last place the previous season. No way would he stand for a second-rate team in this first-class facility. But never in his wildest dreams could he ever imagine the unbelievable season that was about to unfold.

1937-38 SEASON

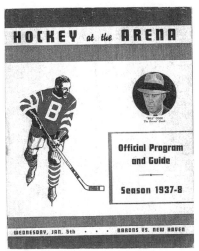

The Barons needed a leader. Al Sutphin was looking for a new coach to head his team out of the doldrums.

Since getting into hockey, Al had become good friends with Lester Patrick, Manager of the New York Rangers of the NHL. After listening to what Sutphin was looking for in a coach, Patrick, without hesitation, recommended his star player and assistant coach, Bill Cook.

Captain Bill Cook is presented the Stanley Cup by NHL President Frank Calder after New York defeated Toronto three games to one in 1933. Cook's goal in overtime gave the Rangers a 1-0 victory in Game Four at Toronto. On Bill's right is his brother, Fred (Bun). Both Cooks would later coach the Barons. On Bun's right is Frank Boucher. This trio composed one of the greatest lines in the history of hockey. James Peter Hendy collection. Photo by Bobbitt.

Born on October 9, 1896 in Brantford, Ontario, Cook went on to become the greatest right wing in hockey during his 11 years with the Rangers. Playing on a line with his brother, Bun (who would later succeed Bill as coach of the Barons) on left wing, and Frank Boucher at center, Bill twice led his league in scoring. Although he didn't begin playing in the NHL until he was almost 30, Bill made up for lost time and held the respect of everyone connected with the game.

Sutphin was completely sold on the man. During the summer of 1937, Bill Cook was named Coach of the Barons. Sutphin was further amazed when Bill said he never signed contracts. He believed a man's word was his bond and would have it no other way. His agreement was sealed with a handshake. An honest man, this Bill Cook.

The first order of business for Sutphin and Cook was to find talent to bolster the team. Holdovers from the 1936-37 team were Moe Roberts in goal; Freddie (The Bull) Robertson, Joe Bretto, and Harry (Yip) Foster on defense; and forwards Bill Cunningham, Walter Brenneman, Emory Hanson, Earl Bartholome, Bud Cook and Earl Roche.

Six important additions to the Barons were made during the off-season. Lorne Duguid and James (Peggy) O'Neil were purchased from the Boston Bruins. Phil Hergesheimer was purchased from Minneapolis. Les Cunningham, who started the previous year in Cleveland but was sent up to the New York Americans, was brought back. These four forwards would be the backbone of the team's offense. Lastly, Art Berlet was obtained from Buffalo to shore up the defense, along with Jean Baptiste Pusie.

Bill Cook – First Coach of the Cleveland Barons. Cleveland Public Library collection – Photo by Glen Zahn.

After a grueling three-week training camp in Winnipeg, Canada, Bill Cook and his Barons were ready to begin the 48-game 1937-38 season in the International-American League. The circuit consisted of 7 teams in two divisions. In the East were the Philadelphia Ramblers, Springfield Indians, Providence Reds, and New Haven Eagles. In the West were the Cleveland Barons, the Syracuse Stars, and Pittsburgh Hornets. Buffalo was scheduled to be in the West division, but a snowstorm destroyed their arena during the previous season. They would return in 1940.

The Barons opened the season with a four-game East Coast road trip.

On November 14, 1937, the Barons defeated the Providence Reds 2-0 on goals by Les Cunningham and Peggy O'Neil. The game was especially significant in that it was the first win ever by the Cleveland club as the Barons.

Coming home with a 1-1-2 record, the club was looking forward to a November 17th exhibition game against the New York Rangers. This would be the first hockey game ever played at The Cleveland Arena.

Over 6,000 fans showed up to see the Barons lose a hard fought game to the Rangers, 4-3. Star of the game was Les Cunningham, who scored all 3 Cleveland goals. Les felt he had something to prove. Although happy to be with Cleveland, he felt the

New York Americans made a mistake by not keeping him after the previous season. During the Ranger game, Les got into numerous scraps to go along with his 3 goals. Although he would later become one of the League's cleanest players, Cunningham was a hellraiser early in his career. On this night his point was made.

After 3 straight ties on Arena ice, the local fans began to have their doubts about this team. They seemed to be able to bring the puck up the ice in fine shape, but they just could not seem to put it in the net. Despite their lack of scoring, one thing was truly evident. This club would not back down to anyone. The games were fast and furious and filled with numerous roughhouse antics. But Cleveland fans were hungry for victory.

The first home victory came on December 4th in a 3-1 victory over Providence. When the Barons came back and defeated the Stars in Syracuse the next afternoon, also 3-1, in a bloody affair, the team found itself only one point out of first place. This set up a battle for first place against the Hornets in Pittsburgh on December 8th. The game ended in a 2-2 tie to stretch the Barons' unbeaten streak to six games and gave notice to their fans that the team indeed was beginning to gel.

Cleveland fans adored the Barons. Here is a typical sellout crowd during the Al Sutphin era. Cleveland State University archives.

On December 12, 1937, Cleveland was firmly planted on the map as a hockey-mad city. 10,003 fans jammed their way into the Arena to see the Barons defeat the Philadelphia Ramblers 2-1. This game was significant in two distinct ways. First of all was the huge crowd. By far the biggest throng to witness a hockey game in Cleveland, it put the city on a level of fan interest seen only heretofore in the NHL.

Secondly, this was the first time the Barons had defeated Philadelphia in two years. The Ramblers were the most feared team in the League. When Bud Cook scored on a pass from Earl Barthelome at 6:05 of the 3rd period, the fans went wild. An old jinx had been slayed.

As the season headed into the new year, the biggest story was how the fans had taken to the team. When Al Sutphin was making plans for his new arena, he hoped the Barons would draw at least 5,000 per game. Attendance far exceeded that figure. After 8 home games (1/3 of the season), the team had drawn 68,850 fans.

There were two main reasons for the fan hysteria. One was the new arena. Every game was a chance to show off the new ice palace. The building had become the crown jewel for the entertainment-seeking public.

More importantly was the team itself. It never stopped battling. Up and down the lineup were exciting and colorful players.

The fans especially had taken to Peggy O'Neil and Lorne Duguid.

O'Neil was the scrapper. His hard, fierce play made him immensely popular. Although a small player of 160 lbs., Peg always seemed to take on the biggest players on opposing teams. He was also an expert stickhandler and goal scorer. Coach Cook would always send O'Neil on the ice to stir things up whenever the team would appear flat.

Duguid was leading the team in scoring. The handsome and debonair icer was especially popular with female fans. He was a class act on the ice but never would back off when the going got rough.

January 6th and 9th saw goalie Moe Roberts rack up back-to-back shutouts to extend the Barons' unbeaten streak to 10 at the Arena.

The January 6th game, a 2-0 triumph over New Haven, saw Bud Cook score the winning goal on a 60-foot slapshot past Eagle goalie Paul Gauthier. Cook, Coach Bill's brother, was the first player purchased by Al Sutphin in 1934. Although never a huge scorer, he had a knack for coming through time and again in the clutch.

The 1-0 triumph over Providence on January 9th was a tribute to goalie Roberts. This may have been his greatest game in his 5 years to date in Cleveland. After a goal by Lorne Duguid at 1:45 of the first period, the Reds were relentless in their pressure to tie the game. But Moe seemed to be everywhere at once. Leaping and sprawling, side to side, the Reds were totally frustrated.

After Yip Foster deliberately held the puck during a goal mouth scramble, Roberts stopped Bud Jarvis on a penalty shot, and the 9,300 in attendance went wild. The victory left the Barons 1 point behind Pittsburgh.

Moe Roberts was the captain and backbone of this team. He had been tending goal in Cleveland with the Indians, Falcons, and now Barons since November, 1933. Now 29 years old, he was just reaching his peak.

When Moe registered his fourth shutout of the season in a 2-0 win over Syracuse on January 30th, the undefeated streak at home reached 13 games. Even more remarkable was that Moe had only given up 12 goals in those 13 games.

Barons sparkplug James (Peggy) O'Neil. Cleveland Public Library collection. Cleveland News photo by Perry Cragg.

New Haven goalie Paul Gauthier makes a sliding save against Cleveland's Bud Cook (R). Note cap worn by Goalie Gauthier. Cleveland State University archives – Photo by Herman Seid.

Close battles were common in hockey's early days. The game itself was much more defensively orientated than it is today. The red line, which would open up the game considerably, did not come into existence until 1943. The ice was divided into 3 zones by 2 blue lines: offensive, neutral, and defensive.

The main difference from the modern game was that the puck had to be stickhandled over each line. There was no dumping the puck in and chasing it; no passing from one zone to another. This made stickhandling an art and the short passing and weaving game a necessity.

Players had to work extremely hard to get the puck out of their defensive end and into the attacking zone. They were usually pounded as they crossed each line. This tighter checking produced lower scores.

To Cleveland's credit, they seemed to be winning most of the close games. A record of 15-8-6 was carried into February. Their first place lead over Pittsburgh was now 4 points.

What was the secret for this new-found success? Al Sutphin and all of his players agreed that the lion's share of the credit should go to Coach Bill Cook. He was proving that a great ex-player could, indeed, become a great coach.

He never expected his players to play at the level that he once played. None of them could. He just insisted that they do the best job of which they were capable. He could yell, shout, and curse with the best of them, but he never expected miracles.

Still, all of the players held over from the 1936 last-place team were now playing the best hockey of their careers. Bill knew how to bring out the best in his team.

The fans and the media had been clammering all season long for Cook to put on his skates one more time. But Bill had resisted the temptation. He was finally talked into playing one more game by Al Sutphin.

The fact that the Barons won the game 5-4 over New Haven on February 2nd took a back seat to Cook's debut as a Cleveland player. He failed to score but clearly took a back seat to no one at the age of 41.

One play symbolized the total spirit of Cook and the Barons. Frank Beisler, a defenseman with the Eagles, tried to embarrass Cook by knocking him down when he wasn't looking. Frank soon found out he was messing with the wrong man.

A short time later, Beisler and Cook ran into each other in the corner. Up went Bill's elbow, and down went Frank Beisler. He was helped from the ice with a mouth full of loose teeth and a head wound that required 3 stitches. An eye for an eye. This was the team's philosophy. They followed the lead of their coach. Never give in and never give up.

On February 9th, Cleveland stretched its lead over Pittsburgh to 6 points by defeating the Hornets 2-1 before a monster crowd of 10,677 at the Arena. This made it 16 straight games without defeat at home – 3 ties to open the home season and 13 straight wins. Phil Hergesheimer, the Barons' flashy rookie, scored first at 10:09 of the first period. After the Hornets tied the score, Lorne Duguid once again became the hero by scoring past Pitt goalie Alphie Moore at :50 of the second period.

Still, there was never a dull moment as Pittsburgh sent wave after wave of attacks on Cleveland's goal. But Moe Roberts held on as the crowd was held breathless. Coach Cook was forced into action once again due to an injury of defenseman Art Berlet. He thought this would be his last game. He had no idea how wrong he was.

In their very next game on February 11th, the Barons wove their magic again. Earl Bartholome scored at 1:48 of a ten-minute overtime period to extend the home unbeaten streak to 17 games by defeating the vaunted Philly Ramblers 2-1 before 10,472 fans. These last-second one-goal victories were stunning. The fans were on the edge of their seats game after game, and the good guys kept coming through in unbelievable fashion. This win gave Cleveland an 8-point lead over Pittsburgh and Syracuse as they headed East on a four-game trip. They would make the trip without goalie Moe Roberts, who twisted his knee in the Philadelphia game.

Bill Cook as a player during his first season as Coach of the Barons. Cleveland Public Library collection – Cleveland News photo by Perry Cragg.

In hockey's early years, teams would carry only one goaltender on the roster. If a goalie was hurt and could not finish the game, a teammate would have to fill in. For longer term emergencies, the league had a spare goalie who could be "drafted" by any team to fill a short-term need. Thus, the Barons used Paddy Byrne to fill in for Moe while his knee mended.

In Byrne's first game at New Haven, the teams battled to a 5-5 tie. Battle is the right word. Prior to Phil Hergesheimer finally tieing the score midway through the third period, the 3,000 fans were treated to an all-out war.

Les Cunningham and Glen Brydsen of the Eagles were given 5-minute penalties for a fight that touched off a bench-clearing brawl. After another fight, Baron defenseman Jean Baptiste Pusie climbed into the stands to chase a heckler.

Pusie was another player that Cleveland fans loved. They never knew what to expect from him. After one road trip, he returned with a full beard. For a later game he was clean-shaven and bald. If given a plaid shirt, blue jeans, lumberjack boots, and an ax instead of a hockey stick, the Frenchman would become a spitting image of Paul Bunyan.

Since there was no screen along the sideboards at the Arena (only behind the goal), Pusie would shake hands with fans and kiss ladies' hands after goals. The fans loved his act. But "The Great Pusie", as he was called, could play some hard-nosed hockey when needed. Coming back from a broken leg suffered in a car accident, Pusie was a mainstay on defense for the Barons along with Art Berlet, Joe Bretto, Freddie Robertson, and Yip Foster.

Pusie only spent one year in Cleveland. Unfortunately, in later years, fooling around on the ice began to cost his teams games. When his limited skills began to decline, teammates tired of his act and the "Clown Prince of Hockey" was forced to retire.

The Barons returned home, and on February 27th stretched their unbeaten string on Arena ice to eighteen with another hard-to-believe ending.

It looked like the streak was over as Springfield held a hard-fought 2-1 lead into the game's last minute. But during a wild scramble in front of the net, Cleveland's super rookie Phil Hergesheimer somehow poked the puck past Indian goalie Benny Grant with 1 second left in regulation time. The 7,158 fans brought the house down.

Coach George Boucher of Springfield was livid. He violently contended that the goal was scored after the game had ended. Referee "Rabbit" McVeigh disagreed, and the goal stood.

When the Barons returned for the 10-minute overtime period, they were alone. Coach Boucher refused to continue the game, and the Barons were awarded a 3-2 forfeit victory.

This was the only forfeit in the League's history, and Boucher was heavily fined as a result. This game eventually cost him his job.

Jean Baptiste Pusie – The "Clown Prince of Hockey". Walt Voysey collection.

The Barons' home ice magic was not yet over. On March 5th, fiery Les Cunningham scored a three-goal hat trick as Cleveland came from two goals behind to defeat Syracuse 5-2 before 8,760 fans. The game also marked the return of Moe Roberts to the nets. Captain Moe showed no ill effects from the knee injury as he kicked out 36 shots in the victory.

The next evening in Syracuse, last second lightning struck again. Norm Duguid was the hero as he scored with 3 seconds remaining in at 2-2 tie with the Stars. The teams played a full 10-minute overtime in those days, no matter how many goals would be scored.

This game set the stage for a big 3 games in 5 nights showdown series with second place Pittsburgh. The Hornets were now 5 points behind Cleveland in the West division. The division crown in all likelihood would be settled during this series.

The first game was played in Cleveland on March 8th, and Norm Duguid once again got the home team off to a flying start. His two first-period goals started the Barons off to a 4-0 lead, and the game looked safe.

But near the end of the second period, the Hornets unleashed a barrage that was unparalleled in league history by scoring 3 goals within one minute.

Deed Klein scored at 17:09. Then it was Don Deacon at 17:53 and Klein again at 18:05. Three goals in 56 seconds! The period mercifully came to an end, and the Barons were able to regroup. They scored twice in the third period for a big 6-3 win that stretched their first-place lead to 7 points. It also was their 17th straight home victory and put their Arena unbeaten streak at 20 games.

The two teams met the next night in Pittsburgh and battled to a 1-1 tie. In this game Bud Cook, star center iceman of Cleveland, suffered a broken right leg and was lost for the season. This was a huge blow, since Cook was one of the team's steadiest players and most respected leaders. His season ended with 13 goals and 27 assists, which would place him 7th in league scoring totals.

The third game of this crucial series was played before a record crowd of 11,332 at the Arena. The overflow crowd saw the Hornets dominate the game for a full 55 minutes and hold a 2-0 lead. But hockey is a 60-minute game, and the Barons were able to pull off their magic act one more time.

At 15:52 of the third period, Earl Bartholome scored on a pass from Phil Hergesheimer. The Arena exploded, and the fans screamed and pleaded for their heroes to pull off another miracle. With two minutes remaining, Coach Bill Cook pulled goalie Moe Roberts in favor of a sixth attacker. The strategy worked, as Barthelome scored again with only six seconds left in the game! The crowd was hysterical as the home unbeaten streak reached 21 games.

Time after time, all winter long, the Barons had come up with some sort of unbelievable ending to save one game after another. Unfortunately, you can't win them all, and the team ran out of miracles on March 16th.

Cleveland's great unbeaten streak of 21 games ended when the Philadelphia Ramblers hung on to defeat the Barons, 3-2. This was the team's first loss suffered at the Arena. Ironically, the winning goal for the Ramblers was scored by Bill Carse, whose brother Bobby would become one of the all-time great Barons a decade later.

Goalie Roberts was pulled during the last minute, as Cleveland mounted a furious all-out attack to tie the game. Philly goaltender Bert Gardiner came up big on two great saves on shots by Lorne Duguid and Phil Hergesheimer, and the streak was history.

On March 23rd, the team received more bad news. Earl Barthelome was hit by an attack of appendicitis and had an emergency operation. Along with Bud Cook, Earl was the second star player to be lost for the season. He finished the year with 14 goals and 18 assists for 32 points.

This emergency forced Coach Bill Cook to suit up and play again. Just one week earlier, Bill had stated that he was through as a player. Wrong again!

With first place in the West Division already clinched, the team had one more regular season goal: win the overall point total for the entire League. Who stood in the way? None other than the Pittsburgh Hornets, who wanted badly to spoil the Barons' party.

Shortly before the March 26th showdown, the Barons were once again rocked by injuries. Defenseman Art Berlet's back, that was injured in Pittsburgh a week earlier, had gotten worse. Also, Peggy O'Neil, the team's sparkplug, had come down with a bad case of blood poisoning. This was the result of a hand injury.

The team was now down to twelve players for the big Hornet game. A crowd of 10,558 came to watch the AHL title-clinching contest.

On this night, one man came up with the game of a lifetime. Bill Cunningham, a four-year Cleveland veteran, who never before had a hat trick in his career, scored all three Cleveland goals in a great 3-2 triumph over Pittsburgh.

Leading an undermanned team, minus four regulars, Cunningham scored his first goal at 14:24 of the first period. He scored again in the second period, but the Hornets came back to tie the game at two.

The Barons could have played for a tie and still clinched the point title. But Bill Cunningham would have none of that. Taking a pass from Earl Roche on the left wing with less than three minutes to go in the game, mighty Bill beat Pitt goalie Alphie Moore with a high, hard shot.

30

The victory set off a wild celebration by the fans and made a hero of Bill Cunningham. To make his night even more meaningful, Bill's father had come in from Winnipeg, Canada, to see his son play. He was one proud papa.

Cleveland ended its regular season the next night with a 5-4 win at Syracuse. The victory gave the Barons a total of 61 points in the standings with a 25-12-11 record. They finished 9 points ahead of Pittsburgh in the West and four atop Providence, the East division winner.

Lorne Duguid finished one point behind Jack Markle of Syracuse in the individual scoring race, with 22 goals and 30 assists.

Named to the first all star team were Duguid, center Bud Cook, and coach Bill Cook. Moe Roberts was the second team goaltender. Duguid was also named the league MVP. Total attendance was 196,940 for 24 home games.

THE PLAYOFFS

The Barons were entering the playoffs against the Syracuse Stars in a best-of-three mini-series, with only 12 healthy players. This included Coach Cook, who was still pressed into service. Out for the season were Bud Cook with his broken leg; Earl Bartholome with appendicitis; Art Berlet with a bad back, and James (Peggy) O'Neil with blood poisoning.

League rules prohibited bringing in replacement players, since playoff rosters were already turned in.

Ready or not, the battered Barons opened the play-offs at Syracuse on Sunday, April 3rd. The second and third game, if necessary, would be played in Cleveland.

Game One was a rout. The undermanned Barons were no match for the pumped-up Stars, as Syracuse hung a 6-3 defeat on the Clevelanders.

Even worse than the outcome of the game was the loss of Earl Roche, who suffered a severe eye injury when hit by a stick in the third period. The injury was diagnosed as a contusion of the eyeball. Roche eventually would recover and play hockey again, but he was through for this season.

The Barons were now down to eleven bodies, including coach and goaltender. The two teams headed back to Cleveland by train for what would turn out to be the most remarkable and heroic game any Baron team would ever play.

The game was played at a violent and furious pace. Midway through the first period, Oscar Hanson, the Barons' third line center, was carried off the ice with a knee injury after being hit by Max Bennett. Cleveland was now down to 10 men.

The Barons drew first blood on a power play goal by Phil Hergesheimer at 7:59 of the second period.

Bill Thompson then tied it for Syracuse at 10:19.

Les Cunningham put Cleveland ahead again at 15:23 on a great solo effort. Les sped past both Syracuse defenders to beat goalie Phil Stein.

The Barons held this 2-1 lead until 8:04 of the third, when Bill Thompson scored again. Neither team could score during the remainder of regulation time, and the game went into overtime.

By now the Barons were a severely tired team. The Stars used quick line changes to wear the undermanned Barons down, as all Cleveland players were doing double duty.

Wave after wave of Syracuse players kept attacking the Barons' goal during the first 10-minute overtime. But still the Clevelanders would not crack.

The same was true during a next 20-minute sudden-death overtime; and yet a third. Somehow the courageous home team summoned up the strength to thwart the constantly attacking Stars.

No one was more magnificent than Coach Cook himself. Past his prime and over 40 years old, Bill logged as much ice time as anyone. He and the rest of the Barons just refused to give up.

THE 1937-38 CLEVELAND BARONS.
Front Row (L-R) – Peggy O'Neil, Les Cunningham, Morrie Roberts, Bill Cook, Coach; Walter Robertson, Trainer; Emory Hanson, Earl Bartholome.
Back Row – Lorne Duguid, Phil Hergesheimer, Harry Foster, Art Berlett, Bill Cunningham, Joe Bretto, Earl Roche, Fred Robertson, Alex "Bud" Cook. Note: Walter Brenneman was confined to his bed with an infected toe when this picture was taken.
Dennis Turchek collection.

The team was thoroughly exhausted as the fourth overtime began. The 9,071 fans even got into the act by throwing debris on the ice to give the players a rest. But all was for naught. At 12:42 of the fourth overtime, a 30 ft. goal by little right wing Max Bennett gave Syracuse a 3-2 victory in the longest game ever played here.

After 122 minutes 42 seconds of actual playing time, the game ended at 1:15 a.m.

Ten men against fifteen. Ten men who were dazed by fatigue but full of pride and courage, and a will to win and never give up. The team reflected the image of its coach, Bill Cook. The Barons lost one of the classic games in Cleveland sports history. But never was a city and its fans more proud of their team in defeat. They were simply magnificent.

To a man, the players could not wait for the next season to begin. They were on a mission.

FINAL STANDINGS
1937-38

West	W	L	T	GF	GA	PTS.
Cleveland	25	12	11	126	114	61
Pittsburgh	22	18	8	100	104	52
Syracuse	21	20	7	142	122	49
East	**W**	**L**	**T**	**GF**	**GA**	**PTS.**
Providence	25	16	7	114	86	57
Philadelphia	26	18	4	134	108	56
New Haven	13	28	7	93	131	33
Springfield	10	30	8	96	140	28

Top Baron Scorers	G	A	PTS.
Lorne Duguid	22	27	49
Les Cunningham	19	28	47
Phil Hergesheimer	25	20	45
Bud Cook	13	27	40
Earl Bartholome	14	18	32

Calder Cup Champion – Providence Reds

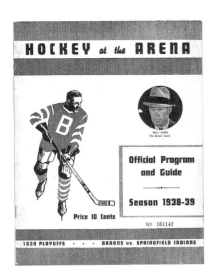

1938-39 SEASON

The core of the Cleveland hockey team was kept intact, but during the off-season, several player moves were made by Al Sutphin. Left wing Bob Blake and center George Patterson were brought up from the Minneapolis farm club.

On defense, Jean Pusie was sold to St. Louis, and Joe Bretto was released. Dick Adolph, who would be a Baron star for nearly a decade, was signed as a replacement.

Right wing Bill Cunningham was traded to Syracuse for defenseman Mickey Blake. Right wing Ossie Asmundson was purchased from New Haven.

When the Montreal Maroons of the NHL ceased operations, Sutphin purchased center Paul Runge and goalie Bill Beveridge from the defunct team. Beveridge became a holdout during training camp and was beaten out by Moe Roberts in the battle for #1 goaltender. Bill was subsequently loaned first to Providence and then to New Haven, where he finished the season. Cleveland retained his rights, and he would return to the club a few years later in a starring role.

Spirits were high as the Barons opened training camp on October 16th. But by the end of the first practice, the team was stunned as the injury jinx, which had ruined the previous season, had struck again. Bud Cook broke his right leg for the second time.

The all-star center had spent the previous summer rehabilitating this same leg that he had broken last March 9th during a game in Pittsburgh. Cook reported to camp a week early in great shape and was expecting a big year. It was a crushing blow to both Bud and the team.

The jinx was not through yet. On October 30th, new wing Ossie Asmundson also broke his leg. Once again the team was shorthanded as it opened its season in Pittsburgh on November 5th.

Cleveland lost this game 5-1 and also lost the services of James (Peggy) O'Neil for 6 weeks with a cracked ankle.

These three injuries were instrumental in the team getting off to a so-so start. By mid-December, the Barons were in third place with a 4-6-2 record. During a 4-2 loss to Syracuse at the Arena, the local icers were hearing boo's for the first time by the hometown fans.

Only Phil Hergesheimer, with seven goals, was playing up to his potential. Phil, who was now the crown jewel in the American League, had NHL scouts drooling. On December 16th, after Hergy scored his 10th goal, the Detroit Red Wings made a bid for the budding superstar. Al Sutphin rejected this trade offer. Later in the season, Hergesheimer would be caught in a bidding war for his services that ultimately would change the course of hockey in Cleveland.

Coach Cook realized that it was time to shake up the team. He made two line changes that turned things around.

Peggy O'Neil, who had just returned to the line-up from his ankle injury, was reunited with Les Cunningham and Lorne Duguid on the first line.

This was the line that tore up the League the previous season.

Phil Hergesheimer, who had been playing on Cunningham's line, was now teamed up with Earl Bartholome and Paul Runge. The key to this line was the shifting of Bartholome from wing to center. This put Runge, who had been at center, back to his natural position at left wing.

The results were instantaneous and spectacular. First game with the new lineup was against the League's new team, the first-place Hershey Bears, on December 10th.

Hershey came to town ready to play and led after two periods, 1-0. The 8,266 Arena fans were restless, and the boo's began again. Two minutes into the final period, defenseman Mickey Blake fed O'Neil the puck near the net. Peg found an open Les Cunningham, who ripped in a beautiful shot to tie the score.

The fans and team finally began to pick up the pace. No one more so than Peg O'Neil. The little Irishman began playing like a man possessed, hitting everyone and anything in a Hershey uniform. He personally had the crowd in a frenzy.

Midway through the period, the Barons were a man short. While killing the penalty, O'Neil intercepted a pass at center ice and broke into the clear. He bested goalie Alphie Moore from five feet out to break a three-game losing streak and give Cleveland a 2-1 win.

The entire spirit of the club was lifted, and the new lineup really began to click. The next night Peg and Bartholome scored in a 2-2 tie at Syracuse.

Phil Hergesheimer then scored the winner in a 1-0 thriller against New Haven at the Arena. This game was the battle of two Cleveland goalies – Moe Roberts of the Barons and Bill Beveridge, Cleveland owned, but on loan to New Haven. Both goaltenders wanted this game badly as a matter of personal pride. Each man made one great save after another. After the game, the two goalies shook hands at center ice and skated off together. Everyone at the game knew they had witnessed a special effort by each of these two great competitors.

When Hergy scored his 13th goal in a 5-1 humiliation of the Eastern division leading Ramblers in Philadelphia on December 21st, there seemed no stopping the Barons. This was their first victory in Philadelphia in over two years. They now felt they could beat anyone, anywhere. Since the beginning of their streak on December 10th, the Barons had outscored their opposition 21-9, with most of the credit going to the new lineup changes.

The Cleveland icers took over first place by defeating Hershey in a back-to-back series December 25th and 26th. The first game was a 5-1 romp at the Arena in a savage match that erupted into a full-scale brawl with five minutes left in the game.

The next evening, the two teams went at it again in Hershey with the Barons pulling out a 4-3 thriller on Phil Hergesheimer's late goal. This was Cleveland's sixth straight triumph over the Bears, who were completely frustrated.

January 7th became a landmark game for both Hergesheimer and the Barons. A record crowd of 11,860 saw the Barons thrash the hated Philly Ramblers 5-2. The huge crowd, that included over 2,000 standees, came away from the game in awe of Phantom Phil (as he came to be known).

For the first time in his career, Hergy scored the three-goal hat trick. He completely dominated the game from start to finish. Every time he stepped on the ice, electricity filled the air. This overpowering performance gave Phil 20 goals in 26 games as the Barons' record climbed to 14-8-6.

The team played streaky hockey for the next month, losing four in a row and then winning three. But all this took a back seat to the controversy surrounding Phil Hergesheimer.

Playing in the American Hockey League, every other year the Barons were subject to the National Hockey League secondary draft. In this process, for the price of $4,000, an NHL team could claim any player from any minor league team. Once a team lost one player, no one else could be taken off the roster. $4,000 was a lot of money in those days, so not many players were lost in the draft. Unfortunately for Cleveland, everyone wanted Hergy.

On January 17th, a meeting was held in New York with Al Sutphin and representatives from the Rangers, New York Americans, Detroit, and Chicago – all making offers for the services of the Barons' star. Cleveland's owner listened but wanted more time before making a decision.

Al Sutphin's back was up against the wall. If he didn't make a trade for players, he would lose Hergy at the end of the season for nothing but money. To complicate matters, if he did make a deal for his star before the season ended, the Barons would still be subject to the draft and would wind up losing another player, most likely Les Cunningham. It was a no-win situation.

On February 6th, a deal with Chicago was announced. Phil Hergesheimer would remain with Cleveland for the remainder of this season but would report to the Blackhawks next Fall. In return, the Barons would receive two Chicago-owned players after this season was completed. They were Charlie Mason, now playing for Pittsburgh, and 21-year-old defenseman Harold Jackson, now with Providence. Mason was a first team all-star last season, and Jackson was a bright prospect. Also, veteran Blackhawk center Bob Gracie would report to Cleveland on February 25th of the current campaign. In return, it was agreed that the Blackhawks would take Les Cunningham when the draft was held after the season.

Bud Cook (L), Phil Hergesheimer (C), Earl Bartholome (R). Hergesheimer was one of the most popular Barons ever and the center of controversy during his great 1938-39 season. Cleveland Public Library collection.

The final result was Phil Hergesheimer and Les Cunningham for Charlie Mason, Harold Jackson, and Bob Gracie.

It was the best deal Cleveland could make under the circumstances, but Al Sutphin was furious. He was a self-made man and hated to be at the mercy of anyone.

Make no mistake about it – the seeds of Sutphin's discontent with the NHL were planted during the Hergesheimer deal.

When Al bought the team in 1934, his ultimate goal was to bring an NHL team to town. But five years later, he had come to firmly believe that within a few years the American Hockey League would grow by strength and popularity into a second major league. He envisioned all teams in the AHL playing in a big new arena like his own, and Hershey's, and the one being built in Buffalo.

Unfortunately, World War II would change all these plans. Most AHL owners (but not Sutphin) would encounter financial difficulties during the war, and these dreams would go up in smoke. But in 1939, the dream was still alive.

Sutphin stressed total independence from the NHL. He urged his fellow owners to do the same and sign their own players so they would not be subject to any NHL working agreement.

Though he would carry on a professional working relationship with the NHL during his entire tenure as Barons' owner, one thing would always remain true. Al Sutphin was one large headache to the National Hockey League.

Despite all the controversy surrounding Phil Hergesheimer, the Barons were still able to hang around first place.

Hergy set a new Cleveland goal-scoring record with his 26th in a 5-1 overtime rout of New Haven on February 11th.

Cleveland took over first place the next night in Syracuse after a 2-2 draw. This gave the Barons a 19-13-8 record. Les Cunningham was a one-man show as he scored both goals and played a fierce checking game. Night after night, either Les or Hergy seemed to come up big and lift the team. Fans hated the thought of losing them.

After finally taking over first place, the Barons began to falter. They lost five consecutive games at the Arena, to knock themselves out of the race for first place. But it was a road game in Hershey on March 2nd that really did the Clevelanders in. They went into the game only three points behind the first-place Bears and needed a victory.

Things were looking good for Cleveland when Les Cunningham scored at 17:05 of the third period to give the team a 3-1 lead. But then the roof caved in. Two quick Hershey goals in the last minute and a half sent the game into overtime. Cleveland was reeling with the worst yet to come.

During a wild scramble in front of Moe Roberts, Earl Roche tipped in the winning goal for the Bears at 1:39 of overtime. This was the same Earl Roche who had performed so admirably for Cleveland the previous season. He nearly lost an eye during the playoffs, and his career was thought to be over.

He fought back from the injury and made the Barons team. Unfortunately, Earl was caught in a numbers game. When all of the early season injuries had healed, Roche was released. He landed on his feet in Hershey, had a good season, and on this night his revenge was sweet.

The low point of the season came on March 8th as Cleveland lost its fifth straight game on home ice, 4-3 to New Haven. Hergesheimer scored two goals to bring his total to 32, but it was not enough. The fans were upset and throwing programs on the ice as the game ended.

The main reason for the slump was a change in their attacking strategy. The Barons began sending both defensemen deep into the offensive zone in an all-out effort to score goals. They were constantly caught up ice, leaving their defensive zone unguarded. After the New Haven loss, Coach Bill Cook decided to go back to a close-checking defensive style game, and the move paid off.

Cleveland finally clinched a playoff spot on March 11th with a thrilling 3-1 victory over Syracuse at the Arena. 11,317 fans witnessed a savage battle and Les Cunningham's finest game as a Baron to date. Les scored all three Cleveland goals and was brilliant throughout the game. But it was the wild display put on by Syracuse "bad man" Basil (Bummer) Doran that had the crowd in a rage.

Doran didn't come to play hockey on this night. He carried his stick like an ax and used it on any Baron he came near. In the first period he skated the length of the ice to flatten an unsuspecting Phil Hergesheimer. After getting into altercations throughout the game, Doran crashed into Peggy O'Neil. O'Neil suffered a split mouth and broken teeth and was helped off the ice. Yip Foster came to Peg's aid and went after Doran but was dragged away before he could exact his revenge. O'Neil also wanted to go after Doran but was restrained from going back on the ice in his battered condition.

With this victory, the Barons clinched third place and a playoff spot against Springfield. After leading the League on February 12th with 46 points, Cleveland finished out the year with a 4-9-1 record. This included losing 6 of their last 7 at the Arena. No one gave them much of a chance in the playoffs. No one, that is, except themselves.

THE PLAYOFFS

No Cleveland team had gone beyond the first round of the playoffs since the 1930-31 season. This was a huge monkey on the backs of the local team. To a man, the Barons felt that they could go all the way this year. But their play was so lackadaisical down the stretch, could they turn the jets back on? The answers would begin to unfold in Springfield, where they would meet the Indians in the first game of a two-out-of-three game mini-series.

Springfield finished a poor third in the Eastern division with a 16-29-9 record, but one would never know it by watching the opening game.

The game was scoreless until 16:38 of the second period when Lloyd Jackson took a pass from Ted Saunders and beat goalie Moe Roberts to give Springfield a 1-0 lead. From that point on, the Indians sat back and played defensive hockey until Norm Schultz scored at 16:12 of the third period to give Springfield a 2-1 victory. Goalie Benny Grant was superb in continually frustrating the Clevelanders.

The Barons were one game from elimination when Coach Bill Cook called a meeting to try and fire up the team. He appealed to their pride. Privately he knew that they needed someone to come to the forefront and carry the team on his back. That man turned out to be Moe Roberts.

Roberts was flawless in a 4-0 victory at the Arena. Moe kicked out 18 shots in the scoreless first period alone. The team seemed to rally around its goaltender.

Referee Eddie Burke disallowed a Cleveland goal late in the first period and again early in the second. Coach Cook rushed onto the ice to protest Burke's second call to no avail. With 7,123 fans in an angry mood, the Barons finally broke through at 13:11 of the second period on a 55-foot shot by Art Berlet that bounced off Goalie Benny Grant into the net.

The game turned into a rout in the third period as Bob Gracie, Phil Hergesheimer, and Emory Hanson scored. The team had finally found its old spark, and everyone pointed to the great goaltending of Roberts as the catalyst.

The deciding game of this series was played at the Arena on March 25th. 9,382 fans witnessed another spectacular performance by Moe Roberts as the great Cleveland goalie led the Barons to a 3-0 victory. Recording his second straight shutout, Moe stood head and shoulders above everyone in this series.

Phil Hergesheimer scored twice for Cleveland, with the other tally knocked in by Bob Gracie. With these two hot scorers and their goaltender on fire, the Barons were extremely confident as they headed into the second round against the Providence Reds, defending Calder Cup Champions.

The semi-final series against Providence was another two-out-of-three affair that had two unusual angles of interest. The Reds, who finished the regular season with a 21-22-11 record, were coached by Fred (Bun) Cook, brother of Barons' coach Bill Cook. They had just finished their first-round series by defeating Syracuse two games to one.

The rival brothers, who played together on one of hockey's all-time great lines with the New York Rangers, were facing each other for the first time as coaches in a playoff series. With the Reds holding a

3-2-1 edge during the regular season, the series figured to be a dogfight with each coach fighting for family-bragging rights.

The other unusual angle had Providence using Cleveland-owned Bill Beveridge in goal. This was a situation that could only happen in hockey.

During hockey's early years, teams in any league carried only one goaltender. The #1 goalie played every game. The system of rotating goalies was still years away. Why pay a second goalie a full salary to sit on the bench and never play? It was strictly for financial reasons.

How Beveridge wound up playing for the Reds was a story in itself.

Cleveland purchased Bill from the Montreal Maroons when the NHL club disbanded and loaned him to New Haven for the season when Moe Roberts won the battle for #1 goalie.

Providence started the year with Frankie Brimsek in goal. When Brimsek was called up to Boston, the Reds obtained Nick Damore on loan from Hershey. The Bears were using Alphie Moore, who was owned by the NHL New York Americans, and would rather have Damore play somewhere else than be sitting on their bench.

Just before the NHL playoffs opened, the Americans recalled Moore to replace their own injured goalie, Earl Robertson. Hershey, in turn, took Damore back from Providence, leaving the Reds without a goalie.

Since New Haven had not made the American League playoffs, Reds President Jean Dubuc asked permission of Al Sutphin to use Cleveland-owned Bill Beveridge for the balance of the season. Sutphin, always willing to help out his fellow owners for the good of the League, agreed. He never thought this decision could come back to haunt him.

Cleveland Coach Bill Cook strongly protested, wanting Providence to find another goalie for the series against his Barons. He knew how good Bill Beveridge was. But Sutphin was a man of his word. He said Providence could use Beveridge for the balance of the season, and he meant it – even if this meant hurting his own team. Sportsmanship always came first with Al.

The stage was set, and the series opened on March 28th at the Arena. The 9,582 fans in attendance would witness one of the most memorable games in team history.

Things looked bleak for Cleveland, as Providence jumped out to a one-goal lead and held this advantage for nearly half the game. But at 9:56, only thirty-two seconds after the Reds had tallied their second goal, Les Cunningham scored during a wild scramble in front of the net to put the Barons back in the game.

Cleveland went back on the attack and kept the Reds pinned in their own zone. Suddenly, Phil Hergesheimer intercepted a pass behind the Providence net. He spotted Paul Runge open in front of the cage and passed him the puck. Paul deked twice and beat Bill Beveridge to tie the score at 13:08 of the second period.

After a scoreless third period, the game went into a full 10-minute overtime. Still, no one scored.

After that, the fierce battle went into a twenty-minute sudden death period. Still, no score. Again, during a third overtime, no score. The fans and players were exhausted. This was a game of non-stop action, up and down the ice, featuring unbelievable goaltending by Moe Roberts and Bill Beveridge.

Finally, Cleveland got a break. George (Popeye) Patterson took control of the puck in the Cleveland zone and skated up the left side with Bob Gracie speeding down the center. Patterson flipped a pass toward the net that was tipped in by Gracie at 9:47 of the fourth overtime for a 3-2 victory. Bedlam erupted in the Arena as Gracie was carried off the ice by his jubilant teammates.

The game ended at 1:14 a.m. after 119 minutes, 47 seconds of playing time. This was the second longest game in Cleveland history. Only the heartbreaking loss to Syracuse in the previous season's playoffs lasted longer.

The game also broke the spirit of the Reds. The second game of the series, played in Providence, was strictly no contest.

After spotting the Reds a quick goal at :55 seconds by Art Giroux, the Barons took control of the game and never looked back. Led by Phil Hergesheimer's hat trick and Les Cunningham's two goals, the Clevelanders blew away the Reds by a score of 7-2. Single goals were also scored by Earl Bartholome and Bob Gracie.

The ease with which Cleveland won the game surprised everyone. Both coaches agreed that the overtime loss in Cleveland took the heart out of the Reds.

The Barons were now playing with supreme confidence as they headed into the title round against the vaunted Philadelphia Ramblers.

Cleveland was on a roll, but Philadelphia was still the most feared team in the League. They eliminated the Hershey Bears in a hard-fought series between the League's first-place teams three games to two.

The Ramblers were solid from top to bottom. But it was their high-powered offense that made them so dangerous. They used the New York Rangers' style of sending all three forwards and both defensemen deep into the offensive zone in a constant all-out attack. Their 214 goals during the regular season was far and away the League's best.

But going into the final series, the Ramblers were at a distinct disadvantage. Philadelphia was the only team in the American League that was owned and operated by a National League club – in this case, New York. Due to injuries to the Rangers during their Stanley Cup series against Boston, New York recalled three Rambler stars as replacements. Most notable was All Star goalie Bert Gardiner. Filling the void in the Rambler net would be the very capable Harvey Teno. Also missing would be center Bill Carse and left wing George Allen.

It was not known how long these three would be up with New York, so the Barons felt their best chance to steal a game in Philadelphia would be in the opener.

The first two games of the best of five series were scheduled on Rambler ice with games three and four in Cleveland. If a fifth game was necessary, it would be in Philly.

On April 1st, the Barons launched their title drive with a hard-earned 2-1 victory. The defensive effort put forth by the Clevelanders was nothing short of sensational.

The Ramblers sent their famous five-man charges at the Barons, but they were continually broken up at the Cleveland zone. It was as if they built a brick wall along the blue line. Defensemen Dick Adolph, Yip Foster, Freddie Robertson, and Art Berlet protected Moe Roberts flawlessly.

After Les Cunningham and Lorne Duguid scored in the second period, the Barons were content to play defensive hockey the rest of the way to protect the lead. The strategy worked as Philadelphia was shut out until a harmless goal was scored with three seconds remaining.

Cleveland had won the game it needed. They hoped for at least a road split, and they got the job done.

The Barons were now thinking sweep, but the Philadelphians' silent prayers were being answered. The New York Rangers were defeated by Boston in the NHL playoffs. This meant that goalie Bert Gardiner and forwards Bill Carse and George Allen were returning to the Ramblers for the balance of the playoffs. Also, the recently ill Babe Tapin was returning to action. The team from Philly was loaded and ready to turn the tables on Cleveland.

Game Two had the looks of a rout right from the start. The Ramblers went on an all-out attack right from the opening face-off. Moe Roberts held the fort until 12:56, when George Allen knocked in a rebound of a Bill Carse shot. It didn't take long for the two returning stars to make their presence felt.

Kilby McDonald at 17:11 and Joe Krol 37 seconds later made the score 3-0, and the Barons looked out of the game.

Totally outskated during the opening period, Cleveland staged a sensational second-period rally. Led by the line of Les Cunningham, Lorne Duguid, and Peggy O'Neil, the Barons tied the score in the middle stanza. Each linemate scored a goal, as the Philly fans sat back stunned.

The fiery O'Neil was right back at it to start the third period. Taking a perfect pass from Cunningham, Peg beat Bert Gardiner at 2:09 to put Cleveland on top 4-3. This capped one of O'Neil's greatest nights as a Baron. In a little more than twenty minutes, the Irishman had two goals and two assists.

The lead looked like it would stand up, but McDonald scored again on a pass from Carse at 16:26 to tie the score and send the game into overtime.

The game remained deadlocked through a ten-minute overtime and a twenty-minute sudden death period. Tight checking took over the game as each team waited for an opening that didn't come.

The Barons changed tactics to start the third extra period and went on the attack. Goalie Gardiner made three super stops to save the game for Philly. Cleveland kept attacking, but Lude Waring intercepted a pass in the neutral zone. He whipped a pass to Joe Krol, who beat Moe Roberts from twenty feet out. The Barons had lost a real heartbreaker, as the series moved on to Cleveland for games three and four.

Despite the loss in Philadelphia, the Barons were extremely confident that they would end the series in Cleveland. They had beaten the Ramblers on home ice three straight times during the regular season and saw no reason why the mastery should end.

11,278 fans jammed the Arena for the third game and witnessed a defensive masterpiece by the local boys. Led by Moe Roberts and his air tight defense, the Barons hung a 2-0 shutout on the Ramblers. The game was totally one-sided, as Philly rarely got off a good shot on Roberts . "Up fast and back faster" was the Cleveland playoff motto, and the defensive play never cracked.

Les Cunningham scored his fifth playoff goal at 1:07 of the second period to give the Barons the only goal they needed. Phil Hergesheimer added an insurance marker in the third. This was Hergy's 41st goal of the season, 34 during the regular season and 7 in the playoffs. The Barons were now only one win away from their first Calder Cup.

The City of Cleveland was ready to explode. It had been nineteen years since the baseball Indians won the World Series and since had fallen on hard times. Nine years had elapsed since the hockey Indians won the International League title, but that was no comparison to the love affair that Cleveland now had with its local ice heroes.

Hundreds of fans lined Euclid Avenue on Saturday, April 8th, to buy general admission and standing room tickets for that night's fourth game.

11,421 fans saw one of the greatest exhibitions of goaltending ever put on at the Arena.

The game was fast and furious from the outset. Both teams had several great scoring chances, but both goalies were equal to the task. In all, Roberts had eleven saves, and Gardiner 9, during the first period.

At 4:05 of the second period, the Barons appeared to have taken the lead on a twenty-foot shot by Les Cunningham, but the play was whistled offside. The noise was so great in the Arena that the players could barely hear themselves shout, let alone hear a whistle.

At 10:15 of the second frame, the Barons scored. George (Popeye) Patterson took the puck in his own zone and started up ice. Stickhandling his way through the neutral zone, Patterson then bullied his way through both Rambler defensemen and broke in free on goal. He faked once and lifted a backhander past a fallen Bert Gardiner. The fans went crazy, and the celebration held up the game for several minutes.

The third period was high drama all the way. Philadelphia went on an all-out attack to try to tie the score. This was Moe Roberts' finest hour. The Ramblers were relentless as they continually broke free on Moe. But the great goalie was equal to the task with one miracle stop after another. In all, Roberts had 17 stops in the third period alone, 38 for the game.

When the final seconds ticked away, the Barons had won the Calder Cup with a 1-0 victory. Bedlam was everywhere. Fans raced on the ice and hoisted their heroes on their shoulders.

At 1:00 a.m., George Patterson and Moe Roberts were still signing autographs for the fans, and hundreds still cheered inside the Arena. Partying in downtown went on until daybreak. The Cleveland Barons were champions!

A victory dinner was held the next night before many Cleveland dignitaries, including the Mayor. Moe Roberts was honored as the playoffs' MVP. The championship was a personal triumph for Moe. He had been a Cleveland goalie since 1933 with the Indians, Falcons, and now Barons. After suffering with some poor teams, his loyalty, dedication, and hard work paid off.

His four shutouts were a new record. In nine playoff games, Moe allowed a mere twelve goals, five coming in one game. He was the toast of the town, and nobody deserved it more.

FINAL STANDINGS
1938-39

West	W	L	T	GF	GA	PTS.
Hershey	31	18	5	140	110	67
Syracuse	26	19	9	153	116	61
Cleveland	23	22	9	145	138	55
Pittsburgh	22	28	4	176	166	48
East	**W**	**L**	**T**	**GF**	**GA**	**PTS.**
Philadelphia	32	17	5	214	161	69
Providence	21	22	11	136	153	53
Springfield	16	29	9	121	179	41
New Haven	14	30	10	114	174	38

Top Baron Scorers	G	A	PTS.
Phil Hergesheimer	34	19	53
Norm Duguid	19	32	51
Les Cunningham	26	20	46
Earl Bartholome	17	28	45

Calder Cup Champion – Cleveland Barons

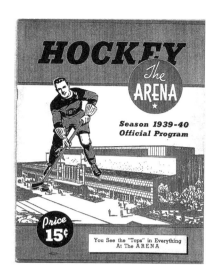

1939-40 SEASON

The departure of Les Cunningham and Phil Hergesheimer to Chicago left a huge void in the Barons' offense. The arrival of Harold Jackson and Charlie Mason, obtained in the Hergesheimer deal, would help stop the bleeding. Also the return of Bud Cook at center was heavily counted upon. Bud's twice broken right leg seemed to be in fine shape.

Leroy Goldsworthy, a twelve-year NHL veteran, was purchased from the New York Americans to help fill the offensive hole. Sutphin felt the 31-year-old Goldsworthy had a few more goals left in him to help out.

Bill Cook and Sutphin also felt that the defense needed restructuring. Although the backline crew was one of the League's strongest last season, especially in the playoffs, the Baron brass wanted a younger, more mobile defense. Art Berlet and Yip Foster were sold to Syracuse, and Mickey Blake was released.

To replace them, Larry Molyneaux was purchased from the New York Rangers, and Joe Jerwa was obtained from the New York Americans.

Just two years earlier, the 24-year-old Molyneaux was a first team AHL All Star with Philadelphia before spending last season with New York. Jerwa was a high-scoring rearguard, having spent the last four seasons with the NHL Americans.

These two newcomers, along with returnees Dick Adolph and Fred Robertson, promised to give Cleveland a rock solid defense.

On a sad note, playoff hero George (Popeye) Patterson was sold to New Haven in an effort to help out the suffering Eagles. Despite his playoff heroics, Sutphin felt the twelve-year veteran was well past his prime. Al was usually right in these matters, but not this time. Patterson scored 25 goals for New Haven and remained a solid scorer for several more years. He would be sorely missed this season.

The Barons were set in goal as Moe Roberts once again beat out Bill Beveridge for #1 goalie. Subsequently, Bill was loaned to Syracuse for the season.

The Barons opened the season with a 2-1 win at Philadelphia, lost their home opener to Pittsburgh, also 2-1, and then rolled to four straight wins. Cleveland was sitting on top of the Western division, and the suspect offense seemed in fine working order.

Especially gratifying was the play of Bud Cook. Bud was skating like his old self. When he scored the team's first goal of the season in Philadelphia, Bud was mobbed by his teammates. They knew how hard he had worked to come back from that twice-broken right leg. Those who thought that his career was over didn't know Bud Cook. He had the heart of a lion and never doubted that he could come back. Cleveland was lucky to have him.

The team's stay in first place was shortlived. A humiliating game on November 22nd at the Arena started the team on a long slide.

The Barons seemed overconfident and lackadaisical in falling behind New Haven 3-1. Eagle goalie Wilf Cude was hit on the right elbow by a wicked shot and could not continue. As was the custom of the day, the Eagles had no spare goalie. They were about to have one of their defensemen play goal when the Barons informed them that an amateur goaltender was in attendance and could be used as a substitute.

Gordon (Sonny Boy) Baxter was a Cleveland Indian goalie in 1931, and not a very successful one at that. A Baron season ticket holder, he was now a car salesman and a weekend goalie in the Cleveland Amateur League.

The crowd, remembering Sonny Boy, let out a collective laugh when it was announced that Baxter would take over in the New Haven net. They wouldn't laugh for long.

From somewhere deep inside him, Sonny Boy Baxter summoned up his dreams and made them reality. He stood the Barons on their ears with save after save. The Cleveland icers were shaking their heads in disbelief and could only score twice on Baxter. By the end of the game, the embarrassed Barons were totally disorganized and could not even complete a pass.

For one brief moment, Sonny Boy Baxter was a hero again. He went out that night to watch the Barons play hockey and went home as the goalie who bested them 6-3! Who said fairy tales don't come true?

The hangover from this game lasted nearly a month. In their next ten games, Cleveland went 1-6-3, and the offense was non-existent. This was the team's biggest fear come true. The loss of Cunningham and Hergesheimer was coming back to haunt them.

As 1939 was drawing to a close, the Barons lost back-to-back games to the first-place Indianapolis Capitals. The Caps were the League's newest team. Owned and operated by the Detroit Red Wings, the newcomers were running away with first place.

The double loss was Cleveland's fourth straight to Indy and gave them an 8-9-3 record as they headed into the new year.

Lack of scoring was not the Barons' only problem. Injuries were mounting up. Charlie Mason banged up his knee, and Paul Runge suffered a broken thumb to further cripple the offense. But the worst was yet to come.

On January 7th, during a 4-2 loss at New Haven, Lorne Duguid suffered an accidental blow to the eye off the stick of Eagle Glen Brydson. He suffered a severely lacerated eyelid, and an operation was needed to close the wound.

One of the most popular Barons, Duguid had played his last game for Cleveland. He came to Cleveland in 1937 after stays in Montreal, Detroit, Boston, and Providence. An instant hit with the fans, Lorne scored 22 and 19 goals respectively during the past two seasons but had slumped to 6 during the current campaign. A pro since 1930, he reported to camp overweight and never really got going.

Al Sutphin thought he was nearing the end of the line and had been working on a deal involving Lorne before the injury. Pittsburgh still had an interest in Duguid, but for cash only because of his now uncertain future. On January 20th, the deal with the Hornets was completed. Hergesheimer, Cunningham, and now Duguid. Three of the most popular players from Cleveland's Calder Cup Champions were gone.

While Indianapolis was in first place by 13 points by mid-January, a real dogfight was developing between Cleveland, Hershey, and Pittsburgh in the battle for the final two playoff spots in the West division. All three teams were playing .500 hockey and were tied for second on January 11th, as Cleveland was in the midst of a three-game winning streak.

While they were the lowest scoring team in the League, the Barons had given up the fewest number of goals. Defense was carrying them. Dick Adolph, Fred Robertson, Larry Molyneaux, and Joe Jerwa were providing great protection in front of goalie Moe Roberts. The team finally seemed on the rise.

Even though they were playing better, Al Sutphin was far from satisfied. He knew the team needed another goal scorer. First, he sold Harold Jackson back to Providence. Jackson was the odd man out in the Barons' defensive rotation and did not live up to his advance billing.

On February 6th, Sutphin made his last big deal of the season. Bob Gracie was dealt to Indianapolis for Don Deacon, last season's scoring champion while with Pittsburgh.

Gracie, who performed so well in last season's playoffs, did not seem to have the same intensity as before and fell out of favor with Coach Bill Cook.

Deacon had been up and down between Detroit and Indianapolis all year. The Red Wings couldn't make up their minds on Don's ability. He was a big, sometimes awkward skater. But he was also an excellent stickhandler and had a gift for scoring goals. Last season his 65 points, on 24 goals and 41 assists, led the AHL. This season, he had 7 goals and 15 assists during his limited time at Indianapolis.

Cleveland fans got their first look at Deacon in a Cleveland uniform that night as the Barons took on New Haven at the Arena.

The game was a close defensive struggle as most Baron games were that season. Regulation time expired with the score knotted at 1-1. It looked like a sure tie when Joe Jerwa brought the puck into the New Haven end and passed to Ossie Asmundson. Ossie then fed a pass to the husky Deacon in front of the net. Don beat Eagle goalie Claude Bourque at 8:48 of overtime and became an instant hero. It was a storybook first game for the big center iceman, who just barely got to Cleveland in time for the game. The win put the Barons alone in second place by one point with a 16-16-7 record.

The fans seemed to sense that the team was finally on the upswing, as 11,115 crowded into the Arena on February 10th to see the Barons play their finest game of the season against 1st place Indianapolis.

Goals by Joe Jerwa, Bud Cook, and Charlie Mason gave Cleveland a 3-1 win. This was the first time in eight games that the Barons had beaten the Capitals. The Indy squad was slipping a bit, and the loss left them only six points ahead of Cleveland. It was now a four-team battle for the top three playoff berths.

The pressure of the race really began to show the very next night in Springfield during and after a 2-1 loss. The game was filled with fighting and stick-swinging. Even Coach Bill Cook got into the act.

During the third period, Cook began throwing hockey sticks on the ice to protest an official's call. While arguing with the referee, an amused Springfield player picked up the sticks and gave them to fans along the boards. This further angered the coach, as the fans refused to give them back.

When a photographer flashed a picture in Bill's face on the way to the dressing room after the game, Cook decked the picture-taker with one punch. The coach later apologized. As the race got tighter, tempers got shorter.

February 16th brought major news in the Barons' front office. Al Sutphin announced the formation of a seven-man scouting staff that would scour Canada for new talent, especially in the western provinces. The staff would be headed by Director Jean Dubuc, former owner of the Providence Reds. Chief Scout would be Hub Bishop. Other staff members were Hobb Wilson, Gail Egan, J. C. Oliver, Al Rogers, and Ollie Campbell. These men, and others who followed, kept a constant flow of talent coming to Cleveland for years to come.

The scouting staff and subsequent minor league system was unheard of in minor league hockey. This infuriated the NHL owners. They realized that Sutphin was attempting to build his team, and the AHL, into a league that would rival their own. This meant more competition to sign talent.

The AHL threat was real. At Sutphin's insistence, Syracuse and Pittsburgh, two former NHL farm teams, had gone independent. Also, a new AHL rule forbade any member club from taking more than three NHL players on loan. All other players must be owned by each AHL club. This did not include Indianapolis and Philadelphia, who were owned and operated by Detroit and New York, respectively.

The biggest insult to the NHL came when the AHL owners voted upon ownership rights to the new Buffalo franchise for the 1940-41 season. AHL officials voted down the franchise bid by Toronto Maple Leaf owner Conn Smythe. Smythe wanted to operate the Buffalo franchise as a Toronto farm club. The vote was 7-2 against Smythe, with Indy and Philly, both NHL operated farms, the only votes for Smythe.

The Buffalo franchise went to Edgar Danahy, who would operate on an independent basis.

AHL teams were putting money into a secret fund for the time if and when their league would totally challenge the NHL. If it had not been for World War II, in all probability there would have been two major hockey leagues.

Indianapolis was able to hold on to its slim lead for first place. Cleveland, Pittsburgh, and Hershey kept climbing or falling into second, third, or fourth.

The Barons were in second place on February 17th after defeating Hershey 5-2 at the Arena before 9,816 fans. They were now only four points out of first. But quicker than you could bat an eye, they lost three straight and fell to fourth. The race was topsy-turvy all the way.

On March 13th, Cleveland won a clutch game at Pittsburgh to move into second place, 1 point ahead of both the Hornets and Hershey. The Barons had two games remaining, while the Hornets and Bears had three games left, two of which were against each other. Cleveland played Syracuse and New Haven during that last weekend and needed wins desperately.

Once again, the Barons would be playing without defenseman Fred Robertson. Three games earlier, Robertson's season was ended with a broken ankle. It was a tough blow, as Fred was having the finest year of his career. He was sorely missed.

Hershey and Pittsburgh split their home and home series, each winning one game. This put both teams one point ahead of Cleveland with one game each remaining.

Standing between the Barons and the playoffs were the Syracuse Stars. The Stars were in last place and came to the Arena with nothing to lose.

The Barons went on the attack early and threw everything at Syracuse but the kitchen sink. But this night belonged to Bill Beveridge. Twice beaten out for the #1 netminding job in Cleveland by Moe Roberts, Bill had something to prove. Last season he was bested by Roberts again in the playoffs. Now he would get his revenge.

Beveridge made 14 saves in the first period and 10 in the second to frustrate the Barons. When the Stars scored twice within one minute midway through the second period, the writing was on the wall.

Cleveland attacked savagely in the third period, but Beveridge stood tall. In all, he kicked out 21 last-period shots for a total of 45 saves. Bud Cook scored in the last minute, but the damage was already done. The 9,647 fans were stunned. The Barons were just about done, but they still had one more chance. If they could win at New Haven the next night, and if either Pittsburgh or Hershey lost their last game, they would be in the playoffs. A slim chance, but a chance nonetheless.

After an all-night train ride to the East Coast, the exhausted Barons gave it all they had.

Down 2-0 after one period, Cleveland got one back at 2:05 of the second period on a goal by Bud Cook. After New Haven scored again, Charlie Mason brought the Barons to within one again at 16:35.

Earl Bartholome tied the score early in the third period. From that point on, Cleveland's attack was all out, but they could not get the elusive game winner. With Dick Adolph in the penalty box during the last minute, the Barons were struck down by an ironic twist of fate.

George (Popeye) Patterson, who fired the goal that won the Calder Cup for Cleveland last season, scored a goal with 30 seconds left to give the Eagles a 4-3 win and knock the Barons out of the playoffs. Patterson, now in his late 30's, was thought to be over the hill by Al Sutphin. In one of his few bad moves, Al sold Popeye to New Haven, and it came back to haunt him.

First Bill Beveridge the night before; now George Patterson. Two ex-Barons made the Clevelanders ex-champs.

FINAL STANDINGS
1939-40

West	W	L	T	GF	GA	PTS.
Indianapolis	26	20	10	174	144	62
Hershey	27	24	5	154	156	59
Pittsburgh	25	22	9	152	133	59
Cleveland	24	24	8	127	130	56
Syracuse	20	27	9	147	169	49

East	W	L	T	GF	GA	PTS.
Providence	27	19	8	161	157	62
New Haven	27	24	3	177	183	57
Springfield	24	24	6	166	149	54
Philadelphia	15	31	8	133	170	38

Top Baron Scorers	G	A	PTS.
Earl Bartholome	17	26	43

Calder Cup Champion – Providence Reds

Fred "The Bull" Robertson as he appeared in a Cleveland Falcons uniform. Extremely popular with the fans, Fred was a rock on defense during the 1939-40 season and earned first All-Star team honors. Walt Voysey collection.

The departure of Les Cunningham and Phil Hergesheimer to the Chicago Blackhawks left a huge hole in the Barons offense during the 1939-40 season. However, the loss was shortlived. Cunningham returned to Cleveland for the next season; Hergesheimer in 1942. Walt Voysey collection.

Les Cunningham

Phil Hergesheimer

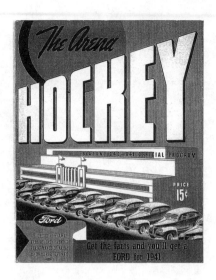

1940-41 SEASON

The failure of the Barons to make the playoffs did not sit well with Al Sutphin. The Barons' owner, along with Coach Bill Cook, had two main goals during the off season – revamp and improve the offense and return the team to the top of the League. The sweeping personnel changes were staggering.

First off and most important, was the re-acquisition of center Les Cunningham. Les had a so-so year in Chicago and welcomed the opportunity to return to Cleveland. He would finish out his career here and become the League's first great superstar. Everyone concerned, including the fans, couldn't be happier.

Sutphin wanted two new wingers for Cunningham. First, he pulled off a blockbuster trade with Syracuse. The Barons sent to the Stars Paul Runge, Emory Hanson, and Leroy Goldsworthy for last season's scoring champion Norm Locking. A super left winger, Locking registered 31 goals and 32 assists for 63 points for the Stars last season. Along with Don Deacon, who led the League in 1938-39, Cleveland now had the League scoring champion for the past two seasons.

Right winger Joffre Desilets was purchased from Chicago to complete the line. These three would terrorize opposing goalies all season long. They had a certain chemistry and jelled as soon as they were put together.

Sutphin wasn't finished. He traded sparkplug James (Peggy) O'Neil to Montreal for right wing Bill Summerhill. Al hated to part with O'Neil. Nobody worked harder than Peg, but his goal production slipped drastically, and Summerhill's potential was too great to pass up. Bill had blazing speed and would become the League's fastest skater. No one could believe Montreal would part with him.

Charlie Mason was sold to Buffalo, which meant the Barons now had no one to show for the Phil Hergesheimer deal. Bob Gracie, Harold Jackson, and Mason looked like good additions the previous season. All were solid players but just did not fit in here. Sutphin was quick to admit his mistakes and move on.

The last major acquisition was defenseman Bill MacKenzie in a cash deal with Montreal. The Canadiens had purchased Bill from Chicago with the intention of dealing him to the Barons. MacKenzie divided last season between Chicago and Providence. It was his goal, with seven seconds remaining in the final game, that won last season's Calder Cup for the Reds. Five feet nine inches and 200 pounds, he was made captain of the Barons and was counted upon to take on the inspirational leader role of the now-departed Peg O'Neil.

As the Barons prepared to open the season against Hershey at the Arena, Sutphin dangled a lucrative carrot in front of the team. If the club was in first place after each or any 14-game quarter of the season, a $1,200 bonus would be awarded to the team to be split up among the players. No other owner in hockey offered his players this incentive. It may not seem like much today, but given the tough

Goalie Moe Roberts chats with Baron Captain Bill Mackenzie. Cleveland Public Library collection.

conditions in the country just prior to World War II, this was a good chunk of change. The players were grateful and went after it.

Sutphin had assembled a potential powerhouse and expected immediate results. He didn't have to wait too long.

Bill Summerhill earned the nickname "Blazin' Bill" on Halloween night, as the Barons started the season with an 8-4 thrashing of Hershey. Teamed with Bud Cook and Ossie Aubuchon, Summerhill and his linemates dominated the game. "Blazin' Bill" himself amazed the crowd with a three-goal hat trick and two assists to boot.

The Barons had changed their entire style of play. No longer putting defense first, Cleveland would send all three forwards and both defensemen deep into the attacking zone in an all-out effort to score goals. Coach Cook knew they would be caught too far up ice on occasion, resulting in the opposition getting breakaways on Moe Roberts; but he had confidence in his players' ability to get back on defense and help out.

Defenseman Bill MacKenzie put an explanation point on this new offensive outlook by scoring two goals himself, while in the first game playing a solid game on the backline.

Cleveland stayed hot, with the wide open attack credited with a 5-0 start. It was during the fifth straight victory, a 5-2 triumph over Indianapolis, that the Barons embarked on a goaltending soap opera that lasted for nearly a month. While making a save against the Capitals, Moe Roberts tore the hamstring muscle in his right leg. Unable to continue, none other than Sonny Boy Baxter was rushed in to finish the game.

The amateur goalie and season ticket holder, who saved a game for New Haven against Cleveland the previous season, had another dream come true as he now helped the Barons to victory.

An emergency call was put into the League office, and Alphie Moore was sent on loan to Cleveland to fill in at goal. Moore, the goalie who led the hockey Indians to the title in Cleveland's first pro season eleven years ago, was playing out the string of a long career. Little did he know of the wild ride and unexpected turn that this season would hold for him.

After a 7-2 defeat at Indianapolis, Moore sprained his ankle during the second period of his very next game, a 4-3 win over New Haven. Once again, Sonny Boy Baxter, who was now practicing with the Barons, was called out of the stands to preserve the win when Moore couldn't continue. The fact that Cleveland had a 6-1 record was amazing.

Al Sutphin got help from Pittsburgh, as Harvey Teno was loaned to the Barons. Teno was the regular goalie for the Hornets last season and the team's MVP. But Harvey was involved in an auto accident six weeks before the start of the season and had yet to see any action, as his substitute, Red McAtee, was playing super.

Teno should have stayed in Pittsburgh, since the goalie jinx was still hanging over Cleveland. In his first game, a 4-2 win over Providence that saw Don Deacon finally score his first two goals of the season, the new Baron goalie broke his hand! He was able to finish the game but was sent back to Pittsburgh for treatment. In the last four games, Cleveland had now gone through four goaltenders! Fortunately, Alphie Moore's sprained ankle had healed sufficiently to allow him to return to action. One wonders if he really wanted to come back here.

A dark cloud was hanging over the Barons. Although the team was in first place with a 9-3-1 record, the injury bug would not leave. In their next game, a 2-2 tie against Springfield before a crowd of 11,423 at the Arena, Norm Locking came within a half inch of losing his life.

Locking was going great guns and was part of the League's top line. Les Cunningham had 15 points, Joffre Disilets had 13, as did Locking.

After being knocked down during a scramble in front of the Springfield net, a teammate's skate pierced the right side of his neck behind the ear. The wicked cut was an inch and a half deep and missed the jugular vein by 1/2 inch. Norm was a lucky man. The cut healed faster than expected, and the courageous winger was back on the ice in a little over a week.

On the plus side, Moe Roberts finally returned to action on December 11th after a 24-day absence to face the fast-charging Hornets at Pittsburgh. The Steel City crew had won five straight, and were now only one point behind Cleveland and Hershey.

The Barons trailed 2-0 with less than six minutes to play, when Joffre Desilets took matters into his own hands. The big Frenchman scored twice within three minutes to tie the score when a loss looked certain. The Barons attacked relentlessly during the 10-minute overtime, and it finally paid off. At the 8:07 mark, defenseman Joe Jerwa slapped in a 50-foot shot that gave Cleveland a 3-2 victory!

Roberts seemed as sharp as ever, and the timing of his return was perfect. December 18th had been declared Moe Roberts Day to pay homage to the star goaltender. Al Sutphin would honor players with a "day" after eight years of service to the club. Moe was the first so honored, and the festivities were grand.

The Parmadale band played with NBC vocalists Dorothea Brooks and Stewart Groshan and the Hermit Glee Club before the game. Sportscaster Tom Manning was master of ceremonies, and speeches were made by AHL President Maurice Podoloff, League VP John Digby Chick, and Al Sutphin himself. Last but not least was Harry (Hap) Holmes. The former owner, who brought pro hockey and Roberts himself to Cleveland, presented Moe a new Ford automobile on behalf of more than 500 fans who contributed toward its purchase.

On this big night, Roberts did not disappoint his fans. The Barons won a big game over the Hershey Bears, 6-3, and held on to first place with an 11-5-2 record. Besides the car, Moe also took home a huge black eye and swollen face after being hit with a puck. Moe was at the top of his game, but he could not shake the injury bug this year.

Roberts was knocked out of the lineup again on January 16th in a game at Pittsburgh. For the past month, the Barons were either in or around first place in their three-way battle with the Hornets and Hershey. On this night, Les Cunningham led the way as the League's leading scorer racked up four assists in a 6-3 victory. But it was another painful night for Cleveland's battered goalie.

Moe was hit in the Adam's apple on a shot by Eddie Convey and suffered a slightly cracked larynx. He somehow stayed in the game and played superbly despite being in great pain. His teammates were amazed by Moe's heroics, but the great goalie would miss the next three games. Alphie Moore was called in again as a replacement and went 1-1-1 in his latest stint with the club.

Although only able to talk in a whisper, Roberts returned to action in a 1-1 overtime tie that finally saw Bud Cook resurface. Cook was having a real

"Moe Roberts Night" – The great Baron goalie is congratulated by Harry "Hap" Holmes, who brought professional hockey to Cleveland with the old Indians.
Cleveland Public Library collection – Photo by Clayton Knipper.

tough luck season. Goalies always seemed to come up big on Bud, and he probably led the League in hitting goalposts. But his playmaking was as good as ever, and nobody on the team hustled more. The fans gave Bud an extended standing ovation when he tied the score at 6:27 of the third period. They appreciated his hard work and let him know that he was still one of their favorites.

Cook rewarded his fans again two weeks later when he scored the winning goal in a 1-0 victory over Springfield. Bud's score came at 10:26 of the third period. He won a face-off in front of the Indian net, passed to Earl Bartholome, who gave it back to Cook fifteen feet in front of the net. The shot was perfect.

Perfect was also the word for the Cleveland defense as they allowed only nine shots on goal the whole evening. Goalie Roberts made five saves in the first period and two saves in each of the second and third. The big win put Cleveland 12 points (or six full games) ahead of Hershey in the West division.

When Cleveland defeated Hershey 4-1 in overtime at the Arena on February 15th, the race appeared over. The Barons had a 24-11-8 record. They were 12 points in front of the Bears with only 13 games remaining.

Everything was going well. Roberts was outstanding in goal. The defense was smothering opponents. The offense, led by the League's top line of Les Cunningham, Norm Locking, and Joffre Diselets, was in high gear. The Cunningham line was the best in League history up to that time. What could go wrong? Well, winning only two of their remaining 13 games was one thing.

The Barons started their tailspin during a 6-4 loss in New Haven. The most crushing blow of the night was not the score but a serious injury to Norm Locking. The ace left wing, who scored his 22nd goal in

Barons great defense of 1940-41 – Larry Molyneaux, Fred Robertson, Joe Jerwa, Dick Adolph, and Bill Mackenzie. Cleveland Public Library collection.

The American Hockey League's top line of 1940-41 was the trio of Joffre Desilets (L), Les Cunningham (C), and Norm Locking (R). Cleveland Public Library collection – Cleveland News photo by Eddie Dork.

the second period, suffered a partial torn ligament in his right knee after being body-checked to the ice. He would miss only four games all year, but the knee would always give him trouble in the future.

After losses at Springfield and Pittsburgh, the Barons came home to face the Hornets with a chance to clinch a playoff berth. Though there was no danger of missing the playoffs, it always felt good to have it official.

The Hornets were fighting for their playoff lives, and the game was a nip-and-tuck affair.

The visitors jumped on top in the first period when Scotty Bowman fired a shot that Moe Roberts misplayed for a goal. The fans got on Moe a bit, but he settled down and played a great game. Norm Locking, bad knee and all, tied the game at 1-1 on a rebound off of Les Cunningham's shot at 3:31 of the second period.

The game remained tied until Big Fred (The Bull) Robertson thrilled the crowd with an end-to-end rush to get the game winner. The fans loved Fred. Sort of a bull in a china shop on skates, Robertson had refined his game in recent years. Once only a banger, he worked tirelessly with Coach Cook to become a complete defenseman.

Bud Cook scored an insurance goal, and Cleveland secured its playoff spot with a 3-2 win.

Another loss and a tie preceded a dismal six-game losing streak. Everything seemed to be falling apart. Their one-time 12 point lead over Hershey had dwindled to two, and they had fallen behind Providence and New Haven in the race for overall point champion.

Worst news during the losing streak was the loss of Joffre Diselets. Jof broke his right hand during a 7-3 loss at Indianapolis. He finished the regular season with 15 goals and 29 assists for 44 points. This meant the break-up of the League's top line.

The Barons headed into the last weekend of the regular season needing a victory to hold off the Hershey Bears for first place and to give the team's morale a lift heading into the playoffs.

Cleveland got the big win and division championship at the expense of the Indianapolis Capitals. A crowd of 10,093 fans saw the Barons win a 2-1 squeaker. After Earl Bartholome scored a shorthanded goal at 11:41 of the second period, both teams went on the attack in an effort to get the winner. The game went back and forth at breakneck speed and kept the fans breathless.

Finally, at 10:06 of the third period, Joe Jerwa scored the title-clinching goal. This was the 13th goal of the season for the Polish backliner, a huge total for a defenseman. The fans were jubilant, but the best was yet to come.

The Barons now prepared to meet the Providence Reds, Eastern division winners, in the first round of the playoffs.

Individual honors went to several Clevelanders. Les Cunningham won the scoring championship with 64 points on 22 goals and 44 assists. Norm Locking and Bill MacKenzie were named to the first All Star team and Cunningham, Joffre Diselets, and Fred Robertson to the second team. Les was edged out of the first team by Fred Thurier of Springfield.

Total attendance for 28 home games was 231,471, for an average of 8,267 per game.

Defenseman Dick Adolph with Barons owner Al Sutphin. Cleveland State University archives – Photo by Herman Seid.

THE PLAYOFFS

The Barons were decided underdogs heading into the best of five opening playoff round against the Reds. During the regular season, they had beaten Cleveland four out of six games. With the first two games being played out East, where they had dropped all three regular season games, Cleveland was really up against it. Having lost seven of their last eight games, they weren't given much of a chance. Their chances were even more remote after the first game.

The game opened with the Barons attacking furiously. Unfortunately, Reds goalie Mike Karakus was equal to the task. Near the end of the first period, Hub Wilson put Providence on top 1-0.

That lone goal looked like it would hold up; but at 15:47 of the third period, Les Cunningham took a pass from Norm Locking to tie the game and send it into a full 10-minute overtime. The Barons seemed to have the momentum, but the Reds had other ideas.

Just 31 seconds into overtime, Hub Wilson blasted a shot past Moe Roberts to give the Reds the lead. Since the first ten-minute overtime was not sudden death, Providence had time to turn the game into a rout. Two more goals gave Providence a 4-1 victory.

This put the Barons' backs against the wall. They could not afford to go back to Cleveland down two games. To make matters more complicated, Moe Roberts' sprained ankle was getting worse. He suffered the injury in practice ten days before, but it seemed to be getting better. No such luck.

Game Two in Providence was a real roughhouse affair. Five major penalties were called for fighting, featuring a long and bitter bout between Doug Young and Bud Cook. The fight started with a stick-swinging duel and ended with Young decking Cook with a solid punch to the face. In all, 18 penalties were called in the wild contest.

When they weren't beating each other silly, some great hockey was played. High-scoring defenseman Joe Jerwa put the Barons on top midway through the first period. This was the game's only goal, until Jack Shill took the puck behind his own net and carried it the length of the ice to beat Moe Roberts to tie the score in the third period. For the second game in a row, overtime was played.

Nobody scored during the first 10-minute extra period that was played without Dick Adolph. As regulation time expired, Dick got into an argument with a fan and poked his stick at the heckler. He received a 10-minute misconduct penalty and missed the first overtime period. He redeemed himself in the second.

As the sudden death second O.T. was nearing its conclusion, Adolph took a pass from Bill Summerhill at center ice and fired from the blue line. The shot fooled Mike Karakas at 19:11 and gave Cleveland a 2-1 victory. The win was sweet because the Barons achieved their goal – a split in Providence.

Dick Adolph made big news in Cleveland just a few weeks earlier. Although Cleveland and Buffalo were completely independent, the seven other teams in the League had three players each on loan from NHL clubs. This made all clubs subject to the NHL draft again this year.

Speculation arose as to who Cleveland might lose for the new $7,500 price tag. Fearing it could be him, Adolph came out and said he was happy in Cleveland and did not want to be drafted. That a bright young star would prefer to stay in the American League was a kick in the face to the NHL. It pointed out that the AHL was getting stronger and that players loved it in Cleveland. Adolph got his wish and remained a Baron for the rest of his career.

The series shifted back to Cleveland, and 11,882 fans turned out to see their heroes win a big one, 4-2.

After Earl Bartholome opened the scoring early in the first period, Providence took the lead on goals by Normie Mann and George Johnston. Down 2-1 entering the third period, the Barons took the offensive and forced the play in the Reds' zone. Taking a pass from Les Cunningham, Joe Jerwa beat Mike Karakas from 30 feet to tie the score. Counting regular season and playoffs, Big Joe now had 15 goals, and most of them were clutch markers.

Bill Summerhill got the game winner at the sixteen-minute mark. Mired in a season-long slump after his blistering opening month, Summerhill was mobbed by the entire team. They knew his frustration and stood by him all year because he never quit.

When Jake Milford scored into an open net to clinch the game, the fans were once again seeing a Baron team that resembled the one that ran rampant through the League earlier in the year.

The only down note was that Moe Roberts could barely walk after the game. The great goalie was in severe pain but somehow was able to block the ankle injury out of his mind once the game started. But now the Baron management was worried. Just in case, Alphie Moore was brought in should Roberts not be able to continue.

Game Four was simply a classic. 10,712 fans saw a titanic struggle that see-sawed back and forth and kept them literally on the edge of their seats from start to finish.

The thrills began at the :32 mark on a Cleveland goal by Ossie Asmundson. Three minutes later, Earl Bartholome made it 2-0, and it looked like a laugher.

But no one was laughing as the Reds stormed back with three unanswered goals to take a 3-2 first-period lead.

As the fans were settling into their seats for the second period, they were shocked by an announcement that Moe Roberts could not continue and that Alphie Moore would take over in goal. Roberts had reached the end of his endurance. The courageous goalie had given his all, but the pain had overwhelmed him. His severely sprained ankle had left him immobile. It was good foresight that the Barons had Alphie Moore on hand in case of such an emergency.

As the second period began, Cleveland launched an all-out five-man attack. The major offensive was rewarded by a Bill MacKenzie goal at 2:46 to tie the score 3-3.

Cleveland kept attacking relentlessly, and Providence did not even get a shot on goal until the 8:45 mark. At 9:40 Red Defenseman Ed Bush tackled Ossie Asmundson on a breakaway, and Cleveland was awarded a penalty shot. A penalty shot is very rare and the most exciting individual play in hockey. In those days, when one was called, the shooting team could pick any player to take the shot. Coach Cook chose Les Cunningham.

Everyone cleared the ice except Cunningham and Red goalie Mike Karakas. Les started alone at center ice as the crowd held its breath. They were delirious when he scored on a short shot to give the home team a 4-3 lead.

But Providence wasn't through. The third period began by MacKenzie and Earl Bartholome drawing penalties that gave the Reds a two-man advantage. Art Giroux cashed in at the five-minute mark to tie the score.

A few minutes later, Mr. Clutch, Joe Jerwa, came through again to put Cleveland up by one at 9:51. Still it wasn't enough. At 14:10, defenseman Ed Bush rifled a 25-footer past Alphie Moore to tie it at 5-5.

Then came the play of the season to that point. Only a few seconds after Bush's goal, Joe Jerwa got hold of the puck on the right side of the rink. As if possessed, he bullied his way through both Providence defensemen. At an angle that looked impossible, Joe fired an incredible shot that somehow got past Karakas. Bedlam ensued. But at the same instant he shot, Jerwa was knocked into the boards and lay on the ice writhing in pain as the crowd celebrated. After being helped up by his teammates, the hero skated to the dressing room with his right arm limp at his side. Alphie Moore held off the Reds the rest of the way, and the Barons were in the finals with a dramatic 6-5 victory.

After the game, it was learned that Joe Jerwa, that heroic son of Poland, had suffered a broken hand after his great game-winning goal. His greatest individual moment in 14 years of hockey had ended his season. But the Barons' season moved on. They dedicated the championship final against the Hershey Bears to the man who made it possible, Big Joe Jerwa.

Hershey made it to the finals by beating New Haven in two straight games and then getting past Pittsburgh two games to one. The Bears were a healthy team, but the same could not be said about Cleveland. In addition to the loss of Joe Jerwa, Bill Summerhill was out after having two teeth pulled, and Joffre Diselets was going to try to play with his broken hand.

But the most distressing news came in the announcement that Moe Roberts would give way to Alphie Moore in goal. His injured ankle would not come around in time to start the series. The fate of the Barons would be in the aging hands of the man who won Cleveland's first pro title back in 1930. It was a long, twisting road back to Cleveland for Moore. Although he played well while substituting for Moe throughout the year, could he come through one more time? The first game in the best of five series would start revealing the answer.

Moore played a fine game in the opener by kicking out 31 saves in Cleveland's thrilling 4-3 overtime victory at the Arena. Jake Milford, Les Cunningham, and Ossie Asmundson tallied for Cleveland in regulation time. Gordon Pettinger sent the game into overtime when he scored at 14:32 of the third period.

Unheralded Oscar Aubuchon got the game winner at 7:44 of overtime, but it was the ever-hustling work of Bill MacKenzie that made the goal possible. Bill took a pass from Bud Cook at mid ice and barged through the Hershey defense on the left side. He carried the puck behind the net with a Bear defender all over his back before passing out to Aubuchon. Captain Bill would not be denied, and the Barons had a win.

The ankle injury to Moe Roberts turned out to be more serious than was first believed. At first thought to be a sprain, x-rays revealed a chipped bone in the ankle. This left no doubt that he was through for the year. It was all up to Alphie Moore now.

Alphie was more than up to the task in Game Two in Cleveland as the Barons won 3-1 to move within one game of the championship.

Moore was called on to make only 20 saves, as the Barons kept up the pressure all night. The score would have been much higher had it not been for the great goaltending of the Bears' Nick Damore. Nick kept his teammates in the game with one big save after another. With the score tied 1-1 after two periods, Hershey had a good shot at victory. But quick goals by Ossie Asmundson and Bud Cook sealed the victory for Cleveland.

The series shifted back to Hershey for two games, and the Barons should have stayed home. During the regular season, their record in Chocolate Town was 0-3-1, and it didn't get any better just because it was playoff time.

Cleveland never really was in Game Three, as the Bears blasted the Barons 4-0. Nick Damore was the big story as he kicked out 27 shots for the whitewash. Cleveland was beaten in every facet of the game and needed a much better effort in the next contest, or the score would be even higher.

The Barons got the effort in Game Four, but not the win. Nothing went right for most of the game; and with Hershey ahead 4-1 with twelve minutes remaining, the situation appeared hopeless. But the Barons finally staged a rally that nearly pulled the game out.

A goal by Fred Robertson at 8:22 of the third period, and another by Dick Adolph at 10:09, put the Barons back in the game. However, the great goaltending of little Nick Damore saved the day, and the game, for the Bears. The 4-3 Hershey win sent the series back to Cleveland for the fifth and deciding game for the Calder Cup.

Both teams were battered for the title game. Hershey was without Gordon Bruce and Jack Shewchuck with leg injuries suffered in the last game. For Cleveland, hard-luck Bill Summerhill, who sat out Game Four after having his right wrist severely slashed in game three, was doubtful for the big game. He would dress, but he could not grip a stick, as the wrist was braced but badly cut and bruised.

10,743 fired-up fans saw a game they would not soon forget.

The Barons went on the attack right from the opening face-off but could not beat the super Damore. Nick made 11 stops in the scoreless opening period, and none was easy. By comparison, Alphie Moore had only five saves.

It seemed only a matter of time until Cleveland would score, as they again pressed the attack in the second period. Finally, at 7:16 Don Deacon fed a pass to Jake Milford in front of the net. Jake deked Damore out of position and put Cleveland up 1-0.

The Hersheys came out of their defensive shell after Milford's goal and opened up their offense. They finally got on the board in the last minute of the second period. Joffre Diselets, playing with his broken wrist, attempted a pass out from behind his own net that was intercepted by Gordon Pettinger. Gordon wasted no time in beating Alphie Moore to tie the score.

Hershey took the lead at 12:51 of the third period on a goal by Harry Frost. It appeared the Bears would have their first title, but the Barons would not give up.

Coach Bill Cook decided to take a huge gamble. At the end of the bench sat Bill Summerhill with his badly damaged wrist. Bill hadn't played all night, but he had fresh legs. At 14:35 Cook sent five forwards onto the ice – Cunningham, Locking, Aubuchon, Asmundson, and the until-now-forgotten Summerhill. Bill was amazed to be called by Cook, but was thrilled for the opportunity.

In storybook fashion, the move paid off. At 17:29, Summerhill was at the right corner of the Hershey net with Locking fighting for position on the left. Norm received a pass from Asmundson. With a defenseman all over him Locking somehow managed to turn to shoot, but goalie Damore had the angle covered. Cool as ice, instead of shooting, Locking slipped a pass to Summerhill. Blazin' Bill slapped the puck into the net before Damore could move. The crowd erupted, and Bill Summerhill had made up for a frustrating, injury-filled season that had looked so promising last Fall.

Earl Bartholome gets a big hug from Barons' Mascot Jackie Kilbane after his overtime goal won the Calder Cup for Cleveland on April 10, 1941.
Cleveland Public Library collection – Photo by Jerry Horton.

The game remained tied, and a full ten-minute overtime ensued.

Early in the overtime, Don Deacon took hold of the puck in the neutral zone and fed a pass to Jake Milford. Both Milford and Earl Bartholome were racing down the left side, Bartholome closest to the boards. As they crossed the blue line, Jake gave Earl the puck and cut to the middle. At that moment, near the face-off circle, Earl let go a high, hard shot that beat Damore at 1:25 of overtime. Pure bedlam let loose. But the game was not over yet. This was not sudden death.

Barons celebrate after winning 1940-41 Calder Cup.
Cleveland Public Library collection.

Rush after Hershey rush was turned back by Alphie Moore and the Cleveland defense. Finally, the game ended, and the Barons were Calder Cup Champions for the second time.

This truly was a fairy-tale season. The heroes were many. Gallant Moe Roberts ; Joe Jerwa and his clutch goals, only to be lost when his brightest moment ended with a broken hand; Blazin' Bill Summerhill, early-season hero, all but forgotten, gets a last chance while injured and rises to glorious heights; Alphie Moore, over-the-hill spare goalie, wins the Calder Cup in his last game; and last but not least, Earl Bartholome. Earl was often overlooked because of the team's many stars. Never flashy, he would never complain, and would do anything Coach Bill Cook asked. He was the team's best checker, best penalty killer, and steadiest player. In short, he was a coach's dream. On April 10, 1941, Earl Bartholome's dreams came true, and the Barons were champions once again.

FINAL STANDINGS
1940-41

West	W	L	T	GF	GA	PTS.
Cleveland	26	21	9	177	162	61
Hershey	24	23	9	193	189	57
Pittsburgh	21	29	6	156	170	48
Buffalo	19	27	10	148	176	48
Indianapolis	17	28	11	133	168	45
East	**W**	**L**	**T**	**GF**	**GA**	**PTS.**
Providence	31	21	4	196	171	66
New Haven	27	21	8	179	153	62
Springfield	26	21	9	157	149	61
Philadelphia	25	25	6	166	167	56

Top Baron Scorers	G	A	PTS.
Les Cunningham	22	42	64
Norm Locking	25	19	44
Joffre Diselets	15	29	44

Calder Cup Champion – Cleveland Barons

CLEVELAND BARONS 1940-41.
Back Row (L-R): Stickboy Charles Homoniuk, Joffre Desilets, Larry Molyneaux, Dick Adolph, Norm Locking, Joe Jerwa, Bob Blake, Ossie Asmondson, Fred Robertson, Les Cunningham, Trainer Walter Robertson.
Front Row: Bud Cook, Earl Barholome, Bill Summerhill, Moe Roberts, Al Sutphin, Bill Cook, Bill Mackenzie, Oscar Aubuchon, Don Deacon, Jake Milford. Up Front: Mascot Jackie Kilbane. Cleveland Public Library collection.

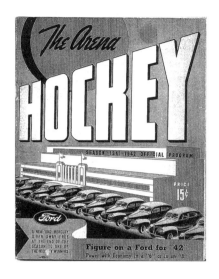

1941-42 SEASON

The first order of business in the off-season was to re-acquire the services of Bill Beveridge from Buffalo. Sutphin did not want to go through another season searching for a spare goalie if his #1 man went down. Cleveland thus became the first team to carry two goaltenders on their active roster. Bill and Moe Roberts battled for the #1 spot, with Roberts getting the nod to open the season against Pittsburgh.

According to Sutphin, when it came to winning and offense, you never had enough. Despite the team's prolific attack last season, he wasn't satisfied with the club's third line. When the Philadelphia Rockets (formerly Ramblers) decided to sell some of their players in order to pay their bills, Al was first in line. He purchased Stan Smith, Lude Wareing, and Herb Foster from Philly. This trio had scored 66 goals the previous season and was the Rockets' #1 line. This would give Cleveland such high scoring depth that it would be hard for anyone to touch them.

Unfortunately, due to the war escalation, only Foster was permitted by the Canadian government to start the season here.

The war was causing havoc in the hockey circles. Although the United States and Canada were not directly involved in the war yet, they were gearing up for the inevitable. Canadian draft boards were denying permits to play hockey in the U. S. to many players under the age of 25 who had not gone through two months of summer military training. In Manitoba and Saskatchewan, permits were refused to all players under 25, regardless of training status. Those who had already undergone the two-month training period could be called into the Canadian army at any time.

Smith and Wareing were denied entry to the states and began military training.

Not one to roll over when knocked down, the Barons' owner traded Ossie Asmundson and Oscar Aubuchon to Providence for 33-year-old high scoring right winger Art Giroux.

Bill Summerhill was sold to the Springfield Indians. Despite his last game heroics in the playoffs, Sutphin lost faith in Summerhill. But this was a case where he should have had more patience, for Bill would become a top performer in the League for the next decade.

Twenty-four rookies were invited to camp. These were all prospects from the Barons' new farm system. Many of these youths pushed the veterans hard. Most impressive were Walter Melnyk and Ed (Whitey) Prokup. Although Prokup was sent to Minneapolis for another year of seasoning, Bill Cook was enamored by Whitey's blazing speed. Bill took one look at the flashy winger and knew this kid was for real. Although he wasn't quite ready yet, Prokup would make his presence felt two years later. Melnyk stayed with Cleveland.

With basically the same team as last season plus Beveridge, Foster, Giroux, and Melnyk, the Barons looked like the team to beat and were picked to win it all again.

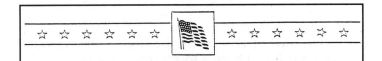

CLEVELAND BARON PLAYERS IN THE ARMED FORCES

George Agar
Sonny Baxter
Don Deacon
Alex Cunningham
Joffre Desilets
Sam Fasano
John Frenette
Oscar Galipeau
Maldwyn Hughes

Ragnar Jonson
Dick Livingston
Wilfred Mattson
Walter Melnyk
A. J. McGerrigle
Joe Metka
Jake Milford
Sandy Milne
Norman Nichol
Harry Dick

Edward Patzer
Ronald Pickell
Whitey Prokop
Wilton Speck, Jr.
Stan Smith
Garfield Shervin
Bernie Strongman
Lude Wareing
Moe Roberts

Cleveland came out of the gate smoking with a 6-4 win over Pittsburgh and did not lose until their 10th game of the season in Springfield. The 8-0-1 start was the best in the team's history with depth and scoring balance heralded as keys to this early success. All three forward lines were a threat at any time. The combinations were Diselets-Cunningham-Locking; Giroux-Cook-Foster; Barthelome-Deacon-Milford. Melnyk was the swing man.

Cook and Giroux had played together eleven years before at Providence in the old Canadian-American League. Their careers went in different directions, but there was a special chemistry between them. Put together again after all this time, they began to click immediately. Neither could explain it. The Barons and their fans were the beneficiaries.

After their first loss, Cleveland got right back in winning form with a 7-1 pasting of Philadelphia in the Quaker City. The game featured a hat trick by Herb Foster and a kidney injury to Joe Jerwa. The mishap would keep Big Joe out of the lineup for over a month, but it did have a silver lining. To replace Joe, the Barons called up Sandy Milne from Minneapolis. The 22-year-old defenseman proved to be a real find, as he showed right from the start that he was someone special. Unfortunately, at 22 years old, he was a prime candidate to be called into the military.

The Western division race was shaping up as a three-team dogfight. After 14 games, Cleveland, Indianapolis, and Hershey all had identical 9-3-2 records. No one else in the entire League was playing above .500. Despite sharing the lead, Al Sutphin decided to give the team its full $1,200 quarterly bonus as a gesture for its great start.

On December 6th, the Barons defeated Providence at the Arena before 10,238 fans. The game featured a sensational exhibition of goaltending by Moe Roberts. Ole Man Moe kicked out 41 shots in the 5-4 win, most of the saves sensational. But one shot, off the stick of Jack Shill, split the middle finger of Moe's right hand. The injury jinx had struck the goalie again, and he would miss the next nine games. But this time, the Barons were prepared. Bill Beveridge would step in, and the team would not miss a beat.

Of far greater concern to everyone than the previous night's game was the bombing of Pearl Harbor by the Japanese on December 7th. The war would ultimately end many a hockey career and change the future direction of the American Hockey League.

Of immediate concern to Al Sutphin was the status of his players. Since most of the team was made up of veterans over 26 years old, they were safe for the time being. But on Cleveland and every other team in the League, players knew that at any moment their hockey careers could end and a future in the military could begin.

Bill Beveridge played his first game in goal as a Cleveland Baron on December 10th in Pittsburgh. Though he lost 3-2, Bill was extremely sharp and would remain in the nets for the next nine games. All nine of these games were 1-goal decisions. With the pressure on, Bill came up with 6 wins and only three defeats. Moe Roberts was ready to play 2 weeks after his injury, but Coach Cook was reluctant to make a change because of Beveridge's great play.

Roberts, who was superb before his finger injury, was itching to get back in the lineup. The coach had a dilemma.

The situation temporarily took care of itself on January 3rd, when Beveridge suffered an eye injury that would keep him out of the lineup for a few weeks.

Moe Roberts returned in the 3rd period of a 2-0 shutout of Buffalo at the Arena. The game saw the Barons stretch their undefeated streak at home to 13 games and give the team a 17-6-2 record. Still, they were 4 points behind Hershey.

Cleveland stayed on Hershey's heels and finally caught them on January 17th, when they defeated the Washington Lions 2-1 at the Arena before 10,688. This marked the 16th straight game at home without defeat. Third-period goals by Jake Milford and Herb Foster put the Barons back in first place.

After a 4-3 loss at Providence and a 5-4 win in Philadelphia, Cleveland came home and put its 16-game undefeated streak on the line against the Springfield Indians, first-place club in the East division. The battle between East and Western division leaders took center stage, but Bill Cook had other worries in the back of his mind.

Although the Barons were still winning, the performance of Moe Roberts in goal had been slipping.

Moe had gotten into some bad habits and had looked shaky in recent games. Bill Beveridge was ready to go again, but Coach Cook was reluctant to make a change because the team still was winning games. Yet he worried as Springfield came to town because the Indians were scoring goals at a record pace. His worries were proved to be justified.

11,895 fans, the largest crowd to ever see a hockey game in Cleveland up to that time, saw a real thriller between the two division leaders. Over 2,000 people were turned away, but a 7-6 loss shattered the Barons' 16-game home unbeaten streak. Led by Fred Thurier's four goals, the Indians also knocked Cleveland out of first place.

Most significant were the seven goals given up by Moe Roberts. They certainly were not all his fault, especially with defenseman Fred Robertson out of the lineup with a sore knee. But the fans were all over Moe and were calling for Beveridge to replace him. How soon they forgot all the great years and great games he had given them. Fans are so fickle.

The pressure was really on Coach Cook to make a change in goal, but Bill was intensely loyal to Moe and really felt for the old goalie. "The situation requires a lot of thought," he said in regard to a switch. "I do not propose to make a hasty decision, and there will be nothing definite for another day or so."

In his heart, the Coach wanted to stick with Moe out of respect for what he had meant to the franchise. But in his mind, he knew that he should go with Beveridge. On January 28th, the day before a showdown with Hershey for first place, Bill Cook announced that he was starting Bill Beveridge and that Moe Roberts would serve as backup for the time being. What nobody knew at the time was that the 7-6 loss to Springfield on January 24, 1942 was the last game that Moe Roberts would ever play for the Cleveland Barons.

A huge Wednesday night crowd of 10,096 saw the Barons drop a heartpounding game to the Bears, 2-1 in overtime. The loss knocked Cleveland 3 points behind Hershey with a 23-11-2 record.

After Joffre Diselets opened the scoring on a beautiful feed from Les Cunningham at 9:54, the game became an old-fashioned, hard-hitting, tight-checking affair with excellent goaltending provided by Nick Damore of Hershey and Bill Beveridge. Goals by rookie Wally Wilson at 16:07 in the second period and 6:51 in overtime gave the Bears the big win.

On the plus side, the game marked the debut of Stan Smith in a Barons' uniform. Purchased by Al Sutphin along with Herb Foster and Lude Wareing in the off-season, Smith was held up from entering the United States by the Canadian government until he finished early military training. He would serve as a spare forward until called to duty.

After going 1-2-1 in their next four games, the Barons dropped six points behind Hershey. They were further rocked by the loss of Joe Jerwa on defense. It had been a tough season for Big Joe. After breaking his hand in last season's playoffs, Jerwa lost 30 lbs. while working in the Canmore Allerta Canadian coal mine. This weakened condition led to a back injury on November 27th. When attempting to come back too soon from that injury, Joe suffered a severely torn groin muscle in early January. The injury was extremely slow to heal, and Jerwa was heading home to Canmore to receive hospital treatment. He announced his retirement but would return when the team was hit hard by injuries during the last week of the season.

Norm Locking was also out of the lineup with an extremely sore back that turned out to be a slight chip of a bone at the base of his spine. Although he would return in the playoffs, Norm was through for the regular season.

Despite the many injuries, the Barons stayed in the hunt for first place with Indianapolis and Hershey. The Bears were further bolstered by the acquisition of ex-Baron Phil Hergesheimer. Al Sutphin had been after Phantom Phil all season long, but when negotiating with Chicago finally broke down, the Blackhawks sold him to Boston, who in turn loaned him to Hershey.

The chief reason for Cleveland staying in the race was the fantastic goaltending of Bevridge. His 1-0 whitewash of Providence on February 16th was a masterpiece. The Reds had gone a record 112 games without suffering a shutout until running into Bill.

Beveridge had now played in 19-2/3 games for Cleveland and had only given up 35 goals, a 1.78 average. Moe Roberts, by comparison, had played 25-1/3 games and gave up 79 goals for a 3.42 average.

After splitting a home and home series with Pittsburgh and defeating Philadelphia at the Arena, the Barons now led the West by two points over the Bears and Capitals with a 29-15-4 record.

This set up a date in Hershey on March 4th that would see Phil Hergesheimer face his former team for the first time.

The Bears dominated play for the first two periods, but the score remained deadlocked at 0-0, thanks to the unbelievable goaltending of Beveridge. Most of his saves seemed impossible, and finally his work fired up his teammates. With Jake Milford in Hergesheimer's face all evening, rendering the star a non-factor in the game, the Barons broke the game open in the third period with five unanswered scores. Goals were scored by Dick Adolph, Les Cunningham, Art Giroux, and Stan Smith twice. The 5-0 win was Beveridge's sixth shutout and put Cleveland in first place by 4 points with six games remaining.

The Barons dropped 2 of their next three games and lost the services of two more players. Center Don Deacon and winger Jake Milford went down with knee injuries in the team's 5-3 win over Washington.

With Norm Locking still hurting with his injured back, Cleveland went into its next game against Springfield with only two healthy forward lines.

Using only seven forwards, the Barons came up with a courageous effort and defeated the Indians behind Bill Beveridge's seventh shutout, 2-0, at the Arena. This put Cleveland 3 points ahead of Indianapolis with two games remaining. Unfortunately, the lead was shortlived. The Capitals had two games in hand, both against Buffalo, and won both. This put them back in first by one point over Cleveland with a big showdown scheduled for the Arena on March 14th.

A valiant but crippled Barons' hockey team fell to Indianapolis 4-2 before a record crowd of 12,225. Despite calling up Sam Fazano and Walter Melnyk from Minneapolis, Cleveland did not have enough firepower to hold off the hard charging Caps.

The game looked promising when Bud Cook scored first at 4:34. But Indy got two lightning quick goals by Jack Keating at 14:01 and 14:17 of the first period and never looked back. Stan Smith scored for Cleveland in the second period, but the Capitals added two more to lead 4-2 heading into the third stanza.

The Barons became unglued and completely disorganized in the final period and could never mount a serious offensive threat. Indianapolis played flawless defense and clinched first place with the decisive win.

Cleveland still had a shot at second place, but a Hershey win coupled with the Barons' 5-4 overtime loss at Buffalo toppled the injury-riddled Clevelanders to a third-place finish.

Despite having their highest point total ever with a 33-19-4 record, the season ended with a thud. But the Barons were never dull. They headed into the playoffs against the Washington Lions, third-place finishers in the East, at the center of a new controversy.

THE PLAYOFFS

A bad practice of "borrowing" players from teams that did not make the playoffs had been going on in hockey for years. If a team had injury problems they would fill out their roster by "loading up" with loaned players. Cleveland never took part in this practice and would usually look the other way if another team bent the rules on occasion, especially if another team needed a goalie. But now the situation was getting out of control.

Some injuries seemed suspicious, and every team seemed to be bending the rules. Sutphin was against the practice of borrowing players and was voted down 9-1 by his fellow owners when trying to make them stick to the eligibility rules.

Since his squad was severely handicapped by legitimate injuries, Al worked out a deal to borrow Kilby MacDonald from Buffalo and Johnny Sherf from Pittsburgh to help out his team. Still he didn't feel right about the situation and called his players together for a team meeting.

The owner spelled everything out to his team. He knew how hard they worked all season and now were up against the wall because of injuries. They could add two star players on loan if they so desired. Regardless of their decision, Al told them he would add $3,000 of his own money to the playoff pot. It didn't matter if they lost in the first round or went all the way – the money was theirs. This meant a possible $9,300 if they won the championship, not bad for 1942. Sutphin then left the room and left the team alone with its coach.

After discussing the pros and cons of adding "loaner" players, the Barons decided to play by the rules and turned down any outside help. Win or lose, they would go with what they had.

Sutphin was relieved and proud of his boys. "I am delighted...this undeniably is the greatest thing that ever happened in the game," he exaggerated. The owner felt that after this season the other teams would follow the Barons' example and quit breaking the eligibility rules. For the most part, he was correct. The glaring exception was Eddie Shore bending the rules at the Barons' expense in the 1944 playoffs. More of that later.

Don Deacon, Jake Milford, and Joe Jerwa were definitely out of the opening best-of-three series. Despite the injuries, the Barons were still favorites to oust the first-year Lions. Washington was so far behind at mid-season that their owner, M. J. Uline, booked the roller derby into their arena the same week that the playoffs opened. He was as surprised as anyone that his team was in the post-season tournament. Thus, all games would be played in Cleveland.

The Barons were high as a kite for the opening game and completely dominated the contest.

At the 15-second mark, Norm Locking, who by his own admission should not have been playing with his bad back, scored on a pass from Les Cunningham.

At 7:51 Joffre Diselets went the length of the ice on a solo dash, circled behind the Lion net, and passed the puck out front. It hit the skate of a Washington player and deflected past a stunned Bert Gardiner.

Rod Lorrain got one back for the Lions in the second period, but after that, Bill Beveridge slammed the door shut. What few chances the Baron defensemen allowed, Bill kicked out with authority. Les Cunningham and Stan Smith added insurance tallies, and Game 1 belonged to Cleveland, 4-1.

Game Two was a much closer affair, but the Barons swept into the semi-finals by defeating Washington 3-2.

Hero of the game was Walter Melnyk, who scored Cleveland's third and deciding goal. The game was especially meaningful to Melnyk, since he didn't know when he would play another hockey game. Earlier in the day, he was served notice to report for his physical exam prior to induction into the Canadian Army.

Walter played well in Cleveland. After 23 early season games, he was sent to the Minneapolis farm when Stan Smith joined the team in January. He kept improving his game, and it payed off when he was recalled later in the season. His next game was anyone's guess.

Cleveland's opponent in the second round was the high-powered Hershey Bears, who had just swept New Haven in two games. The Bears were looking for revenge, having lost the Calder Cup finals to Cleveland the previous year 3 games to 2. The best of three series opened in Cleveland, with Games 2 and 3 in Chocolate Town.

Game One in Cleveland brought back to town old friend Phil Hergesheimer. Phil played the final twelve games for Hershey and scored eight goals plus two more in the final playoff game with New Haven. With Hergey hot, the Barons had a tough road to hoe.

Cleveland opened the scoring on a long shot by Herb Foster at 4:41. Hershey then tied the score at 1-1 heading into the second period.

From then on, the Cleveland defense took over. Holding the Bears to two shots for the entire second period, the Barons attacked in a frenzy. Had it not been for the great goaltending of Nick Damore, the Barons would have won in a cakewalk.

The go-ahead goal was put in by Les Cunningham in an outstanding solo effort. Scrambling for the puck at the blue line, Les got hold of the disc and broke in on Damore with a Bear defender all over him. He somehow got the puck past Damore while at the same time crashing into the boards behind the net. Although stunned, Les kept right on playing. Nothing could keep him out of this game.

Art Giroux scored an insurance goal at 15:41 of the third period that proved vital when Hershey's Gaye Stewart scored with only 26 seconds remaining.

The unsung hero of the game was Earl Bartholome, who checked Phil Hergesheimer furiously. Phil was a non-factor in the game, thanks to Earl.

Cleveland was now only one game from the finals, as the series shifted to Hershey for Games Two and Three.

The Barons were totally outplayed in Game Two and were routed by the score of 4-1. Ex-Baron Bob Gracie, obtained in a trade from Buffalo at mid-season, got revenge on his former team by scoring two goals. Gracie took a fearful pounding from his ex-mates that climaxed with an altercation with Bill Beveridge. Still, Bob had the last laugh, as his goals sent the series to a third-game showdown.

After a scoreless first period in Game Three, where the two teams seemed to feel each other out, Cleveland came out firing in the second period. On several occasions, they seemed sure to get the first goal, only to be thwarted by Bear goalie Nick Damore.

When Bud Cook was called for interference, Hershey got a power play goal at 8:57, as Gordon Pettinger batted in a rebound of a shot by Phil Hergesheimer.

Cleveland kept pouring on the pressure until Les Cunningham knotted the count scoring on a shot from 20 feet in front of Damore at 10:55.

Neither team could score the rest of the way, and the game headed into a full 10-minute overtime. Who would have thought that an 18-year-old kid would end the Barons' reign as champions? But that is exactly what happened.

Gaye Stewart, a skinny 18-year-old, fresh up from the amateur ranks and on loan from Toronto, scored off a rebound of a Gordon Pettinger shot after only 45 seconds of play in the overtime.

The Clevelanders kept pressing to send the game into a sudden death overtime, and on six occasions they appeared to have sure goals only to have Nick Damore come up with miracle saves. Finally, young Stewart ended the suspense with another goal at 7:22, and the Barons were done for the year.

The Barons held their heads high in defeat. They gave it their best shot under very adverse circumstances. Even though they lost, they lost fair and square, with their own players. From Al Sutphin on down the line, everyone was proud of the season just concluded. But with the war now raging, what lay ahead was anyone's guess.

FINAL STANDINGS
1941-42

West	W	L	T	GF	GA	PTS.
Indianapolis	34	15	7	204	144	75
Hershey	33	17	6	207	169	72
Cleveland	33	19	4	174	152	70
Buffalo	25	25	6	182	157	56
Pittsburgh	23	28	5	210	223	51
East	**W**	**L**	**T**	**GF**	**GA**	**PTS.**
Springfield	31	20	5	213	167	67
New Haven	26	26	4	182	219	56
Washington	20	30	6	160	172	46
Providence	17	32	7	205	237	41
Philadelphia	11	41	4	157	254	26

Top Baron Scorers	G	A	PTS.
Les Cunningham	25	40	65
Norm Locking	14	32	46
Earl Bartholome	13	23	36

Calder Cup Champion – Indianapolis Capitals

THE 1941-42 CLEVELAND BARONS

First row (L-R): Earl Bartholome, Joffre Desilets, Captain Bill MacKenzie, Bill Beveridge, President Al Sutphin, Coach Bill Cook, Moe Roberts, Jake Milford, Don Deacon, Trainer Walter Robertson.
Back row: Walter Melnyk, Art Giroux, Herb Foster, Norm Locking, Whitey Prokop, Harry Dick, Dick Adolph, Freddie Robertson, Bud Cook, Les Cunningham, Norbert Stein, Publicity Director.

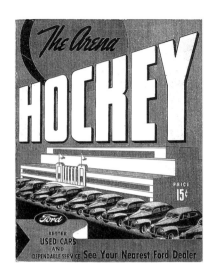

1942-43 SEASON

Al Sutphin faced a fork in the road in his tenure as owner of the Barons. Near the end of last season, the Cleveland Barons and Buffalo Bisons were invited to join the National Hockey League in a proposal by Jack Adams, Manager of the Detroit Red Wings.

It had always been Al's intention to play in the big league. He was refused admittance to the NHL while he was raising funds to build the Arena. NHL executives wanted to see the finished building before letting Cleveland into their exclusive league. After seeing the great structure upon its completion, it was the big league coming to Sutphin and asking him in. But Al refused. He now wanted to see how Cleveland fans would respond to the Arena before he made a great investment in the NHL.

By the end of the 1940-41 season, while averaging 8,267 a game, Cleveland outdrew four of the NHL's seven teams – Montreal, New York Rangers, New York Americans, and Detroit. The AHL was growing in power and popularity and would soon rival the NHL. Unfortunately, the war was now wrecking havoc on professional hockey.

Several owners in AHL cities were experiencing severe financial problems. The Philadelphia Rockets had already ceased operation and left the League. To make matters worse, the U.S. Army, which owned the building where the Springfield Indians played, had taken over the facility and converted it into a huge supply warehouse. Owner Eddie Shore worked out a deal with the financially strapped Buffalo owners to merge his franchise with the Bisons and play out of Buffalo.

New Haven, Providence, and Hershey would experience acute attendance problems because of gas rationing. While Cleveland had a great public transportation system that allowed fans to attend games during the war, people in smaller markets that did not have elaborate public transportation did not want to use their gasoline getting to and from sporting events – thus, smaller crowds and less revenues for team owners.

In short, the League was in trouble and needed the Cleveland franchise.

Al Sutphin knew that the NHL owners had ulterior motives in wanting his team and Buffalo to join their league. While the addition of Cleveland and Buffalo would strengthen the NHL during a time when they needed help, it would also cause the entire American League to fold. At this time, the AHL could not exist without Cleveland. The Barons led the League in attendance and assured a sellout, or near sellout, wherever they played on the road.

Sutphin was completely aware that the future of the American Hockey League rested in the palm of his hand. He also knew that he may never again get the chance to join the NHL if he refused their invitation now.

From a purely business standpoint, he did not need the big league. He was turning a profit with the Arena, while most other building owners were losing their shirts. Also, with the Canadian and American armies taking many of his players, and with more likely to follow, there was no guarantee that he would be as successful in the NHL as he was in the AHL.

In the end, it was his fierce loyalty to his fellow American League owners, and the relative assurance of financial security in the AHL, that led Al Sutphin to turn down the NHL.

It was a tough decision. The NHL owners were furious. Many fans were disappointed. Al only hoped that the American League would survive the war and rival the NHL once again. Only time would tell.

From a player-personnel standpoint, Cleveland was hit hard by the war. Now in the armed services were such standouts as Joffre Diselets, Don Deacon, Jake Milford, Walter Melnyk, and Moe Roberts. Moe joined the Navy and knew that at the age of thirty-five his hockey days were over. Thus ended the career of one of the Barons' all-time great goaltenders. Sandy Milne had joined the Canadian Navy and was also lost to the team. These six players were an important and huge part of the previous year's success and would be greatly missed. Add to the list great young prospect Whitey Prokop, who was now in the Canadian Mounted Police, and it was obvious that the Barons were in trouble.

The team's only recourse was to force feed several youngsters from their farm system and hope they could succeed on the AHL level. Forwards Tommy Burlington, Walter Stefaniw, Mike Shabaga, Ernie Trigg, and defensemen Fred Ferens and Harry Dick would try to fill the bill. To add to the problem of their inexperience, all of these kids, with the exception of Burlington, were on 24-hour recall to the Canadian army. All had completed their basic training and could be called to active duty at any time. Such was life in professional sports during World War II.

With the retirement of Joe Jerwa, the Barons were a little thin on defense. Bill MacKenzie, Fred Robertson, and Dick Adolph were the only experienced backliners, and Adolph would suddenly be lost for the year in one of the most dramatic incidents in team history.

Dick suffered a fractured skull during an exhibition game victory over the Detroit Red Wings at the Arena.

The accident came about when Adolph and Detroit defenseman Alex Motter bumped together in the neutral zone. Dick gave Motter an elbow that hit Alex in the mouth. In retaliation, Motter hit Adolph with the butt end of his stick. Adolph was bending forward at the time, and the blow accidentally hit him in the face and knocked him backward on the ice. He fell on the back of his head with a sickening thud that made the crowd gasp. Adolph lay motionless in a pool of blood and later was rushed to Huron Road Hospital, where the skull fracture was treated. Dick was fortunate to be alive.

Motter was crushed by the accident. He and Adolph lived within seven miles of each other in Canada and had been close friends for years.

In an act of sportsmanship seldom seen before or since, Motter asked permission of Jack Adams, the Red Wing manager, to play the first two games of the season for Cleveland while the Barons sought a replacement for their fallen defenseman. Permission was granted, and Alex Motter attended a luncheon with Baron players and the media, and wore Adolph's number 4 in the home opener against Pittsburgh. The Arena crowd gave Alex a standing ovation when he came on the ice. Motter was a class act, and the fans appreciated his sincere grief for Adolph.

The game itself was a rousing success as the Barons trounced the Hornets 7-2. Les Cunningham and Norm Locking each scored two goals in the contest, where all gate receipts were donated to the American and Canadian Red Cross. Unfortunately, only 3,280 fans showed on opening night. The defense was also bolstered for one night by an appearance from Sandy Milne, whose ship was docked near Toronto and who was given a one-day pass to play the game.

The new kids looked fast and sharp, but optimism that was garnered by a 3-0 start was displaced by gloom as the defense was ripped apart by the third game.

Sandy Milne was back in the Navy after his one-game stay. Alex Motter had returned to Detroit. After the team's third straight win in New Haven, Harry Dick was called by the Canadian Army on 24-hour notice. He left the team immediately after the game and reported for active duty in Toronto the next day.

To make matters worse, Bill MacKenzie broke his hand in the game and would be lost for three weeks. This left Fred Robertson and rookie Fred Ferans as the team's only defensemen. Bud Cook was dropped back on the blueline to help out, but the team was in dire straits and lost four of their next five games.

It got so desperate that old time ex-Baron Yip Foster, who was working in a factory in Detroit, was signed to help stop the defensive bleeding.

This team had a lot of young talent that was suffering through its growing pains. They could look great one night and seem lost the next. But their speed and enthusiasm was always present.

The Barons had loaned 19-year-old Pete Horeck to Providence to start the season and recalled him when the kid caught fire. He was teamed with lightning-quick center Tommy Burlington, and the results were stunning. Pete scored his 11th and 12th goals in a 3-2 win over defending champion Indianapolis on December 7th. Even more impressive was the fantastic stickhandling of young Burlington. He left the experienced Capitals shaking their heads in disbelief. Tommy was a true rising superstar.

Still the team was giving up way too many goals. The fans were all over Bill Beveridge during a 6-3 loss at the Arena. It was true that he was not getting much support from his teammates. Backchecking by the forwards seemed a dirty word, and the defense was leaky. But Beveridge was not totally blameless. He was not playing with the same fire as last season when he had a League-leading eight shutouts. Something was missing.

The bottom dropped out on December 13th when Coach Cook decided to start spare goalie Lloyd Storie in New Haven. The Eagles had won only three games all season; yet they humiliated the Barons 9-2.

The coach was incensed after the defeat. He closed the dressing room after the game and verbally lashed out at his underachieving players. The team was now 2-10-2 in its last 14 games. If ever a team needed a lift, this was one.

Al Sutphin was not the type of owner to sit back and watch his team disintegrate. On December 15th, he stunned his team and had the city's hockey fans rejoicing out loud. Phil Hergesheimer was returning to the Barons!

Happiest of all was Hergesheimer himself. Known as the "Flying Dutchman" in 1937-38 and 1938-39, Hergy never wanted to leave. He was perfectly happy here and considered Cleveland his home.

While playing a game here last season while with the Hershey Bears, Hergesheimer stated, "To me there is no place in all hockey quite like Cleveland. To me it will always seem like home. I would be quite content to wind up my career right here. No where else have I received such fine treatment – and often, when things weren't going just right, I thought of my days with the Barons."

Hergy finally got his wish when Sutphin borrowed him from Chicago for the balance of the season. He would buy his contract outright from the Blackhawks at season's end.

Things hadn't worked out for Hergesheimer in Chicago after he was traded following the 1938-39 season. His style of play did not fit in with the Blackhawks; and in 1942 he was sold to Boston, who in turn sent him to Hershey. His rights then reverted back to Chicago. Sutphin had been trying to re-acquire Phil ever since he lost him. Finally, after three long years, Hergy was back, and everyone was happy.

It took Hergesheimer four games to score his first Cleveland goals. He knocked in two, as the Barons defeated Indianapolis on December 28th, to improve their record to 9-13-2. To show what a perfectionist Phil was, he sat dejected after the game. "I should have had at least three goals before I got the first one. I seem to have lost something," he said. If he did, every Baron should find it.

Hergy was back at it on January 4th, as he scored a three-goal hat trick in a 7-6 loss to the Capitals at Indy. This gave Phil 6 goals and eight assists in eight games since coming back to Cleveland. He certainly was doing his part. But the team remained inconsistent.

In the 7-6 loss to Indy, the Barons spotted the Caps two goals, rallied and went ahead 6-5, only to lose in overtime. This game typified the whole season. Though the loss was only the third in its last nine games, the team remained in last place at 11-14-3, but only six points behind first-place Buffalo.

On January 13th, the League announced that the New Haven Eagles were suspending operations. Beset by financial problems brought on by the war and gasoline rationing that resulted in poor attendance, the Eagles would play their last game on January 17th against Providence.

As a result, the League would now regroup into one seven-team division. The top six clubs would make the playoffs. This shakeup put Cleveland in sixth place and virtually assured them of playoff competition, as Washington was running a poor seventh, a full 10 points behind. The Barons did not really deserve this break in the standings, but were not about to complain.

One final sad note on the New Haven situation: Eddie Powers, the Eagles' 58-year-old coach, died of a cerebral hemorrhage at 5:15 p.m. on January 17th, just hours before New Haven's last game. He had suffered a heart attack 10 days earlier brought on by stress. To their credit, the grief-stricken Eagles dedicated the contest to their late coach and beat Providence in their last game, 9-4.

The New Haven players were sold off throughout the League, and Cleveland purchased goaltender Frank Ceryance, who was actually owned by Hershey but on loan to the Eagles. Originally slated to back up Bill Beveridge, it would not be long before he would see regular action.

Ceryance took over as the Barons' #1 goalie on January 27th, when Bill Beveridge was loaned to the New York Rangers, who were having problems in goal of their own. Bill's fall from grace in Cleveland was stunning. After standing the League on its ear last season while taking over for Moe Roberts, Beveridge had been playing fair at best this season. His own teammates had lost confidence in him, and he welcomed a change of scenery. In his first game in New York, he lost 10-1.

Ceryance's first game as a Baron was a memorable one in that he only had to make seven saves during the entire game – one save in the first period, four in the second, and two in the third. The Barons won the game 9-2 on Les Cunningham's biggest night of the year. Les had three goals and three assists, while rookie Tony Leswick also had the hat trick.

This game started Cunningham on a real tear for the rest of the season. At the end of January, Les had 19 goals, 35 assists for 54 points. In the next one and a half months, he would add 16 goals and 12 assists to finish 35-47-82 points.

No one in the League was playing better hockey than Les. After scoring three goals against Washington, he had another hat trick in his very next game, a 6-1 victory over Indianapolis before 10,690 at the Arena. He followed this big night with two more goals the next evening in a 6-2 win at the Hoosier capital. This gave him 8 goals in three games and moved him into third place among League scorers.

This last win improved Cleveland's record to 16-17-5 and moved the Barons into fifth place. Third-place Pittsburgh was only 3 points ahead. A mile out in front was Hershey with a 22-7-8 ledger.

Owner Sutphin felt that the team was on the rise and pulled off a big deal by trading Herb Foster to Washington for high-scoring winger Lou Trudel. This was a real steal, as Trudel was one of the League's top marksmen and had scored 21 goals and 28 assists already this season. Last season, he led the League with a record 37 goals.

Just as everything appeared in place for a great stretch drive, the Barons collapsed – and closed the year in sixth place. From their high point at the end of January, they finished with a 5-12-1 record. With the exception of a few individuals (notably Les Cunningham, Norm Locking, Lou Trudel, Earl Bartholome, and Tommy Burlington), the team fell apart in all areas. Ceryance was not strong in goal, the defense was like a sieve, and the forwards failed to backcheck to any degree.

Cleveland did win its last two games of the regular season by defeating second-place Buffalo twice, 6-1 and 6-5. This gave the Barons a bit of confidence going into the playoffs against the fifth-place Providence Reds. But nobody expected them to hang around long.

A Few of the Men of the Press and Radio Who Have So Greatly Assisted Cleveland Hockey

SAM D. OTIS
Plain Dealer Sports Editor

ED BANG
New Sports Editor

FRANKLIN LEWIS
Press Sports Editor

JOHN DIETRICH
Plain Dealer

HOWARD PRESTON
News

CARL SHATTO
Cleveland Press

TOM MANNING
WTAM

JACK GRANEY
WHK

BOB KELLY
WGAR

THE PLAYOFFS

The Barons opened the playoffs at the Arena against a Providence team that was in serious trouble. The Reds were on the verge of bankruptcy, and owner Lou Pieri had given up hope of having a team next season. In order to recoup some of his losses, Pieri sold his entire first line of Ab DeMarco, Oscar Aubuchon, and Norm Calladine to Boston for $20,000. The cash deal was completed just before playoff time.

Although Pieri did come up with enough money to save the franchise during the off-season, he was widely criticized as the playoffs approached. The Reds' firepower was greatly reduced by the deal, and the Barons were ready to pounce on their apparent misfortune.

Game One at the Arena was strictly no contest, as Cleveland completely dominated play in a 3-1 victory.

The Barons backchecked, as they seldom had all season, to make life easier for goalie Frank Ceryance.

The local icers jumped on top early on goals by Tony Leswick and Les Cunningham. Tony scored his goal as his pass from behind the net struck the skate of Red goalie Mike Karakas and bounced into the cage at the :57 of the third period to put the game on ice.

Cleveland expected a tougher contest in Game Two at Providence, and they were right. The Barons had lost all four previous regular-season games to the Reds in their building.

Only 2,970 disgruntled fans showed up to see if the Reds would stave off elimination in the 2 out of 3 series. They were barely in their seats when the Reds' Windy Steele scored for the home folks at the :32 second mark. Cleveland tied it two minutes later on a shot by Walter Stefaniw.

After Providence took the lead again, the Barons came back, as Pete Horeck sent the game into overtime with a third-period goal.

Both teams pressed hard for the go-ahead goal. The Reds thought they scored first, but the goal judge disallowed a shot by Alex Ritson. As the Reds continued to grumble as play resumed, Tommy Burlington seized the moment. Young Tom backhanded a shot off Karakas' stick for the winner at 4:34. This was a full 10-minute overtime, and the game continued as the Reds pressed desperately for the equalizer. The end came in the closing moments as Tony Leswick sewed up the 4-2 win with an empty net goal as the Reds pulled their goalie.

In the second round of the playoffs, Cleveland was facing an Indianapolis Capital team that was on fire. The Caps had won their final ten regular season games and then swept Pittsburgh in two straight playoff games.

The first game of the best of three set was played at Indianapolis and turned out to be not much of a contest. The Barons played poorly in all facets of the game and lost 4-1.

This sent the series back to Cleveland with the Barons' backs against the wall. To make matters worse, Earl Bartholome was scratched because of a sciatic nerve problem.

To the end, the Clevelanders put up a tough stand and carried the game into a second overtime. Les Cunningham and Phil Hergesheimer scored for Cleveland, but a goal by 36-year-old Hec Kilrea at 11:56 of the second overtime sent the Barons home for the summer.

Despite their poor record and playoff failure, the Barons had reason to hope during the off-season. While they lost many players to the service and to injuries, several youngsters brought up from the minors got their feet wet and showed great promise. First and foremost was Tommy Burlington. Big things were expected from Tom, and he would not disappoint.

The biggest worry was how many more men would be lost to the military.

FINAL STANDINGS
1942-43

West	W	L	T	GF	GA	PTS.
Hershey	35	13	8	240	166	78
Buffalo	28	21	7	189	143	63
Indianapolis	29	23	4	211	181	62
Pittsburgh	26	24	6	183	203	58
Providence	27	27	2	211	216	56
Cleveland	21	29	6	190	196	48
Washington	14	34	8	184	272	36

Top Baron Scorers	G	A	PTS.
Les Cunningham	35	47	82
Norm Locking	26	40	66
Lou Trudel	29	34	63
Earl Bartholome	21	38	59
Tom Burlington	12	31	43

Calder Cup Champion – Buffalo Bisons

THE 1942-43 CLEVELAND BARONS

First row (L-R) – Earl Bartholome, Herb Foster, Bud Cook, Captain Bill MacKenzie, President Al Sutphin, Bill Beveridge, Coach Bill Cook, Norm Locking, Les Cunningham, Art Giroux, Freddie Robertson.
Back row – Norbert Stein, Publicity Director, Mike Shabaga, Tommy Burlington, Ernie Trigg, Hal Dewey, Heck Pozzo, Fred Ferens, Harry Dick, Pete Horeck, Tony Leswick, Trainer Walter Robertson.

Barons Coach Fred "Bun" Cook. Collections of Bobby Carse and Bill Hudec.

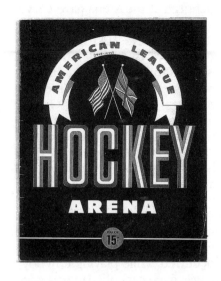

1943-44 SEASON

The biggest news of the off-season was the making of the Barons a Cook family affair.

Bill Cook, coach of Cleveland since 1937, was moved up to general manager, and his younger brother Fred (Bun) became the new coach of the team. Youngest brother Bud was entering his ninth season with the team but would soon be entering the Coast Guard.

In his new job, Bill's main responsibility was lining up new talent for the Cleveland farm system. After the press announcement, the new general manager left immediately on a scouting assignment in Western Canada.

In order for Providence to release Bun from his contract, the Barons had to give the Reds veteran right wing Art Giroux as compensation. It was well worth it. In Bun (he got the nickname when Bill stated that his brother "looks like a bunny" while scampering over the ice during his playing days), the Barons were getting a coach who was held in the highest esteem by the players in the League. For four consecutive years – 1939, 1940, 1941, and 1942 – Bun was named "Coach of the Year" at Providence. While there, he also won two Calder Cup championships.

Bun was also noted as a master strategist and a great developer and motivator of young players. While brother Bill was an explosive coach who could lose his temper quickly, Bun was more soft-spoken and took a fatherly approach in motivating his players. Bun would never bawl out a player in front of his teammates. Instead, he would rather sit down next to a player in the locker room after a game and quietly discuss that player's mistakes and build up his confidence.

The 39-year-old coach could be tough as nails if the situation so merited. While playing on early hockey's greatest line with brother Bill and Frank Boucher in New York, many a hockey player skated the other way when the Cooks got riled. The same respect was given Bun as a coach.

There were several changes on the ice as well. Most notable was the sale of goaltender Frank Ceryance to Buffalo. Taking his place was Paul Gauthier, who was signed when the Washington Lion franchise suspended operations for the duration of the war. The League would operate as a six-team loop, same as the NHL. The only difference was that the AHL would have 2 three-team divisions.

Strengthening the forward lines were center Mike Shabaga and wings Ed (Whitey) Prokop and Eddie Emerton.

On defense, the Barons lost Captain Bill MacKenzie, who retired following his injury-filled 1942-43 season. Taking his place was 28-year-old rookie Danny Sprout. Sprout seemed a longshot, since he spent the past year working in a Calgary brewery while only playing 12 games in a Sunday commercial league. But Danny fooled everyone and became one of the Barons' greatest defensemen ever during his long and distinguished career.

Backbone of the Barons defense during the war years was Danny Sprout (L) and Dick Adolph (R). Cleveland State University archives.

The other big change for the 1943-44 season was in the game itself. The new red line ruling now permitted passing from anywhere in the defensive zone to the red line at center ice. Designed to open up the game, it completely changed the style of hockey previously played. Players no longer had to carry the puck out of the defensive zone but could pass to streaking forwards near center ice. Speed and a mobile defense were even more important than before.

The season got off to a rousing start with a 6-3 ambush of the Pittsburgh Hornets at the Arena. Bud Cook had two goals for the Clevelanders, but the victory had a sad note. These were the last goals scored by Bud in his great career. Despite being 36 years old, the patriotic Cook enlisted in the U. S. Coast Guard and would report for duty on November 5th. After nine seasons with the team, Bud would say goodbye after a 5-5 tie at Indianapolis on October 30th.

After the tie with Indy, the team and its fans got a real jolt when nine-year veteran Freddie (The Bull) Robertson was traded to the Pittsburgh Hornets for "bad man" defenseman Pete Bessone.

Al Sutphin announced the deal, saying that he and Coach Bun felt that the team's biggest need was a tough banger who would hit anything that moved. Bessone answered the bill and was extremely happy to be coming to Cleveland. This despite the fact that he was as popular in Pittsburgh as Robertson was here.

Sutphin hated to part with The Bull. His rink-long dashes, goal or no goal, always thrilled the fans. But Fred, whose game improved dramatically under Bill Cook, was getting on in years and slowing down. While still a dependable defenseman, speed was more important than ever with the new red line in effect.

Robertson was the second player signed by Sutphin after Al purchased the team in 1934. Bud Cook was the first. Now both were gone. Only Les Cunningham and Norm Locking remained from the days when the team was known as the Falcons.

The only other negative note in an otherwise excellent early season was the condition of Locking's right knee. This was the same knee that Norm hurt a few years earlier. The problem was now diagnosed as a loose cartilage, and the knee could only bend with great difficulty. Locking was ordered off skates and began treatment that would keep him out of the line-up for five weeks.

Cleveland and Hershey began to pull away from the other teams in their respective divisions early on in the season. By mid-December, after a 4-2 win at Providence, the Barons boasted a record of 9-3-3, their most points yet after 15 games.

On January 1st, 2nd, and 3rd the Barons won three games on three consecutive nights for the first time in their history. They won at Indianapolis 2-1 on a Friday night, came home to shut out Providence 4-0, and then went up to Buffalo to hand the Bisons a 4-2 defeat. The team seemed to thrive on hard work.

A 9-3 rout of Pittsburgh at the Arena gave Cleveland their second four-game winning streak of the year and improved their record to 16-6-5. The game saw Tommy Burlington score two goals and three assists to increase his totals to 14 goals, 25 assists for 39 points and a tie with Hershey's Walter Kilrea for the League lead in scoring.

Tommy was centering a line that had become the sensation of the League. With Lou Trudel on his left side and Earl Barthelome on his right, the trio had accumulated 40 goals and 63 assists. They clicked as a unit from the minute they were put together by Coach Cook.

The key to the line's success was Burlington. What made everything all the more remarkable was that Tommy was playing hockey at all. He only had one eye! The injury occurred while playing cowboys and Indians when he was five years old. He was accidentally shot in the eye with an arrow by another little boy.

Despite this horrible setback, young Tom never stopped playing the game he loved. While playing in junior leagues in Canada, he used to worry about injuring his good eye, but that was behind him now.

"I used to think about my eye, I'll admit it," said Tom. "But when I went to the Eastern Amateur League in the U. S., I began to think differently. Then I got married, and my wife helps me get over any worry I might have about it. Now, I just figure that I've had about all the tough luck I'm entitled to...my mind is on other things than my own troubles."

At Atlantic City in the Eastern Amateur League, Tom set a record with 65 goals. He had scouts everywhere drooling. But the NHL had an unwritten rule about players with eye injuries. The liabilities were great. The AHL had no such rules, and Al Sutphin took a chance on the one-eyed wonder. He never made a better personnel decision in his life.

After a 12-goal, 31 assist season in his rookie year, Burlington hit his stride in 1943. A real dynamo on skates, and a clever stickhandler to boot, Tom was in a class by himself. He had everything – speed, power, intestinal fortitude, and class. Ex-teammate Whitey Prokop today describes Burlington as "the Wayne Gretzky of his day." And the 23-year-old was just beginning to blossom.

Norm Locking, who had just returned to action, re-injured his right knee again during a 6-2 loss to Buffalo before 12,006 at the Arena on January 10th. Norm knew that his playing days were numbered, but he again went into rehab hoping to give it one more try later in the season, and he succeeded.

The loss to Buffalo ended Cleveland's four-game winning streak, but the highlight of the season was about to begin.

The next night at Indianapolis, the Barons beat the Capitals 4-3 on a goal by Phil Hergesheimer at 17:22 of the third period. This was the beginning

The great Tommy Burlington.
Cleveland Public Library collection.

of a record eleven-game winning streak for the Clevelanders.

Game Two of the streak against Hershey was one of the most dramatic games of the season and a personal triumph for Tommy Burlington.

Although the Barons were far in front of Indianapolis in the West division, they still trailed the Bears by two points for the overall AHL leadership. An added incentive was that they had not beaten Hershey since February of the previous season.

Cleveland got off to a rocky start, and 9,690 Arena fans figured another loss to Hershey was inevitable. Before the game was a minute old, Mike Shebaga was carried off the ice with a broken leg. Then goals by Gaston Gauthier and John Harms had given the Bears an early 2-0 lead, and things did not look good.

Cleveland got another scare when Burlington suffered a badly bruised knee when Bill Moe of the Bears fell on his leg during a pile-up in front of the net. Big Tom was helped off the ice and did not return until the second period.

Burlington returned and put the home team on the board off a feed from Dick Adolph. After Pete Bessone tied the game up, Tom was hurt again as he was checked hard into the boards and sustained a badly pulled chest muscle and bruised ribs. Once again, he retired to the dressing room. No one thought he would return, including Tom himself.

After the game Burlington stated, "I never would have come back for the third period except for Bun. I was in tough shape, but I knew that Bun really wanted to win this game. And with the score tied 2-2, I thought if I could help out any, I should be back on the ice. Believe me, I don't know of anyone else I would have gone back for." You might say he had great respect for his coach.

Come back on the ice he did, and then some. With his left wrist encased in a reinforcing harness brace from a previous injury, his ribs taped up, and skating with a limp, the great Burlington inspired his teammates by scoring the go-ahead goal. Two insurance goals followed, as the Barons overwhelmed their rivals 5-2. Burlington received a great ovation from the crowd after every shift on the ice. They knew the great pain he was in and realized they were witnessing a very special performance by a great, gutsy athlete.

Tommy needed a rest, but with the injury to Mike Shabaga, he decided to keep on playing. He registered two more assists in the next game, as Cleveland scored 5 third-period goals to come from behind and defeat Indianapolis 7-4 at the Arena before 10,971. The game also saw Les Cunningham come up with two goals and three assists to increase his point total to 37, fifth in the League.

Prior to the next game, goalie Paul Gauthier was diagnosed with a case of pleurisy and was advised not to play that night by his doctor. But determined to play, Paul gave it the old college try. After giving up two quick goals, he knew he should have stayed in bed. Spare goalie Lloyd Storie was rushed into the game at the 12:04 mark. Storie was equal to the task and held the fort, as the Barons rallied to a 4-3 victory.

10,654 fans witnessed Cleveland's fifth straight victory over Providence, 5-3. Lloyd Storie remained in goal, and the fans got their money's worth as a fight between the Barons' Pete Bessone and Red's Bill Whitlet touched off a near riot. Every player on each team began battling, with only 16 seconds remaining in the game. It took nearly 30 minutes to restore order.

The team's sixth straight win, a 5-2 win over Hershey, was a milestone of sorts. It was the first hockey game in Cleveland to be sold out 3 days in advance of gametime. Hundreds of fans were turned away, when the last of the reserve seats were sold on the Saturday before the Wednesday night game.

Cleveland was now the talk of the hockey world. After 19 home games, the team had drawn 171,133 fans. The City was ga-ga over its hockey team. Al Sutphin never dreamed his team would ever be so popular when he bought the Barons in 1934. And they were drawing the great crowds when times were tough in the middle of a war!

The win over Hershey saw Paul Gauthier return from his sick bed earlier than expected and play a great game. The eventual game-winning goal was scored by the ever hustling Ed "Whitey" Prokop. Whitey had speed to burn but was used mainly on the checking "kid" line during his rookie year. One of the best skaters in the League, Ed was often used to counter the opposition's top scorer. Later in his career, he would blossom into a top-notch goalgetter himself.

The Bears were hurting even more after the game as their top scorer, center Wally Kilrea, was called into the service.

The team kept winning, and the eighth straight came at the expense of Buffalo, 4-2, before 11,687 at the Arena. Once again, the Burlington line did the damage. Earl Bartholome scored two goals and Lou Trudel one in the victory. Trudel's goal gave him 50 points, only 2 behind Burlington.

The club record was nine straight wins, set during the 1937-38 season. This mark was tied after a thrilling 7-6 win over Providence before 10,525.

This game belonged to Phil Hergesheimer. With a three goal hat trick, Hergy joined the 100-goal club. He was finally regaining his old scoring touch and looking like the player he was back in 1937-38-39.

A new team record was set on February 7th in Buffalo, as the Barons blanked the Bisons 3-0 for their 10th straight win. Despite being outshot 27-12, Cleveland rode the back of Paul Gauthier as the goaltender posted his second shutout. Eddie Speaker scored the only goal the team needed with a rebound of a shot by Whitey Prokop. Lou Trudel and Les Cunningham got insurance tallies.

The eleventh and final win of the great streak came over Hershey before 10,189. The Bears became victims for the third time by dropping a 5-4 squeaker. Hero for the local icers was Pete Horeck with the game winner at 7:18 of the third period.

The victory gave the Barons a 27-7-5 record; and for all intents and purposes, the Western division race was over. Cleveland now led Indianapolis by a full 18 points with only 15 games remaining.

The Bears got their revenge by ending the streak with a 5-0 whitewash of the Barons in Hershey. Cleveland had to lose sooner or later, and the Bears really clawed a flat Baron team that was never really in the game.

Cleveland headed to the East coast and handed Providence a 9-3 whipping in a game Pete Horeck would never forget. Pete set a team record by scoring five goals. He actually could have had several more but missed a few easier chances than the goals he did tally. His two assists gave him a total of seven points for the night. This game, more than any other, put Horeck in the NHL as the Chicago Blackhawks drafted him in the off-season, much to the chagrin of Al Sutphin.

Life for the Barons was a head-spinning parade of victories and goals. It was easy for them to forget their surroundings amidst so much adulation from their fans. But they were brought back to earth and reminded of the grim realities of the world around them. On February 16th, Phil Hergesheimer was called to active duty in the Canadian navy. Hergey had joined the reserves in the last Fall, but had hoped to make it through the season before being called, if he was called at all.

It was a sad blow for Phil and the team. He was scoring goals in bunches again and had looked as good as ever in recent weeks. He departed with 21 goals and 19 assists, for 40 points. After waiting three years to get him back from Chicago, Hergy was gone again after one short year. The team, and especially Al Sutphin, took his departure hard.

Despite the loss of Hergesheimer, the Barons kept rolling along, until March 5th. In this 11-5 loss at Buffalo, goalie Paul Gauthier suffered a leg injury that would keep him out of the rest of the regular season and part of the playoffs. He tore ligaments in his knee early in the game, but continued to play, which made the injury worse. Lloyd Storie would finish the season in goal.

With the season all but wrapped up, it was hard for the Barons to get up for their remaining games. But they did clinch the overall AHL regular season title with a 7-5 victory over Pittsburgh at the Arena. This climaxed a record-breaking season for Cleveland with 73 points. The 33 wins tied the 1941-42 club for most victories.

Tommy Burlington was the League's leading scorer, with 33 goals and 49 assists for 82 points. Pete Horeck led the team with 34 goals.

Unfortunately, Cleveland lost its last three regular season games to finish at 33-14-7. Despite leading the League, they were entering the playoffs against Hershey playing inconsistent defense with a goalie who was shaky at best.

THE PLAYOFFS

Down through the years, the Cleveland-Hershey rivalry produced many a hard-fought series. This best of seven tussle between division champions ranked among the best.

During the regular season, the two teams split their games, going 4-4-2. But the Barons entered the playoffs without Paul Gauthier, putting backup Lloyd Storie on the spot in goal. Also, Norm Locking was less than full strength. Norm came back during the last two months of the season and finished with nine goals and nine assists. However, his ailing knee was still giving him trouble.

Hershey, on the other hand, was at full strength for the first time in weeks. Top-notch left wing Gaston Gauthier, out for a month with a bad back, was returning to the lineup. Also, top defenseman Bill Moe, who had missed two weeks with a shoulder injury, was ready to play.

The Bears closed the season with a rush, losing only one of their last seven games. With the League's top goalie Nick Damore in peak form, Hershey was rated a slight favorite entering Game One at the Cleveland Arena.

To pardon the expression, the opening game before 8,776 had a true "storybook" ending. Lloyd Storie, who asked for a tryout during the 1942 training camp and wound up as the Barons' spare goaltender, registered his first career shutout as Cleveland edged the Bears 2-0. Lloyd played at a confidence level not seen during the regular season. Although the Barons gave him great protection, Storie came up big whenever called upon. He had his greatest moment near the end of the game, as Hershey's Hec Pozzo broke free at the blue line and skated in alone on the Cleveland goalie. Pozzo faked and shot from ten feet out, but Storie did the splits and made the save.

The first goal of the game was a fluke. Tommy Burlington passed the puck in front of the Hershey net from the corner boards. Ex-Baron Peggy O'Neil, in attempting to clear the puck away from the goal, accidentally tipped it past a stunned Nick Damore. No one was more surprised than Burlington, who was credited with the score at 13:16 of the first period. It was all the Barons needed, although Earl Bartholome gave Cleveland some breathing room by scoring an insurance marker.

Game Two at Hershey saw Storie continue his great goaltending, but it wasn't enough as Cleveland dropped a 3-1 decision. The game was fast-paced from the word "go", with end to end action.

The Bears got on the board first, when Gaston Gauthier, bad back and all, beat Storie on a pass from Peg O'Neil at 12:58 of the first period. Hec Pozzo made it 2-0 early in the second, as he put in a rebound after Storie made a super stop on O'Neil.

Storie was at his best when he stopped a penalty shot that was awarded to Hershey's Gauthier after he was pulled down on a breakaway by Yip Foster.

The save inspired the Barons. Coach Cook sent four forwards out with only one defenseman in an all-out effort to score. Finally, the move paid off early in the third period, when Earl Bartholome was credited with a goal. Earl passed the puck from behind the Hershey net while a scramble for position was taking place. The disc hit a Hershey skate and bounced into the net.

For the balance of the period, Cleveland pressed hard, but could not beat Damore. Peg O'Neil got an insurance tally when he scored into an empty net at 19:05 when Coach Cook pulled Storie in favor of an extra attacker.

Cleveland took a one-game lead in the series by winning Game Three in Hershey 4-3. This was another knock-down, drag out affair that saw Danny Sprout and Pete Horeck put the Barons in front in the first period. After Mike Shabaga and Earl Bartholome scored in the second, Cleveland used a solid defense to hold off the Bears. Once again, Lloyd Storie was the difference, as he held off wave after wave of Hershey attackers.

The series shifted back to Cleveland for Game Four, and 11,208 fans witnessed a true thriller.

Things looked dark for the home team, as Hershey took a 2-0 lead in the second period and held onto the advantage for half of the third. Then the Barons put on a spectacular rally that sent the fans into a frenzy.

A hustling Whitey Prokop carried the puck into the Hershey zone and passed to Les Cunningham, who in turn slid the puck to Lou Trudel on the left side. The passing was lightning quick and caught the Bear defense off guard. Trudel, who was an expert marksman rifled home the shot at 11:39 and gave Cleveland new life.

It was Prokop again who set up the tying goal. From an extreme angle on the right, Whitey took a shot that hit the side of the Hershey net. The puck bounced to the side, and Nick Damore dove after it. At the same instant Nick dove, Les Cunningham got his stick on the disc and flipped it into the open cage.

The full ten-minute overtime was non-stop action. Cleveland got the winning score off the stick of Pete Horeck at 4:47 after Tommy Burlington made a dazzling dash down the right side and passed to an open Horeck in front. Lloyd Storie and the defense held off the Bears the rest of the way, as Cleveland won 3-2 and was now only one game away from the finals.

10,553 fans showed up at the Arena for a Game Five victory party, but went away shaking their heads. Nick Damore was a party-pooper, as the Hershey goalie played an unbelievable game.

Les Cunningham scored for Cleveland at 2:06 of the first period, but that was it for the Barons. From that point on, it was all Damore as the little netminder stopped at least a dozen shots that had "goal" written all over them. The Bears countered with one goal in each period to send the series back to Hershey for Game Six after the 3-1 victory.

After Pete Horeck tallied in the first period, Earl Barthelome gave the Barons a 2-0 lead at 5:35 of the second period in the sixth game at Chocolate Town. But from there on out, it was all Bears.

Hershey erupted for four straight goals in the second stanza and added another early in the third. Lou Trudel scored late in the game, but it was far too little, too late, as the Bears evened the series at three games apiece with the 5-3 win.

Game Seven in this classic series was set for the Cleveland Arena, and Coach Bun Cook was faced with a big decision. Paul Gauthier was ready to go again in goal. Should he go back to his regular netminder, or stick with the Cinderella Lloyd Storie, who had performed so admirably throughout the series but who looked ever so shaky in Game Six? It was a tough choice, but experience won out and Paul Gauthier started in goal for Cleveland. Coach Cook crossed his fingers that the month layoff for Gauthier wouldn't spell doom for his team.

His decision proved a wise one, as an aroused bunch of Barons played an inspired game and defeated a proud Hershey team, 4-1.

Mike Shabaga and Lou Trudel each scored in the first period to give the local icers a lead they never relinquished.

After Gaston Gauthier made it close, with a quick goal at 1:29 of the middle period, Tommy Burlington made the play of the series. Tommy carried the puck to the Hershey blue line, slid the disc between two Bear defensemen, skated around them and retrieved the puck. He then flipped a pass to Pete Horeck, who scored to make it 3-1.

Lou Trudel sewed the game up with a goal at 3:27 of the third period. From then on, it was all over. The Barons were back in the finals against the powerful Buffalo Bisons.

Cleveland was wary of the Buffalo team, and they had every right to be. The Bisons had gained strength as the season wore on and were at peak form for the finals.

The two teams met twelve times during the regular season with the Barons holding the upper hand, 7-3-2. But this was a deceiving record. Much of this dominance occurred early in the season before Buffalo had reached full strength.

Three early acquisitions put the Bisons over the top. Center Fred Thurier was discharged from the

Canadian army and scored 33 goals during the season. Also, the acquisition of Roger Leger and Gordon Davidson from New York beefed up the defense and made Buffalo a powerhouse.

One need look no further than the last two games between the two teams to get a read on the Bisons' improvement. The Buffalo boys whipped the Barons 11-5 and 9-7 in March. They carried their momentum into the playoffs and made quick work of Indianapolis, four games to one. Momentum was on their side, as was a new goalie.

When Buffalo goalie Frank Ceryance was lost to military duty, owner Eddie Shore appealed to the League to let them borrow a goaltender from another team that did not make the playoffs. Al Sutphin was against such practices, but under the unusual circumstances cast the deciding vote in letting Buffalo use Pittsburgh's Roger Bessette. This was a costly move, as Bessette played tremendous hockey during the upcoming series. It would be the last time this "borrowing" practice was ever used.

Game One at the Arena had 9,572 fans groaning in their seats as Buffalo dominated the game for a 4-2 victory. For some reason, Cleveland didn't play the hard checking game used against Hershey and consequently were skated into submission by the faster Bisons.

Les Cunningham played a fine game, scoring both Cleveland goals; but the rest of the team seemed to be standing around. Only 35 saves by Paul Gauthier kept them in the game.

As the series shifted to Buffalo for Game Two, team followers thought things could not get worse. How wrong they were!

After an early goal by Whitey Prokop gave the Barons a 1-0 lead, the Buffalos skated over, around, and through Cleveland as if they weren't even there. The Barons put on a disgraceful performance; and when the dust had cleared, the Bisons had a 12-2 victory. 12-2! This was the worst playoff defeat in Cleveland's history. Everything that could go wrong did. Add bad play to lack of effort, and the result was justified. Buffalo scored seven unanswered goals in the third period to totally humiliate the Clevelanders.

Just to prove to their fans that the disaster in Buffalo was no fluke, the Barons came home and got clobbered by the Bisons 8-1. 11,270 angry fans witnessed the debacle. The game saw Lloyd Storie return to nets to take over for a shell-shocked Paul Gauthier, but his efforts were fruitless as well.

With the fourth game being played in Buffalo, it was a foregone conclusion that the Barons were dead. To their credit, the Clevelanders made a game of it to save some face in the series.

Bun Cook's club actually had a 3-1 lead after two periods thanks to a hat trick by Tommy Burlington. But the inevitable happened, as the Cleveland defense came unraveled as the Bisons struck for five straight goals and a 6-4 triumph. The win gave Buffalo its second straight Calder Cup and left all of Cleveland bewildered.

What happened? Only Everything. Everyone from top to bottom needed to do his share of soul-searching. What had been a great regular season and first-round playoff victory over Hershey now seemed light years away. Not even a new regular season attendance record of 254,480 for 27 games could make Al Sutphin smile. To be sure, it was a long summer for everyone connected to the Cleveland hockey club and its fans.

FINAL STANDINGS
1943-44

West	W	L	T	GF	GA	PTS.
Cleveland	33	14	7	224	176	73
Indianapolis	20	18	16	156	156	56
Pittsburgh	12	31	9	140	181	33
East	W	L	T	GF	GA	PTS.
Hershey	30	16	8	181	133	68
Buffalo	25	16	13	201	168	63
Providence	11	36	5	126	214	27

Top Baron Scorers	G	A	PTS.
Tommy Burlington	33	49	82
Les Cunningham	26	52	78
Lou Trudel	29	47	76
Earl Bartholome	20	47	67
Pete Horeck	34	29	63
Phil Hergesheimer	20	19	40
Ed Prokop	7	19	26
Mike Shabaga	10	12	22
Norm Locking	9	9	18

Calder Cup Champion – Buffalo Bisons

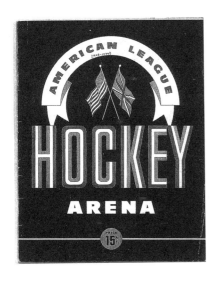

1944-45 SEASON

Despite the collapse of the club in last season's playoffs, the nucleus of the team was kept together. After all, the Barons did win the AHL regular season title. But Al Sutphin was not shy when it came to trying to improve his team, especially when he had two important holes to fill.

One was the retirement of star winger Norm Locking. His knee injury did not improve over the summer. Rather than risk permanent damage to his leg, he decided to hang up his skates.

The other main departure was Pete Horeck. The League's leading goal-getter was drafted by the NHL's Chicago Blackhawks. Since the American League was still subject to the National League draft every other year, Sutphin had no choice but to let him go.

The Barons tried to fill these gaps in the lineup by bringing up three youngsters from their farm system. Roy Kelly, Leo Gasperini, and George Agar were promoted from Minneapolis, and all had fine seasons.

One trade was made with the Buffalo Bisons. Eddie Emerton and defenseman Fred Ferens went to the Bisons for forwards John Horeck and Leon Richard. The deal was of little consequence, as Horeck was sold to the new St. Louis Flyers after eighteen games, and Richard was used sparingly.

Defenseman Orville (Rusty) Waldriff was purchased from Buffalo to fill the opening on the backline due to the retirement of Yip Foster and the trade of Ferens.

Last but not least was the signing of former Pittsburgh star goaltender Harvey Teno only three days before the start of the season. Teno sat out the previous season to tend to his gas station business back in Canada. He missed the game greatly, and Cleveland jumped at the chance to sign him. Last year's starting goalie Paul Gauthier had a so-so training camp and was relegated to backup duty behind Teno.

Teno was the star in the season opener, as the Barons got off and running with a 6-1 victory over Pittsburgh. 7,093 fans, the largest opening day crowd to date, brought in a total gate receipt of $10,350.31, which was donated to three local war charity agencies. Everyone had to pay to get in, including the players themselves. When it came to a good cause, Al Sutphin was one of this City's great contributors.

After their opening night success, the Barons began to flounder. As the end of November approached, their record stood at 5-6-1. But Bun Cook was not worried. He remembered what a great start the team had the year before, and how they burned themselves out near the end of the season. He also recalled a quote from a supremely confident Eddie Shore before the finals began last Spring. "Cleveland won't win a single game from us. The Cleveland club was at its peak all winter, but is past it now while my team has been coming along gradually and is at its peak form for the playoffs." He proved a wise prophet.

But you can't keep a good team down for long, and Cleveland was good – very good.

Les Cunningham with admiring fan Douglas Patterson. Cleveland Public Library collecton – Cleveland News photo by Glen Zahn.

They rattled off 22 goals during three straight wins that climaxed with a 7-3 victory at Pittsburgh. While still under orders to concentrate on his checking, Whitey Prokop broke through for two goals to lead the Clevelanders over the Hornets.

The big story during the first half of the season was the play of Les Cunningham. The League's all-time leading scorer to date was playing the best hockey of his great career. After eighteen games, Les had 12 goals and eight assists. It was on December 9th that Les, the team, and the fans all got a big scare, as Cunningham's career and life could have all ended.

The Barons were playing the expansion St. Louis Flyers at the Arena. Early in the day, Johnny Horeck, the little-used forward Cleveland had received from Buffalo in a trade during the summer, was sold to the Flyers. He suited up for St. Louis that evening.

The game started out rough and tumble, with some of the Barons seeming to go after Horeck. Johnny was incensed by the harsh treatment from his former teammates and lost his cool. While being bothered by Cunningham near center ice, Horeck turned and swung his stick with one hand and clubbed it over Les's head with full force. Cunningham went down face first as if shot by a gun. He laid on the ice as blood gushed from a wound on his skull.

After being carried to the dressing room, Les came around and had the wound stitched up. Although woozy for awhile, Cunningham returned to the game for the start of the second period. Les was lucky; he could have been killed. After the game, Horeck was all remorse. He called Cunningham personally to apologize, and later wrote a letter to Bun Cook expressing his regrets for the incident.

Cleveland won the game 5-2 and, inspired by Cunningham, went on a winning tear that lasted the rest of the season.

Les kept right on scoring. After a 5-0 shutout win at Hershey in late December, Cleveland followed with a 5-2 victory over Buffalo at the Arena. This game saw Cunningham register four points, and the team improved its overall record to 14-8-5.

On January 3rd, it was announced that the Barons would honor their star center with a "Les Cunningham Night" on January 17th.

It was a fitting tribute to the man known as "Cocky." The 31-year-old Cunningham was the first superstar of the American Hockey League. Playing most of his career before the red line ruling opened up scoring, Les had scored 176 goals and 255 assists for 431 points by the evening he was to be honored. 19 of the goals had come during the current season.

When Les first came to Cleveland in 1936, he was a temperamental, stick-swinging ruffian. He always seemed to play as if he had a chip on his shoulder.

"I wouldn't take anything from anybody," he recalled. "If I got a bodycheck, I'd retaliate – and get a penalty."

But he was older and wiser now. He realized the value he had to the team was on the ice, not in the penalty box. He changed his game around and rarely got a penalty late in his career.

On his special night, Les was honored during pre-game ceremonies and received a $1,000 war bond among his many gifts. He responded by assisting on Lou Trudel's late goal to give Cleveland a 1-1 tie with Hershey. This was the fourth tie in five games with the Bears, as the Barons improved their record to 16-9-7, five points behind front-running Indianapolis.

Sort of lost in all the commotion over Cunningham was the super season and scoring streak being put together by Lou Trudel. During a 6-3 win over Providence on January 20th, Trudel registered one assist. This was the 15th consecutive game in which Lou had scored a goal or assist. He broke the old team mark set by Phil Hergesheimer just the year before. This gave Lou 21 goals and 30 assists already this season. The game also saw Les Cunningham score his 20th goal for the campaign. This was the sixth time Les had scored at least twenty goals in a season, a new League record.

The win put Cleveland only three points behind Indy in the battle for first place. In the Barons' favor was the fact that they had played six fewer games than the Capitals. Cleveland had now lost only three games in their last 22 starts, going 13-3-6 since late November.

They finally caught the Caps on January 24th by beating Pittsburgh 4-3 in the Steel City. Lou Trudel contributed one goal and one assist, to stretch his scoring streak to eighteen games, one shy of the League mark held by Bill Thompson of Indianapolis. Unfortunately, the streak ended after Lou tied the record.

Slowly but surely, the Barons began to pull away from Indianapolis. On February 9th, just before the midnight trading deadline, Cleveland made its last move to gear up for the stretch drive. They traded Mike Shabaga to Hershey for 27-year-old veteran center Tom Forgie.

A bright young prospect, the 22-year-old Shabaga was playing center on the Barons' third line. His five goals and eight assists were far off the pace of Forgie, who had 16 goals and 25 assists. Why would Hershey make such a deal? Forgie had reached his peak as a player, while Shabaga had a bright future. But Al Sutphin was not thinking about the future. He wanted a title this year.

On February 15th, 11,888 fans, the largest crowd of the season to date, turned out to see if Indianapolis could get back in the race against the Barons. What they saw was Cleveland just about wrap things up with a 4-2 victory. George Agar led the attack with 2 goals, as Cleveland boosted its lead over the Capitals to 10 points. Indy put up a good fight, actually leading 2-1 after two periods. But the Barons had too much for them to handle.

The main objective for the team during the last month of the regular season was to stay as sharp as possible going into the playoffs.

This was never more evident than in a 12-2 massacre of St. Louis at the Arena. 11,648 fans saw the Barons score their all-time high total for goals in a game since the League was formed. In fact, it was the first time they had hit in double figures.

It was a banner night for many, but most of all for Tommy Burlington. Tom rapped home four goals and an assist, to move into third place in League scoring totals with 74 points.

Earl Bartholome scored numbers 30 and 31. After nine seasons with the team, this was the first time Earl had scored 30 goals.

Also, Lou Trudel scored his 33rd and now set his sights on the League record of 43.

One had to feel sorry for St. Louis goalie Hec Highton. Despite the score, Hec came up with 55 saves – and it's almost scary to think what the score might have been had he had a bad game. To his credit, he hung in there despite the fact that his defense forgot to show up.

Cleveland officially wrapped up their West division crown by going into Indianapolis on March 5th and destroying the Capitals 9-0. This accomplished the first of the team's three goals set during training camp. The second goal was reached on March 11th before 11,241 fans at the Arena.

Cleveland locked up its second straight American Hockey League regular season title by blanking Buffalo 2-0. Goals were scored by Harvey Fraser and Whitey Prokop. This was goal number two. It gave the Barons the all-important home ice advantage throughout the playoffs.

It also meant that Cleveland could rest its walking wounded for the balance of the regular schedule. Les Cunningham and Danny Sprout were nursing sprained knees, while Dick Adolph had a bad hip. With a little rest, all would be ready for the playoffs.

All that remained to be seen during the last three games was if Lou Trudel could break the goal scoring record of 43 set by Harry Frost of Hershey during the 1942-43 campaign. Trudel had 39 goals heading into the final weekend.

Lou wasted no time in his pursuit of the record, as he scored three goals in a 5-5 tie with St. Louis. Although meaningless in the standings, the game was a milestone, as Trudel became the first Cleveland Baron to ever score 40 goals in one season. His eighth career hat trick put him at 42 for the season, only one shy of the record.

The following night in Cleveland was a record-breaking game in more ways than one. Lou Trudel became the League's single season record holder for goals scored, as he rifled home three more to lift his total to 45. This also gave him hat tricks on two consecutive nights, another record. But as great as Lou's individual heroics were, they almost took a backseat to the game itself.

In the most spectacular shootout in Arena history, Cleveland stung the Pittsburgh Hornets by the unbelievable score of 12-10. This set a new League record of 22 goals in one game. The old record was 19.

Cleveland had nothing to lose in the game, but it was crucial to Pittsburgh. It was the Hornets' last game, and they needed to win to clinch a playoff berth. They held nothing back, but were unable to match Cleveland's great firepower. As it turned out, the loss to Cleveland, coupled with the Barons' 8-4 loss at Indianapolis the next night, knocked Pittsburgh out of the playoffs.

Individual honors were many for the Barons. Tom Burlington, Lou Trudel, and Coach Bun Cook made the first All-Star team. On the second team were Les Cunningham, Danny Sprout, and Dick Adolph. Cleveland's 78 points in the standings were a new team and League-tying record.

All the honors were nice, but there were far more important matters at hand. The Barons were entering a first-round playoff battle between division winners. Their opponents were none other than the Buffalo Bisons. This was the team that humiliated Cleveland just one year ago. To a man, none of the Barons had forgotten.

THE PLAYOFFS

Cleveland entered the best of seven Buffalo series without star center Les Cunningham. Les was still hobbled by a bad knee, and his status was day to day.

The Barons waited a year for this game, but it was over almost as soon as it started. In the fourth minute of play, defenseman Danny Sprout was called for tripping Buffalo's Eddie Emerton. In hockey's early days, minor penalties were served to their completion, no matter how many goals were scored. This two-minute penalty proved to be a disaster.

The Bisons poured in three goals during the next 61 seconds to all but sew up the game. Buffalo knew they were in the driver's seat and played a flawless defensive game the rest of the way.

Roy Kelly got one back for the home team, but it was too little, too late. A goal by Buffalo's George Pargeter at 16:10 of the third put icing on the cake.

If Cleveland was discouraged by their play in the opening game, they didn't let it show in Game Two at Buffalo. The Barons came back with their most brilliant and hardest fought game of the year. Comeback is the operative word here. Four times Cleveland found itself behind in the game only to fight back and tie the score.

After Len Halderson put the Bisons in front while shorthanded, Earl Bartholome tied the score early in the second period with the first of his two goals. Buffalo took the lead on a power play goal, but this was answered by George Agar at 2:32 of the third period.

When Paul Mundrick got his second goal at 5:56, it looked like curtains for Cleveland. The Bisons held onto the lead for the next ten minutes, as 6'3" goalie Bill Fraser repeatedly came up with the big save. Finally, at 15:43, Cleveland rallied to tie the score on some super heroics by Whitey Prokop. Taking a pass from his good friend Pete Bessone, Whitey cleanly beat Fraser to send the game into a full 10-minute overtime.

Once again Buffalo grabbed the lead at 1:11 of overtime on a goal by Ken Kilrea. It was then that Lou Trudel took matters into his own hands. Skating on a bad leg injured in the opening game, Lou grabbed a loose puck at center ice, worked it behind the net, and found Earl Bartholome alone in front of Fraser. Earl's shot was true, and once again the score was tied. But not for long.

This time Trudel did the honors himself by picking up a loose puck and whipping home the winning score at 3:32. Goalie Harvey Teno took over the heroics for the rest of the overtime with several outstanding saves. When the final gong sounded, Cleveland had a game it had to win.

The Barons had a much easier time of it in Game Three at the Arena before 11,931. Led by Leo Gasparini, who scored the team's first and last goals, Cleveland dominated a 5-1 win. The Bisons obviously had not recovered from their overtime loss in the previous game. Cleveland sensed this and kept Buffalo off balance all game. Sandwiched between Gasparini's goals were singletons by Tommy Burlington, George Agar, and Roy Kelly.

Game Four in Buffalo saw the great Tommy Burlington wear the king's crown, as the Barons came away with a 3-1 series lead after a highly dramatic 5-3 victory.

After Leo Gasparini gave Cleveland a 1-0 lead early in the second period, the Bisons came back with two of their own to carry a 2-1 lead into the third period. Lou Trudel took a pass from Whitey Prokop at 2:09 to tie the game at two each. For the next ten minutes, each team looked for an opening only to be foiled each time by some great goaltending.

Buffalo went ahead at 13:39, only to have George Agar of the Barons tie the count at 3-3 just 39 seconds later. Then Burlington took over.

On a lightning quick rush, Earl Bartholome brought the puck down the right boards. He passed to Gasparini, who found Burlington streaking toward the net. Leo passed to the brilliant Cleveland center iceman, and big Tom was perfect with his shot to put the Barons on top 4-3 at 18:47.

Buffalo sent five forwards into the Cleveland zone in an effort to tie the game. Their strategy backfired when Burlington stole the puck, skated the length of the ice, and beat Goalie Fraser at 19:49.

10,889 came to the Arena for Game Five to see the Barons put the clincher on Buffalo. They came away disappointed. The Bisons' surprising 5-3 victory was achieved in much the same way as Cleveland won twice in Buffalo, by coming from behind. The Barons had leads of 1-0, 2-1, and 3-2, but could not hold on, and the series went back to Buffalo for Game Six.

A long year's wait for the Barons and Tommy Burlington came to an end on March 28th. Cleveland became the first team to win three games on an opponent's ice with a dramatic 6-4 victory that ended Buffalo's two-year reign as champions. They finally had their revenge for losing last year's finals in four straight games.

The victory was especially sweet for Burlington. A year ago he won the scoring crown but had slumped in the playoffs against Hershey and Buffalo.

Tom didn't let this get him down. He went out and had a sensational 90-point season, and was the outstanding player in this year's Buffalo series with five goals and five assists. With the score tied 3-3 in the final game, it was Tom who scored the go-ahead goal at 17:46 of the second period while his team was shorthanded. After the Bisons pulled within one at 5-4, it was Burlington who delivered the knockout punch by taking a pass from Earl Bartholome at center ice. After faking around defenseman Roger Leger, Tommy beat goalie Yves Nadon at 18:57.

Revenge for Cleveland was sweet, but the celebration did not last long. They had a date in the playoff finals against the Hershey Bears.

This was the fourth time that the Barons and Bears met in the playoffs. The first time was in the finals of 1941, won by Cleveland three games to two. Hershey returned the favor the next year, two games to one. Last but not least was the classic seven-game set won by the Barons 4-3 the previous Spring. This certainly put the revenge angle in Hershey's corner this time around.

During the regular season, the two teams were about as even as they could be. Cleveland won three games, Hershey two, with five ending in ties. The Barons had the more potent offense, but the Bears boasted the best goalie in the League in Nick Damore. Hershey also was the more rested of the two clubs, having taken care of Indianapolis in five games.

The stage was set, and 10,625 at the Arena saw a nip and tuck battle in Game One. Hershey outplayed the Barons for the first half of the game and had a 2-0 lead when Cleveland finally got its break.

Hershey's Bill Goodfellow was called for high sticking to give the Barons their first power play. They struck quickly, as Leo Gasparini converted a long pass from Tommy Burlington to put the home team back in the game.

The score remained the same until early in the third period when that man Burlington did it again. Tommy broke free in front of Damore on a pass from Gasparini with no defensemen in sight. He faked one way, then the other, and beat a completely fooled Damore at 4:05.

Cleveland won it late in the third period when Lou Trudel took a soft pass from Les Cunningham while flying down the left side. His aim was true, and the Barons had a hard-fought 3-2 victory.

Game Two in Cleveland saw Nick Damore come up with one of his greatest games. 10,727 saw the little Hershey goalie kick out 44 shots in a 5-3 Bear victory. Despite giving up goals to Tom Forgie, Lou Trudel, and Tommy Burlington, Damore continually came up with one great save after another as the Barons were on the attack all night. Only Nick's stellar effort saved Hershey as at least six shots seemed sure goals. But on this night, Damore would not be denied victory; and the series shifted to Hershey, deadlocked at one game apiece.

Cleveland had not lost two games in a row since late October, but that streak was broken when Damore shut the door on the Barons again 3-1. Although he only had 24 saves this time, Nick was just as tough as in Game Two.

Les Cunningham scored first in Game Three after just 59 seconds elapsed. But from then on, it was all Hershey. The Barons seemed a bit demoralized by the great goaltending of Damore. They were well aware that a hot goalie could mean the difference in a series.

Hershey's goaltender remained hot in Game Four, but he was matched save for save by Harvey Teno, as the Barons won the critical fourth game 2-1.

After Hershey took a 1-0 lead in the first period on an Art Strobel goal, George Agar tied it at 18:01 of the second stanza.

Cleveland came out for the third period with fire in their eyes. This time it was Earl Bartholome's turn to wear the hero's wreath. Earl got the game winner at 4:23 off a great pass from Leo Gasparini. Then Harvey Teno took over and held the fort, as Hershey threw everything but the kitchen sink at him.

A huge crowd of 11,805 at the Cleveland Arena saw the Barons climb to within one game of the title with a 5-3 victory in Game Five.

Leading 3-2 heading into the third period on goals by George Agar, Harvey Fraser, and Tom Forgie, Cleveland sewed things up in the final 20 minutes on goals by Les Cunningham and Tommy Burlington. It was Tom's eighth playoff goal, one short of the record. Just as he had in Game Four, Harvey Teno was magnificent down the stretch to preserve the win.

Game Six in Hershey saw the Bears come out firing, but it was Cleveland that got on the board first. The great Burlington got the Barons rolling with his ninth playoff score at 10:40. This tied the League record set in 1942 by Jack Keating of Indianapolis.

Hershey program cover of Game #4 of 1944-45 Calder Cup Finals at Hershey.
Whitey Prokop collection.

Hershey Sports Arena

Calder Cup Championship Playoff

Hershey Bears vs. Cleveland Barons

Line-up for Tonight's Game: Saturday, April 7th, 1945

at 8:00 o'clock

	Hershey Bears			Cleveland Barons	
No.	Player	Position	No.	Player	Position
1	NICK DAMORE	Goal	1	HARVEY TENO	Goal
4	BILL WARWICK	Left Wing	2	PETE BESSONE	Left Defense
5	BILL GOODEN	Left Wing	3	RUSTY WALDRIFF	Right Defense
6	MIKE SHABAGA	Center	4	DICK ADOLPH	Left Defense
7	WILF HOCH	Right Defense	5	DAN SPROUT	Right Defense
8	HAL JOHNSON	Right Wing	6	GEORGE AGAR	Center
9	HY BULLER	Right Defense	7	EARL BARTHOLOME	Right Wing
10	ART STROBEL	Left Wing	8	LOU TRUDEL	Left Wing
11	HAL COOPER	Right Wing	9	TOMMY BURLINGTON	Center
12	CHUCK SCHERZA	Left Wing	10	LES CUNNINGHAM	Center
14	FRED ROBERTSON	Left Defense	11	TOMMY FORGIE	Right Wing
15	JIM DRUMMOND	Right Defense	12	ED PROKOP	Right Wing
16	NORM CALLADINE	Right Wing	14	LEO GASPARINI	Left Wing
17	ALEX RITSON	Center	16	ROY KELLY	Center
18	JACK RILEY	Right Wing	17	VIRGIL JOHNSON	Right Defense
19	PEGGY O'NEIL (Captain)	Center	19	GORDON PETTINGER	Left Defense
20	DOUG MAHER	Left Defense	20	HARVEY FRASER	Left Wing
				PAUL GAUTHIER	Alternate Goal
	Coach: Ralph (Cooney) Weiland			Coach: FRED (BUN) COOK	
	Trainer: Tom Sharkey			Trainer: WALTER ROBERTSON	

SPORTS ARENA INFORMATION

Music by the Hershey Sports Arena Orchestra.

Referees and linesman: Eddie Burke, Mel Harwood, George Hayes, Rabbit McVeigh, Bert Hedges, Norval Fitzgerald, Gordon Parsons.

Goal judges: Cy Davidson, "Patty" Miller, John Showalter. Official scorer, Paul H. Brewer. Scoreboard operator, August F. Meyer. Announcer, Ralph L. Hoar. Physician in attendance, Dr. Wayne D. Stettler.

Admission prices for hockey (including tax): Promenade—Side boxes, $1.80; side seats (brown and blue) and end boxes, $1.40; end seats (brown and blue), $1.10; Mezzanine—Side, $1.00; all other Mezzanine reserved, 90 cents; general admission, upper west end Mezzanine, 60 cents. Children under 12 years of age, 35 cents. All unpaid reservations must be taken up by 7 p.m. on the night of the game.

Public skating every Monday, Tuesday, Friday and Sunday evening at 8 p.m. Matinees on Saturdays, Sundays and holidays at 1:30 p.m. Admission (for those using their own skates): Adults, 50 cents; children, 12 to 16 years, 35 cents; under 12 years, 30 cents. Tax included in admission prices. Skating hours: 1:30 to 4 p.m. and 8 to 10:30 p.m. Skates may be rented at the Arena. Free skating for one-half hour after hockey games.

Skating classes: Mondays, for beginners, 6:55 to 7:55 p.m.; ladies, Tuesdays, 2 to 4 p.m.; kiddies, Saturdays, 9:30 to 11:30 a.m. Ice Professional, Miss Ailsa G. McLachlan, who is available for private skating instruction by appointment.

The Hershey Sports Arena Box Office is open daily, except Sunday, from 11 a.m. to 9 p.m. On Sunday from 1 to 9 p.m.

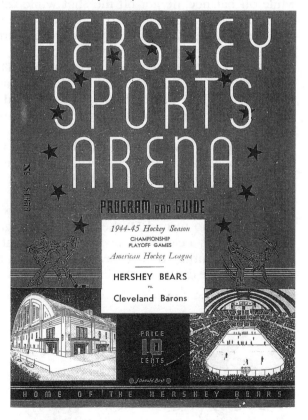

Lineup card for Game #4 of the 1944-45 Finals at Hershey.
The Barons won, 2-1. Whitey Prokop collection.

Lou Trudel continued his fine series by making it 2-0 just shy of two minutes later. Heading into the second period up two goals, the Barons looked to be on Easy Street, but Hershey had other ideas.

The Bears stunned the Clevelanders by scoring two goals within ten seconds during the period's first minute. Chuck Scherza scored at the 42-second mark, with Alex Ritson following suit just ten seconds later.

To their credit, the Barons immediately regrouped and went on top 3-2 on Lou Trudel's eighth playoff goal. Roy Kelly made it a two-goal cushion again by hitting the twine at 10:01.

Once again, Cleveland's lead looked secure, but Hershey refused to die. Ex-Baron Mike Shabaga made it 4-3 at 15:51. The second period ended with Hershey one goal down but on fire.

The Bears attacked relentlessly at the start of the third period. When Dick Adolph of Cleveland drew the game's only penalty for holding, Hershey seemed sure to score. But some fine penalty killing by Earl Bartholome and great goaltending by Teno kept Cleveland in front.

What looked like an insurance goal, but what turned out to be the game winner, was scored on a spectacular play by Tommy Burlington. Cleveland's great center iceman took a pass from Earl Bartholome and faked around a Hershey defender. As he was ready to shoot, he was tripped. Somehow, while off balance, he got off the shot while falling down and beat Damore at 13:01. Tom's record-setting 10th goal amazed everyone. His magic on ice seemed endless.

But the Hersheys would not give up. They pulled within one again at 15:51 on Mike Shabaga's second goal of the game. Hershey pressed hard for the rest of the game, but to no avail as the Barons held on for a dramatic 5-4 win.

The victory gave Cleveland its third Calder Cup title. This one was a true Grand Slam, as the Barons won everything: West Division title, AHL regular season percentage title, and the Cup.

It was also a special birthday present to owner Al Sutphin, who turned 50 the day after the great win. As the City celebrated, no star shined brighter than Tommy Burlington. He clearly stood head and shoulders above everyone else in the League.

FINAL STANDINGS
1944-45

West	W	L	T	GF	GA	PTS.
Cleveland	34	16	10	256	199	78
Indianapolis	25	24	11	169	167	61
Pittsburgh	26	27	7	267	247	59
St. Louis	14	38	8	157	257	36
East	**W**	**L**	**T**	**GF**	**GA**	**PTS.**
Buffalo	31	21	8	200	182	70
Hershey	28	24	8	197	186	64
Providence	23	31	6	241	249	52

Top Baron Scorers	**G**	**A**	**PTS.**
Lou Trudel	45	48	93
Tommy Burlington	30	60	90
Earl Bartholome	38	43	81
Les Cunningham	35	45	80
Tom Forgie	21	37	58
Leo Gasparini	20	24	44
George Agar	18	25	43
Whitey Prokop	13	28	41
Roy Kelly	15	20	35

Calder Cup Champion – Cleveland Barons

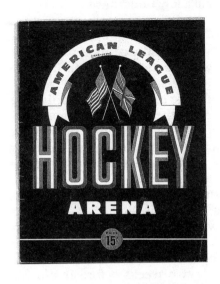

1945-46 SEASON

The defending champion Barons were starting the first peacetime hockey season in five years. They appeared to be loaded with talent again, but the rest of the League had gained in strength also. Although Cleveland remained a strictly independent club, many teams took players on loan from the NHL in order to strengthen themselves quickly. Add to this the return of many players from the war, and suddenly there was a surplus of hockey talent in the League.

Sutphin could see that the nucleus of his team was getting a little long in the tooth. The older players were bound to slow up a bit, so a few changes on the squad were deemed necessary.

Fred Thurier and Walter Atanas were purchased from the New York Rangers. Thurier was the key man here. Before playing in New York, Fred starred with Buffalo and Springfield of the American League. He would continue his great play here for many years to come.

To bolster the defense, Gordon (Moose) Sherritt was purchased from Indianapolis. Sandy Milne, who began to blossom just before the war broke out, returned from the military. One game into the season, Sutphin purchased blueliner Alex Motter from Detroit. This was the same Motter who was involved in the near-tragic incident where Dick Adolph received a fractured skull in 1942. Alex played two games with Cleveland in retribution before returning to Detroit. He also was just returning from military duty.

The returnee who Cleveland fans longed to see most was Phil Hergesheimer. Phantom Phil had been discharged from the service and was returning for his third stint with the Barons.

Coach Bun Cook summed up his team by saying, "We'll be the goingest team in the League, but I don't know how we'll be in the matter of coming back." What he meant was that he was worried. The team had plenty of scoring punch, but it was lacking in speed to backcheck and get back to play defense. He also had many one-way hockey players who loved to score but weren't all that much into stopping the other team.

Starting in goal against Hershey in the opener was 21-year-old Johnny Kiszkan. (This same player changed his name to Johnny Bower during the following off-season and went on to become the American League's greatest goalie ever. After 13 years in Cleveland and Providence, he went up to Toronto at the age of 34. There he played 11 years and was elected to Hockey's Hall of Fame in one of the sport's greatest careers. He will be referred to as John Kiszkan for this season only.)

John was a raw country boy who was subbing for Harvey Teno. Teno was suffering from an infected toe.

The new season got off to a rocky start for Kiszkan and the Barons, as they dropped their home opener to Hershey 4-3 and looked bad in doing so despite the close score.

Harvey Teno returned to the nets a few games later, but the team was still giving up way too many goals. By the end of November, they stood at 5-7-4 and only one point out of the cellar. To make matters worse, the defense was in shambles.

Pete Bessone and Danny Sprout were playing well. Moose Sherritt was ineffective and getting too many unnecessary penalties. Dick Adolph, long a big standout, was beginning to slow down and was having trouble keeping up with the many fast forwards now in the League. Worst of all, Alex Motter broke his ankle in a game at New Haven on November 11th.

Owner Sutphin saw trouble ahead and stepped in to improve the backline. Al traded Sandy Milne and Harvey Fraser to the New Haven Eagles, who were back in the League after a three-year absence. In return he received All-Star Gordon Davidson. Davidson was familiar to Cleveland fans as a longtime nemesis with the Buffalo Bisons.

Unfortunately, it didn't take long for the injury jinx to hit Davidson, as he suffered a wicked face cut in his first home game with his new club. The wound along his jaw required 15 stitches to close and forced Gordie to miss several games. This left Pete Bessone as the only healthy rearguard, and the team continued to stumble. By mid-December, their record stood at 7-9-5.

Near the end of the month, the defensive play began to improve, and the team's offensive pyrotechnics kicked into high gear. Leading the pack, of course, was Tommy Burlington, who went on a goal-scoring rampage during the weekend before Christmas. Tom fired three goal hat tricks in consecutive games against Indianapolis and Providence.

The December 22nd game against the first place Capitals had been declared "Dick Adolph Night" to honor the eight-year veteran defenseman. After spending two years playing in London, England, Dick came to Cleveland in 1938 at the urging of Bill Cook. He became the leader of the defense with his hard-hitting style.

Unfortunately the years had caught up with Dick, and he announced that his retirement would begin after the current campaign.

"Yes, this is going to be my last season," announced Adolph. "I've slowed up so much this year – I can tell. A defenseman has to skate around a lot these days in hockey. It's not like the earlier years when you just had to stand on the blue line and bop 'em when they came in." Despite this handicap, Adolph still was a force on the backline during his final year and always made his presence felt.

The game was a huge success, as the Barons destroyed Indianapolis 11-4 behind the hat tricks of Burlington and Earl Bartholome. The victory moved Cleveland to within eight points of the first place Caps.

The team boarded a train for a long ride to Providence for the next night's game. Long ride turned out to be an understatement. Due to transportation problems, the Barons did not arrive at the Red's arena until shortly before midnight. Their delay was announced to the crowd well before the 8:00 starting time. The game would be played upon their arrival, which was still a few hours away.

That most of the 3,999 fans stuck around was a testament to the popularity of both the Barons and the sport of hockey in Providence. As it turned out, most of the fans wished they had gone home as Cleveland beat the Reds 4-2.

After dressing for the game on the train, the dog-tired Barons were led by the red hot Burlington, who hit for three more goals. The game itself did not end until after 2:00 a.m. After going through so much just to get to the game, Cleveland figured they might as well win the thing, and they did.

The Barons stretched their winning streak to five games with a Christmas Night 3-0 shutout of Indianapolis. This was their most polished victory of the season and left them only six points behind the Capitals. Not bad for a team that was only one point out of the cellar only two weeks before. It also was the second shutout of the season for Johnny Kiszkan. His first was against Buffalo earlier in the month, and it was the same Eastern division leading Bisons who were next up on the schedule.

12,356 fans jammed into the Arena to see if the red hot Barons were for real. They witnessed a hard-fought battle but came away disappointed as Buffalo ended the Barons' five-game winning streak 5-3. It also was their first defeat on home ice since the opening night loss to Hershey, a stretch of 12 games.

Cleveland bounced back from the Buffalo setback and started the new year off on the right foot by blanking Indianapolis at the Arena 6-0. John Kiszkan shut out the Caps for the second time in a row, the last time being on Christmas Night. This set up a big weekend against Buffalo at home and Indy on the road.

11,612 Cleveland fans saw Les Cunningham reach another milestone in his great career. In an 8-5 victory Les poured in four goals in one of his finest games ever. The third goal gave him 500 points in his career. No other player was even close to this total at the time.

This gave Cleveland seven wins out of their last eight games as they headed on an important four game road trip. The trip started out on a sour note, as the Barons were manhandled by the Capitals 9-0. Indy shot three goals in each period, and they made it look easy.

The Barons were falling into an aggravating pattern. They were playing great hockey at home but were getting bombed on the road. Thus, their record continually hovered around the .500 mark. Why the Jekyll-Hyde routine?

Two words summed up the Barons' problems: defense and checking. At home, the team had a big advantage playing in front of a noisy full house game after game. The crowd always got the players up in a hurry. While there was little checking, fore or back, they got away with their wide open, loose style of play.

But when the Barons went on the road, the lack

of hitting was killing them. Other teams knew that the older Barons had trouble getting back on defense after their all-out attacks. They also knew that they were free to roam the ice without getting hit. Unless Cleveland tightened up on the road, they would keep having trouble, and they did.

After the Indianapolis debacle, the Barons dropped back-to-back games in Hershey, 7-4 and 5-1. They finally broke through at New Haven with a 3-2 win on Dick Adolph's third-period goal.

Near the end of January, Cleveland hit rock bottom as they fell into last place. Al Sutphin was fed up. He sent Moose Sherritt and Walter Atanas to their farm club at Minneapolis. A team meeting was called, and the players were told in no uncertain terms to bear down. The message seemed to get through.

In four games during the first week of February, the Barons scored a whopping 32 goals. The onslaught began with an 11-0 rout of Hershey. They then lost to Providence 7-5 before blasting Hershey again 9-5. This set up a showdown with St. Louis, who trailed Cleveland by one point in the standings.

After spotting the Flyers a first-period score, the Barons bombarded St. Louis with eight consecutive goals enroute to a big 9-3 win. Phil Hergesheimer and Fred Thurier led the way with two scores apiece.

The Barons all but ended the Flyers' playoff hopes on February 13th by taking a 4-2 win at St. Louis. The fact that Cleveland won in St. Louis, where they had lost four previous games this season, seemed to take the air out of the Flyers' sails. They faded fast and no longer were a threat to Cleveland.

After Whitey Prokop scored two goals to lead the Barons to an 8-2 romp over New Haven, the Clevelanders began to believe they could catch second-place Pittsburgh. The Hornets were eight points ahead. Although Prokop would not develop into a big scorer until two years later at Providence, Whitey was one of the few players on the team who could be counted upon to check both ways. If some of the big guns backchecked like the fleet white-haired winger, the team would have had no problems winning on the road.

Fans packed the Arena throughout the 1940's. During the 1945-46 season, the Barons averaged 10,146 per game. Seating capacity was 9,739. James Peter Hendy collection.

If Cleveland had any hopes of catching Pittsburgh, they needed to sweep a home and home series between the two clubs on the last two days of February.

The Barons moved to within six points of the Hornets with an easy 7-0 shutout at the Arena. This was the fourth shutout of the season for Johnny Kiszkan. One would have thought that the Clevelanders would be hard to beat the next night in Pittsburgh. Momentum was on their side. But momentum is useless if a team does not check.

A mere twenty-four hours later, these same two teams met in Pittsburgh, with the Barons getting clobbered 11-3. Talk about night and day! There really was no excuse for this type of turnabout except lack of effort. Whatever the case, Pittsburgh's lead over Cleveland went back up to eight points, as the Barons settled into third place for good.

Throughout all the up and down play, fans were following a great scoring streak that Tommy Burlington was building. Game by game Tom was getting closer to the consecutive game point record of 19 shared by Cleveland's Lou Trudel and Bill Thomson, now of Hershey. As the pressure kept mounting, Burlington finally got the record he treasured in a 6-5 win over Pittsburgh on March 6th. It was his 20th consecutive game with either a goal or an assist. The record-breaking point was an assist on a goal by Dick Adolph.

Almost forgotten in the hoopla over Burlington's record were the heroics of Phil Hergesheimer. It was Hergy's goal with only 20 seconds left in the game that gave Cleveland its 6-5 victory. But the night belonged to Tommy Burlington. Once again, his light shined brightest among all the Barons' stars.

Tommy scored in all of the team's remaining four games to stretch his consecutive game scoring streak to 24 games. The team finished in third place with a 28-26-8 record, six points behind Pittsburgh.

While Al Sutphin was disappointed by the team's finish, he was beaming when it came to attendance figures. The Barons drew 314,538 fans for 31 home games. This is an average of 10,146 per game. To say the least, Cleveland was mad about its Barons.

The Barons were mad too, at themselves. They were not happy with their mediocre record. Their one chance to save face was in the playoffs that began with a best of three mini-series against the Providence Reds.

THE PLAYOFFS

Rumors were rampant that owner Al Sutphin was going to tear apart the club after the playoffs. This was a little drastic, but the players were aware that changes would be made. Where the shoe would fall was anyone's guess. The only thing for sure was that some of them would not be back and that next year's team would have a different look.

The team was determined to rally together for one last stand. They vowed to put the season's disappointments behind them and to play up to their potential in the playoffs. This meant tough, hard-nosed defensive hockey. If they did this, the offense would take care of itself.

The one major lineup change made by Coach Cook was starting Harvey Teno in goal. Having played most of the year behind John Kiszkan, Teno's selection was a surprise. But Cook was a big believer in experience in pressure situations. He was consistent with this philosophy all through his coaching career.

Bun Cook looked like a genius in Game One, as Teno played one of his greatest games ever in goal. Harvey was the Rock of Gibralter as the Barons won in Providence 2-0. Time after time the pudgy goaltender shut the door on the Reds as he made an incredible 54 saves. He was particularly outstanding in the first period when he kicked out 27 shots.

The Reds came out attacking relentlessly, but came away empty. Teno had excellent help from his teammates as every man tended to his particular assignment.

After Les Cunningham scored at 13:26 of the first period, Cleveland began to play its strongest two-way game of the season. Despite the high number of Reds' shots, the forwards checked furiously to preserve the shutout. Still, the game wasn't over until Gordon Davidson fired a 125-foot shot into an open net with 1 minute 16 seconds left to play. The Reds had pulled their goalie in favor of a sixth attacker, but the move failed.

Cleveland wrapped up the mini-series by taking Game Two 5-3 before 10,827 at the Arena. As was commonplace by now, the game was a showcase for Tommy Burlington. The great Cleveland pivotman hit for a goal in each period, for a three-goal hat trick. Other scores were by Whitey Prokop and Phil Hergesheimer.

Burlington was at his best on his third-period tally. As the Reds were bringing the puck out of their own zone, Tommy intercepted a pass at the Providence blue line and broke in alone on goalie Gordon Bell. Bell was helpless. As he took a fake and sprawled one way, Burlington deposited the puck on the other side for the coup de grace.

This win set up a two out of three semi-final series against the Pittsburgh Hornets. The Hornets were a formidable foe, having just eliminated Hershey two games to one. With a 30-22-10 record, Pittsburgh was enjoying its greatest season ever. Although the first game of the series was to be played in Cleveland, Games Two and Three, if necessary, were in Pittsburgh. This gave the Hornets a huge advantage in that the Barons were 0-4-1 at Duquesne Gardens that season.

The series was a thriller all the way, with Game One setting the tone. 12,224 witnessed a back and forth affair, with Cleveland finally winding up on top 6-5 in overtime.

The hard-fought victory saw the Barons take a 1-0 first period lead and 4-2 advantage after two. But the roof caved in during the third period. Pittsburgh got two goals from Joe Klukay to send the game into a full ten-minute overtime.

Things looked bleak for the home team, when Hornet John Mahoffey scored at 2:44. But Cleveland kept plucking away and tied the score on a 60 foot blast from the blue line three minutes later by Alex Motter. Although each club had several more scoring opportunities, the game went into "sudden death".

The Barons took to the offensive and pressed hard for the winner, but goalie Aldege (Baz) Bastien was equal to the task. Ironically, Cleveland got its break when the Hornets went on the attack.

With their entire team packed into the Barons' zone, defenseman Jim Thompson tried to pass in front of the Cleveland net. Lou Trudel intercepted and burst into the clear at center ice with Tommy Burlington on his right. Using Tommy as a decoy,

Ed "Whitey" Prokop about to backhand a shot at Buffalo's Connie Dion during fourth game of 1945-46 Calder Cup Finals. #21 Ernie Trigg waits for rebound.
Whitey Prokop collection – photo by Herman Seid.

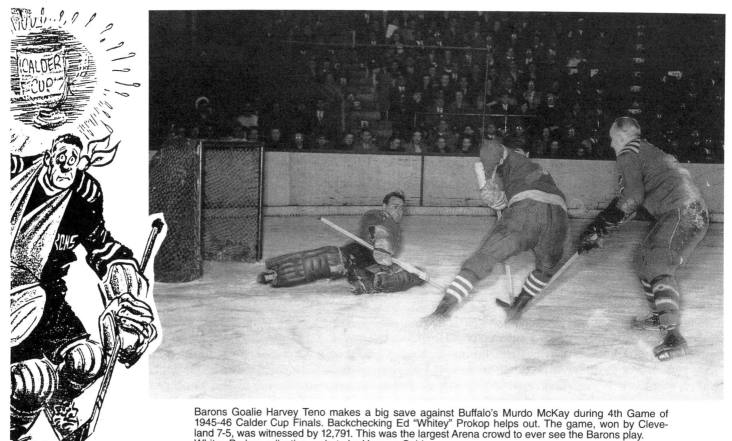

Barons Goalie Harvey Teno makes a big save against Buffalo's Murdo McKay during 4th Game of 1945-46 Calder Cup Finals. Backchecking Ed "Whitey" Prokop helps out. The game, won by Cleveland 7-5, was witnessed by 12,791. This was the largest Arena crowd to ever see the Barons play. Whitey Prokop collection – photo by Herman Seid.

Lou cut loose with a wicked shot that beat Bastien at 5:08 of the second overtime.

Game Two saw Pittsburgh even the series by taking a 6-5 decision of their own.

After taking an early lead on a score by Earl Bartholome, Pittsburgh tallied four unanswered goals to lead 4-1 entering the third period. Hornet fans were whooping it up, thinking the game was over, but the Barons had other ideas. Within four and a half minutes Cleveland had tied the score on shots by Motter, Trudel, and Danny Sprout. This stunned the crowd into silence.

With Fred Thurier off for tripping, Pittsburgh went on top; but Cleveland came back with Trudel once again coming through in the clutch. One would have thought Cleveland had the momentum, but a penalty to Dick Adolph proved their undoing. With the Barons a man short, and Harvey Teno screened, Hornet defenseman Pete Backor fired in the game winner at 14:49.

A crowd of more than 6,000 jammed little Duquesne Garden for the frantic series finale. They witnessed a highly dramatic game that saw both teams leave every once of energy they had out on the ice.

Twice during the contest, the Barons found themselves down by a goal. On both occasions, it was Fred Thurier who tied it up. His second goal tied the score at 2-2 early in the third period.

From that point on, neither team held back. Each seemed to want to avoid overtime, as the game was back and forth, non-stop action. With the period nearing its end, Dick Adolph broke up a Pittsburgh rush and gave the puck to Burlington near center ice. The lightning quick center broke into the Hornet zone and whipped a pass to Lou Trudel speeding down the left side. Lou slapped a shot from 25 feet out to give Cleveland its final advantage.

The last couple of minutes were nerve-wracking as Pittsburgh stormed the Barons' nets. But Teno and the Cleveland defense somehow kept the puck out, and the Barons won 3-2. This clincher put Cleveland in the finals for the third straight year. Their opponent? The Buffalo Bisons.

The Cleveland-Buffalo rivalry was at its peak in 1946. There was absolutely no love lost between the two teams. Adding fuel to the fire was a Buffalo newspaper article ridiculing the Barons as a bunch of old men and that the Bisons should win in a romp. Bun Cook's boys were incensed by the story. They wanted to shove the old-men baloney down the Bisons' throats. Motivation was definitely on Cleveland's side.

Heading into the opening game, the only negative was the condition of Les Cunningham. The veteran center missed the final two games of the Pittsburgh series and would not dress for Game One. Les was suffering from a severely pulled groin muscle. He could barely walk, let alone skate. His status was listed as game-to-game.

With Cunningham out, Bun Cook went with only two centers in Game One. Tommy Burlington and Fred Thurier took turns centering the third line. The strategy paid off as Cleveland took a stirring 3-2 victory from Buffalo before 12,359 at the Arena.

Thurier was especially effective, as Burlington's line was bottled up all evening. The game was fast and furious.

Buffalo was loaded with speedsters, but somehow the Barons were able to stay with them. It was Thurier who scored the eventual game winner after Cleveland went ahead 2-1 early in the third period on shots by Danny Sprout and Phil Hergesheimer. The Bisons made it close with a late goal, but the Barons edge in experience seemed to be the difference.

Unfortunately, experience didn't help in Game Two at Buffalo, as the Bisons won easily 8-2.

Cleveland made a game of it for 30 minutes as the teams were deadlocked 1-1, the Barons' goal coming off the stick of Thurier. But a penalty to Pete Bessone proved their undoing. While Pete was in the penalty box, Buffalo scored twice.

Being two goals down, the Barons opened up their play; but this played into Buffalo's hands. Constantly catching Cleveland far up ice, the Bisons tallied three more times in the third period before Phil Hergesheimer made it 7-2.

Once again the Barons took offense to derisive comments in the Buffalo papers. Called an "ancient collection of pushovers" who can't win on the road, Cleveland players were once again spurred on to greater heights by the press.

One never would have known it, as the Barons fell behind 4-1 early in the second period of Game Three, once again played in Buffalo. Frankly, Cleveland looked dead. This was before Fred Thurier put the team on his back and carried them to victory. Scoring once in the second period and twice in the third, Fred tied the score at 5-5 to send the contest into overtime. The Fox, as he was nicknamed, was relentless. He would not let the team die.

In the full 10-minute overtime, each team had golden opportunities – only to be thwarted by the great goaltending of Harvey Teno and Connie Dion.

Finally, with only 22 seconds left in the extra session, Lou Trudel took a pass from Phil Hergesheimer and fired in the winner for a 6-5 victory. This one was sweet, for it took a lot of pressure off and made the Buffalo press eat their words. It also gave Cleveland a 2-1 edge in games, and a big upset now really seemed possible.

The upset possibility seemed probable after Game Four, as an all-time record crowd of 12,791 saw Cleveland take a 3-1 lead in games with a 7-5 victory. The April 9th gathering was the largest crowd ever to witness a Barons' hockey game at the Arena.

Highlight of the contest was two third-period goals by Tommy Burlington. These were Tom's first goals since his hat trick in the Providence series. With the great center pressing, the scoring slack had been picked up by Fred Thurier. But the team needed Burlington, and he came back when they needed him most.

The game also saw a goal by Les Cunningham. Les was giving it a game try, but his groin injury was severely handicapping his play.

The Barons could smell the title; they were that close. But Buffalo had other ideas. The Bisons staved off elimination by bombing the Clevelanders 6-1 in Buffalo. Only the badly limping Cunningham could score for the Barons, who were never in the game. Obviously, the team let down, knowing Game Six was back home. This was a fatal mistake, for the momentum swung over to Buffalo. They firmly believed that they were now going to take the series.

Buffalo's strategy in Game Six at Cleveland was to gang up on Tommy Burlington and to hit everything that moved. 12,372 fans saw a hard-hitting battle from start to finish.

The Barons attacked ferociously but were denied repeatedly by Buffalo goalie Connie Dion. Time after time he robbed Cleveland of sure goals and kept the Bisons in the game.

After a scoreless first period, Buffalo was first to score. Tom Cooper took a pass from Murdo McKay and beat Harvey Teno at 4:18 of the second. The Bisons hit for one more score, but goals by Fred Thurier, Alex Motter and Burlington gave Cleveland a 3-2 lead after period two. The Barons were only twenty minutes from winning the Cup.

The Bisons came out flying in period three and tied the game at three each on a goal by McKay at 3:18. From then on, the checking was tight and hard. It was especially hard on Burlington. With Les Cunningham slowed to a walk when his groin injury flared up again, the Bisons concentrated on stopping Burlington. Tom took a terrific beating.

Finally, with just over seven minutes to play, Buffalo succeeded in knocking Cleveland's star center out of the game. After being crashed into the boards by defenseman Bob Blake, Tom collapsed in a heap. After being revived, he was carried to the dressing room. This seemed to fire up Buffalo and deflate the Barons.

The end came at 15:49 when Buffalo's Paul Mundrick broke free at the Cleveland blue line and skated in alone on goalie Teno. His aim was true, and the 4-3 win put the Bisons firmly in the driver's seat.

With their backs against the wall, the Barons needed a miracle, but they had run out. Tommy Burlington was so beat up from Game Six that he was left home for Game Seven in Buffalo the next night. Les Cunningham's groin injury was bad, and he could not play either. Without their two ace centers, the battered Barons were only a shell of the team that began the series.

Despite these handicaps, the Barons gave it all they had, but it was not enough. Buffalo played a near flawless game and skated away with a 5-2 victory and their third Calder Cup in four years.

Although they lost the series after leading 3 games to 1, the Barons held their heads high. While never quite living up to expectations during the regular season, the team gave a spirited run in the playoffs and came one victory from the championship. So close, yet so far away.

As the players went home for the Summer, they all wondered who would be back next year. It was no secret that owner Al Sutphin was going to make some changes. Deals would be made – deals that would shake the team to its very core.

FINAL STANDINGS
1945-46

West	W	L	T	GF	GA	PTS.
Indianapolis	33	20	9	286	238	75
Pittsburgh	30	22	10	262	226	70
Cleveland	28	26	8	269	254	64
St. Louis	21	32	9	198	266	51
East	**W**	**L**	**T**	**GF**	**GA**	**PTS.**
Buffalo	38	16	8	270	196	84
Hershey	26	26	10	213	221	62
Providence	23	33	6	221	254	52
New Haven	14	38	10	199	263	38
Top Baron Scorers				**G**	**A**	**PTS.**
Tommy Burlington				36	46	82
Lou Trudel				33	46	79
Les Cunningham				33	44	77

Calder Cup Champion - Buffalo Bisons

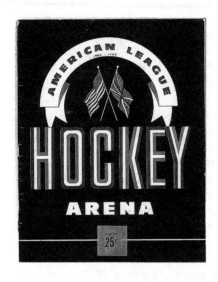

1946-47 SEASON

During the Summer of 1946, Al Sutphin dropped a bombshell by trading the great Tommy Burlington to Providence for Jack Lavoie and Roger Gagne. The shock waves were felt by every hockey fan in Cleveland. The fans' knew changes were coming, but no one expected Burlington to go.

Lavoie and Gagne were both solid two-way players, but neither approached Burlington's status. Then why the trade?

The standard party line given out by the club was that the Barons were going to go with more team-oriented players. Solo artists would take a back seat to unselfish players who checked as well as scored. The reasoning didn't wash.

For one thing, Burlington was one of the most unselfish players in the game. Often he would pass up shots in order to let his linemates score. He didn't get all those assists by hogging the puck. Secondly, Tom was also a pretty fair backchecker. While not a big hitter, he would often break up plays with his great speed.

Burlington himself was never told the real reasons for the trade, but to this day he believes money played a major role in his being dealt – money that hadn't even been discussed at the time.

To understand a likely scenario, one must understand that above all else, Al Sutphin was a businessman. He was well aware that the only reason Burlington was not playing in the National Hockey League was because of his only having one eye. If he had been allowed, there was no doubt that he would have been a big star. Tom would have been a star in any League. Along with NHL status would be an NHL salary. This was the key.

Sutphin probably reasoned that it was only a matter of time before Tom would demand an NHL level salary that he should be making if it were not for his eye handicap. And if he did give the star center such a salary increase, how would this affect his other star players? Would they not follow suit and demand big pay increases? The Barons were the highest paid team in the AHL; but when it came to dollars, players were only human.

It was entirely possible, if this scenario did unfold, that the entire salary structure of the team would be blown out of whack. To avoid a possible problem such as this, the deal was made.

Sutphin knew that the Barons could win without Burlington. The team's talent reservoir was great, and he was also purchasing many top stars to replace talent that was leaving. Still, the trade was a gamble.

As for Tom, the great center went to Providence and broke his hand early in the season. Despite missing two months, he still scored 22 goals and 43 assists for 65 points.

The next year Burlington held out for more money. He missed the entire 1947 training camp. When Reds' owner Lou Pieri was ready to pay Tom an NHL salary, Burlington stunned the hockey world by quitting the pro game.

Tom had a wife and two young children. He frankly was tired of being away with all the travel. So he packed his bags and went home to Owen Sound, Ontario, where he regained his amateur status and starred for the local Senior Amateur team. He also went into partnership with two other former players in a new car dealership. From there he branched into racetrack operations and made more money than he ever could have made playing hockey in the States.

As great as the Barons were over the next decade, they never could replace the great Burlington. He was one in a million. The sky was the limit for Tom, and he could have set standards that would have stood for years in the AHL. But alas, it was not to be. Let it just be said that Tommy Burlington was one of the brightest lights ever to shine in the history of the American Hockey League.

Two other longtime local heroes also departed. Earl Bartholome, one of the team's all-time great two-way players, retired and returned home to Minneapolis. Earl did get antsy and played a bit for the Millers, the Barons' farm club in his home town. Bartholome played ten strong years in Cleveland. Known primarily as a defensive player early in his career, he blossomed into a top scorer in his later years when the game opened up with the red line ruling. Earl would be missed.

Also to be missed was Phil Hergesheimer. One of the most popular Barons ever, Hergy played a total of five years with the club in three different periods. His was a career of "could have been's."

Once the League's most dynamic player, he was taken away by Chicago. After three years in the NHL, Sutphin brought him back. It took a while; but just as Phil was beginning to look like his old self, he was called to military duty. He returned to Cleveland after the war and had a fair year.

Sutphin thought that Hergy's best days were behind him. With the new Philadelphia Rockets coming into the League and needing players, the Barons' owner sold Phil, Whitey Prokop, Pete Bessone, and Paul Gauthier to the Rockets. Hergesheimer fooled all the experts and won the scoring title in 1946-47 with 48 goals and 44 assists, his greatest year. It truly was sad to see Phil leave, but everyone, including Sutphin and his many fans, were overjoyed by his great success late in his career.

Only seven players remained from the 1945-46 club. They were Lou Trudel, Les Cunningham (who was moved to defense), Ernie Trigg, Fred Thurier, Danny Sprout, Gordon Davidson, and Johnny (Kiszkan) Bower.

Included among the new players was an entirely new first line of Bobby Carse, Johnny Holota, and Pete Leswick. Holota, Leswick, and defenseman Roly McLenahan were purchased from the Detroit Red Wings. Carse played for Chicago in the NHL before going off to the war. His rights went to Montreal when the Blackhawks thought he would never play hockey again after being a prisoner of war in Germany. Getting Bobby from Montreal was one of Al Sutphin's greatest moves.

Other new players were Hank Goldup, purchased from the New York Rangers, and forward Bob Walton. Two youngsters up from the junior ranks were defensemen Julian Sawchuk and Doug Lane. Of course, Jack Lavoie and Roger Gagne came over from Providence for Burlington.

Lastly, Roger Bessette was purchased from Pittsburgh to share goaltending duties with Bower.

The Barons had the look of a very strong team. They had speed to burn and appeared to be an overall better defensive group than in the past. Their only possible weakness was lack of size on the forward lines. Except for big Hank Goldup, the Barons' forwards were all rather small. Bun Cook privately wondered if the team would be able to hold up over the long haul.

A huge opening night crowd of 10,207 saw the team's eldest statesman, 33-year-old Lou Trudel, score two goals to lead Cleveland to a 9-5 victory over Philadelphia. Seven other players scored in a rather sloppily played game.

The "new" Barons got a stiff early-season test when they played the champion Buffalo Bisons three straight games. The Bisons were once again favored to take the title, and this early series was used as a gauge to see just how far the Barons had grown together.

Two victories in Cleveland, 2-0 and 5-2, plus a 2-2 tie in Buffalo, had the Barons really believing in themselves.

With their record steadily improving, little used forward Wendell Jamieson fired a hat trick in a 7-2 win over Philadelphia on November 20th that started the Barons on a brilliant nine-game winning streak. The victory over the Rockets gave Cleveland a 10-4-2 record, good for a first-place tie with Pittsburgh.

The most impressive victory in the streak was the December 5th game at Hershey. The Barons had won five in a row while the Bears had a seven-game victory streak of their own. The early season battle of division leaders had both players and fans all hopped up for their first encounter of the year.

Before a full house in Hershey, the Barons proved they were for real. Their 5-3 victory over the Bears was not as close as the score indicated.

Main man for Cleveland was center iceman Johnny Holota with three goals. The hat trick gave Johnny 19 goals in the Barons' first 21 games. But he was not alone in Cleveland's scoring rampage. Linemates Bobby Carse and Pete (The Pony) Leswick had 10 goals each for the number one scoring line in the League.

This trio of super talent was the talk of the AHL. They had that innate special chemistry between them that few linemates had. Each seemed to know instinctively what the other was going to do in any given situation. They were like a fine wine together.

They kept getting better with each and every game.

What made this line all the more impressive was their fine defensive play. Leswick and Carse, in particular, were terrific backcheckers besides being top-notch scorers. Holota, while not a gifted skater like his linemates, had an uncanny knack for getting open in front of the net for short-range goals. The line would stay on fire all season long.

After a 6-4 win over New Haven at the Arena, the Barons ventured into Pittsburgh seeking win number eight in a row. The second-place Hornets were now five points behind Cleveland and wanted a victory badly.

A wild first period saw each team score three times. Cleveland's tallies were by Carse, Trudel, and Leswick. The winning score came at 19:18 of the second period. Julian Sawchuk fired a wicked shot from the point that was stopped by goalie Baz Bastien. Once again, Holota was Johnny-on-the-spot with the rebound for his 20th goal and the win.

The final win in the nine-game streak gave Cleveland a tremendous 18-4-2 record. The 5-2 victory over Providence before 11,265 at the Arena featured a rare penalty shot that was made by Johnny Holota for his 21st goal.

Only two games short of tying the record for most consecutive wins in a row, the Barons went into Pittsburgh seeking number 10. But, as the saying goes, you can't win them all.

One never would have known it the way Cleveland opened the game. Striking for three first-period goals, the Barons looked on the verge of a rout. Their play was nearly flawless. But the Hornets came to play. Banging home three goals of their own, the teams entered the third stanza tied at three. Both clubs had numerous opportunities to score, but the goaltending was superb, especially Cleveland's Roger

Bobby Carse – A prisoner of war during World War II, Bobby returned to hockey during the 1946-47 season and became one of the the greatest Barons ever. Bobby Carse collection.

Bessette. Roger kicked out an amazing 51 shots as the Hornets were buzzing furiously. Unfortunately, Bessette missed one at 18:50 of the final period on a shot by Laurier Archembault. It was a heartbreaking defeat, but the Barons got over it quickly.

Cleveland came home to face Hershey before 11,066 and got right back on the winning track. This time it was Johnny Bower's turn to show off some goaltending wizardry as he rang up his third shutout as the Barons won a 1-0 thriller.

Pete Leswick (6), Johnny Holota (14), Bobby Carse (16) – This super trio terrorized opposing goalies from 1946-47 through 1949-50. Bobby Carse collection – Photo by Conner-Geddes.

Bobby Carse (7) fights for the puck against Hershey. Johnny Holota (14) is in background. Bobby Carse collection – photo by Bill Nehez.

The Bears tried to intimidate the much smaller Cleveland club, but the Barons held their own. Their backchecking was tenacious as they continually broke up Hershey rushes. In the end, Bower had only 24 saves, although a few were rather unbelievable. The winning score was off the stick of big Hank Goldup at 5:27 of the third period.

Cleveland upped its record to 20-5-2 and stretched its 1st place lead to 9 points by routing Springfield 7-2 at the Arena. The first line was at it again as Pete Leswick and Bobby Carse each struck for two goals. Carse also picked up two assists on Leswick's scores to give him 14 goals and 27 assists for the year – good for third place in the League.

The Christmas night win over Springfield was especially satisfying to Bobby for another reason. Just two years previous, he spent Christmas in a German prisoner of war camp.

After playing for the Chicago Blackhawks in the NHL, Carse was taken into the military during World War II. He was taken prisoner by the Nazi's and held for over 6 months. It was during this time that he lost 60 pounds. Hockey was the least of his worries. Only the memory of his lovely wife, Betty, and family back home in Edmonton kept him going. He was determined to survive.

During his time as a prisoner, the Nazi's decided to transfer all of the men in his camp to another location completely on the other side of Germany. Off the tortured soldiers marched from one side of the country to the other. To make matters worse, it was the dead of Winter, and the prisoners had only one set of clothes. They slept outside in the freezing cold except for one lone night.

The Germans stopped at a farm house and herded all of their captives into a barn for the night. Bobby recalls being near death until he and some others caught and ate a chicken found in the barn. The next morning, while leaving the farm house, the owner was passing out raw potatoes to all of the prisoners. Carse remembers thinking how generous the woman was and how guilty he felt for eating her chicken. Here was a man on death's doorstep still thinking about his fellow man! Carse truly had a heart of gold – and still does.

Bobby pulled through the war and finally regained his strength and weight. The Blackhawks thought his playing days were over, and Sutphin's securing of his rights was a real coup. In his four years with the Barons, Carse proved to be one of the team's and the League's greatest players.

After a 5-1 triumph over Philadelphia, the Barons hit the halfway point in the schedule with a superb 24-6-2 record. There seemed no stopping them, as their systematic passing game and team-oriented defense was working to perfection.

Before the Philly game, Al Sutphin presented Rocket goalie Nick Damore the Harry (Hap) Holmes Memorial Trophy in recognition as the League's top goalie the previous year. Damore won the award while playing with Hershey.

In true Al Sutphin form, the Barons' owner pulled a surprise by handing out trophies to Phil Hergesheimer and Les Cunningham. Both players were winding down their careers, and Al wanted them to know how much he appreciated their contributions to the team. In fact, this would be Cunningham's last season as an active player. While he was now playing solid defense, his legs were almost gone. He was switched to the backline because he could no longer keep up with the many speedsters now in the League. A true professional, Les made the switch from star center to defenseman without any difficulty.

The pace they were setting was unbelievable, so it seemed inevitable that the Barons should slip a little. They went 1-4-1 in their next six games and actually fell out of first place behind Indianapolis. On January 21st, they found themselves only two points ahead of Buffalo and six up on Pittsburgh. It seems incredible that these teams kept within striking distance when the Barons were so hot. Yet, here they were, knocking on Cleveland's door.

After Julian Sawchuk broke his leg in Providence, and fellow rookie Doug Lane began to falter, the Cleveland defense needed a boost. Sutphin provided just that by getting rugged veteran backliner Bill Allum from St. Louis in exchange for right winger Wendell Jamieson and the aforementioned Doug Lane.

Allum proved a splendid shot in the arm as the Barons went 6-1-2 in their next nine games. Their 31-11-5 record on February 9th was good for a six-point first place lead over Pittsburgh. But just as soon as the lead seemed comfortable, the team lost three in a row.

Bun Cook's pre-season fear that the small Barons might wear down as the season progressed seemed to be coming true. But not in the case of the first line. The Leswick-Holota-Carse trio never cooled off. Holota, in particular, was on fire. He scored his 40th goal in a 4-3 loss to St. Louis. With 14 games remaining, Johnny seemed a good bet to break the League record of 46 set by Joe Bell of Hershey last season.

The by now up and down Barons came back from the three-game slump to win three straight. Highlight was a 3-1 victory over Hershey at the Arena before 10,964. While Cleveland was busy fighting off Indianapolis, Buffalo, and Pittsburgh in the tight Western division race, the Bears were running away with the East, some 20 points over second-place Springfield.

Hershey had recently been strengthened by the acquisition of long-time NHL star Walter (Babe) Pratt. Pratt had starred with New York and Toronto before being traded to Boston and sent on to Hershey. Although near the end of his career, the huge defenseman would be a name to remember come playoff time.

The win over the Bears put Cleveland two points up on Hershey in the overall League standings, and five points up in the West. But the game was costly, as goalie Roger Bessette sprained an ankle and would be lost for three weeks.

The injury bug hit again in a 9-2 win over St. Louis on February 27th. Lou Trudel, somewhat overlooked this season because of the success of Leswick, Holota, and Carse, suffered a torn Achilles tendon in a collision with the Flyers' Jack Sawchuk. When the two fell to the ice, the skate of Sawchuk somehow sliced through Lou's tendon, ending his season. The great clutch scorer would be missed. His season ended with 20 goals, 29 assists for 49 points.

Walt Voysey collection.

The heated Western division race went into March, with Cleveland, Indianapolis, Buffalo, and Pittsburgh breathing down each other's necks. Pittsburgh, in particular, was on fire with a 19-game undefeated streak that was finally ended by St. Louis on March 2nd.

March 2nd was also a record-setting day for Cleveland as a team, and Johnny Holota in particular. The Barons' 5-2 win at Indianapolis was their 18th road win of the season, a new League record. Holota's goal at 12:07 of the first period was his 47th and broke the League mark of 46 set by Hershey's Joe Bell. Johnny would cap his season by scoring five more times and finish the year with an amazing total of 52 goals. This would be a Baron record that would never be broken.

Cleveland sewed up a spot in the playoffs with a 5-3 win over Providence on March 8th before 11,663 at the Arena. It was the Barons' 38th win of the season, tying the League record set last season by Buffalo. With five games remaining, Cleveland seemed a cinch to set a new record. But it was not to be. The team went flat and went winless in their remaining games.

A most embarrassing loss was a 10-2 shellacking administered by the Hershey Bears. Ironically, Cleveland clinched the Western division crown with the loss. Combined with losses suffered by Buffalo and Pittsburgh, Cleveland now held a four-point lead in the standings over both clubs with only two games remaining. Either club could tie the Barons in points, but not on number of victories. Since number of wins is used as the first tie-breaker in the standings, Cleveland was in. But they were embarrassed by the game and circumstances.

The Barons backed into their 5th regular season American League title in much the same manner. Their 10-6 loss at Indianapolis combined with a 6-1 Hershey loss at New Haven gave Cleveland its title.

Although they hated backing into a championship, the Barons would take it. After all, a title is a title. However, Cleveland faced an uphill battle in the playoffs. Their foe was Eastern division champion Hershey, and the Bears were on fire. Despite their season-ending loss to New Haven, Hershey was playing great hockey, attested by their 10-2 pasting of Cleveland the week before. The Barons, on the other hand, were showing the effects of being such a small team. In plain English, they were worn out.

THE PLAYOFFS

During the regular season, Johnny Bower played in all six games against Hershey, going 3-1-2. The only loss was in the 10-2 blowout. Despite the fact that he played more games and had a lower goals against average than Roger Bessette, Coach Cook decided to start Bessette in the playoff opener. Bun always leaned toward experience in a money series. Despite the fact that he had played only one game in the last three weeks, a classic 0-0 tie with Pittsburgh, Roger appeared ready for the Bears.

10,487 fans showed up for the series opener in Cleveland, and none of them could believe their eyes. The Barons dropped a 3-0 decision to Hershey. It wasn't the loss itself that stunned them, but the manner in which it was achieved. The Bears thoroughly dismantled the Cleveland offense that was so high-powered all season long. The Hershey defense lined up along the red line and pummeled any Baron who tried to cross it with the puck. If a Cleveland attacker did break through this wall of defense, a backchecking forward was sure to be all over him. The strategy paid off as the Barons only had 15 shots on goal, none

of them tough. Goalie Gordon Henry had an easy time of it as huge Babe Pratt knocked down any Cleveland player who came near the Hershey net.

It was more of the same in the first period of Game Two at the Arena. Cleveland didn't even get a shot on goal until the seven-minute mark, while Hershey poured in three first-period goals to lead 3-0.

The Barons finally got a spark when defenseman Bill Allum scored at 5:02 of the second period. Cleveland finally woke up and began to play the brand of hockey they were capable of playing. From that point on, Cleveland pressed the attack. Johnny Hotola made it 3-2 at 6:24 of the third period. The last 13 minutes were nail-biting time, as the Barons swarmed all over Hershey. Only the great play of Pratt and Henry kept the home team off the scoreboard.

In the end, the Bears hung on for a 3-2 victory and headed back to Hershey with a huge 2-0 series lead. The trip to Chocolate Town was one of the lowest points in Barons' history.

In Game Three, Cleveland trailed 3-1 after two periods. Their only goal was scored by Pete Leswick. But then the roof caved in during the third period as the Bears tallied six unanswered goals to win going away 9-1.

If that score wasn't bad enough, the Barons proved it was for real by getting demolished 9-0 in Game Four. Cleveland was totally humiliated in the four-game sweep.

"We were beaten by a Hershey team that's coached tough, plays tough, and is tough," said Coach Cook after the debacle. "Next year...we'll have to get some heavier men – aggressive men."

Thus the Barons went home for the summer with their tails between their legs. A season that looked so great in February had gone up in smoke. Gloom settled over the club. If they only knew what a difference a year would make.

FINAL STANDINGS
1946-47

West	W	L	T	GF	GA	PTS.
Cleveland	38	18	8	272	215	84
Buffalo	36	17	11	257	173	83
Pittsburgh	35	19	10	260	188	80
Indianapolis	33	18	13	285	215	79
St. Louis	17	35	12	211	292	46
East	W	L	T	GF	GA	PTS.
Hershey	36	16	12	276	174	84
Springfield	24	29	11	202	220	59
New Haven	23	31	10	199	218	56
Providence	21	33	10	226	281	52
Philadelphia	5	52	7	188	400	17

Top Baron Scorers	G	A	PTS.
Bobby Carse	27	61	88
Johnny Holota	52	35	87
Pete Leswick	32	41	73
Fred Thurier	18	33	51
Hank Goldup	30	19	49
Lou Trudel	20	29	49

Calder Cup Champion – Hershey Bears

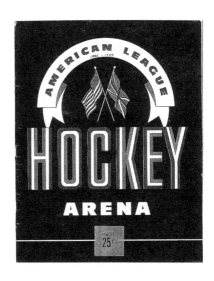

1947-48 SEASON

During the Summer of 1947, Les Cunningham, the last original member of the Barons' first team of 1937-38, decided to retire. Les probably could have hung on, but the constant pounding on his legs had taken its toll. He simply was not the skater he used to be.

Al Sutphin gave Les the opportunity to stay in the game by making him coach of his San Francisco farm club. Cunningham jumped at the opportunity.

It wouldn't be the same without Les around. He was the League's first true superstar. While not blest with blazing speed, he held his own and was one of the most clever stickhandlers the League had ever seen. A roughhouse terror early in his career, Les later became the most respected man on ice, the epitome of class.

He left the game as the AHL's highest career scorer with 233 goals, 346 assists, for 579 points. During the playoffs he tallied 29 goals, 33 assists, for 62 points. In recognition of his great contribution to the AHL, the League's Most Valuable Player is awarded the Les Cunningham Trophy each year.

Another glaring hole that needed to be filled was left by Bobby Carse. Bobby, owned by Montreal, was actually loaned to Cleveland for the 1946-47 season. The Canadiens' had the right to give him a tryout before the 1947-48 campaign if they so desired. After Carse's great season, they decided to keep him even though Bobby made it clear that he preferred playing in Cleveland. He would stay in Montreal for 19 games before Sutphin could get him back permanently.

During the off-season, Sutphin and Coach Cook decided to beef up the squad so as not to repeat the playoff disaster to Hershey. First off, three big defensemen were brought in. Babe Pratt, who ran rampant over the Barons in last season's playoffs, was purchased from Hershey. Along with Joe Cooper, purchased from the New York Rangers, and Eddie Wares, Cleveland now seemed to have a large, hard-hitting backline.

Up on the forward lines three new players would play a significant role in the team's upcoming fortunes.

Ab (The Count) DeMarco, one of the trickiest stickhandlers in hockey, was purchased from the Rangers. Ab would center for two youngsters brought up from the farm system, Bob Solinger and Roy Kelly. Kelly was with the Barons for two years prior to last season, but was sent to Minneapolis to refine his game. This trio would form a dynamite second line for the club all season long.

Cleveland opened the season by dropping a rough 4-3 decision to their long-time nemesis, the Buffalo Bisons. This was the beginning of an up and down first month of hockey. A 5-2-1 spurt brought their record to 12-7-3 by mid-December.

On the plus side was the play of DeMarco and Solinger. Ab was leading the team in points with 27 on 9 goals and 18 assists. Chief benefactor of The Count's great playmaking ability was rookie Bob Solinger. Bob, a big, fast, aggressive skater, was leading the team in goals with 14, one ahead of Johnny Holota and Fred Thurier. Solinger was the best-looking rookie to come into the League for a long time.

He was exactly what Sutphin was looking for when the owner decided to bulk up the team.

The negatives were twofold. First, despite their good record, Cleveland was running a distant fourth in the standings, 6 points behind Indianapolis. Buffalo and Pittsburgh were far out in front. Except for a strong Providence club, all of the power in the League was in the Western division.

Chief reason for the fourth-place standing seemed to lie in the failure of the big defensemen, who were brought in to beef up the backline. Eddie Wares was playing well, but Babe Pratt and Joe Cooper were having their troubles. Pratt, 31, was woefully out of shape and showed no signs of working hard enough to get back into playing condition. Cooper, on the other hand, was beginning to show his age. The 33-year-old defenseman also was financing a new bowling alley in his home town of Winnipeg. He seemed to be preoccupied with the condition of his new business venture, and his hockey playing suffered. Both were rumored to be on the trading block.

City his adopted home. To this day, he and his wife, Betty, still live in the Cleveland area.

In his first game back in front of the Cleveland fans, Carse wasted no time in showing how happy he was to be back. At 2:45 of the opening period, Bobby took a pass from George Allen and scored the first goal in an 8-2 romp over the Washington Lions. He also scored a second goal in a triumphant return before 9,368 adoring fans.

The reacquisition of Carse had a domino effect on the club. First, it allowed him to be reunited with Johnny Holota and Pete Leswick. This trio was the scourge of the League the previous season, with a total of 111 goals. This move made it possible to move George Allen back to defense. He had been playing left wing on Holota's line in place of Carse.

With Allen back on defense, Sutphin was able to make one of his best trades as owner of the Barons. He sent Babe Pratt back to Hershey along with Joe Cooper for 21-year-old Hymie Buller.

Buller was a seasoned veteran despite his young

The return of Bobby Carse to the Barons on December 17, 1948 spurred the team on to its greatest heights. Here Bobby (2nd from left) scores against Buffalo's Connie Dion. Pete Leswick (6) celebrates. Bobby Carse collection – Photo by John Nash.

On December 17th the first of several events transpired that would set the club onto whirlwind heights. Al Sutphin announced that he had purchased the contract of Bobby Carse from the Montreal Canadiens. The return of the star left winger was just what the doctor ordered. As happy as the fans were, no one was more elated than Carse himself. He loved playing in Cleveland and made this

age. He turned pro at the tender age of 17 and first played with Detroit and Indianapolis. He landed with Hershey during the 1944-45 season. During Hershey's title year of 1946-47, Buller banged in 12 goals and 32 assists. Defensively Hy was extremely rugged despite being very offensive-minded. He could mix it up with the best of them.

Sutphin added his last piece to the puzzle by purchasing Churchill Russell from the New York Rangers. Church was a great skater who had good size and a love of banging bodies.

The Barons' owner now had the type of team he dreamed about – team oriented, with blazing speed and good size to boot. The defense was extremely mobile and as rugged as they come. Sutphin expected good things in 1948, but not even he could foresee the amazing events about to transpire.

The new year got off on a bang with one of the most riotous games ever played at the Arena.

The Cleveland-Pittsburgh battle got off to a quiet start. The Hornets held a 1-0 lead after one period. Pittsburgh scored again in the second period, as did Bobby Carse and Danny Sprout for the Barons. This ended the scoring.

The main event began when Pittsburgh coach Bill Davidson called referee Hugh McLean a "homer" along with a host of other choice adjectives. McLean ordered Davidson off the players' bench. The coach complied by standing in the aisle next to the bench. This wasn't good enough for the referee, and a shouting match ensued. Finally, a policeman was called to remove Davidson. By this time the fans surrounding the scene got more than vociferous, and the situation got out of control. Hornet players climbed into the stands to help their beleaguered coach, who was by now swarmed over by the angry fans. Five more policemen entered the fray as the fans and players battled each other. Finally, order was restored, and Hornets' general manager Johnny Mitchell took over as coach.

Just a few minutes later, a feud between Ab DeMarco and Pittsburgh's Stan Kemp erupted into a fierce fight. After the combatants were separated and sent to the penalty box, they went at it again. When a policeman seated between the two players in the penalty box tried to break up their second fight, all hell broke loose.

Kemp, thinking this was none of the cop's business, began firing punches at the peacemaker. At this point the players and fans all converged on the penalty box area, and sticks and fists were flying everywhere. Somehow in the melee, Baron goalie Roger Bessette thought Johnny Mitchell was attacking DeMarco, and he then proceeded to trade punches with the Hornets' general manager. Kemp then attacked Bessette.

After the riot was finally cleared, only Bessette was thrown out of the game. An intermission was called, and Johnny Bower finished the 2-2 tie game.

The old ice house on Euclid Avenue had never seen a game like this.

The season reached its halfway point on January 7th, with the Barons squaring off against the Hershey Bears. Including the humiliating four-game sweep in the playoffs, Cleveland had not beaten the Bears in eight straight games dating back to last February.

This was a determined bunch of Barons that let out all of their frustrations on the powerful defending champions. Led by Pete Leswick's four goals and two assists, the Barons annihilated the Bears 12-1. This tied their all-time high for goals in one game. Although they were still in fourth place, the Clevelanders were only eight points behind first-place Pittsburgh.

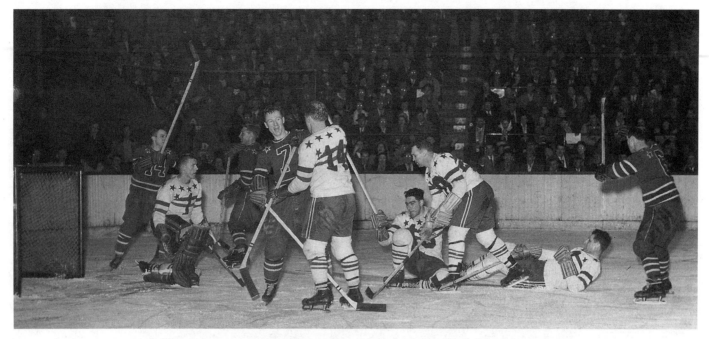

A familiar sight during the late 1940's was the line of Holota (14), Carse (7), and Leswick (6) celebrating another goal. Here they light the red lamp again against St. Louis.
Bobby Carse collection – Photo by John Nash.

The Barons kept up their terrific scoring by routing the Washington Lions 9-2 and the Philadelphia Rockets 10-3 in their next two games. This gave them an incredible 31 goals in their last three games. This tied the three-game record for scoring set by Pittsburgh in 1945.

Heroes in the Philly win were Johnny Holota, who poured in four goals, and Bob Solinger with three. Holota's second goal was the 100th of his career. Solinger's hat trick gave him 25 for the season and made him the odds-on favorite to win "rookie of the year" honors.

Fred Thurier took his turn in the spotlight during the next two games. First, he scored three goals to lead Cleveland to a 7-4 victory over Buffalo before 12,142 at the Arena. Buffalo had been tied with Pittsburgh for first place, and the win left the Barons only one point behind third place Indianapolis.

On January 18th, the Fox became only the third player in League history to score 200 goals, the others being Les Cunningham and Lou Trudel. Thurier's historic goal came at 6:26 of the second period in a 4-2 win at New Haven, the team's fifth straight.

In all the joy surrounding the team's excellent play, a sad note occurred when 34-year-old veteran Lou Trudel suffered a broken ankle during a 2-2 tie at Washington. This put Lou out for the season and ended his brilliant career. His 222 goals ranked him second behind Les Cunningham's 233. One of Al Sutphin's favorite players, Lou was one of the League's deadliest marksmen before age and injuries caught up with him.

Cleveland's seven-game unbeaten streak came to an end on January 26th during a 6-1 loss at Hershey. This game is significant because it was the last game the Barons would lose during the regular season.

The Barons went into Springfield on January 28th and beat the Indians 6-4 to begin the most glorious stretch in the team's history. 21 victories and 6 ties later, the Barons headed into the playoffs with an unbelievable 27-game unbeaten streak.

The Streak started innocently enough with four wins and four ties, but the Barons were building momentum. After finally passing Indianapolis in the standings, Cleveland set its sights on second-place Buffalo.

They finally realized this goal after a 5-2 win against Philadelphia on February 18th. This was the 11th straight game without defeat and was a special night for The Count, Ab DeMarco. Ab blasted home the 100th goal of his career in the first period. This gave The Count 19 for the current campaign and placed him in the top 10 among the scoring leaders. The victory left the Barons only five points behind Pittsburgh, as they drove onward toward the promised land, first place.

Cleveland had the lead down to three points when they faced Pittsburgh in a showdown at the Arena before 11,072. The crowd was pumped up, and so were the Barons as they shut out the vaunted Hornets 6-0. Led by Bob Solinger's two goals, this was Roger Bessette's first shutout of the year. The flamboyant ex-Pittsburgh goalie loved sticking it to his old team. Number 14 in The Streak left Cleveland

Fans line up to buy tickets during the record-breaking 1947-48 season. Notice the prices – How times have changed!
Cleveland State University archives.

only one point out of first, as they headed into Hershey, their jinx rink, the next night.

If anyone had any doubts about the Barons, they were erased that night in Hershey. With the score tied 1-1 after two periods, Cleveland blitzed the Bears with four goals in the third to take #15. Led by Johnny Holota's 38th goal of the season, they now believed they could win anywhere in the League.

Pittsburgh had held first place since November 11th except for one week in January when Buffalo snuck in. Their perch on the top spot came to an end on February 29th when Cleveland finally scaled the mountain they had been climbing all season long. With their 17th straight undefeated game, a 5-2 win at St. Louis, the Barons finally overtook the Hornets and climbed into first place for the first time that season.

It was a long and sometimes frustrating climb up the ladder because Pittsburgh, Buffalo, and Indianapolis had also played great hockey all season long. The Barons now had a record of 34-13-11 with 10 games left to play, and it was still anybody's ball game. Top gun in the St. Louis win was Johnny Holota with two scores, his second being his 40th of the season. The victory not only put Cleveland in first place but left them only 2 games shy of Pittsburgh's record of 19 straight games without a loss set the previous season.

The Barons got a scare going after #18 straight as Phil Hergesheimer almost did in his ex-teammates. Turning back the clock to an earlier time, Phantom Phil scored three goals and assisted on another as Cleveland just nipped his Philadelphia Rockets 6-5 at the Arena. The hat trick gave Hergy 37 goals for the season.

After the Philly game, the Barons headed down to Pittsburgh for a battle with the Hornets. Ironically, in order to tie Pittsburgh's record of 19 straight undefeated games, Cleveland would have to do so on the Hornets' home ice.

Cleveland had not lost to Pittsburgh in six games that season, two wins and four ties. Also, the Hornets were now three points behind the Barons and wanted this game desperately. Every indication pointed to a real dogfight and a supreme battle it was.

Pittsburgh played its hardest and most determined game of the year. They did not want their hated Cleveland rivals tying their record in their own building. After two scoreless periods, the Hornets took the lead at 1:21 of the third on a long, screened shot by defenseman Pete Backor.

The one goal loomed ever large, so the Hornets continued to attack. Only the sensational netminding of Roger Bessette kept Cleveland within one goal.

The Barons finally got the break they needed when Phil Samis received a two-minute penalty for tripping Johnny Holota behind the Pittsburgh cage. On the ensuing powerplay, Church Russell, playing in place of the injured Pete Leswick, passed to Holota, who in turn gave the puck to Bobby Carse. Carse's aim was true, and at 11:22 the score was tied.

Slightly more than a minute later, at 12:29, Russell put on the hero's crown once more. Taking a pass by Roger Gagne from behind the Hornets' net, Church shot once; but goalie Baz Bastien made the initial save. Russell snared his own rebound; and as Bastien went down for the save, Church shot one over the falling goalie for the winning score.

The epic 2-1 win put Cleveland five points up on Pittsburgh with 8 games left. The defeat was a

BARONS SEEK 28TH STRAIGHT TONIGHT IN PLAYOFF OPENER WITH PROVIDENCE

crushing blow to the Hornets, who gave it everything they had. The Cleveland express just would not be derailed.

The record-breaking victory came at the expense of the Providence Reds, runaway winners of the Eastern division. The game was promoted as a preview of the first round of the upcoming playoffs, but the matchup fizzled because the Reds had goaltender problems. Both goalies, regular Harvey Bennett and backup Mike Karakas, were out of the lineup; and 21-year-old forward Jack Stoddard was forced to guard the nets. Stoddard played remarkably well making 50 saves, but in the end the Barons came away with an 8-3 victory before 11,818.

After beating Pittsburgh 4-2, the Barons went into Philadelphia and dismantled the Rockets by the score of 11-0. This overwhelming shutout by Johnny Bower put Cleveland 8 points ahead of Buffalo in the division race.

The division-clinching victory was achieved over the Bisons before 12,119 at the Arena on March 13th. Two early goals by Roger Gagne and Church Russell held up as Cleveland took a 2-1 thriller. Biggest hero in the game was goalie Roger Bessette, who was brilliant with 34 saves.

The victory climaxed an unbelievable rally that led to the Western division and AHL regular season championships. Back in December, Cleveland's chances of winning a title seemed slim and none. Just how good Pittsburgh and Buffalo were is found in the fact that it took until their 40th win for the Barons to clinch the championship. And this was the first time any team had won 40 games in League history! This great triumph was a great reward for total dedication and teamwork never seen before or since.

All that remained for the Barons before the playoffs was to keep the unbeaten streak alive. A 3-3 tie at Buffalo, a 6-1 win over St. Louis, and a 9-5 laugher over Indianapolis led up to the season finale against the Capitals.

When the dust had cleared after a 10-6 win over the Caps, all sorts of records were achieved. The victory was the 27th straight game without a defeat for Cleveland. It also was their 19th road victory of the season, a new record. Their season record of 43-13-12 set new milestones for wins and total points, 98.

On an individual note, Johnny Holota's third period goal was his 48th of the season. Combined with the previous season's 52, his two-year total of 100 goals was a feat never before achieved in professional hockey.

Other Baron teams had won the regular season title only to be defeated in the playoffs. But this year's team seemed invincible as they headed into the playoffs against the Providence Reds.

THE PLAYOFFS

The Barons entered the playoffs heavily favored, but they were playing a first-rate team in the Reds. Providence boasted six of the League's top 15 scorers. Led by Carl Liscombe, whose 118 points on 50 goals and 68 assists was a new League record, the Reds were a veritable scoring machine. As a team they amassed a record 342 goals, although they did give up a rather large total of 277.

This is where Cleveland held its biggest edge. The Barons played a much better team-oriented defense in only giving up 197 goals while scoring 332 themselves.

During the regular season Cleveland held a 4-2 edge in victories, having won all three games at the Arena and once in Providence.

One other interesting aspect to the series was the return of an old favorite, Whitey Prokop.

The Barons gave up on the right winger a little too soon. Whitey never developed into a big scorer in Cleveland because Bun Cook constantly drummed it into his head to think backcheck before scoring. He was afraid to get trapped in the offensive zone and not be able to get back. But his job on the team was to stop his opposing wing from scoring, and he was one of the best on the team in this regard.

After being sold to Philadelphia, Whitey wound up in Providence and soon found his nitch. Playing on a totally offensive-minded club, Whitey was leading the League in scoring in December. In his team's first 27 games, he had 24 goals and 21 assists. Unfortunately, a knee injury slowed him down, but Whitey came back to finish with 41 goals, 38 assists, for 79 points. Al Sutphin was so impressed that he tried to get the speedy winger back before the February 10th trading deadline. But Providence owner Lou Pieri said no way, and Whitey remained a Red.

Game One at the Arena saw Cleveland stretch its gigantic undefeated string to 28 games with a 6-1 rout of the Reds. Actually, Providence was in the game for two periods. The Barons grabbed the lead on two quick goals by Rookie of the Year Bob Solinger, and the Reds countered with one by Pete Kapusta near the end of the second period.

But as so often happened to a Barons' opponent, the Reds wore down, and Cleveland jumped on them for four third-period goals to win going away. The Clevelanders just had too much depth for any team in the League. Two goals by Bobby Carse and singletons by Ab DeMarco and Church Russell blew out Providence in the third period.

Game Two at the Arena before 11,051 saw Roger Bessette turn in a gem, as he blanked Providence 2-0. The Reds came out flying and playing rough, but the first period was scoreless.

Cleveland got a break when Red Harry Taylor was called for tripping. Shortly thereafter, Maurice Arcand joined his teammate in the penalty box. With a two-man advantage, the Barons buzzed around the net until Bobby Carse slipped a pass to Johnny Holota for the first score at 13:17 of the second period.

Change in venue meant nothing to this bunch of Barons, and Cleveland won again 4-2 at Providence, stretching their unbelievable unbeaten streak to 30 games. But the Reds made them earn it.

The Barons took an early 2-0 lead on goals by Jack Lavoie and Bobby Carse. Providence got one back late in the second. This set the stage for another big third period when Cleveland usually wore its opponent down, and they didn't disappoint. Scores by Fred Thurier and Gordon Davidson were too much for the Reds to overcome. But they went down fighting. There was no quit in this Providence club.

The Reds knew that the end was near, but they were determined not to be swept. They dearly wanted to be the team to end Cleveland's streak.

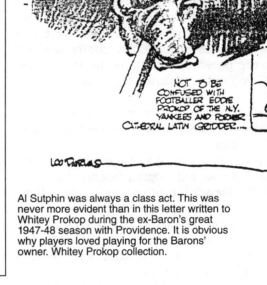

Al Sutphin was always a class act. This was never more evident than in this letter written to Whitey Prokop during the ex-Baron's great 1947-48 season with Providence. It is obvious why players loved playing for the Barons' owner. Whitey Prokop collection.

Before a sellout crowd of 5,850 wild and boisterous fans in their small Rhode Island arena, the Reds played like a team possessed. The Barons only trailed by one goal, 4-3, entering the third period. If previous form meant anything, they would wear Providence down and win the game. But on this cold night of March 30th, it was not to be. The Reds, skating like never before, struck for four unanswered goals to blast Cleveland 8-3.

Thus, the longest undefeated streak in hockey history finally came to an end. After more than two glorious months, the end was bound to happen. In a way, the team seemed to loosen up as the great pressure of the streak was lifted.

There were no bowed heads. The defeat just made the Barons that much more determined to keep on winning and capture the Calder Cup.

All of the enthusiasm displayed by the Reds in their great upset was missing in Game Five. The Barons completely outclassed their rivals and won going away at 8-1. Leading the attack was Johnny Holota's 2 goals and 2 assists.

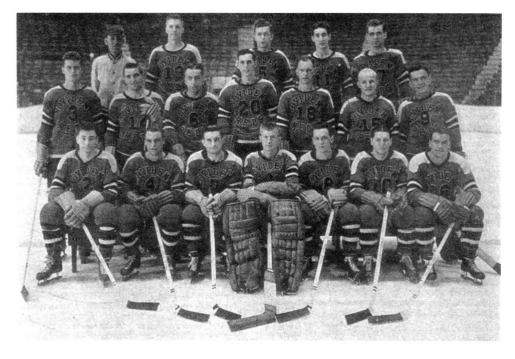

The 1947-48 Providence Reds who ended the Barons 30-game unbeaten streak with an 8-3 victory in Game Four of 1947-48 Playoffs.
Front (L-R): Coach Terry Reardon, Billy Arcand, Johnny Chad, Harvey Bennett, Ray LaPlante, Carl Liscombe, Ab Collings. Second: Allan Stanley, Chuck Scherza, Jack Church, Jack Stoddard, Art Michaluk, Whitey Prokop, Mike Karakas. Top: Trainer George Army, Pete Kapusta, Harvey Fraser, Roger Bedard, Harry Taylor. Whitey Prokop collection.

But the real hero of the series was goaltender Roger Bessette. Roger played in all five games and was positively brilliant. He surrendered a total of 12 goals, and 8 of them came in one game. In the other four games, he was a stone-wall force.

Thus the Barons entered the finals for the third time in five years against their old friends, the Buffalo Bisons.

During the regular season, the Bisons held a slight edge over Cleveland, winning 4, losing 3, while one game ended in a draw. However, all of Buffalo's wins came before the Barons started their Herculean streak. Although many of these Barons were not around when the Cleveland-Buffalo rivalry was still at its peak, the present rivalry was still plenty hot. However, Cleveland was now clearly in a class by themselves.

The cream rose to the top in Game One, as the Barons neatly disposed of the Bisons 6-1 before 11,675 at the Arena.

Buffalo actually outplayed Cleveland during a scoreless first period. But Roger Bessette closed the door. The lanky French-Canadian goalie called "Beeg Steek" by his teammates was reaching new heights of stardom in the 1948 playoffs. At one point, he raced 50 feet out of his cage to beat Les Hickey of Buffalo to a loose puck. The fans loved Roger's flamboyant style. He was a real crowdpleaser.

Bob Solinger and Fred Thurier tallied in the second period to give Cleveland all the goals they needed. But for good measure, the Barons poured home four more in the third. They played nearly flawless hockey in one of their finest performances of the season. Only a goal by Fred Hunt with two seconds remaining deprived Bessette of a shutout.

Game Two was a little closer and a little more exciting; but in the end, the too-powerful Barons had the edge, winning 5-3.

After Bob Solinger and Les Brennan gave Cleveland a 2-1 first-period lead, the two clubs traded goals the rest of the way. The Bisons actually held the advantage of play in the third period. But once again "Beeg Steek" Bessette was remarkable. At times he seemed to be everywhere as he was called upon to make 19 saves, many of them miraculous.

Game Three at Buffalo was a classic and a personal show for Bob Solinger. If there was any doubt that "Sollie" was the Rookie of the Year, it was erased in this game. The rookie, who scored 40 goals during the regular season, put on a dazzling display before some select company. Clarence Campbell, President of the National Hockey League, and most members of the Toronto Maple Leafs and Detroit Red Wings were in attendance. The Wings and Leafs were between games in the NHL Stanley Cup playoffs. Both teams wanted to see the club that went 30 games without losing. Cleveland, indeed, was the talk of the hockey world.

The game itself was full of fury. Buffalo stormed out of the gate and scored quickly at 1:18 on a powerplay goal by Murdo McKay. The Bisons were determined to run the Barons out of their rink and savagely hit any Baron that moved. One hit was just the break that the Barons needed. Mike McMahon was given a two-minute penalty for crosschecking; and by the time it was over, Cleveland had two goals. Danny Sprout assisted on tallies by Roy Kelly and Solinger to give the Barons a 2-1 lead.

The second period was wild and hectic hockey from start to finish. Only the great goaltending of Buffalo's Connie Dion and Roger Bessette kept the period scoreless.

The third period was more of the same as the Bisons desperately tried to tie the score. It was at the 9:13 mark that Solinger took the game in his own hands with a play that left everyone shaking their heads.

Taking the puck behind his own net, Sollie built up a head of steam and weaved his way up ice at full speed through the entire Buffalo team. His final fake on the last Buffalo defenseman spun the player completely around. With a final burst of speed, he skated in alone on Dion and fired home the game winner, his seventh of the playoffs. This goal finished the Bisons. They were not the same team after Solinger's beautiful dash.

Cleveland's remarkable Barons gave owner Al Sutphin the Calder Cup as his birthday present on April 11, 1948. As had been their custom throughout the playoffs, the Barons turned a close Game Four into a rout with a powerful third period.

After two periods of slam-bang hockey, the score was deadlocked at 2-2. Cleveland's goals came off the sticks of George Allen and Fred Thurier.

The action went back and forth for the first eight minutes of the third period, each club looking for an opening. Suddenly at 8:05 George Allen, the wheat farmer from Western Canada, let loose with a long shot from the blue line that a screened Connie Dion never saw. The puck hit the net and crushed the Bisons.

The Barons added three more goals, two by Church Russell and one by Jack Lavoie, to win by a 6-2 margin.

Al Sutphin, Coach Cook, and Norbert Stein, the team's general manager, rushed onto the ice to join their celebrating teammates. The ensuing victory party at Buffalo's Lafayette Hotel lasted well into the night, and everyone had just cause to celebrate.

If ever a case could be made for the rewards of teamwork, this was it. After falling between third and fourth place for half a season, this team rallied to perform feats never before or after seen – 30 straight, undefeated games; only one loss in their last 36 games; and three in their last 48.

Most of all, it was a team of players who put team achievement ahead of individual glory – a team that knew backchecking and defensive play was just as important as scoring goals. The 1947-48 club was Al Sutphin's crowning achievement, the greatest Baron team of all time.

1948 became a very special year in Cleveland sports history. After the Barons won The Calder Cup, the Indians won baseball's World Series, and the Browns won football's All-American Conference. It was then that Cleveland, Ohio became known as "The City of Champions."

THE 1947-48 CLEVELAND BARONS

Front (L-R): Augie Herchenratter, Fred Thurier, Church Russell, General Manager Norbert L. Stein, Roger Bessette, President Al Sutphin, Johnny Bower, Coach Fred "Bun" Cook, Ab DeMarco, Roy Kelly, Roger Gagne. Second: Publicity Director Eddie Coen, Eddie Wares, Julian Sawchuk, Les Brennan, Gordon Davidson, Dan Sprout, Hy Buller, Tony Bukovich, George Allen. Third: Chief Scout Gail Egan, Jack Lavoie, Pete Leswick, Bob Solinger, Johnny Holota, Bobby Carse, Lou Trudel, Trainer Walter Robertson. Bobby Carse collection.

FINAL STANDINGS
1947-48

West	W	L	T	GF	GA	PTS.
Cleveland	43	13	12	332	197	98
Pittsburgh	38	18	12	238	170	88
Buffalo	41	33	4	277	238	86
Indianapolis	32	30	6	293	260	70
St. Louis	22	36	10	242	291	54

East	W	L	T	GF	GA	PTS.
Providence	41	23	4	342	277	86
New Haven	31	30	7	254	242	69
Hershey	25	30	13	240	273	63
Philadelphia	22	41	5	260	331	49
Springfield	19	42	7	237	308	45
Washington	17	45	6	241	369	40

Top Baron Scorers	G	A	PTS.
Johnny Holota	48	38	86
Ab DeMarco	20	61	81
Pete Leswick	36	40	76
Fred Thurier	36	38	74
Bob Solinger	40	29	69
Roy Kelly	31	38	69
Bobby Carse	21	32	53

Calder Cup Champion – Cleveland Barons

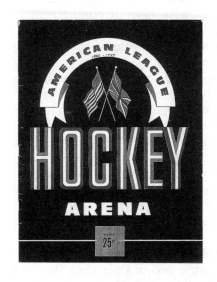

1948-49 SEASON

Out of respect to the previous year's record-setting club, Al Sutphin opened the new season with essentially the same team that won last year's Calder Cup. Although the team was beginning to show its age, there were only three new additions to the roster.

Right wing Bryan Hextall was purchased from the New York Rangers. Ralph (Bus) Wycherley and Johnny Black were promoted from Minneapolis and Edmonton, respectively.

The only questions in the minds of Coach Bun Cook and Sutphin were 1) Would the veteran players begin to slow up as the season progressed, and 2) Would and/or could they play with the same intensity and enthusiasm as last year? It was so hard to repeat as champions, especially for Cleveland. The Barons were by far the biggest draw in the League. They still drew full or near-full houses wherever they played. Also, opposing teams invariably got psyched up a bit more when they were playing the Barons. Everyone wanted to knock off the top dog. Thus, Cleveland had to be at the top of its game night in and night out, or they could be in for a long evening. It was a tough grind being defending champion.

Since regular season and playoff records are kept separate from each other, the Barons opened the 1948-49 campaign with their 27-game regular season unbeaten streak intact. With the team starting with four straight games on the road, the Streak didn't figure to last long. But the Barons fooled the so-called experts.

After opening the season with a 5-2 win at Washington, they defeated Hershey, Springfield, and New Haven. The last victory over the Ramblers was especially satisfying. Down 5-4 with under four minutes to play, Bobby Carse came through with the tying score at 16:15. Then, at 18:32, Pete Leswick blasted home the game winner. The Streak had now reached 31 games.

Coming back home to face Pittsburgh in the Arena opener, the Streak figured to grow even larger. But, alas, it was not meant to be. After being honored in pre-game ceremonies for last season's heroics, the Barons fell flat and were beaten by the Hornets 5-3. There was no crying the blues in the locker room afterwards. Actually, once again, the team seemed to be relieved that the pressure of the Streak had been lifted. It figured that they could now pick up where they left off last year. Once gain, the Barons fooled everyone.

They went 2-3-1 in the next six games to fall into a last-place tie with the Buffalo Bisons. Although a 6-4-1 record wasn't bad and the season was still young, it was becoming clear that this season's race would be no picnic. Once again, except for Providence, the best teams in the League were in the Western division. The only change in Western power was that the aging Buffalo Bisons had fallen off somewhat, and the much improved St. Louis Flyers were now a force to be reckoned with.

The Cleveland team fell into a strange pattern for the next month of the season. They would play good hockey for a short stretch; and just when they looked like they were ready to take off, they would get clobbered.

In mid-November, the good guys went 3-1-1 before visiting Providence and getting their ears pinned back 9-2. They regrouped from that shellacking to put together a six-game unbeaten streak of three wins and three ties. Then came an 11-3 pounding on the chin by the Indianapolis Capitals. These inconsistent performances were adding gray hairs to Bun Cook's already growing collection.

The most pleasant surprise of the early going was the scoring of Ralph (Bus) Wycherly. Bus had played with several teams before landing in Cleveland. When promoted from the Minneapolis farm club, the journeyman forward was expected to play a minor role. Yet by mid-December, Bus had 14 goals and was third on the team in scoring. His surprising output somewhat offset the shocking fall-off of Bob Solinger.

Last season's Rookie of the Year with 40 goals, Solinger was mired in an awful slump. By the end of December, Bob had only registered one goal and looked completely lost. His dramatic plunge had a lot to do with the Barons' early inconsistent play. His center, Ab DeMarco, was also having his troubles.

On the plus side was the superb play of the The Pony, Pete Leswick. Pete had 21 goals by late December and was leading the team in scoring. Unfortunately, his linemate Johnny Holota was having a rough time.

After last season's great streak, the fans seemed to expect perfection. They were frustrated whenever the Barons didn't win and began to take their wrath out on Holota.

Johnny was an easy target. Not a great skater like his linemates Leswick and Carse, he sometimes appeared to be in slow motion in comparison to them. He wasn't loafing – he was just a slower skater. John also took a tremendous beating from opposing defensemen while jockeying for position in front of the net. But he never fought back. When his scoring totals dropped off during the present campaign, the fans figured Johnny was dogging it and began booing him. The heckling became louder as the season progressed. They really got to John. When he tried even harder to please the fans, the more he pressed and the worse it got. He finally wanted out of Cleveland but didn't get his wish until 1950. It was sad. If only the fans knew of the deep secret Holota carried with him, they never would have thought that he lacked courage.

The Barons finally began to play the hockey they were capable of near the end of December. They ran off a four-game winning streak that pushed their record to a very good 17-8-5. The fourth win of the streak was a game of extremes for center Fred Thurier.

Fred fired three goals within 1 minute 44 seconds during the first period to lead Cleveland to a 6-3 victory over Philadelphia. The win moved the Barons into third place, only seven points behind first-place St. Louis.

The hat trick also gave Thurier 227 career goals, tying him with Phil Hergesheimer in their race to break Les Cunningham's record of 233. Unfortunately, Thurier also was whacked on the wrist by the Rockets' Ken Kilrea, and post-game x-rays revealed a fracture. Fred would miss almost three weeks.

During Cleveland's move upwards in the standings, the team was receiving splendid goaltending from Johnny Bower. Called The Panther Man

Johnny Holota (14) and Bobby Carse (16) battle for the puck against Providence. Bobby Carse collection – Photo by John Nash.

because of his quick, smooth moves, Johnny racked up consecutive shutouts during the first week of January as the Barons improved their record to 20-9-5.

After blanking New Haven 4-0, Bower followed that up with a 3-0 gem over first-place St. Louis. This was by far the team's best game of the season to date. Besides Johnny's great goaltending, the forwards were backchecking fiercely, and the defense was belting bodies with gusto.

After losing at home to Providence, the Barons went into St. Louis and up-ended the Flyers again 4-3. The win left Cleveland only five points out of first place and saw Bob Solinger begin to regain his form of last year. Sollie scored two goals. While this only gave him five on the year, he showed signs of breaking out of his season-long slump.

The Barons defeated Springfield at the Arena and then headed East on a four-game journey. It was a successful trip that saw Cleveland temporarily take over first place. But the team that left Cleveland was hardly the one that returned. Although the team was playing its best hockey of the season, Al Sutphin and Coach Cook were unhappy with the play of several veterans. They felt it was necessary to introduce some new young blood to the team.

Just before his team defeated Hershey 5-4 behind a three-goal hat trick by Bobby Carse, Sutphin announced a blockbuster deal with the Washington Lions. Going to the Lions were five veteran players: 35-year-old Bryan Hextall, Ab DeMarco, Julian Sawchuk, Augie Herchenratter, and Tom Forgie. Coming to Cleveland were Ken Schultz and the Porteous twins, Frank and Dan.

Key to the deal from Cleveland's standpoint was Schultz. Ken had scored 18 goals and 29 assists for the Lions and was one of the up and coming young centers in the League. Most noteworthy departure from Cleveland was DeMarco. A mainstay the year before, Ab had mysteriously slumped this season. For whatever reasons, he didn't appear happy, and his sub-par play was partially blamed for Bob Solinger's slump. A few years down the road, the trade was viewed as a dud because Schultz never fulfilled his promise due to injuries. DeMarco, on the other hand, regained his touch after landing in Buffalo and had several great seasons, including one scoring title.

The immediate impact of the trade was minimal, as the Barons continued the same steady play that they showed before the deal. But on January 29th, they hit the jackpot with a record-breaking night. Johnny Holota quieted the boo birds for a night when he erupted for four goals; and Fred Thurier added three in a 14-4 bombardment of Washington. The 14 goals were the most scored in one game by a Cleveland club. The three scores by Thurier tied him with Les Cunningham at 233. However, he lost his race with Phil Hergesheimer. On the same night, Hergey also fired a hat trick and now had 234. With the win, the Barons moved back into first for a night with a 27-12-6 record.

In one last effort to bolster his club, Al Sutphin purchased the contract of veteran defenseman Eddie Bush from Philadelphia. A mild-mannered type off the ice, Eddie was a holy terror on it. Last season was a milestone year for Bush. His 24 goals and 48 assists for 72 points were records for a defenseman. However, this season he had slumped to 2 goals and 16 assists with 83 minutes in penalties. Sutphin hoped a change in scenery would rekindle the spark in Bush. It did for a while, but soon it became evident that Eddie was over the hill. His performance

Bobby Carse scores against Pittsburgh's great goalie Baz Bastien during 1948-49 season. Notice the "City of Champions" moniker.
Promotional photo from "The Cleveland Craftsman". Bobby Carse collection – Lithographed by D.E. Robinson.

dropoff was no accident, and he did not return to the club for the next season.

In late January and early February, the Barons went into an alarming road slump. In consecutive games, they were massacred by Philly 9-5, Buffalo 11-3, and Providence 9-3. This stretch had the wolves out, but they were quieted when Cleveland went back into first with a 3-2 win over Hershey on February 9th.

This was the pattern for the next month of the season – win a few, lose a few, a .500 pace. Cleveland, Pittsburgh, St. Louis, and Indianapolis kept trading places on top. No team could sustain a winning streak and kept knocking each other off.

To illustrate just how close the teams were, the standings on March 9th, with five games remaining, read as follows:

Indianapolis 83 points, Cleveland 82, St. Louis 81, and Pittsburgh 80. It couldn't be much closer.

The Barons moved into first on March 10th by defeating Philadelphia 6-3. Cleveland looked terrible for the first half of the game, falling behind 3-0. It wasn't until midway through the second period that the Barons scored, but then they caught fire. Led by Johnny Holota and Pete Leswick with two goals apiece, the Barons finally wore down the Rockets and won going away.

Cleveland then defeated New Haven and was upset by the last-place Buffalo Bisons 4-3. This set up the final showdown weekend between the four clubs. The Barons and St. Louis would play a home-and-home series against each other, while Pittsburgh and Indianapolis would do the same. With each team having two games remaining, St. Louis led with 89 points, Indy 88, Cleveland and Pittsburgh 86 each. This put the Barons' backs against the wall. They had to win at least one game against the Flyers. If they wound up tied with either Indy or Pittsburgh for the final third-place playoff berth, Cleveland would be awarded third place by virtue of having the most wins. Neither the Capitals or Hornets could top Cleveland's number of victories for the season.

Pittsburgh defeated Indianapolis to pull even with the Capitals at 88 points. The Barons shocked 11,877 fans at the Arena and themselves by laying a huge egg against St. Louis. The Flyers clinched first place by scoring four third-period goals and embarrassing the Barons 5-2. The third-period collapse took everyone by surprise. Usually it was Cleveland who surged to victory in the third period. But on this night, the Flyers would not be denied, and deserved the title.

The loss left the Barons in desperate shape. The only way they could make the playoffs was to win in St. Louis on the season's final night. This would tie them at 88 points with the loser of the Indianapolis-Pittsburgh matchup the same night. But there was one catch. Even if the Barons beat St. Louis, they could still miss the playoffs if Indy and Pittsburgh played to a tie. Since both clubs already had 88 points in the standings, a tie would give each team one point for a total of 89 each. The best the Barons could do was 88. If the Barons beat St. Louis, they would wind up with 41 wins. It seemed impossible for a team with 41 wins to miss the playoffs. But the possibility was real.

Cleveland went into St. Louis determined to make amends for the humiliation they suffered at home the night before. Fighting for their playoff lives, the Barons came through with a rousing 7-3 victory before 13,912 hostile Flyer fans. Led by Bobby Carse, Pete Leswick, and Bob Solinger, the Clevelanders won their biggest game of the year. But they were not in the playoffs yet. There was the matter of the Indianapolis-Pittsburgh game that was still in progress.

After the St. Louis arena emptied out, all of the Barons, some still in uniform, went up to the pressbox to find out the results of the Indy-Pitt game. Since there was no television, and the game could not be picked up on radio, they had to rely on phone calls from the Indianapolis arena.

The first call put a huge damper on the Barons' hopes. With five minutes left in the third period – Indianapolis 1, Pittsburgh 1. This was the worst news possible. If the game ended in a tie, the Barons were out.

The phone rang again. Two minutes to go, the game was still tied 1-1. One could hear a pin drop in the pressbox. With sweaty palms, the players silently prayed for a miracle. One final time the phone rang. The voice on the other end shouted out, "You're in!" Don Morrison of Indianapolis scored a goal with 1 minute 40 seconds left in the game to give the Capitals a 2-1 win. The Barons, of course, rejoiced; and the long road to the playoffs was over.

A Cook Who Knows His Broth — By Darvas

THE PLAYOFFS

The Barons entered the playoffs as heavy favorites in a best of three mini-series against the Springfield Indians, third-place club in the Eastern division. The Indians did not defeat the Barons during the regular season, managing only a tie in six games. Their 22-37-8 record made this series look like a mismatch.

Yet despite their fine record, this Barons team remained a mystery.

They experienced a wide range of highs and lows. One day they could get buried, and then start a series of brilliant games the very next day. Fans never knew which team to expect from one game to the next.

Game One in Springfield saw the playoff debut of goaltender Johnny Bower. Although he was now in his fourth season with Cleveland, Coach Cook had decided previously to use his more experienced goalies, first Harvey Teno and then Roger Bessette, in the big post-season games. But this season, Bower moved to the forefront and took over as the team's #1 puck stopper.

Unfortunately, his teammates spoiled the party by playing one of their worst games of the season. Although they were beaten 8-4, the score could have been much worse. If it were not for the play of Bower, who made 40 saves, the Indians would surely have scored in double figures.

The Barons' offense was dismal, managing a meager 19 shots on goal, only two in the second period. The defense was pathetic also. At times they appeared to be sleep-walking, as Springfield completely dominated play. The poor showing left the Barons only one game from elimination.

Just as they had done all season long, the Barons bounced back from a bad loss to register an unexpected win. Playing Game Two on their home ice at the Arena, Cleveland got up off the floor to defeat Springfield 6-5 in overtime. The winning goal was scored by Frank Porteous at 1:32 of the full 10-minute overtime.

Trailing 3-1 midway through the second period, the season appeared to be over. Fred Thurier's goal, which gave him a new League record of 63 playoff points, passing Les Cunningham's 62, was the only bright light for the home club.

But in the second period's final four minutes, the Barons finally caught fire. Scores by Roy Kelly and Johnny Holota tied the score. Ken Schultz put Cleveland out in front early in the third only to see Rene Trudell and old friend Bill Summerhill put the Indians back on top 5-4. Once again the Barons' immediate future appeared bleak.

However, the day was saved when Johnny Holota silenced his vocal critics by netting the tying goal at 16:04. His tally was a thing of beauty. Taking a pass from Bobby Carse at center ice, Johnny soloed in alone to score and save the day. Frank Porteous took over in overtime, and the series was tied.

The deciding game in the 2 out of 3 series was a comeback of sorts for tough-luck Bob Solinger. A victim of the "sophomore jinx", with only 9 goals during the regular season, last year's Rookie of the Year came through in Game Three.

Solinger scored three goals as the Barons routed Springfield 6-2 before 10,922 at the Arena. A victim of some terrible luck during the season, Sollie never quit hustling, and his hard work finally paid off as the Barons entered the semi-finals against their old rivals, the Hershey Bears.

Based on season records alone, Cleveland appeared to hold the upper hand on the Bears. The Barons defeated Hershey 5 out of 6 games, although 3 were by one-goal margins. The Bears' 28-35-5 record made them big underdogs, but they were still a dangerous opponent. They had just swept Indianapolis out of the playoffs and were looking for another big upset.

The Bears proved just how tough they could be in Game One at the Arena. 9,118 fans saw a sensational contest that was decided in sudden-death overtime.

Hershey took the lead on a first-period goal by Silvio Bettio. This lead held up for the rest of the first stanza and most of the second. After not getting a shot on goal for the game's first 12 minutes, the Barons peppered Bear goalie Gordon Henry furiously the rest of the evening. They finally broke through on a goal by Bobby Carse during the last minute of the second period.

Johnny Holota, enjoying a fine playoff in spite of the boo birds, put Cleveland on top at 3:11 of the third period during a scramble in front of Henry. Gordie Bruce tied the game less than two minutes later. Each team had many opportunities to win the game, but great goaltending by Johnny Bower and Henry sent the game into overtime.

The first ten-minute session was scoreless, and the teams headed into sudden death. The first team to score would win.

Cleveland went on a relentless attack to get the winner, only to be turned back by the sensational Gordon Henry. Hershey's goalie made at least a half dozen miraculous saves to keep his team in the game. And it paid off.

The end came for Cleveland at 9:24 of the second overtime when Arnie Kullman jumped on a rebound in front of Johnny Bower and beat the fallen Cleveland netminder with the winning goal.

The game was a real heartbreaker from which the Barons did not recover. The series shifted to Hershey for Game Two, and Cleveland had nothing left. The fight was taken out of them with the overtime loss, and they lost to Hershey 5-1.

The two-game loss to the Bears put an end to an up and down year. Although they did have 41 wins, this Barons club seemed to lack that special "something" to make them a great team.

A shakeup was expected, since everyone knew that Al Sutphin hated to lose. A shakeup did occur. Less than a month after the season ended, Al Sutphin laid a blockbuster on the City of Cleveland.

FINAL STANDINGS
1948-49

West	W	L	T	GF	GA	PTS.
St. Louis	41	18	9	294	192	91
Indianapolis	39	17	12	288	209	90
Cleveland	41	21	6	286	251	88
Pittsburgh	39	19	10	301	175	88
Buffalo	33	27	8	246	213	74
East	**W**	**L**	**T**	**GF**	**GA**	**PTS.**
Providence	44	18	6	347	219	94
Hershey	28	35	5	256	261	61
Springfield	22	37	9	240	276	53
New Haven	20	40	8	223	286	48
Philadelphia	15	48	5	230	407	35
Washington	11	53	4	179	401	26

Top Baron Scorers	G	A	PTS.
Pete Leswick	44	35	79
Bobby Carse	19	47	66

Calder Cup Champion – Providence Reds

Farewell to the Iceman...

During the last month of the 1948-49 regular season, Coach Bun Cook took turns resting his star players for one game each in order to keep their legs fresh. On one such occasion, Bobby Carse sat up in the pressbox with Al Sutphin during a home game. During the course of the game, Al stared out at the ice and uttered a strange comment. "You know, Bobby," said the Barons' owner, "I think the bloom is off the rose." Carse thought the comment odd, and it bothered him. When he got home that night, Bob told his wife Betty that he had the feeling Al Sutphin was going to sell the club. The thought seemed inconceivable, because Sutphin WAS the Barons.

On April 25, 1949, Bobby Carse's suspicions came true. Al Sutphin announced that he had sold the team and the Arena to three prominent businessmen from Minneapolis for a price tag of $2,000,000. The new owners were George Heller, George Drage, and Lyle Z. Wright. In charge of the day-to-day operations was new general manager Jim Hendy.

Al Sutphin left behind him a huge imprint on Cleveland's way of life. More than any other individual, Sutphin made the Cleveland sporting scene thrive. During the 1930's, when baseball, football, and boxing were at a low ebb here, he built the magnificent Arena when everyone told him he was crazy. They said he would go broke. But Al proved that there was big money to be made through promotion. Along with the Indians' Bill Veeck, Sutphin was the epitome of promotional genius.

The new Arena had class, and the people of Cleveland were proud to be associated with it. They came in droves to watch their beloved Barons play hockey. The founder of the Ice Capades, Al also brought basketball, boxing, six-day bike races, track and field, and school sports to his sports palace. But first and foremost, Barons' hockey was #1 in his sporting life.

He made the Barons into the dominant force in the American Hockey League. Sutphin, in fact, was the main man in the AHL. He kept the League afloat during the war years. When other teams got into financial trouble, Sutphin would bail them out, usually for players in return for cash. It was his undying loyalty to his fellow owners that led him to turn down the National Hockey League's invitation to join their league.

"If it weren't for them, I might make the break for the National League," Sutphin stated. "But I think Cleveland's withdrawal would collapse the American League, and I can't let my fellow owners down."

He was morally correct at that time, but his decision to turn his back on the NHL would have repercussions on Cleveland's hockey future for years to come.

Still, without Al Sutphin, the glory days of Barons' hockey may never have come about. He was one of a kind and surely would be missed by all.

HELLO, JIM HENDY

In charge of running the Barons in place of Sutphin was Jim Hendy.

Hendy got his start in sports as a telegrapher handling the sports copy of Hype Agoe and Damon Runyon from ringside at Madison Square Garden fights. A man with a gift of gab, he later became chief publicity man for the NHL's New York Rangers. From New York he moved on to become president of the United States Hockey League.

Al Sutphin became friends with Hendy while Jim was in New York. Their relationship continued when Jim moved to the United States League, as the Barons' Minneapolis farm club was in this league. Al knew that Hendy was the right man to take over the Barons when he decided to step down.

The choice of Hendy proved to be a wise move. A strong and gracious man, Jim would keep the Barons a powerful force for years to come. A new era in Cleveland hockey had begun.

THE JIM HENDY ERA: CONTINUED SUCCESS

Jim HENDY HAS BARONS HEADED FOR BIG TIME.

1949-50 SEASON

In his first season at the helm of the Barons' ship, Jim Hendy changed many of the faces on the Cleveland squad. Always well stocked with veterans either in their prime or with a few good years left, the Barons usually needed an influx of young talent every few years. Last year's team began to show chinks in its armor, and Hendy came to the rescue.

His most important acquisition was obtaining center Les Douglas from the Buffalo Bisons for defenseman Gordon Davidson. Davidson was just about done as a player, while Douglas was still in his prime. The 5'9", 165-pounder won the scoring title with 90 points while with Indianapolis in 1945-46. He would anchor a fantastic Barons' scoring machine in his first year with the club.

Three young, hard-hitting defensemen were brought in to help Danny Sprout and Hy Buller on the blueline. Steve Kraftcheck, Eddie Reigle, and Tommy Williams would be strong forces in the League for years to come, although all did spend time with other clubs.

Bobby Carse scores against Springfield goalie Phil McAtee.
Bobby Carse collection – Photo by Bill Nehez.

Harry Taylor, Ray Ceresino, and Tod Sloan came in a trade with Toronto for Bob Solinger. With holdovers Carse, Leswick, Holota, Thurier, Kelly, and Schultz, the Barons had the makings of another powerhouse.

Cleveland got a hint of things to come while opening the season with three games out East. Al Sutphin flew to Springfield to drop the puck in pre-game ceremonies and then watched his former team overpower the Indians 6-1. Les Douglas led the way with 2 goals and 3 assists as Cleveland outclassed the home team. When Springfield tested the Barons' muscle, they got more than they asked for in return. Fights between Cleveland's Tod Sloan and Indian Bill Gooden and the Barons' Eddie Reigle and old friend Bill Summerhill were decidedly one-sided in Cleveland's favor. This team showed size, speed, scoring punch, and hard-hitting defense – a deadly combination.

The Barons came back for their home opener with a 3-0 record. A 7-5 triumph in Hershey and a 6-3 win at Providence showed a team of great promise. When Cleveland easily handled the St. Louis Flyers, last season's West division winner, eyebrows were raised. The 5-1 victory could easily have been much worse. Were the Barons really this good, or was this just another fast start?

The answer became clear as Cleveland began to steamroll through the opposition. A fight-filled 8-2 win over the new Cincinnati Mohawks boosted the Barons' record to 12-2-1. Roy Kelly had a hat trick and Les Douglas two goals in the rout. When the Mohawks found it impossible to beat the Barons with goals, they tried with their fists. This proved a failure also. Cleveland seemed unstoppable.

By November 26th, the Barons were sporting an incredible 15-2-2 record. Their latest ambush, another 9-3 drubbing of Cincinnati which featured Harry Taylor's hat trick, gave the team a fine 12-game unbeaten string. Inevitably, comparisons sprung up comparing this team to the 1947-48 squad.

Bobby Carse, who played on both teams, offered an observation. "I think our present team is almost as good as the other one," said the great left winger. "Our team of two years ago had more finesse...more experience. There's one thing we haven't found out yet. That club of two years ago was awful tough when the chips were down. There were lots of games in which we had to rally from two or three goals behind. This club hasn't been tested much in this way...But we'll find out before too long."

The 1947-48 club was a group of veteran stars who played the finesse game better than anyone before or since. The current Barons of 1949-50 were a bunch of rough, tough scramblers mixed in with a few seasoned vets like Carse, Leswick, Douglas, and Thurier. Comparisons aside, this team was loaded.

As good as things were going, Jim Hendy felt that the defense needed a bit more veteran leadership, so he swung into action on the trading front. Hendy sent brilliant prospect and backup goalie Al Rollins to the Toronto Maple Leafs for 25-year-old defensive specialist Bob Dawes. The acquisition of Dawes proved a fortunate one, when Hy Buller suffered a broken ankle later in the month. Dawes filled in beautifully. The Barons had the great Johnny Bower, so Rollins was expendable. Al didn't stick with the Leafs at first and was sent to Pittsburgh where he excelled. He would later become a big star with the Chicago Blackhawks.

During a four-game stretch, where the Clevelanders lost one and tied three, the League sighed with relief. But the League's break didn't last for long, as the Barons started their winning ways again.

Fred Thurier (back to goal) tips home a goal past St. Louis goalie Don MacDonald. #16 is Bobby Carse. Bobby Carse collection.

One of the amazing facets of this Barons' team was that they kept winning despite a variety of injuries. During an 8-2 triumph over New Haven, Cleveland lost two important players. The worst blow was a broken ankle suffered by star defenseman Hy Buller. This would cause him to miss almost six weeks. Johnny Holota suffered a shoulder separation and would miss a month. These two injuries, added to the knee miseries of Ray Ceresino, would be enough to cripple many clubs. But not Cleveland. The Barons had tremendous depth. Almost everyone on the team was capable of playing more than one position. In fact, they had seven men who could step in and play center if needed. Several wings were equally adept at either side of the ice. This depth was one of the reasons Johnny Holota's days with the team were numbered. He would finish out the season here, but would never again be the great scorer he was in the past. When Johnny went down with his shoulder injury, Fred Thurier stepped into his spot, between Leswick and Carse, and went on a scoring tear. This made Holota, who was still the target of the boo birds, expendable.

Many of Cleveland's games were blowouts, so it was a good sign when the team had to come from behind. One such rally on December 20th at St. Louis proved that this team had intestinal fortitude as well as a wealth of talent.

The Flyers were already 11 points behind the Barons in the standings and needed this game desperately. They jumped out to a 4-2 first period lead and looked to have the Barons' number. In fact, they were leading 7-4 late in the game. This was the first time Cleveland had given up more than six goals in a game all year. But St. Louis' joy was shortlived.

Late in the third period, the Barons roared back with a vengeance. At 14:40, Pete Leswick took a pass from Fred Thurier to close the gap to 7-5. Shortly thereafter, Steve Wochy stole a Flyer pass and found Harry Taylor wide open in front of goalie Ralph Almas. Taylor's goal made it 7-6.

With 50 seconds remaining, Coach Cook pulled Johnny Bower and sent six attackers on the ice. The move paid off when Les Douglas tied the game at 7-7 at 19:33 with his 500th career point. The tie completely deflated the Flyers, who would not be a threat to Cleveland the rest of the year.

The end of December saw another first for Cleveland. The top five scorers in the League were all Barons. If anyone needed a reminder of just how dominant Cleveland was, this was it. Les Douglas 54 points, Bobby Carse 42, Roy Kelley 40, Pete Leswick 39, Ken Schultz 39. No team had ever had five players heading the scoring parade.

An 11-2 massacre of St. Louis on January 4th gave the Barons a 24-6-7 record. This gave them a 15-point lead over second-place Indianapolis and just about ended the Western division race. The only fear that Bun Cook had now was that the club would get overconfident. But this squad was filled with extremely hard workers, and a let-down seemed remote.

While the scoring machine was getting most of the attention, the Cleveland defense was playing tremendous hockey as well. Anchored by the great Danny Sprout, in his last season, two newcomers also played a prominent role in the backline brigade.

Rough and tumble Steve Kraftcheck and Eddie Reigle were blossoming into first-class defensemen. The 20-year-old Kraftcheck was already one of the biggest hitters in the League, and he didn't even learn to skate until he was 14 years old!

Larry Smith Collection

Reigle was regarded as one of the best fighters in his day. Eddie was as tough as nails, but off the ice one would never know it. The hard-hitting rookie soothed his temper by playing the piano. The thought of the fiery Reigle playing the ivories would raise some eyebrows. But he really was quite good.

After blowing away the Indianapolis Capitals 10-0, the Barons lost a rare game at home by the score of 5-3 to Pittsburgh. This gave them a 28-7-7 record as they headed East for a six-game road trip.

The second contest of the trip, a 7-2 rout of Springfield on January 21st, was a landmark game for two Clevelanders.

At 16:48 of the second period, Pete Leswick scored the 200th goal of his career that began with New Haven in 1936. Assisting on the goal was Fred Thurier. This was no ordinary assist. The point was #580 for The Fox, breaking the all-time career mark of 579 set by Les Cunningham three years earlier.

Thurier came to Cleveland in 1945 after spending a year with the New York Rangers. The French-Canadian began his career in 1937 with the Springfield Indians, and later played with Buffalo. He was one of the mainstays of the 1943-44 Bison team that destroyed Cleveland in the playoffs. It was then that Al Sutphin decided he had to have the speedy center. After a year's wait, Al got his wish; and Thurier was a class act from his first day with the club. Sometimes overshadowed by the scoring exploits of some of his explosive teammates, Fred was as steady as a rock and now held the title of all-time scoring king.

With the regular season race all but over, there wasn't much left for Cleveland to prove. Standing tall with a 35-11-9 record, the club looked forward to a February 15th game with Pittsburgh. The Hornets were considered the League's top defensive outfit. They were further strengthened by the acquisition of goaltender Al Rollins.

Rollins started the season with Cleveland but was traded to Toronto. The Leafs then sent him to Pittsburgh on January 28th for more seasoning. Since that time, Rollins and the Hornets were on fire. With three shutouts to his credit, Rollins had allowed only 9 goals in his nine games with his new

Fred Thurier was known as The Fox for good reason. His clever and tricky stickhandling made him one of the top centers in the history of the American Hockey League. When Fred called it quits after the 1951-52 season, he retired as the League's leading scorer with 319 goals and 425 assists for 744 points. His record would stand until broken by another Baron, Fred Glover, in 1959.
Dennis Turchek collection.

team. Pittsburgh rolled to a 7-1-1 mark during this stretch.

The Pittsburgh game shaped up as a true test for Cleveland, and they were ready for it. The game was a fast and hard-hitting battle. Led by a three-goal hat trick by Tod Sloan, the Barons played one of their best defensive games in years and blanked the Hornets 6-0.

Sloan was the scoring hero, but the night belonged to Johnny Bower and the team's penalty killers. The Panther Man was at his lightning-like best as he recorded his 5th shutout of the year. He received all kinds of help while the team was short-handed. Twice the Barons played two men short due to penalties. Each time Eddie Reigle, Red Williams, and Pete Leswick were superb in killing the clock. The Barons even scored twice while short a man on goals by Fred Thurier and Steve Wochy. In the end, the Barons looked invincible.

The official crowning of Cleveland as regular season kings came on March 1st. For the fifth time in Bun Cook's seven years as coach, the Barons won the Western division and over-all American League title by defeating Indianapolis 4-2. 7,121 fans braved a huge snowstorm in Cleveland to see their heroes win the championship against an Indianapolis team that seemed to be gaining momentum as the playoffs approached. They had improved dramatically over the last month and needed to be watched closely.

Instead of coasting through the end of the season, the Barons set their sights on the 1947-48 club's mark of 98 points in the standings. It was a lofty goal, but this team achieved it on the last night of the regular season. A hard-fought 5-3 win over Indianapolis gave this team a host of records. New all-time marks set were most points in a season (100); most wins (45); and most victories on home ice (30).

Individual honors went to Les Douglas, who led the League in scoring with 100 points and was elected Most Valuable Player. Roy Kelly led the League in goals with 46.

Cleveland finished with a record of 45-15-10 and would face the Eastern division champion Buffalo Bisons in the first round of the playoffs.

THE PLAYOFFS

The Barons opened the playoffs against a Buffalo team that nosedived at the end of the season. Although they were in first place for most of the year, the Bisons lost seven of their last eight games and finished only two points ahead of Providence. A team equal to Cleveland defensively, Buffalo was at a great disadvantage when it came to scoring. They finished seventh in the League with 226 goals scored, compared to Cleveland's record 358. This fact, along with their mediocre 32-29-9 record, made them a huge underdog.

The Bisons tried to run the Barons out of the Arena in Game One and paid dearly. Although Cleveland was the least penalized team in the League, they could bang bodies better than anyone when the situation called for it.

Buffalo stormed out of the gate, and bodies flew everywhere. Cleveland would have none of that and retaliated fiercely. The first period saw some of the hardest bodychecks in years with the Barons' defense eventually delivering most. They wore the Bisons down and dominated the game.

Ray Ceresino and Buffalo's Sid McNabney traded goals before Cleveland broke the game wide open late in the second period. Roy Kelly, Pete Leswick, and Tod Sloan scored in rapid-fire succession to take a 4-1 lead at the second intermission. Kelly, Sloan, and Bobby Carse had scores in the third period as the Barons skated away with a 7-1 victory.

Game Two was Johnny Holota's last hurrah as a Cleveland Baron. With the boo birds unfairly on his back, it was a foregone conclusion that Johnny would not be back next season. But he still went out every game and gave it his all, even if the fans didn't appreciate him.

The second game at the Arena saw Cleveland surprisingly outplayed for most of the game. They trailed 4-1 with less than four minutes to play. Suddenly, to everyone's surprise, the Barons came alive on goals by Holota and Bobby Carse. The crowd was going wild as Coach Cook sent five attackers on the ice during the final minute in a desperate attempt to tie the game up. After a frenzied minute and save after save by Bison goalie Gordon Bell, Tod Sloan's goal saved the day with only six seconds remaining. The game went into overtime, tied at 4-4.

When Johnny Holota scored the game winner in overtime, the fickle fans roared their approval. It would be his last game-winning goal for Cleveland.

One would think that such a heartbreaking defeat would demoralize the Buffalos. But just the opposite occurred as the Bisons bounced back in Game Three with a 3-2 victory over Cleveland. The Barons were thoroughly outplayed in this one, although they were in the game until the end. Only the outstanding goaltending of Johnny Bower kept the score close.

Buffalo opened the scoring after only 44 seconds, and then proceeded to pound the Clevelanders at every turn. But the skillful Barons tied the score on Tod Sloan's fifth goal of the playoffs. They even took a 2-1 lead into the third period on Ken Schultz's goal.

The game turned vicious in the last stanza as the Bisons dominated play. They tied it up at 3:03 on defenseman Lloyd Finkbeiner's screen shot. The winning score came off the stick of ex-Baron star Ab DeMarco at 9:46.

Cleveland took a severe physical pounding in the third game, but they bounced back in fine form in Game Four.

Taking a 3-0 first-period lead, the Barons never looked back. Fred Thurier, back with the team after four games due to the death of his sister in Quebec, opened the scoring at 6:06. Goals by Harry Taylor and Ray Ceresino followed. Ceresino and Les Douglas scored in the third period in a game that never saw the Barons threatened. What a reversal from the previous game.

Buffalo took a chance in Game Five and started Connie Dion in goal. Dion was a big star in previous years, but was now near the end of the line. He served as backup to Gordon Bell this season, and it was hoped he could inspire his teammates at the Arena in Cleveland. But Connie could not come up with any of his old magic as the Barons won big 6-1.

They won the game and the series riding the hot stick of Tod Sloan. The lightning-quick winger scored three goals in Game Five, giving him eight for the series. He was now only two away from the playoff record set by Tommy Burlington.

Cleveland now entered the championship finals against the dangerous Indianapolis Capitals. This was a Capital team that had been building momentum during the entire second half of the season. After defeating Providence and St. Louis in two straight games each, they rolled into Cleveland with the strength of a tidal wave.

If the Capitals were hot, then their goaltender Terry Sawchuk was simply scorching. In his four previous playoff games to date, Terry had allowed a miniscule total of four goals. In Game One of the finals he remained ablaze. Behind Sawchuk's 43 saves, Indianapolis stunned the Barons 4-1 at the Arena. The Indy goalie was stupendous. Time and time again he turned back the powerful Clevelanders, who actually held a wide advantage in play. The only goal for the home team was scored by Tod Sloan, his ninth of the playoffs.

Cleveland figured to bounce back in Game Two, but once again they were denied by Terry Sawchuk. That the Barons weren't far ahead after two periods was solely because of the Capital goalie's stellar play. As it was, the score was 2-2 entering the third period.

The Caps figured that Cleveland would come out firing in the final period and were ready. Indy continually caught the attacking Barons up ice with short, quick passes to an open man at center ice. Johnny Bower was left unprotected in goal, and Indianapolis turned the game into a rout. Four unanswered goals gave the Capitals a 6-2 victory.

Adding to the misery was a rash of knee injuries suffered by the Barons. Ken Schultz, Roy Kelly, and Fred Thurier would all miss the rest of the series.

Cleveland gave it all they had in Game Three at Indianapolis, but once again they came up empty.

"Somewhere along the way we lost that finesse," said Bobby Carse. This obviously was true, but the Barons never lost their hustle and drive. Fighting hard to the bitter end, Cleveland still wound up on the short end of a 4-3 score.

The Barons led 2-1 midway through the second period on two goals by Steve Wochy. Indy then tied the score on the second of two goals by Pat Lundy.

Period three was a tense struggle, as each team looked for a break to seize the lead. The lucky break went the Capitals' way at 10:02. A wild shot by Nelson Podolsky that had no chance of going in hit the stick of Danny Sprout and deflected past a bewildered Johnny Bower. Gordon Hoidy made it 4-2 just a few minutes later.

The Barons refused to quit. They stormed the Capital goal with a ton of shots. Finally, at 19:05, Bobby Carse scored to make it 4-3. But it was a little too late. Coach Cook pulled his goalie, but the Barons could not tie the score in the last minute.

Cleveland now faced the embarrassment of being swept in the finals after having one of the greatest and most dominating seasons in the history of the League. The proud Barons threw everything they had at the Capitals, but once again Terry Sawchuk slammed the door in their collective faces during a 3-2 series-winning Capital victory.

Besides Sawchuk, most of the damage was done by a hustling winger named Fred Glover. A young man whom Baron fans would get to know quite well a few years down the road, Fred scored Indy's first and last goals. Sandwiched in between was a singleton by constant nemesis Pat Lundy. Scoring for Cleveland were Bob Dawes and Tod Sloan. Tod's goal was his 10th of the playoffs, tying him with Tommy Burlington for most in a playoff.

What never could have been envisaged only one week earlier had come to pass. The mighty Barons had been swept in four straight games. It just didn't seem possible.

But when analyzed, the answer to what happened came in two words: Terry Sawchuk. In becoming the first AHL team to sweep through the entire playoffs without a loss, Sawchuk only gave up a total of 12 goals in eight games. This was phenomenal. Terry got hot at the right time and carried his team to victory. His was one of the greatest displays of goaltending in AHL history. The Barons had nothing to be ashamed of. They gave it their all, but were stopped by an amazing performer, Terry Sawchuk.

FINAL STANDINGS
1949-50

West	W	L	T	GF	GA	PTS.
Cleveland	45	15	10	358	230	100
Indianapolis	35	24	11	267	231	81
St. Louis	34	28	8	258	250	76
Pittsburgh	29	26	15	215	185	73
Cincinnati	19	37	14	185	257	52
East	**W**	**L**	**T**	**GF**	**GA**	**PTS.**
Buffalo	32	29	9	226	208	73
Providence	34	33	3	268	267	71
Springfield	28	34	8	245	258	64
New Haven	24	36	10	196	250	58
Hershey	21	39	10	229	310	52

Top Baron Scorers	G	A	PTS.
Les Douglas	32	68	100
Pete Leswick	36	50	86
Bobby Carse	30	52	82
Fred Thurier	30	52	82
Roy Kelly	46	34	80
Tod Sloan	37	29	66
Ken Schultz	27	38	65
Harry Taylor	27	27	54
Steve Wochy	21	23	44
Johnny Holota	14	28	42
Ray Ceresino	17	24	41

Calder Cup Champion – Indianapolis Capitals

1950-51 SEASON

The off-season following the playoff loss to Indianapolis brought many changes to the Barons. First and foremost, the team was rocked by the retirement of three longtime stars, Danny Sprout, Bobby Carse, and Pete Leswick. Sprout's leaving was somewhat expected. Danny had been with the team since 1943 and was 35 years old. Although he enjoyed one of his greatest seasons in 1949-50, Sprout wanted to go out on top and devote his time to his hotel business in Vancouver.

Carse and Leswick were another story. Both had enjoyed outstanding seasons when they announced their retirements one day after the past season ended. Bobby decided to devote all of his time to his job at the Cleveland office of the Great West Life Insurance Co. He remained a highly successful insurance executive and made Cleveland his permanent home. Bob stayed close to the game by becoming a linesman and official scorer at the Arena. He also was very active in the Parma youth hockey program. One of hockey's class individuals, Bobby Carse was and is a man of whom the City of Cleveland can be truly proud.

Leswick, on the other hand, got the itch to play again and was traded to Buffalo for Murdo McKay. The 33-year-old McKay had one more good year left in him after a sterling career with the Bisons. Leswick, however, really didn't have his heart in playing anymore and retired again for good midway through the 1950-51 season.

Leswick and Carse played on one of Cleveland's all-time great lines. The third man of the trio, Johnny Holota, was sold to New Haven. This was expected because Johnny had lost favor with the Cleveland fans. He had come off a poor season brought on by a shoulder injury, as well as the fan's booing.

The booing started because John would never retaliate when pounded by opposing players. Instead, he would camp in front of opposing goalies and score goals. This should have been enough. But Cleveland fans liked aggressive hockey players and began to get on the great center iceman. They thought he lacked heart.

Holota's career nosedived, and he was sent to Denver of the United States League when the New Haven team disbanded later in the year.

On a dreary early morning of March 7, 1951, Johnny and four other hockey players from Denver and Omaha were injured in a car crash in Broomfield, Colorado. The auto in which they were traveling at a high rate of speed hit a construction sign. Holota was the most seriously injured, with a skull fracture. He was taken to Colorado General Hospital where he died three days later.

News of the tragedy shocked everyone and puzzled his doctors. Although his injuries were serious, they should not have been enough to kill him. An autopsy was performed. It was discovered that Johnny's heart had given out. It turned out that Holota had a heart disease that had begun in his childhood and had been getting progressively worse. It could have caused his death at any time, and he knew this. No wonder he took such a beating during his career.

Getting into fights could have made his condition worse. Still, with knowledge of his ailment a secret, he went out and played the most violent game around. Now that was courage. The fans thought Johnny lacked heart. In the end, his courageous spirit and heart knew no boundaries.

Three players were lost to the National Hockey League. Tod Sloan was drafted into the big league; and Steve Kraftcheck, along with Eddie Reigle were sold to the Boston Bruins.

The Barons had a long-standing position that they would never stand in the way of a player going to the NHL. Sometimes trades were made. On other occasions, cash deals were arranged with the money used to purchase players at a later date. In later years, when attendance problems arose, the money was used to pay bills.

The loss of Kraftcheck and Reigle hurt, but Phil Samis and Joe Lund were brought in as replacements. Teaming with Hy Buller and Tommy Williams, the Barons would still have a formidable defense. With the great Johnny Bower in goal, Cleveland could stop the opposition cold.

The question marks arose on offense. With the departure of Carse, Leswick, Holota, and Sloan, would the Barons still have a powerhouse attack? It was doubtful. But Wally Hergesheimer (brother of ex-Baron standout Phil) and Glen Sonmar would add youthful exuberance. Both were added from the Minneapolis farm team, and Wally especially had a knack for scoring goals.

Holdovers Les Douglas, Roy Kelly, and Ken Schultz were once again counted on to carry the offensive load.

The Barons seemed to be a faster club than last year's and much smaller. In physical stature they were similar to the 1946-47 team. In that regard, the same question arose: Could they hold up to the wear and tear of a whole season? The answers would begin to come as the Barons opened their season in Cincinnati against the Mohawks.

Playing without MVP Les Douglas, who was in Perth, Ontario, attending the funeral of his father, the Barons blew a 3-0 first-period lead and lost to Cincy 5-3. The boys seemed a little nervous in their first game, but many of the young players looked good. Glen Sonmar and Wally Hergesheimer seemed especially quick, and each scored one goal.

After returning to the Arena from a season opening road trip that saw them go 2-2-1, the Barons defeated St. Louis 3-1 in their home opener. This win over the Flyers was the beginning of a long, steady stream of victories.

By mid-November, the team's record was 11-5-2. One hot Baron during the early going was Ray Ceresino. The good-looking, black-haired Italian winger, who was a favorite of the ladies, scored the game-winning goal three times in early November. Ray missed the first seven games of the season and then scored six times in the next nine.

Ceresino was one of the most improved players during the early going. One of the League's fastest skaters, Ray had a bad habit of skating too close to the boards when carrying the puck. This made it easy to take him out of plays. After working tirelessly with Coach Cook, the quick winger was able to adjust his style to using all of the ice on his side of play. This adjustment allowed him to use his great speed and become more elusive. The goals naturally followed.

Pre-season skeptics predicted that Cleveland would have a hard time scoring goals and registering victories. By the end of November, the Barons had proved the doomsayers wrong on both accounts.

1,640 hearty souls braved the elements to see the Barons blast New Haven 9-3 after the great Thanksgiving snowstorm of 1950. Cleveland State University archives.

Only Buffalo had scored more goals while the Cleveland team was steamrolling to a 15-5-2 mark. By this time they were also beginning to pull away from the pack in the Western division race.

On November 29th, the Barons defeated New Haven 9-3 behind a three-goal hat trick by defenseman Hy Buller. Of greater importance than the game itself was what was occurring outside the Arena. Three days earlier, on Thanksgiving Eve, it began to snow in Cleveland. It snowed hard and did not let up. When citizens woke up the next morning, they looked outside and couldn't believe their eyes. The Great Thanksgiving Snowstorm of 1950 dumped 23 inches of snow on the City in less than 24 hours. Cleveland, for all intents and purposes, was shut down as the people began to dig out. The National Guard was even called in to help plow the streets. About 50 of these guardsmen were free guests at the Arena for the Saturday New Haven game. They were among the 1,640 spectators who braved the vicious weather to see the game. It was a lonely night among the empty seats, but at least it was warm.

Although the Thanksgiving weekend crowd of 1,640 was an extreme occurrence, the Barons, the League, and all of sports were having attendance woes caused by another source. The influence of television on the American public was affecting the sporting world in general, and hockey in particular, in a big way. People were now inclined to stay home after a hard day's work. Why go out and spend hard-earned money when they could be entertained at home for free? Comedies of the early 1950's and the quiz shows of the mid '50's kept Americans at home and out of the sporting arenas. Blue-collar towns like Cleveland were affected the most. Attendance at Barons' and Indians' games fell off dramatically. Even the Browns had trouble drawing in the NFL after sell-outs were common in the old All-American Conference. During the early 1950's, the baseball Indians regularly won over 90 games a year, yet would draw only slightly more than 1,000,000 fans. Barons' attendance declined gradually and hit its low during the 1954-55 season. Eventually, the novelty of watching television at home wore off, and it later helped make NFL football and major league baseball the blockbuster sports they are today. But during the early 1950's, TV was a huge drawback to organized sports.

When Al Sutphin told Bobby Carse that "the bloom was off the rose," he foresaw what was coming. He got out just in time. Economic hard times for the Barons were just beginning. However, the team on the ice was powerhouse entertainment.

By the end of December, Cleveland had padded its lead over Cincinnati to eight points, with a 6-5 thriller over Springfield. Once again, Les Douglas was the hero with three goals. His last was the game winner coming with only 21 seconds left in the contest. Also scoring for the Barons was the new darling of the fans, Wally Hergesheimer.

Wally Hergesheimer only played one year with the Barons, 1950-51. But in that one season, he truly became the darling of the fans. Only 5'6", the little dynamo chalked up 42 goals and Rookie of the Year honors – and he didn't stop there. In leading the Barons to the Calder Cup, Wally set a new league playoff record with 11 goals.
Dennis Turchek collection.

The smallest Baron, at 5'6" and barely 150 lbs., Wally was known as "Hergey's kid brother" when he broke into pro-hockey in 1947. This was in reference to brother Phil, the great Ex-Baron star, now with Cincinnati.

But Wally was now making a big name for himself. With 21 goals, he ranked second in the League behind another ex-Baron, Ab DeMarco. Wally, along with fellow rookie Glen Sonmar, was on a line centered by the great old Fox, Fred Thurier. Fred, spurred on by his new young wingers, was playing his best hockey in years. Biggest beneficiary of Thurier's great playmaking ability was Hergesheimer. With the Fox feeding him the puck, Wally had a good shot at Bob Solinger's rookie record of 40 goals set in 1947-48.

By January 8th, the Barons had stretched their first place lead to 15 points while sporting a record of 26-11-3. This was similar to the lead held by last year's team at this stage of the season. But this time around Bun Cook thought his team had a long way to go before reaching its peak. He also felt that the team needed more size for the tough stretch run and playoffs ahead.

With this in mind, Cleveland took a big gamble and traded high scoring but lightweight right wing Roy Kelly to St. Louis for rough and tumble Eddie Olson.

Kelly scored 46 goals the previous season, playing with Les Douglas and Ken Schultz. This season his game had slipped, but he still had 19 goals and 17 assists. The 155-pound Kelly was the last Baron player remaining from the war years.

Olson, who could play either forward or defense, was just what the Barons needed – a high-scoring player who could belt opposing players while protecting the Barons' lighter forwards.

After completion of the trade, the Barons embarked on a five-game road trip. They came home as conquering heroes. The 4-0-1 trip gave Cleveland a record-tying 19 victories on the road for the season. This tied the mark set by the 1947-48 club. The trip had many heroes. Murdo McKay fired a hat trick in a wild 9-8 win over Providence. The game also saw Wally Hergesheimer score his 30th goal in the team's 30th win.

In the Baron's 5-2 win at Cincinnati, Hy Buller tallied the 72nd goal of his career. This gave him the record for most career goals by a defenseman, one more than Eddie Bush. Wally Hergesheimer also registered his 32nd and 33rd goals to give Cleveland a 33-12-4 record. This was good for a 20-point lead over Indianapolis.

Hy Buller became the American Hockey League's highest scoring defenseman during his four years with the Barons. Cleveland Public Library collection.

Johnny Bower rang up his fifth shutout of the season with a 2-0 whitewash of Pittsburgh on January 31st. The game also saw Les Douglas register his 600th career point with an assist on Harry Taylor's goal. Only teammate Fred Thurier had more.

Cleveland's 22-point first-place lead was insurmountable. There were a variety of reasons for this team's success. First was the great Johnny Bower in goal. The Panther Man had risen to the top of AHL goalies. Second was the team's strength at center ice. Thurier, Douglas, and McKay were as strong a trio of middlemen as anywhere in the League. Thirdly, the defense was solid as a rock. Fourth was Bun Cook.

The veteran Cleveland coach was getting the absolute most out of his talent. After all, this team was not expected to go anywhere when the season began.

The Barons clinched the Western division crown on February 24th with a 7-6 win over Indianapolis. The game was a see-saw affair that saw the Capitals tie the game with only four seconds remaining. The League was now using sudden death in regular season overtime games. This allowed Fred Thurier to score the big title-winning goal in the overtime's last minute.

Cleveland clinched the over-all AHL pennant on March 6th with a 4-1 win over Providence. Les Douglas scored three goals to give him 30 on the year.

This was a special group of players that loved playing together. Everyone pulled for everyone else. Morale was as high as on any Bun Cook team. "You know," said Cook, "I couldn't ever hope to have a better bunch of boys than this team. The morale is wonderful...I can honestly say that I've never heard one word of discord all season." This was the sixth over-all regular season crown in Cook's eight years as coach. But it wouldn't mean a thing if the team collapsed in the playoffs again.

The only negative was that the Barons lost their last eight road games to remain tied with the 1947-48 club for most road wins at 19. In the last loss, 6-5 at Indianapolis, Fred Thurier scored his 300th career goal. This capped off his greatest season at age 34.

His 32 goals and 63 assists gave him 95 points, fourth in the League.

The Fox was the main man feeding Wally Hergesheimer. Wally, with 42 goals, was elected Rookie of the Year.

This set the stage for another playoff showdown with the rugged Buffalo Bisons.

THE PLAYOFFS

By virtue of their 40-26-4 record, Buffalo figured to be a tough opening-round opponent for Cleveland. Only the Barons' final mark of 44-22-5 was better. Offensively, the two teams were relatively equal. The Bisons led the League with 309 goals compared to Cleveland's 281. The Barons' big advantage came on defense. Their 221 goals against was second only to Pittsburgh's 177. Buffalo, on the other hand, had trouble keeping the puck out of their own net. Their giving up 284 goals was second worst in the League. The Barons figured to score big.

Game One in Cleveland was a titanic struggle. The two clubs went at each other with a fury during a scoreless first period. The Barons especially did a lot of hard hitting. They figured that the only way to stop the League's leading scorer, ex-Baron Ab DeMarco, was to keep The Count on the seat of his pants.

The second period saw the Bisons hit for two scores, while Ray Ceresino got one for the home team. Early in the third period, Harry Taylor tied the score on a pass from Joe Lund. The score remained tied at two and went into a full 10-minute overtime.

The overtime had barely started when Baron defenseman Sam Lavitt fired a long shot from the point that beat goalie Connie Dion to give the good guys the lead. The lead looked good, as Johnny Bower made several great saves, and the fans whooped it up. But with only 20 seconds left in overtime, Buffalo's Grant Warwick stunned everyone by scoring from an extreme angle.

After intermission the Bisons came out for "sudden death" determined to pull off an upset. They forced the play and caught the Barons sleeping. A careless pass by Cleveland was intercepted by Bison Gordon Pennell at center ice, and he broke in alone on Johnny Bower. Pennell faked twice and fired a bullet. SAVE! The Panther Man somehow got a foot on the shot to foil a sure goal. The crowd went wild. So did Bower's teammates.

Inspired by the miraculous save, the Barons took over the play. At 3:29 Phil Samis hit Les Douglas with a beautiful pass at the Bison blue line. Les found Ray Ceresino near the Buffalo net, and Ray lit the red lamp to give Cleveland a breathtaking 4-3 sudden death victory.

The overtime thriller took the starch out of the Bisons and set the stage for the Wally Hergesheimer Show in Game Two at Buffalo.

The Bisons thought that they would give the Barons a little of their own medicine by throwing their weight around, but the Barons handed the bodywork back with full force. The Bisons were thoroughly frustrated and began to take foolish penalties. This was their downfall.

Three times Little Hergey scored while Buffalo had a man in the penalty box. Wally was a ball of fire all evening as he led the Barons to a lopsided 7-2 victory. His linemates, Fred Thurier and Glen Sonmor, also scored. This line was like a blur the entire game, and the Bisons never did figure out how to stop them.

It was more of the same in Game Three at the Arena. 9,402 fans saw Hergesheimer wear the hero's hat twice in a genuine thriller.

With the Bisons nursing a slim 3-2 lead late in the third period, Little Hergey took over. On passes from Hy Buller and Fred Thurier, Wally tied the game at 15:03.

The Barons' Lloyd Doran and Bison Sid McNabney swapped goals during the first 10-minute overtime before Hergesheimer scored again in sudden death to give Cleveland a 5-4 win. This gave Hergesheimer five goals in the last two games and just about sealed the Bison's coffin.

The coffin was nailed shut by Wally and the gang in Game Four at Buffalo. The Bisons put up a game fight, but the Barons were just too much and skated away with a 3-2 win. Once again Cleveland's big line was the difference. Hergesheimer fired his sixth playoff goal in the first period, and Glen Sonmor got the eventual game winner at 2:40 of the third. In between, defenseman Phil Samis scored the Barons' second goal.

Les Hickey of Buffalo made it very interesting by scoring at 14:31, but Johnny Bower shut the door the rest of the way. The clean sweep put Cleveland in the finals against the surprising Pittsburgh Hornets.

Pittsburgh got into the playoffs the hard way. With a 31-33-7 record, they finished one point ahead of St. Louis. The Flyers argued that the Hornets used an ineligible player in one of their games. The third place playoff series against Springfield was delayed a full week while the League office studied the formal protest. Finally, the protest was not allowed, and Pittsburgh got to start their playoffs. They defeated the Indians and then the Hershey Bears to earn the right to face Cleveland.

The Hornets were strictly a defensive-oriented team. Their 212 goals scored was second lowest in the League. Their strength was in their defense. Allowing only 177 goals against was by far the least in the AHL. Anchored by goalie Gil Mayer and his 2.45 goals against average, the Hornets were usually in every game.

The big question heading into Game One was whether or not the Barons would be sharp. Due to their own quick sweep of Buffalo, coupled with Pittsburgh's protest-delayed start of the playoffs, Cleveland had been idle for two weeks.

The answer was obvious to all in Game One at the Arena. The home team was sluggish all night, and their passes were usually just a hair off the mark. Pittsburgh, on the other hand, was flying; and the Hornets upset the Barons 3-2 in overtime. Still, this was a game Cleveland should have won.

Cleveland center Lloyd Doran opened the scoring in the first period. Ex-Baron Bob Solinger tied it up in the second stanza.

The third period was high drama. When Hy Buller put the Barons on top 2-1 at 14:12, the Arena crowd sensed victory. The precious seconds ticked away, and the Barons held on. With 51 seconds remaining, the Hornets pulled their goalie, and the gamble paid off. At 19:36 George Armstrong poked the puck through a maze of players and past Johnny Bower to tie the score.

The full 10-minute overtime was all Pittsburgh. The winning Hornet score was fired by old friend Solinger at 5:31, his second goal of the game. Sollie looked just as dangerous as he did during his great 1947-48 season in Cleveland. And the Barons were all the worse off for it.

For more than two periods in Game Two at the Arena, the Barons played terrible hockey. Passes were errant, and their intensity was somewhere far away. They were full of jitters, and the possibility of another playoff disaster was staring them in the face as they trailed 3-1 early in the third period.

In an effort to shake up his lethargic club, Bun Cook moved hard-hitting defenseman Joe Lund up to right wing. On his first shift up front, Big Joe took a pass from Phil Samis at the blue line and fired a desperate 60-foot shot from along the boards. The puck glanced off the pads of a stunned goalie Gil Mayer and into the net. Suddenly, the Barons caught fire like never before, and the game turned into a barnburner.

Cleveland tied the score at three each. But soon after, Bob Solinger's pass-out was accidentally deflected into the net by Baron Hy Buller, and the Hornets led again 4-3.

The Barons rallied to tie the score at 4-4 on a powerplay goal by Harry Taylor with less than four minutes to play. Bedlam reigned at the Arena as the walls seemed to shake from the noise.

With the seconds ticking away in regulation time, Cleveland's mighty mite, Wally Hergesheimer, stole the puck from Pittsburgh backliner Pete Backor as every voice in the crowd shrieked. Wally then poked the puck past another Hornet defender, Hugh Bolton. While falling down in front of the net, Hergey somehow got off his off-balance shot, and it went in! How the Arena walls stayed up was amazing in itself as the crowd went completely wild.

Little Hergey was a huge hero now. But not to be overlooked was the goal by Joe Lund. His score was the shot in the arm that the Barons needed. Until then, they looked like a dead team.

The series shifted to Pittsburgh for the next three games. One would have thought that the Barons would have had the advantage in Game Three due to their thrilling second-game victory. Instead, they lapsed back into their lackadaisical play. If they were flat when the game began, they were certainly flatter than a pancake when it was over. The Hornets slaughtered Cleveland 9-2. Coach Cook blasted his team. In no uncertain terms he told them that he expected a much better effort in the next game, or else.

The Barons celebrate their 1950-51 Calder Cup victory.
James Peter Hendy collection.

The message must have gotten through because the Barons were a different team in Game Four. They out-hustled, out-hit, and out-scored the Hornets to the tune of 4-1.

A change in strategy seemed to confuse the Pittsburghers. Instead of trying to stickhandle the puck over the blue line, as had been their year-long style, the Barons instead dumped the puck into the attacking zone and chased after it. This new tactic paid dividends, as play was usually in the Hornet end.

Once again Wally Hergesheimer led the way. His two goals gave him ten for the playoffs. This tied ex-Barons' Tommy Burlington and Tod Sloan for the League record. Joe Lund and Murdo McKay also tallied for Cleveland as the series now stood at two games apiece.

The Barons were in mid-season from in Game Five at Pittsburgh as they defeated the Hornets 3-1. They played with the well-oiled precision of the team that raced to the regular season title. Who else but Wally Hergesheimer took center stage!

After Joe Lund gave the Barons a 1-0 at the 51 second mark, Hergey stepped forward. On passes from Red Williams and Fred Thurier, Wally set a new AHL record by scoring his 11th playoff goal at 10:48. Pittsburgh's Andy Barbe and Cleveland's Ray Ceresino traded second-period goals. Then Johnny Bower and a great Cleveland defense took over. The Hornets appeared discouraged near game's end as the Barons played a near-perfect defensive game. Pittsburgh rarely got near the Cleveland net. When they did, Bower was equal to the task. Only one game now separated the Barons from the coveted Calder Cup.

There was champagne on ice in the Cleveland dressing room as Game Six began at the Arena. It remained on ice when the game was over. Pittsburgh skated rings around the Barons and won 3-1 behind Bob Solinger's two goals.

Although they led 1-0 after two periods, thanks to Joe Lund's first-period goal, the Barons skated as though they had cement shoes. Only the great goal-

L-R: Coach Bun Cook, Team President Al Kroeson, General Manager Jim Hendy, AHL President John Digby Chick, Captain Hy Buller.

Team Captain Hy Buller speaks to the fans while accepting the Calder Cup after Cleveland's thrilling 3-1 cup-winning victory over Pittsburgh on April 21, 1951. Unbeknownst to all concerned, Buller had just played his last game as a Cleveland Baron. He would soon become a New York Ranger. James Peter Hendy collection.

tending of Johnny Bower kept them ahead. But the roof caved in during the third period as the Hornets struck for 3 well-deserved goals.

"It's impossible to play any worse," understated Fred Thurier. He was right. Now there was no tomorrow. Game Seven on April 21st would decide the champion of the American Hockey League.

The Barons came out firing in Game Seven at the Arena before the season's biggest crowd, 9,689. Phil Samis broke up the middle with a pass from Eddie Olson and beat Gil Mayer at 1:06.

Olson was an unsung hero in the game. He was given the task of being Bob Solinger's shadow. Coach Cook felt it imperative to stop Solinger if Cleveland was to win. "Wherever Sollie goes, I want you in his hip pocket," the coach instructed Olson. And Eddie did the job. Solinger was no factor in the game.

The Barons took a commanding lead in the second period on goals by Les Douglas and Ray Ceresino. From that point on, Cleveland sat on the lead and played perfect defense. Only a late goal by Hornet Andy Barbe at 17:50 of the third period spoiled Johnny Bower's shutout. As the final gong sounded, the Barons had won the precious Calder Cup with a 3-1 victory.

In the wild celebration afterward, Coach Bun Cook locked the dressing room door for a few minutes and personally thanked his players for the victory. "...Thank you from the bottom of my heart and God bless you all," cried the Coach.

It was then that Hy Buller led a toast for Bun as the players cheered along. The coach was overwhelmed with emotion.

Heroes for the Barons were many – Hergesheimer, Bower, Lund, Olson, and on down the line. But this title was won for the coach. After the previous year's disappointing loss to Indianapolis, this championship made the world all right again for one Bun Cook.

THE 1950-51 CLEVELAND BARONS

Front (L-R): Walter Robertson, Trainer; Hy Buller, Captain; James C. Hendy, General Manager; Floyd Perras, Richard L. (Dick) Kroesen, President; Johnny Bower, Fred (Bun) Cook, Coach; Fred Thurier.
Second: Edward J. Coen, Publicity Director; Lex Cook, Chief Scout; Kenny Schultz, Glen Sonmor, Murdo MacKay, Joe Lund, Lloyd Doran, Tom Williams, Phil Samis, Sheldon C. Fullerton, Promotional Director; Les Robinson, Stick Boy. Third: Walter Hergesheimer, Sam Lavitt, Ray Ceresino, Steve Wochy, Eddie Olson, Nick Tomiuk, Harry Taylor, Les Douglas, Eddie Busch, Walter Samanski. James Peter Hendy collection.

FINAL STANDINGS
1950-51

West	W	L	T	GF	GA	PTS.
Cleveland	44	22	5	281	221	93
Indianapolis	38	29	3	287	255	79
Pittsburgh	31	33	7	212	177	69
St. Louis	32	34	4	233	252	68
Cincinnati	28	34	8	203	228	64

East	W	L	T	GF	GA	PTS.
Buffalo	40	26	4	309	284	84
Hershey	38	28	4	256	242	80
Springfield	27	37	6	268	254	60
Providence	24	41	5	247	303	53

New Haven – DISBANDED – December 10, 1950

Top Baron Scorers	G	A	PTS.
Fred Thurier	32	63	95
Wally Hergesheimer	42	41	83
Les Douglas	31	39	70
Murdo McKay	25	36	61
Hy Buller	16	41	57
Steve Wochy	26	30	56
Glen Sonmor	14	35	49
Ray Ceresino	21	27	48

Calder Cup Champion – Cleveland Barons

1951-52 SEASON

The Barons received another overhaul during the off-season despite their Calder Cup success.

Willing to give Wally Hergesheimer and Hy Buller a shot at the big time, the Barons reluctantly traded the two young stars to the New York Rangers. Both players were loved by the fans, but Jim Hendy would not stand in their way. Buller would star for four years on the Ranger blueline before calling it a career. Hergey was a shooting star in the NHL. An early success, he later returned to the AHL with Buffalo.

In return from the Rangers, Cleveland received center Jackie Gordon, left wing Fernand Perreault, and defensemen Eddie Reigle and Fred Shero. The deal really was a good one for both teams. Gordon, Reigle (in his second turn with the club), and Shero put in many solid years here. Perreault was soon traded.

Another deal saw Glen Sonmor and Harry Taylor go to St. Louis for left wing Paul Gladu. Three years previous, Paul scored 51 goals, although injuries held him to 25 in 1950-51.

Les Douglas, Murdo McKay, and Eddie Busch decided to regain their "amateur" status and play for the Quebec Aces in the Quebec Senior Amateur League. This was amateur in name only, as the players were well compensated.

The farm system reaped a harvest as four solid prospects were promoted to fill out the roster – defenseman Bob Chrystal, right wing Ike Hildebrand, center Bob Bailey, and his brother John Bailey, a left wing.

Holdovers from the previous year's club were goalie Johnny Bower, defensemen Phil Samis, Sam Lavitt, and Red Williams; forwards Fred Thurier, Joe Lund, Ken Schultz, Steve Wochy, Eddie Olson, and Ray Ceresino.

With half of the team new, Cleveland took a little time to jell as a unit. They dropped their first two games on the road before winning their next two at home. Arena fans soon found another darling, as little Ike Hildebrand did his imitation of Wally Hergesheimer as he scored two goals in a 5-3 win over Buffalo. Playing on a line with center Fred Thurier, Ike was a buzzsaw on the ice and also showed a lot of fire as he would back down from no one.

Unfortunately, injuries began to hit the team early. Worst of all was a torn cartilage in the knee of Jackie Gordon on October 28th at Buffalo. The expert playmaker underwent knee surgery and would not return until mid-February.

Three weeks later the Barons recalled center Cal Stearns from Seattle to replace Gordon. Ray Ceresino was loaned to the West Coast club in Cal's place. The Barons only hoped that Stearns could hold the fort until Gordon returned. Cal fooled everyone. He starred with Cleveland all through the 1950's.

On November 28th the Barons were geared up to play the first-place Pittsburgh Hornets. The Hornets had become the scourge of the League. After winning their first eight games of the year, they built up a big first-place lead and came into Cleveland with a 15-2-2 mark, 14 points up on the Barons. Once again, the key to their team was defense. Rarely would a team get more than 20-25 shots on goal in a game against them. They had defensemen who would knock down anyone who went near their goal. The great record was no fluke.

The Barons dented the Pittsburgh defense for six goals before an encouraging Ladies' Night crowd of 7,805. Unfortunately, Pittsburgh ripped Cleveland for nine. The unexpected high-scoring loss left the Barons 16 points, a full eight games, behind the Hornets; and December had yet to begin. The hole they were in was a deep one. Still, their 10-7-2 record was not really bad. Pittsburgh was just setting a phenomenal pace.

After dropping back to back games to St. Louis, the Clevelanders appeared in trouble. Ken Schultz re-injured his shoulder and had to be carried off the ice. The team was in need of some new bodies, as injuries were beginning to take their toll.

Jim Hendy, in the Al Sutphin vein, was not one to stand idle. Disappointed in the play of Joe Lund, a hero in last season's playoffs, and Paul Gladu, Hendy traded the two players to St. Louis for center Ken Davies and left wing Vic Lynn.

The trade had a positive effect on the club as they rattled off four consecutive wins. The fourth win in the streak was a tough 4-3 victory over Pittsburgh. Little Ike Hildebrand scored the game winner with only two minutes left to play. The game, which left Cleveland 10 points behind the Hornets, saw Johnny Bower at his best. He stopped 20 shots in the third period alone. Bower had now become the most dominant goalie in the League.

The Barons went 1-2-1 in their next four games and then received a big Christmas present from Jim Hendy. The irrepressible general manager secured the services of Gerry Couture from Montreal for Fern Perreault. The Canadiens liked Perreault as a future prospect and were able to part with Couture because their roster was loaded with stars. A six-foot-two-and-one-half-inch, 185-pound center, Couture was a dangerous scorer.

As was the case when the Barons acquired Vic Lynn and Ken Davies, Couture's arrival spurred the team to instant results. The Barons rolled to six straight victories and closed to within 8 points of Pittsburgh. During the streak, the Cleveland defense was brilliant, and Johnny Bower was the leader. During back to back wins over Indianapolis, the Panther Man played despite being in severe pain. During a pileup in front of his goal, Johnny was gashed in the chin by a skate and helped to the dressing room. Seven stitches were required to close the cut, and a loose tooth was pulled out. Johnny then returned to the game and led his team to a 5-1 win! Goalies were a tough breed, and Bower was as tough as they came.

It seemed that every time the Barons got on a roll, they would run into Pittsburgh, and their streak would end. They, along with everyone else in the League, had enormous problems with the Hornets.

The latest setback ended their six-game winning streak. George Armstrong scored all three Pittsburgh goals as the Hornets nipped Cleveland 3-2. The winning goal set off a wild rhubarb that saw Coach Bun Cook get thrown out of the game after rushing on to the ice to protest the third Hornet goal.

After Vic Lynn and Cal Stearns scored to tie the game in the third period, a fight broke out between Ken Schultz and Pittsburgh's Tim Horton at one end of the rink. As the players brawled in one corner, play moved to Cleveland's end of the ice, and Pittsburgh scored. Cook protested that Referee Maurice Walsh should have stopped play when the fight broke out. Cook was right, but the goal still counted. The loss left the Barons ten points out of first with a 21-12-3 record.

Cleveland bounced right back with an 8-2 thrashing of the Syracuse Warriors behind Steve Wochy's hat trick and Gerry Couture's two goals. The Warriors were actually the transplanted Springfield Indians. With the Korean War raging, the Army once again took over the Springfield Arena and converted it into a storage warehouse. Eddie Shore moved his team to Syracuse for the duration of the conflict with Korea. Three years later, he moved back to Springfield.

Cleveland suddenly went on a five-game losing streak that included back to back losses to Pittsburgh. This dropped their record to 23-17-3, 16 points behind the Hornets. The race for first place certainly seemed over. But nobody told the Barons.

The Clevelanders went into Buffalo determined to break out of their slump. Their 7-3 victory on January 20th started a glorious unbeaten streak that lasted nearly the rest of the season.

Johnny Bower's second shutout of the season, a 6-0 whitewash of Hershey, extended Cleveland's unbeaten streak to five games and brought them to within 11 points of Pittsburgh. The game also saw Eddie Olson score his 100th career goal.

The Barons were gaining momentum, and two of the reasons were Cal Stearns and Steve Wochy. Stearns didn't even make the club out of training camp and was sent to Seattle. After being recalled after 16 games, Cal turned into the find of the year. In his first 32 games in Cleveland, Stearns had 17 goals and 20 assists to rank second on the club.

Wochy was on a tear. His two third-period goals led the Barons to a 3-1 win at Hershey. The scores gave Wochy 28 for the year, only two behind League leader George Armstrong of Pittsburgh. More important, the Barons' eight in a row without a loss left them only 9 points back of the Hornets.

Defenseman Phil Samis suffered a hairline skull fracture during a fight with Chuck Scherza of Providence. This necessitated the recall of Fred Shero from Seattle. Shero started the season in Cleveland but broke a rib and was sent to Seattle for conditioning. The rugged rearguard would become a fan favorite. The addition of Shero, along with the return to action of Jackie Gordon, finalized Cleveland's roster for the stretch run.

The unbeaten streak reached 13 when the Barons won at Buffalo 5-2. Johnny Bower was magnificent with 44 saves, and Vic Lynn led the attack with two goals within 63 seconds. The victory left the Barons with a 35-17-3 record, 6 points behind Pittsburgh. As torrid as the Barons were, Pittsburgh was almost as hot. Catching the Hornets was one mean task. But drive on the Barons did to the tune of four more wins in a row. Their tremendous unbeaten streak reached 18 with a 3-1 win over Syracuse on March 1st. This gave them 16 wins and 2 ties in those 18 games. Incredibly, they were still six points behind Pittsburgh, as the Hornets refused to fold.

Standing between the Barons and number 19 in the streak was none other than the Pittsburgh Hornets themselves. Back to back games with their first-place rivals would most likely decide first place. Only seven games remained in the season. The Barons needed a sweep of the two games.

The first game in Pittsburgh was all it was expected to be. But in a fierce and violent game, the great Cleveland streak came to an end when the Barons lost a 3-2 heartbreaker. The end came at 10:05 of the third period when John McLellan broke in alone on Johnny Bower and scored the go-ahead goal.

This was Cleveland's eighth loss in nine games to the Hornets and put them 8 points behind the leaders.

The Barons came back the next night and shut out Pittsburgh 3-0 in Cleveland, but the damage was done. Still, the Barons would not give in. They won their next three games and headed into the last weekend of the season only 2 points behind Pittsburgh.

The final dagger in the Barons' hearts came when the Hornets defeated Hershey 6-4 while Cleveland was defeating Indianapolis 7-3. This closed the door on the Barons in one of the greatest pennant races the League had ever seen. The final standings showed Pittsburgh with 95 points to Cleveland's 93.

The Barons gave it all they had. They gave every last ounce of fight and grit in their spirited run to catch the Hornets. But while their effort was valiant, they entered the playoffs against Providence as an exhausted team.

Ike Hildebrand (8) attempts to score against Pittsburgh's Gil Mayer. Cleveland State University archives.

THE PLAYOFFS

On paper, the Barons were heavily favored to defeat Providence in the opening three out of five playoff series. Losers of only two of their last 25 games, Cleveland also had a 6-1-1 record against the Reds during the regular season.

Their 32-33-3 record notwithstanding, Providence was no slouch. They had seven players with over 20 goals, including scoring champ Ray Powell. Ray racked up 35 goals and 62 assists while centering the League's top line. Linemates Barry Sullivan with 25 goals and Paul Gladu with 31 made a powerful combination. Gladu was cast off by Cleveland earlier in the year, but wound up strong at Providence.

In Game One at the Arena, the Barons grabbed an early 2-0 first period lead on goals by Steve Wochy and Gerry Couture. When Eddie Olson scored at 3:36 of the third period, Cleveland appeared to have it made.

Then, within a span of 30 seconds, the Reds were back in the game. Goals by Chuck Scherza at 7:35 and Ray LaPlante at 8:05 made it too close for comfort. For the rest of the game Providence attacked ferociously. However, Johnny Bower held them at bay, and Cleveland escaped with a 3-2 victory.

Game Two was all Cleveland. Led by Cal Stearn's two goals and one goal and three assists from Vic Lynn, the Barons were in command all of the way during a 7-2 win. This was a roughhouse game that seemed to take something out of the home team despite the big score.

This was more than evident in Game Three at Providence. The game turned in the Reds' favor after a stick-swinging melee between Cleveland's Ken Davies and the Reds' Jack McGill. After clubbing each other first with sticks and then with fists, Davies received 2 two-minute penalties, one for slashing and the other for high sticking. McGill only received 1 two-minute penalty for high sticking.

This was all the opening Providence needed. Ex-Baron Paul Gladu wrecked havoc on his old team as he struck for three goals in the span of 87 seconds. If ever revenge was sweet, this was it. The Reds never looked back and routed the Barons 5-1.

As bad as Cleveland was in Game Three, they managed to look even worse in Game Four. Having lost their scoring punch completely, the Barons were blanked 4-0. It wasn't just the score that raised eyebrows. The Clevelanders just looked totally inept. It was obvious that the long drive of trying to catch Pittsburgh had finally taken its toll. There was no way that the team could sustain such a feverish pace, but they picked a bad time to go stale.

Game Five was more of the same, but Cleveland went down fighting. The Reds jumped out to a 3-0 lead before Ken Schultz got one back late in the second period.

The Barons' hopes were raised when Ike Hildebrand brought Cleveland within one at 16:01 of the last period. Coach Cook gambled and pulled Johnny Bower with two and one-half minutes remaining. The Barons thrilled the Arena fans with several close calls but could not get the tying goal past Red goalie Harvey Bennett. Finally, an open net goal gave Providence a 4-2 series-clinching victory. Leading the Reds in celebration were Paul Gladu and Joe Lund, who were traded to Providence in December.

It certainly was a disappointing end to an extraordinary season. But grief was soon forgotten as the Barons announced that they would officially apply for entry into the National Hockey League.

FINAL STANDINGS
1951-52

West	W	L	T	GF	GA	PTS.
Pittsburgh	46	19	3	267	179	95
Cleveland	44	19	5	265	166	93
Cincinnati	29	33	6	183	228	64
St. Louis	28	39	1	256	262	57
Indianapolis	22	40	6	232	273	50
East	**W**	**L**	**T**	**GF**	**GA**	**PTS.**
Hershey	35	28	5	256	215	75
Providence	32	33	3	263	270	67
Buffalo	28	36	4	230	298	60
Syracuse	25	42	1	211	272	51

Top Baron Scorers	G	A	PTS.
Steve Wochy	37	41	78
Ken Davies	18	45	63
Cal Stearns	22	35	57
Ike Hildebrand	32	15	47
Eddie Olson	12	35	47
Gerry Couture	24	21	45
Eddie Reigle	9	36	45
Fred Thurier	19	23	42
Vic Lynn	17	25	42

Calder Cup Champion – Pittsburgh Hornets

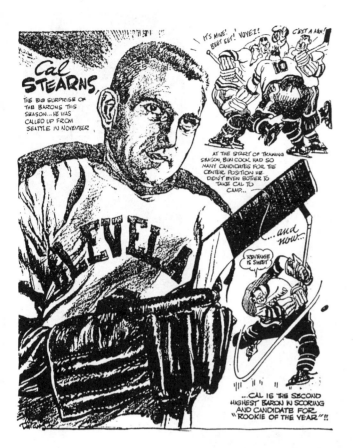

1951-52 CLEVELAND BARONS

Front (L-R): Tony Webner, Publicity Director; Joe Carveth, Ken Schultz, Jim Hendy, General Manager; Floyd Perras, Promotion Director; Dick Kroeson, President; John Bower, "Bun" Cook, Coach; Fred Thurier, Steve Wochy, Lex Cook, Chief Scout. Second: Shel Fullerton, Program Editor-PA Announcer; Chas. Homenuk, Trainer; Ed Reigle, Ike Hildebrand, Phil Samis, Ray Ceresino, Jack Gordon, Sam Levitt, Ron Cook, Radio Announcer. Back: Ed Olson, Tom Williams, Bob Chrystal, Fern Perreault, Joe Lund, Jerry Reid, Paul Gladu. Larry Smith collection.

The NHL Strikes Back

After all of the preliminaries had been taken care of, the Cleveland Barons officially applied for entry into the National Hockey League on May 14, 1952. The NHL had in its possession $425,562.12 in Cleveland funds that were placed on file to back up the Barons' application.

The NHL issued this statement: "It was moved by Mr. Conn Smythe, Toronto, and seconded by Mr. James Norris Sr., Detroit, and passed unanimously, that Cleveland Arena Inc. be admitted to membership in the National Hockey League upon fulfillment of the following conditions..." The conditions were spelled out. The Barons fulfilled every condition and awaited formal confirmation at the NHL's annual July meetings.

The Cleveland management, its fans, and the media were overjoyed. It had been the present ownership's dream to join the NHL. It had been Al Sutphin's dream also. Yet, due to circumstances out of his control, Sutphin had turned his back on the big league when the NHL came knocking at his door. Now, at long last, the Barons were going to "the Promised Land."

On July 2nd, all of these dreams came crashing down. The NHL formally denied Cleveland's entry into their exclusive club. Everyone connected with the team was shocked.

"Well, they slapped us down," understated a dejected Jim Hendy. "All I can hope now is that the people of Cleveland will get behind us to prove to the National Hockey League that we are a major league city in every respect."

The NHL's party line for rejection centered around the fact that the $318,000 submitted for working capital was borrowed money rather than cash in hand. The NHL, acting as judge and jury, determined that money obtained on long-term notes was not working capital. However, no mention of this was made at the May 14th formal application meeting.

Cleveland State University archives – Photo by Paul Tepley.

Hendy stated that working capital could be raised, if not on hand, by 1) selling stock, or 2) borrowing money. Under the Barons' corporate setup, they couldn't sell stock.

Toronto General Manager Conn Smythe stated, "The Barons would be assuming a financial burden too great to overcome."

In this regard, Cleveland did have one drawback – the size of their arena. Once a palace on a par with most NHL facilities, the Arena was now deemed too small by NHL standards. All National League arenas now had over 12,000 seating capacity, while Cleveland's was 9,700. However, Hendy scaled the Arena at higher ticket prices to offset any loss in revenue. He assumed that the ticket-buying public would pay higher prices for NHL hockey. The big league doubted they would. After all, attendance was down in every hockey league due to television.

The Globe and Mail

Overcast, Showers
High 65

Final Edition   TORONTO, THURSDAY, MAY 15, 1952.   5 Cents Per Copy   36 P

$107,000 Plus for Franchise

NHL Will Admit Cleveland If League's Cash Terms Met

Norris Interests Block Cleveland From N.H.L.

By DAN PARKER

CLEVELAND, a fine sports town, should be a welcome addition to any big league group, but the way the National Hockey League is handling the Cleveland Barons' application for membership, you'd swear it was a leper colony.

The Barons have complied with every condition imposed by the N.H.L., often facetiously referred to as the Norris House League, but they have run up against a situation that looks like a combination of the Chicago Chill and the Detroit Run-Around. If their latest application for admission is turned down, I have it on the authority of a Canadian well posted in hockey matters that the owners of the Barons will sue the league as a combination in restraint of trade. Should this come about, some of the secrets involving ownership of several National League clubs would probably be dragged out into the open, and that would hurt some of the magnates as much as it would help hockey.

Cleveland's Barons are the classiest team in the American League. They have operated independently of the N.H.L. because they couldn't afford to function as a farm club and let a major league club take players they developed. So, the Barons have had their own farm system, which is as good as those of at least three major league clubs. The Barons have one professional club—Seattle in the Pacific Coast League—and four amateur teams on their chain. The club is operated by the Cleveland Arena Corporation, which owns the 10,000-capacity rink where its home games are played. Stock in the arena is owned mostly by Clevelanders. A local sports goods dealer owns a block, Shipstad...

...oard of C... voted that ...used their cash reserve to $425,652.12, of which 60 percent had to be Cleveland capital, they would be admitted to the league. It looked like such a sure-thing that on May 28, the Cleveland Press ran an 8-column banner line reading: "Barons Join National League."

When the Board met again June 17th in Montreal, the Cleveland delegation was on hand, loaded with cash and certified checks, and ready to be welcomed into the fold. Imagine their chagrin, therefore, when they ran into a chill that would freeze a rink in Hades. Gen. John Reed Kilpatrick, representing the Rangers, wanted to know where they had raised the money and thought there should be a thorough audit of the Barons' books before any action was taken. Of the six clubs represented, three —Toronto, Boston and Montreal—were in favor of admitting the Barons. Jim Norris's Detroit Red Wings were opposed to taking them in and Jim's tenants, the Chicago Black Hawks lined up with him. Gen. Kilpatrick remained on the fence. Because the Norris interests own a large block of stock in Madison Square Garden, it probably wasn't considered politic in view of the danger of anti-trust suits for the Rangers to show their hand. But the General's abstention from voting could have served as a subtle warning to the Barons that in a show-down, the best they could hope for was a deadlock which would mean defeat.

The Barons' legal department considers the Board of Governors' motion in Toront^ offer and t^ ^osition th^' ^illing th^

...s league.

Nor.. ...terests bought the Chicago Stadium, the Detroit Olympia and the St. Louis Auditorium in bankruptcy, and converted them into goldmines through ice shows, hockey, boxing and other sports. Television opened up new nugget-rich lodes. The feeling prevails, therefore, that Old Jim has his eye cocked for the Cleveland Stadium to round out his major league TV circuit. Besides, as Gord Walker of the Toronto Globe and Mail pointed out, "With Cleveland in the N.H.L., along with the other 'Independents', Toronto, Montreal and Boston, the Norris interests (they run the Detroit club, Chicago Stadium and have stock in Madison Square Garden) could be outvoted 4-3 on questions that need only a majority vote."

Meantime the National Hockey L^ signs of

So when all was said and done, the Barons were forced to remain in the AHL. The truth was, this was not bad at all. The American Hockey League was a great league! But the damage had been done.

It seems that the Barons were the victims of inside NHL politics. A majority vote was needed in order for them to be admitted to the big league.

When the NHL Board of Governors met in Montreal on June 17, 1952, Toronto, Boston, and Montreal voted in favor of admitting Cleveland. Detroit and Chicago were against, with New York unsure. The Rangers later voted no. This 3-3 standoff meant a crushing defeat for the Barons. But it was predictable.

At the time of Cleveland's application for entry, the NHL was facetiously referred to as "the Norris House League." This was because James Norris Sr. owned and operated the Detroit Red Wings, the Chicago Stadium (where the Blackhawks played), and owned a large block of stock in Madison Square Garden (home of the Rangers). Thus, when it came to matters of league policy, Chicago and New York would always side with Detroit. This made it possible for Norris to dictate NHL policy. He could always propose new policy and hope for a vote from Toronto, Boston, or Montreal to win a majority. On the other hand, he could also block anything he was against with the help of Chicago and New York.

This would prove to be the Barons' downfall.

Dan Parker, columnist for the New York Daily Mirror, pointed out in his column on June 26, 1952 that "With Cleveland in the NHL, along with other 'Independents', Toronto, Montreal, and Boston, the Norris interests could be outvoted 4-3 on questions that need only a majority vote." This could have put an end to James Norris Sr.'s influence over the NHL. He would not let this happen and the end result was that the Cleveland entry bid was denied.

Deep down, Hendy, and everyone in Cleveland, knew another reason why Cleveland's NHL bid was rejected. Certain powers that be in the big league still held a grudge against Cleveland. Their pride was hurt when Al Sutphin rejected them during the 1940's when they came knocking at the Barons' door.

Sutphin's motives were pure. The AHL would probably have folded if he had joined the NHL. Besides that, he was making a good profit where he was. This galled the NHL. Some day, they would have their revenge. On July 2, 1952, they did.

1952-53 SEASON

The Barons entered the 1952-53 American League season in a circuit that had been reduced to seven teams. Indianapolis and Cincinnati had to bite the financial bullet and cease operations. Each city had a drastic drop in attendance that was too great to overcome. Leading cause of the drop in fans was television. People were staying home everywhere. The AHL would now operate as a one division, seven team loop.

Cleveland was going with basically the same lineup that finished the previous year, with one glaring exception. Fred Thurier, the great Baron center, had decided to call it a career. He began his professional career in 1937 with the Springfield Indians and came to Cleveland in 1945-46. One of Al Sutphin's greatest acquisitions, The Fox left the game with 319 goals and 425 assists for 744 points. A gentleman of class both on and off the ice, the loss of Thurier left a void in the Barons and the League as well.

Two old friends returned to the team. Glen Sonmor was purchased back by Jim Hendy. His fierce determination and spirit were a welcome addition. Ray Ceresino also was back in the fold from Seattle. Once again, Cal Stearns started the year out west only to return later in the season.

Cleveland started the year off on the right foot by defeating the defending champion Hornets in Pittsburgh 2-1.

Baron goals were scored by Ray Ceresino and Ike Hildebrand. But it was the tough, hard-driving defensive play that pleased Coach Bun Cook the most. It was obvious early in the season that this was a club to be reckoned with.

While the team played a bit above .500 hockey for the first month of the season, the home crowds were encouraging. After three home games, the Barons had drawn 24,210 fans. While attendance did not stay at an 8,000 average all year, the increase in fan interest showed what hard work could do. Industrial and business groups were coming back to the Arena. This was the result of intense promotion that began during the summer under Jim Hendy. Hendy and his staff hit the streets, and their long hours of work seemed to be paying off.

On the ice, a swift upturn in the team's fortunes began on November 18th. Their 3-2 win over Pittsburgh was the start of a fine eight-game winning streak. The start of the game was held up 15 minutes as a flash crowd showed up for the midweek game. Fans formed a line one block long down Euclid Avenue. While not a sellout, 8,441 fans saw Ike Hildebrand score two goals to lead the home team. This gave him 11 for the young season, and the team stood at 8-5-0.

The Barons had many contributors to the eight-game streak. But one who stood out among the rest was goalie Johnny Bower. The Panther Man was superb as he yielded a scant 10 goals in the 8 wins. He now led the League with a 2.33 goals against average. His 6-0 whitewash at Syracuse gave him 3 shutouts for the year as the Barons led the League with a 15-5-0 record.

The eight-game streak came to an end in Hershey. The Bears defeated Cleveland 3-2 in overtime on a goal by Duncan Fisher.

High point of the first half of the season came when Bower recorded his fifth shutout of the season on December 17th. His 1-0 blanking of the Hornets at Pittsburgh put the Barons seven points ahead of second-place Hershey. Their record stood at 18-7-0. Bower tied his season high for shutouts. Twice before, in 1949-50 and again in 1950-51, he recorded five blankings in a season.

"I've said it before and I'll say it again, that Bower is the best of them all," declared Bun Cook after the game. And he meant the NHL as well as the AHL. "Bower is every bit as good as Terry Sawchuk of Detroit, and I would pick Bower over Sawchuk," the coach added for emphasis.

Bower was just reaching his peak. While he shared duties with Harvey Teno and Roger Bessette during his first four years in the League, John now played nearly every game. He would work for hours on what he thought were weaknesses in his game. The extra practice was paying off. He was now as good as anyone at his profession.

Just as quick as Cleveland built up its seven-point lead, it was gone. The team went into a 1-5-1 tailspin and was suddenly tied for first with Hershey. Chief cause of the slide was a rash of nagging injuries – not the critical kind, but those muscle pulls and large bruises that slow a player down. Most everyone on the club was banged up, and it showed in the team's play.

Despite the team being rejected by the National Hockey League, fans returned in big numbers to see the powerful 1952-53 team. Here a flash crowd formed a line one block down Euclid Avenue to see the Barons defeat Pittsburgh 3-2 on November 18, 1952.
Cleveland State University archives – photo by Fred Bottomer.

The great Johnny Bower makes a diving save against Syracuse's Harry Pidhirny. #18 Eddie Olson defends. Cleveland State University archives – photo by Fred Bottomer.

The Cleveland offense was faltering, and a shot in the arm was needed. Jim Hendy, never shy to pull the trading trigger, engineered a deal that would turn out to be the most important player personnel acquisition in the team's history. On January 13th, it was announced that Vic Lynn had been traded to the Chicago Blackhawks for a yet unnamed player. Two days later, on January 15, 1953, Fred Glover became a member of the Barons. He would remain a Baron through the 1967-68 season. During his 16 seasons here, Fred would become the highest scorer and most penalized player in League history.

Glover turned pro in 1947-48 at Omaha in the U. S. League. The next season he was promoted to Indianapolis. He was a member of the 1949-50 Capital squad that upset Cleveland four straight in the League finals. The next season his 48 goals led the AHL. Owned by Detroit, he bounced back and forth from Detroit to Indy. He was thought to be a step too slow for the Red Wings and was sold to Chicago. The Blackhawks loaned Fred to St. Louis before he was traded to Cleveland. Glover didn't know it then, but he had found a home.

The 25-year-old forward's debut as a Baron on January 18th was a memorable one. Before a Sunday matinee crowd of 7,175, Cleveland took over first place again by besting Syracuse 8-6. Playing on left wing, Glover scored one goal and assisted on two others.

Fred also engaged in a savage fight with Sam Casanato of the Warriors. In the battle, Glover pulled the jersey of Casanato over the Syracuse player's head and pounded him into oblivion. This was the first of countless fights Fred would engage in over his years with his new team. Whether he was scoring, fighting, or delivering a vicious bodycheck, Fred Glover knew only one way to play – all out, 100% all of the time. The man was a total inspiration to his teammates.

During the last week of January, the Barons lost back-to-back games in Pittsburgh to drop three points behind the Hornets. Both losses were by the score of 3-1. The wild, penalty-filled games were hard fought bruising battles.

In the second contest, Cleveland not only lost the game, but Johnny Bower as well.

Midway through the third period, Hornet John McLellan fired a bullet from 10 feet that struck the great goalie just above the upper lip. Blood poured out of the gash, as an almost unconscious Bower was helped to the dressing room. Twelve stitches were required to sew up the wound. Also a dental plate and two teeth were broken. Still, Johnny wanted to finish the game! Fortunately, spare goalie Floyd Perras finished.

Bower was sent back to Cleveland after the game where delicate oral surgery was performed. The courageous netminder only missed three games. John was one tough cookie.

Fans were pleased when the Barons acquired Fred Glover during the 1952-53 season. But no one could have dreamed that he would play with the team for the next 15 years and become the greatest player in American Hockey League history. Bill Hudec collection.

Johnny Bower was an unbelieveable force in goal for the Barons. In all, he would play 400 regular season games and record a 2.43 goals against average in Cleveland. During the Playoffs, he would get even more stingy. In 41 Calder Cup tests with the Barons, he posted an incredible 1.91 average and nine shutouts. Kay Horiba collection.

In his place for three games, Lou Crowdis was recalled from New Haven, now in the Eastern League. Crowdis played admirably in front of an inspired Cleveland defense, and the Barons won all three games that Lou played. Eddie Reigle, Red Williams, Fred Shero, and Bob Chrystal were magnificent in protecting the substitute goalie. The three victories gave Cleveland a 26-16-1 record, one point ahead of Pittsburgh.

With Johnny Bower back in goal after a 3-0 loss to Springfield, the Barons went on a six-game winning streak during mid-February. Still they could not shake Pittsburgh. Their 31-17-2 record was still only two points better than the Hornets. The two clubs were pulling away from the rest of the League. It would be a two-team race for first place the rest of the way.

Two bright spots in the Barons' attack were Jackie Gordon and Eddie Olson. Both players, along with Ike Hildebrand, were challenging St. Louis' Guyle Fielder for the scoring lead.

Gordon, one of the smoothest playmakers in the League, had bounced all the way back from knee surgery the previous year. Olson was invaluable. Equally adept at forward or defense, the hard-hitting battler played anywhere Coach Cook needed him. This season he played mostly up front and was piling up the points.

A 10-2 thrashing of Hershey on February 24th put Cleveland four points up on Pittsburgh. The game featured hat tricks by Eddie Olson and Ike Hildebrand. Jackie Gordon also chipped in with two goals.

Hildebrand was a man on a mission. All season he played with the goal-scoring title as his main objective. The previous year he was snubbed in the All Star and Rookie of the Year voting – this despite scoring 31 goals while missing nearly 1/3 of the season due to injuries. He was determined to make everyone take notice of him this year, and he succeeded.

After defeating Hershey, the Clevelanders slumped a little. Two losses let Pittsburgh tie the Barons for first place. This set up a showdown between the two bitter rivals on March 3rd.

The Barons were up for this one. Riding the coattails of their great goaltender Johnny Bower, Cleveland shut out the hated Hornets 3-0. Bower had 29 saves in his sixth shutout of the season, a personal high.

Leading the lamplighters was Steve Wochy with a pair of goals. Sometimes overlooked because of his quiet ice demeanor, Wochy was a deadly marksman. Rookie Gus Karry's first professional goal started the scoring for Cleveland. The win gave the Barons a two-point lead with a 35-20-4 record.

From the big win over Pittsburgh onward, the Barons were unstoppable. To a man, they now believed that they were the best.

After defeating Syracuse 2-1, their lead was up to four points. A 9-2 pasting of Providence followed by a 4-2 win against Syracuse saw Cleveland's lead jump up to seven points.

The victory over Syracuse saw battling Freddie Glover break out of a scoring slump. He had only scored 4 goals in his first 22 games here. But he fired the tying and winning goals against the Warriors and regained his scoring touch.

The regular season title-clinching victory came at the Arena against St. Louis. The 6-1 win was the team's sixth straight and 40th of the season. It gave Bun Cook his seventh percentage championship in his 10 years as Cleveland coach.

The Barons closed out the season with two more wins to give them eight straight. Their 86 points, on a 42-20-2 record, was six better than Pittsburgh.

In the season finale, a 5-2 victory over Buffalo, Eddie Olson scored the eventual game winner. This capped a dramatic late-season flourish that saw him overtake St. Louis' Guyle Fielder and win the scoring championship with 86 points. The great joke teller scored 32 goals and 54 assists.

The native of Hancock, Michigan became the first American-born player to win the AHL scoring title.

Ike Hildebrand fulfilled his season-long ambition and won the goal-scoring title with 38, one more than teammate Steve Wochy's 37.

The All-Star team was dominated by four Clevelanders. Johnny Bower, Tommy Williams, Eddie Olson, and Ike Hildebrand all made the first team.

The Barons headed into the playoffs as heavy favorites over the third-place Syracuse Warriors. But as all Clevelanders knew, regular season titles did not always mean Calder Cup success.

THE PLAYOFFS

Syracuse was a solid club that finished with a 31-31-2 record. Still, they were not in the same class as Cleveland.

One never would have known it in Game One of the best of five series at the Arena. The Warriors gave the Barons all they could handle before finally losing a hard-fought 2-0 game.

The shutout was the first playoff whitewash for Johnny Bower. Johnny was perfect as he handled everything the Warriors could muster. The only goal he needed was scored by Ray Ceresino at the :53 second mark of the third period.

The rest of the period was frenzied. With 37 seconds left in the game, goalie Gordon Bell was pulled for a sixth attacker. The move backfired when defenseman Fred Shero got hold of the puck after a faceoff and sent a 150-foot shot nearly the length of the rink to ice the victory.

Game Two was another nip and tuck affair. After Bob Chrystal took a Fred Glover pass to score at 11:23 of the first period, Cleveland tried to make the 1-0 lead hold up. But Kelly Burnett spoiled Johnny Bower's shutout attempt at 8:12 of the last period.

The game appeared headed for overtime until a Tommy (Red) Williams shot was rebounded in by Jackie Gordon at 16:36. The 2-1 victory put Cleveland in the driver's seat.

But the Warriors were not through. They rallied for a 5-3 win in Game Three. Down 3-0 after one period, Cleveland rallied to tie it up in the third. A goal by Warrior Armand Lemieux put Syracuse on top to stay at 9:30. An insurance marker at 17:43 gave Syracuse its final margin of victory.

Game Four was a defensive masterpiece by Cleveland. Backed by Johnny Bower's perfect goaltending, the Barons blanked the Warriors 2-0. After Jackie Gordon and Bob Bailey put Cleveland up by two, the Clevelanders went into a defensive shell to protect the lead. Their execution was flawless.

In the third period, the Barons attempted only one shot at the Syracuse goal. Their sole intent was to keep the puck away from Johnny Bower's net. The Cleveland netminder finished with 35 saves as the Barons headed to the finals for the ninth time. Standing between them and the Calder Cup was their bitter rival, the defending champion Pittsburgh Hornets.

For three years running, the Barons and Hornets fought for domination in the American Hockey League. Two years previous, Cleveland won the Calder Cup in a seven-game playoff over Pittsburgh. Last season, the Hornets held off the Barons in a thrilling regular season race. They then went on to win the Cup.

Verbal barbs were being thrown by both clubs, as there was no love lost between them. In terms of strength, the two teams were about as even as they could be. During the regular season, they met 10 times. Pittsburgh held a slight edge, winning 5 to Cleveland's 4 victories. One game ended in a tie. From top to bottom, these teams were solid as a

Cal Stearns scores against Pittsburgh's Gil Mayer in Game #5 of the 1952-53 Finals. Cleveland State University archives – photo by Fred Bottomer

rock. The preliminaries were over. Talk now was cheap. The best team would be decided on the ice.

Game One in Cleveland lived up to its expectations. The game was filled with fire and brimstone as each team tried to gain a physical and psychological edge. In the end, it was the spectacular goaltending of Johnny Bower that was the difference.

The Panther Man remained white hot at the Barons blanked Pittsburgh 2-0. The shutout was Johnny's third of the playoffs. He now had given up a measly 6 goals in five games. But he had plenty of help. The Cleveland defense, playing without Eddie Reigle for the duration because of a knee injury, was like a stone wall.

Second-period goals by rookie Ray Ross and Jackie Gordon gave the Barons all they needed.

Game Two saw more of the same slam-bang action, with a lot more drama added in.

The two evenly-matched squads were deadlocked at 2-2 at the end of regulation time. The game then went into a full 10-minute overtime. Neither team scored, but both came close. Near the eight-minute mark, a Baron shot hit the crossbar and ricocheted out. On the ensuing Hornet rush down ice, Johnny Bower made a super save to send the game into sudden death overtime.

Early on in the second extra session, the Barons worked the puck into the Pittsburgh zone. Bob Chrystal took a pass from Glen Sonmor at the blue line and let fly a bee bee. The puck flew past a screened Gil Mayer and gave Cleveland a 3-2 thriller. Referee Frank Udvari thought the puck tipped in off Ike Hildebrand's stick and gave Ike credit for the goal. No one really cared who scored. The bottom line was that Cleveland won. They now had a big two game lead in the best of seven series, as the teams headed to Pittsburgh.

The Hornets proved in Game Three that they were still a force to be reckoned with as they skated off with a 5-2 victory.

Cleveland was in the game until late in the second period. But with the score tied 1-1, the Hornets struck for two quick goals to take over for good. Frank Mathers at 18:25 and Andy Barbe at 19:44 put the game on ice. The third period was all Pittsburgh as the Hornets thoroughly dominated.

Pittsburgh really stuck it to Cleveland in Game Four as they won again 4-1. The Barons were never really in the game and took out their frustrations in the game's final minute.

Bob Bailey and Ike Hildebrand were assessed five minutes each for fighting with Pittsburgh's Willie Marshall and Chuck Lumsden. These brawls led to a full-scale riot between both teams. Everyone on both squads paired off in a sea of fisticuffs. Even the two coaches, Bun Cook and Frank (King) Clancy, got in on the act.

It took the referee and linesmen 10 minutes to restore order. But all the fighting in the world couldn't hide the fact that the Barons still lost the game. It would be a long bus ride back to Cleveland.

The shaken team had no idea how long. As the team bus pulled to a stop at a railroad crossing, it was smashed in the rear by an automobile. Four passengers in the car were hurt. Everyone on the bus was O.K., except the bus itself. After a delay of over two hours, another bus was brought in to take the players home. The team did not pull into the Arena parking lot until dawn.

The pressure was on both clubs, especially Cleveland. The Barons desperately needed Game Five. With the home team having won all four games thus far, the Barons did not want to return to The Steel City down by a game and facing elimination.

A dog-tired Cleveland team played like it for two periods. They were lucky to only be down 1-0 after two stanzas. A first-period goal by Bob Solinger put the Hornets on top.

But the Barons were a determined group to start period three. At 2:53, Cal Stearns converted a pass from Bob Bailey to knot the score. The team could sense a victory now. They stormed the Pittsburgh net relentlessly until Eddie Olson nudged home the game winner at 13:52. The good guys now

had a 3-2 series lead as the teams went by train to Pittsburgh for Game Six.

The teams went at each other tooth and nail in that sixth game. Never had two so evenly matched clubs battled so hard.

Cleveland looked to be in the driver's seat as defenseman Bob Chrystal scored two first-period goals to give Cleveland a 2-0 lead. But Pittsburgh got one back late in the second period and tied it up early in the third. There was no further scoring, and the teams went into a full 10-minute overtime.

From that point on, it was like two boxers slugging it out at center ring and each refusing to be knocked out. The Barons and Hornets put on a show that only once before was equaled for longevity.

Two stout-hearted clubs battled through one 10-minute overtime and two twenty-minute sudden death periods with still no score.

Cleveland came out for the fourth overtime session with a big second wind and went after the game winner with a vengeance. But time after time Gil Mayer turned them back. Then it was the Hornets' turn to turn on the heat. They bombarded the gallant Johnny Bower. Finally, the cruel end for Cleveland came at 11:46 of the fourth overtime when Dan Lewicki scored to win the marathon for Pittsburgh.

It was a shame anyone had to lose a game like that one. The contest lasted nearly five and one-half hours and ended at 1:55 a.m.. The 121 minutes and 46 seconds of playing time were only 56 seconds shy of the longest game in League history. That was the Cleveland-Syracuse matchup in 1938 that was won by the Stars 3-2.

Biggest hero of the heartbreaking loss for Cleveland was Johnny Bower. The great netminder kicked

Johnny Bower makes a save in overtime against Pittsburgh in Game #7. Pictured is Bob Chrystal (#2) whose overtime goal gave the Barons a dramatic 1-0 Calder Cup championship. Cleveland State University archives – photo by Fred Bottomer.

out 78 saves for his evening's work. More than a dozen had "miracle" written on them.

The season now came down to one game. These two great rivals had already met 16 times this season, including playoffs. The record in Pittsburgh's favor was 8-7-1. It couldn't be much closer.

Game Seven was a close-checking, titanic struggle between the two great clubs. After a few close calls during the first period, the two defenses and goaltenders dominated. Neither squad could muster a goal, and regulation time ended with a 0-0 score. The tension was just unbelievable.

It seems incredible, and in a way somewhat sad, that this great championship would be decided by a fluke goal. But that's exactly what happened.

In the full 10-minute overtime, Cleveland kept the pressure on. After almost scoring, the Bailey-Stearns-Hildebrand line needed a rest. Bailey sent a pass to Bob Chrystal at the point. Coach Cook yelled, "Throw it in." And Chrystal obliged by lifting a long, soft lob in the direction of the Hornet net as the players changed lines "on the fly."

Chrystal turned to skate off the ice when a huge roar from the crowd made his heart jump into his throat. His 70-foot lob "shot" had gone in! Chrystal was stunned, and so was everyone on both clubs as the crowd celebrated in a frenzy.

Chrystal really didn't shoot the puck; he just lifted it in so the players could change lines. At its apex, the 70-foot shot was about 25 feet in the air. It was wide left of the cage. Hornet goalie Gil Mayer came out to trap or clear it on the bounce.

When the puck hit the ice, it took a crazy, almost right-angle bounce past the bewildered goalie and into the net! The score came at 6:23, and the Barons held on the rest of the way to win the championship.

"I didn't see it go in," yelled the ecstatic Bob Chrystal in the Barons' jubilant dressing room.

Coach Cook was still in shock. "It was the kind of series that almost had to be decided by something like that," stated the coach. "So close, and the teams so evenly matched that it took a break to do it."

Sports are strange. One crazy bounce of a puck has one entire city celebrating while another city weeps. Bob Chrystal is a hero, while poor goalie Gil Mayer is heartbroken.

After all the dust had cleared from one of the greatest playoff series in League history, the Calder Cup came to rest in Cleveland, Ohio for the sixth time.

The Barons celebrate their 1952-53 Calder Cup title.
Cleveland State University archives – photo by Fred Bottomer.

THE 1952-53 CLEVELAND BARONS

Front (L-R): Charles Homenuk, Trainer; Ike Hildebrand, James C. Hendy, General Manager; Johnny Bower, Richard L. (Dick) Kroesen, President; Jim Shirley, Fred (Bun) Cook, Coach; Jack Gordon, Captain; Lex Cook, Chief Scout. Second: Phil Simon, Stick Boy; Eddy Reigle, Steve Wochy, Fred Shero, Tom Williams, Cal Stearns, Fred Glover, Armand DelMonte, Ray Ceresino, Edward J. Coen, Publicity Director. Third: Tony Hemmerling, Scout; Frank Kubasek, Ott Heller, Gus Karrys, Ray Ross, Bob Bailey, Bob Chrystal, Glen Sonmor, Eddie Olson, Floyd Perras, Promotional Director. Kay Horiba collection.

FINAL STANDINGS
1952-53

West	W	L	T	GF	GA	PTS.
Cleveland	42	20	2	248	164	86
Pittsburgh	37	21	6	223	149	80
Syracuse	31	31	2	213	201	64
Hershey	31	32	1	208	217	63
Providence	27	36	1	215	254	55
St. Louis	26	37	1	212	258	53
Buffalo	22	39	3	160	236	47

Top Baron Scorers	G	A	PTS.
Eddie Olson	32	54	86
Jackie Gordon	20	58	78
Ike Hildebrand	38	34	72
Steve Wochy	37	31	68
Ray Ceresino	23	35	58
Glen Sonmor	25	26	51
Bob Bailey	11	35	46
Eddie Reigle	3	35	38
Fred Glover	12	19	31

Calder Cup Champion – Cleveland Barons

1953-54 SEASON

There were changes in the League and on the Barons roster since the previous season ended.

The St. Louis Flyers gave up their financial struggle and folded during the Summer of 1953. This made the League a compact six teams, the same as the National League. Rivalries would now be even more intense as every team would now play each other 14 times.

The Barons made a few off-season moves as usual. Most noteworthy was the departure of the great Johnny Bower. John was finally given a chance in the big league. After eight seasons in Cleveland, he really did not want to leave. But he would never know about the National League unless he gave it a try. His reluctant approval was given for a deal to be made.

Ike Hildebrand also went to New York as three Ranger-owned players came to Cleveland. Jim Hendy hated to sell off star players that the fans loved. But in those days when money was short, it was the only way to pay the bills and still get quality players as replacements. Inevitably, this practice took its toll on the team, but it had to be done.

Coming to Cleveland were goalie Emile (The Cat) Francis, Steve Kraftcheck, and Jack Stoddard.

Francis had the unenviable task of replacing Bower, but the flamboyant netminder was a great talent and became a crowd favorite. Defenseman Kraftcheck was back for his second tour of duty with the team. His hard-hitting style would blend in beautifully. Stoddard was a tall (6'3"), high-scoring right winger. Although Cleveland hated to part with Bower and Hildebrand, they received fine talent in return plus a bundle of cash.

The Barons also dealt Steve Wochy to Buffalo for Don Ashbee, a left wing. In one other deal, highly touted center Bob Bailey was sent to Toronto in the NHL. The Maple Leafs sent Chuck Blair to the Barons. Blair was a solid performer with the Leaf's Pittsburgh farm club that faced Cleveland in the previous year's finals.

With the addition of Kraftcheck, the Cleveland defense looked stronger than ever. The offense was a little suspect, but this team definitely looked like a title contender again.

After spending his rookie season of 1949-50 with the Barons, rough and tumble Steve Kraftcheck was sold to the Boston Bruins. He returned to Cleveland for 1953-54 and spent five outstanding seasons on the Barons' backline. Bill Hudec collection.

Emile "The Cat" Francis had big shoes to fill, taking over for the great Johnny Bower in goal. But he responded in fine fashion, leading the Barons to the 1953-54 Calder Cup championship. Here he attempts a save against Pittsburgh's Willie Marshall. #20 Gus Karrys defends. Cleveland State University archives.

The team's opening 2-2 road trip set the tone for the first month and a half of the season. The Barons were up and down and for the most part were inconsistent. One exception was goaltender Emile Francis.

"The Cat" had big shoes to fill. Those belonged to another goalie of the feline variety, "Panther Man" Johnny Bower. But Francis was quickly winning fans over to his entertaining style of play.

Emile was an acrobat on ice. While Bower stayed close to his cage and played the angles, Francis would wander far from his goalmouth to challenge shooters. Sometimes he would be caught hopelessly out of position. But more often than not, he would come up with a sprawling save. A man small in build, he stood out as a leader. Always calling out instructions to his defensemen, he kept every player on his toes, and the fans on the edge of their seats.

After going 9-10-0 in the season's early going, the Barons began to play some of their best hockey of the regular season as November drew to a close. Ten points behind the once-again powerful Buffalo Bisons, Cleveland swept back to back games from the division leaders. Particularly sweet was a 5-3 comeback victory in Buffalo after trailing 3-0.

Fred Glover, out of the lineup since October 28th with a knee injury, came back on December 5th against Hershey and was the center of attention as usual. Besides scoring two goals in a 5-2 win, he carried on a running feud with the Bears' Andy Branigan that nearly touched off a riot. Fred's fierce play was an inspiration to his club.

The team went on a 10-2-0 run in December that culminated in the Barons taking over 2nd place on Christmas night. There was no "good will to men" at the Arena that evening.

Once again Glover led the charge as Cleveland defeated the Bears 6-2. With the Barons up 4-2, a fight broke out between Fred and Hershey's league-leading scorer George Sullivan. As the players were watching, another tussle between Steve Kraftcheck and the Bears' Andy Branigan developed. That was all it took. Both benches emptied and fists flew everywhere.

The fans loved it, especially Fred Glover. While most "bad men" couldn't score a goal if the net was wide open, Fred had talent to boot. He could score, he could fight, he could do everything. His intensity was insidious. It spread to all his teammates. As soon as he stepped on the ice, the crowd would buzz. The fans knew that Fred would always stir things up.

Jim Hendy stirred things up himself when he traded the popular Glen Sonmor to New York for 21-year-old Andy Bathgate. Sonmor had been playing well, but Hendy wanted a forward who could play wing as well as center. The multi-talented Bathgate filled that bill.

Cleveland moved into first place in early January. One of the pleasant surprises on the team was Fred Shero. Previously a defensive defenseman who rarely scored, Fred had developed into a top goal-getter. He had 10 goals by January 8th and credited his switch from glasses to contact lenses. He never felt comfortable in his rough profession wearing glasses. His new found stickhandling and scoring ability was the talk of the League.

Also playing well was the line of Glover-Olson-Gordon. This trio was popping in goals at a super pace. They were a perfect blend. Keyed by the tremendous playmaking ability of Gordon, the threesome could move the puck up the ice with precise passes and set up plays in the offensive zone quicker than any other trio around.

A sudden reversal of form began on January 16th. Don Marshall's sudden death goal gave Buffalo a 5-4 overtime win. This was the first of three straight setbacks to Buffalo in January that sent the Barons into a tailspin that lasted over a month. By the middle of February, Cleveland was twelve points behind Buffalo and still sliding. First place was now out of the question and missing the playoffs a reality.

By February 22nd the Barons had lost 10 of their last 13 games. Jim Hendy and Bun Cook were mystified. Hendy blasted the club during a team meeting and threatened wholesale changes if they didn't get straightened out soon. "I don't know what's wrong, but I'm going to try to find out," stated the frustrated Hendy.

It seemed that there was a general lack of hustle. The team was just going through the motions. Both Hendy and Cook were at a loss as to the reason for the team's lack of spirit. Privately, Hendy questioned whether Cook was losing control of his team.

The tongue-lashing didn't work. The Barons lost seven games in a row and fell to an even 31-31-0 record. This was the worst slump in the team's history up to that point. It seemed as if the Barons' season was going down the drain.

One bright spot during the slump was the continued brilliant offensive output of defenseman Fred Shero. He broke the single season goal scoring mark for backliners with his 17th goal against the Pittsburgh Hornets on March 6th. The old mark of 16 had been held by ex-Baron Hy Buller.

The Barons ended their excursion into the land of Mr. Hyde by turning back into Dr. Jekyll just in time. The big spark was once again provided by Fred Glover.

Although they had lost seven in a row, Cleveland had a chance to clinch a playoff spot by defeating and eliminating the Providence Reds on March 7th. Glover led the attack as the Barons crushed the Reds 10-2. The line of Gordon-Olson-Glover was in high gear, especially Glover.

The tough right winger came up with two goals and four assists to pace a devastating attack. Scoring aside, it was Fred's leadership on the ice that inspired his teammates. He would not let his team lose again. When Fred set the tone, everyone else went along for the ride. Still, he could not do it alone. Eddie Olson chipped in with three goals, and Jackie Gordon scored one to go along with his four assists. The big line was back on the beam.

After losing their next game, Cleveland steamrolled through the balance of the schedule. By winning their last six games, the Barons finished in third place with a 38-32-0 record.

They put an exclamation point on their streak by blasting Syracuse 13-5 in the regular season finale. Hat tricks by Eddie Olson and Ray Ross paced the rout. The three goals by Olson gave him 40 on the season, a personal high. Hitting the jackpot was Jackie Gordon. The playmaker extraordinaire set a new team record with his two assists. His mark of 71 assists was a club mark that would never be broken.

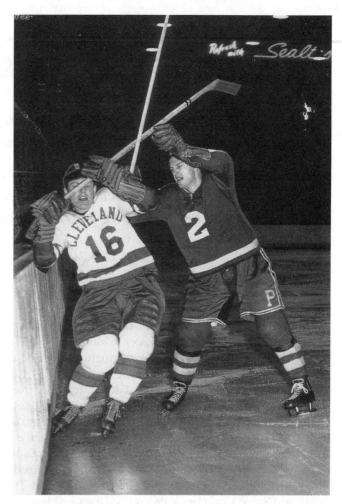

Ken Schultz (#16) takes a hit from Pittsburgh's Frank Mathers. Cleveland State University archives – photo by Fred Bottomer.

THE PLAYOFFS

By finishing third, the Barons faced the first place Buffalo Bisons in the best of five opening round of the playoffs.

Although Buffalo won the season series from Cleveland 9 games to 5, the Barons caught a break in playing Buffalo. The Bison had been reeling as they won only 6 of their last 15 games.

Still, they had built up such a big lead by mid-February that they still won the division by 7 points. Main reason for the slide was the recall of their star goalie Jacques Plante by the Montreal Canadiens. The team never recovered from this. Plante never did return to Buffalo as he launched a Hall of Fame career in Montreal.

Cleveland jumped on this opportunity with a vengeance in Game One and came away with a 7-2 victory. As usual, it was Freddie Glover leading the way. His two goals and three assists paced a brilliant show by his line as Gordon and Olson also scored. This trio dominated every time it stepped on the ice. In Game One, sub-goalie Jean Paul Renaud was completely befuddled by the constant onslaught. Fred Shero, who ended the regular season with a record 21 goals, and Steve Kraftcheck also scored for Cleveland.

In Game Two, Fred Glover became Buffalo's worst nightmare. Entering the third period trailing 3-2, Cleveland tied the game with a blistering goal by Chuck Blair.

The contest had all the earmarkings of an overtime affair until Glover took over. With a scant 32 seconds remaining, Eddie Olson won a face-off deep in the Buffalo end and got the puck over to Fred in front of the net. The great winger faked Renaud out of position and calmly flipped in the game winner. The entire Cleveland bench emptied onto the ice to congratulate the hero. Shortly after, Jackie Gordon scored into an empty net to give the Barons a 5-3 win.

Game Three in Cleveland was all Jackie Gordon and one of Cleveland's greatest comeback victories in their playoff history. Trailing by three goals, the Barons were looking at defeat until they rallied to shock the Bisons. Gordon tallied the game winner in the third period to send Cleveland into the finals for the tenth time. The super center fired two goals on the night and assisted on all of the other three in a great 5-4 win. The three-game sweep put Cleveland in the finals against long-time rival Hershey.

The Bears were coming off a dramatic series win over Pittsburgh. Trailing by two games, Hershey rallied for three straight wins to oust the Hornets. The fifth and deciding game was won 3-2 in two overtimes by the Bears. The biggest hero for the winners was Gordon Henry, and he proved to be the difference in Game One against the Barons in the best of seven finals.

Henry, a ten-year veteran star, hung a 3-0 shutout on Cleveland in the series opener. The Barons frantically tried to stay in the game but could not dent the Bear defense at Hershey.

Game Two at Chocolate Town saw the return to form of the Gordon-Olson-Glover line as the Barons skated to a 4-2 victory. Olson led the way with two goals and Glover one. Jackie Gordon assisted on three goals to give him 15 points for the playoffs, three shy of the record. The split in Hershey was just what Cleveland had hoped for. They now had home ice advantage as the series shifted to Cleveland.

Game Three at the Arena saw Cleveland's number two line rise to the occasion. Trailing 2-0, Andy Bathgate started the home team's comeback with a goal at 7:23 of the second period. After Ray Ross and defenseman Steve Kraftcheck tied the score at 3-3, Eddie Reigle, now playing as a forward, and Chuck Blair put Cleveland on top for a 5-3 victory. With three goals, this was the first time in the playoffs that a line other than Gordon's came to the front. It took so much pressure off the #1 line and gave the team a big lift.

Cleveland did not play well in Game Four, but still came away with a 3-1 win thanks to the great goaltending of Emile Francis. The Cat was spectacular when the Barons needed him most. The Barons looked stale and really couldn't generate much offense as the Hersheys controlled much of the play. But they couldn't overcome the great play of Francis. "I believe Francis played his greatest game for us," stated Coach Cook after the game. "Several times I was just waiting for the goal light to flash."

The Cat couldn't save the Barons in Game Five. Continuing their suddenly poor play, Cleveland was overwhelmed by the Bears at Hershey 7-1.

With star goalie Gordon Henry out with a knee injury, Cleveland thought they would have an easy

time of it against Jim Shirley. They were sadly mistaken as the Hershey defense threw up a brick wall in front of the spare netminder. Suddenly, memories of past playoff disasters confronted the Barons. They went back to Cleveland with a 3-2 series lead and were determined to win the Calder Cup on their home ice.

Things looked dark after one period in Game Six as Hershey led 1-0. But Fred Shero and Chuck Blair put Cleveland ahead before Hershey's Arnie Kullman tied the score again. Soon after Kullman's goal, Gus Karrys and Fred Glover scored to put Cleveland on top 4-2. The Barons appeared over the hump.

When Andy Bathgate scored at 3:06 of the final period, it was all over but the shouting. Hershey did score late in the game, but it was too little too late.

With the 5-3 victory, Cleveland had its seventh Calder Cup and for the first time back-to-back championships. Jackie Gordon, drawing an assist on Glover's goal, scored his 18th playoff point. This tied the record of Fred Thurier, Frank Mario of Hershey, and Barry Sullivan of Providence.

This was not the greatest of Cleveland's championship teams. But it was a team that could pick itself off the floor and play big when it had to. Once again, the Barons had done the City of Cleveland proud.

FINAL STANDINGS
1953-54

West	W	L	T	GF	GA	PTS.
Buffalo	39	24	7	283	217	85
Hershey	37	29	4	274	243	78
Cleveland	38	32	0	269	227	76
Pittsburgh	34	31	5	250	222	73
Providence	26	40	4	211	276	56
Syracuse	24	42	4	215	317	52

Top Baron Scorers	G	A	PTS.
Jackie Gordon	31	71	102
Eddie Olson	40	54	94
Fred Glover	23	42	65
Cal Stearns	21	42	63
Jack Stoddard	23	34	57
Fred Shero	21	33	54
Ray Ross	16	23	39
Chuck Blair	23	15	38
Ray Ceresino	14	22	36
Eddie Reigle	10	26	36
Andy Bathgate	13	18	31

Calder Cup Champion – Cleveland Barons

1954-55 SEASON

The Barons held on to all of their big names from the previous year's Calder Cup squad. Only minor changes were made.

Ray Ceresino was sold to Providence, and Jack Stoddard was dropped. Young Andy Bathgate was returned to the New York Rangers, where he went on to superstardom.

Four new youngsters were brought up to Cleveland from the farm system or amateur ranks. Forwards Gordon Vejprava, Billy Ford, and Jim Farelli gave the Barons new speed and muscle up front. Johnny McLellan was purchased from Pittsburgh.

Rough and tough defenseman Ian Cushenan made the jump from the St. Catherine's junior ranks. He added more muscle to an already strong backline.

Although Cleveland was highly touted coming out of training camp, they opened the season with an unsuccessful 1-3-1 road trip. Things got worse when the Barons dropped their home opener to Springfield 5-1 and heard a few catcalls from the fans. Even though the season was in its infancy, last place was unfamiliar territory for Cleveland. But their stay there was short as they bounced up on their feet with four straight wins.

Still, the Barons were inconsistent for most of the 1954 portion of their schedule, with one large exception. The Gordon-Olson-Glover line was playing phenomenal hockey. They were by far the best line in the League and had picked up right where they left off in last season's playoffs.

By the end of November, the torrid trio was the talk of the AHL. Glover, who earlier had an 18-game scoring streak, was leading the League in scoring with 15 goals and 20 assists for 35 points. Right behind was Eddie Olson with 32 points on 17 goals and 15 assists. The glue between these two great wingers was Jackie Gordon. The great playmaker had 25 assists to go along with his 4 goals. He was content to set up the plays and let his linemates score.

Unfortunately, word was getting around the League that if you could stop Cleveland's big line, you could beat the Barons. They were just not getting much production from their second and third lines.

Two important deals were made to add more punch to the lineup. In mid-November the Barons sent Ray Ross to Providence and farmed out Ian Cushenan to the Quebec Aces. These moves made room for the return of Eric Pogue from Vancouver and Glen Sonmor from the New York Rangers. Glen, in particular, was a joyous sight for Cleveland fans. Now in his third tour of duty with the Barons, Sonmor was extremely popular. His high-spirited play was always a lift to his team. He hoped that his third stint here would be a lucky charm. Instead, fate was playing a cruel game with Glen.

Jim Hendy pulled off one more important deal on December 4th. Cleveland sent Chuck Blair to Buffalo in return for big Joe Lund. Lund played in Cleveland before and was a big hero in the Barons' Calder Cup victory of 1950-51. Conversely, he helped eliminate Cleveland the next year after being traded to Providence.

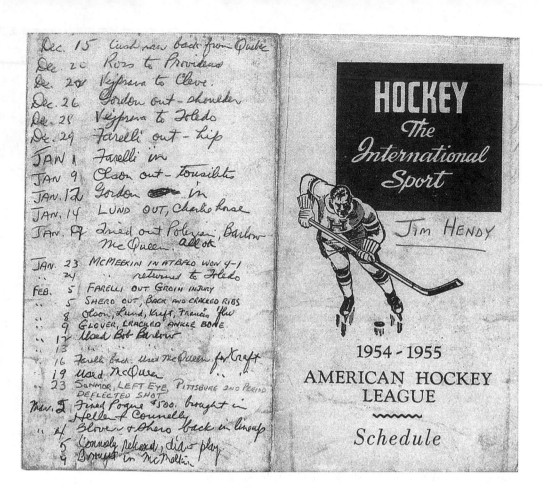

James Peter Hudy collection.

It didn't take long for Lund to make an impression with his new club, as he had a career night one week after joining Cleveland. In a record-breaking game, Big Joe scored 7 points on three goals and four assists in a 12-0 blasting of first-place Springfield. The Indians were back in Springfield for the first time in three years. Relocated to Syracuse when the Army took over their arena during the Korean conflict, Eddie Shore moved back East as soon as the war ended.

The 12-0 whitewash was the largest margin of victory in a shutout in League history and made Joe Lund an overnight celebrity. Once he had been noted only as a hard-hitting defenseman, but this game made him a force to be reckoned with at forward. This was not a flash in the pan. Joe scored 20 goals in Buffalo the year before. His hard work was paying off. The big win evened Cleveland's record at 11-11-2, good for fourth place in the tight race.

Cleveland went 5-3 over the next two weeks and moved into second place on December 31st after an 8-2 win over the Indians at Springfield. Biggest gun for Cleveland was still Freddie Glover. He scored two goals against Springfield to follow up his four-goal outburst against Providence the night before.

Fred was still leading the League in scoring, but it was a game against Pittsburgh at the Arena on January 14th that had people buzzing all around the League.

To set the stage, one has to go back to a game at the Arena against the Hornets on November 11th. In this game, Pittsburgh's rookie defenseman Bill Burega emerged as a "bad man" extraordinaire. Burega had been throwing his huge bulk around all evening. But the big, broad-shouldered rookie hit a new low midway in the second period. With stick raised, he purposely cross-checked little Gordon Vejprava across the mouth, knocking out three of the diminutive center's teeth. It was strictly a cowardly act.

Ian Cushenan tried to come to "Vejy's" aid but could not get full vengeance. One Baron would not forget this night – Fred Glover. Nobody got away with that kind of vicious play against Fred or his teammates. He played the game "an eye for an eye, a tooth for a tooth." He may not be able to pay someone back that same night; but somewhere down the road, the bell would toll. It tolled for Bill Burega on January 14th.

Glover was in a surly mood all night. The team was in the midst of a bad losing streak. They would go 0-7-1 and fall to last place by January 23rd. This put them 13 points out of first.

In the Hornet game, Glover was hit with a 10-minute misconduct penalty after arguing with referee Scotty Morrison over a tripping penalty.

This put Fred near the boiling point. Added to that, he had been carrying on a running feud with Burega all night. Finally, in the third period's first minute, Glover blew his top. Fred and Burega engaged in a long and spectacular fight that even amazed the players with its ferocity. The two combatants were separated once but went at it again. Burega was tough, but Glover clearly was the winner

Glen Sonmor had three tours of duty with the Barons, his last ending tragically with the loss of his left eye. His fighting spirit made Glen one of the most popular Baron players ever. Bill Hudec collection.

as he made the Hornet pay for knocking out Gordy Vejprava's teeth two months earlier. Burega had to be helped to the dressing room.

In all, Glover received a record 31 penalty minutes for the game – three minor 2-minute penalties, one 5-minute major for fighting, and two 10-minute misconducts! The old Arena never saw a wild party like this one. But a point was made loud and clear: If anyone unfairly messed with a Cleveland Baron, he would have Fred Glover to answer to.

Cleveland finally ended its losing ways when they won at Buffalo on January 16th. The victory was noteworthy because Roy McMeekin was in goal. Coach Cook was concerned with the play of Emile Francis. He borrowed McMeekin from Toledo of the International League for a one-game tryout. The 200-pound McMeekin was very impressive in a hint of things to come.

The Barons' visit to the uncomfortable surroundings of the League basement was shortlived. They ended their slump by winning the last three games of a five-game road trip. They didn't stop there, as they added three more wins on home ice. The six-game winning streak was their longest of the season and put them only five points out of first place on February 7th. With a 22-21-3 record, Cleveland was right in the thick of a five-way battle for first place. Only Providence was out of the running. The League was so balanced that a few wins or losses in a row by any team made a big shift in the standings.

Thus, Cleveland could finish fifth just as easily as finishing first.

Reason for the reversal of fortune was defense. "We decided that we'd just have to tighten up our defenses and play the game closer to the vest," said a happy Bun Cook. "...we would have to concentrate a little more on keeping the other fellows from scoring." Obviously, the strategy paid dividends. The Clevelanders only allowed 2.1 goals per game during the six-game winning streak.

Just when everyone figured that the team was about to roll into first place, leading scorer Fred Glover suffered a cracked ankle against Hershey and was lost for three weeks. With Fred Shero already out with a bad back, the new blow was a killer. Without their leader, Cleveland lost three straight and dropped into fifth place.

"That's all it takes...we just have to get mad at somebody," hollered a jubilant Glen Sonmor after the Barons blasted Hershey 7-4 to end their latest losing skein. Cleveland, indeed, got mad. 17 penalties were called in the roughhouse contest. Leading the mayhem was none other than goalie Emile Francis, who got into a wild fracas with Hershey's Norm Corcoran. Eddie Olson led the scoring parade as he now had taken over the League's scoring lead from injured Fred Glover.

As the season wound down to the stretch run, Glen Sonmor met his destiny. After the Hershey win, Glen's wife Margaret gave birth to their first child, Kathleen Ann, on February 19th. Sonmor was on top of the world.

Three days later the Barons suited up for a big game at Pittsburgh against the first-place Hornets, whom they trailed by eight points.

The Hornets jumped out to a 2-0 lead and seemed in command. But the feisty Sonmor put Cleveland back in the game with a beautiful goal at 18:55 of the first period. That the Barons went on to win 3-2 seemed incidental after the game.

At the 5:08 mark of the second period, defenseman Steve Kraftcheck wound up and fired a long hard shot toward the Hornet goal. Along the way, the puck struck the stick of a Hornet defenseman and ricocheted upwards into Glen Sonmor's left eye. Glen went down as if shot by a bullet. One could hear a pin drop in the Pittsburgh arena as Sonmor writhed in pain.

Eventually Glen was carried off the ice and attended by Hornet physician Dr. Phillip Faix. Eleven stitches were needed to close the cuts around his eye before Sonmor was taken to Mercy Hospital.

After examination, doctors reported that Glen had some light perception in the eye but it would be several days before the full extent of the injury would be determined.

Sonmor remained at Mercy Hospital for nearly two weeks before the bad news finally came. Glen had lost all sight in his left eye. Efforts to regain his sight in the injured eye had failed. Sonmor would never play hockey again.

Shock waves were felt throughout all of hockey, for Glen was an extremely popular player. While his teammates won five in a row before losing two after the injury, their hearts were with Sonmor. But still the games had to be played.

As the team prepared for an important three-game road trip, their March 16th game against Pittsburgh was designated Glen Sonmor Night. All gate receipts would be given to the fallen Baron.

Cleveland went 2-1 on the road to pull within three points of Pittsburgh with three games remaining. Glen Sonmor Night was a big night indeed.

165

THE PLAYOFFS

All four playoff teams were so evenly matched that there was no clear-cut favorite. Any team that got hot or caught a break could end up champion.

Bun Cook went against past form and started rookie goalie Roy McMeekin over Emile Francis. Cook had always gone with a veteran netminder in the playoffs. But McMeekin played so well down the stretch that Cook went with his hunch that Roy could get the job done.

Coach Cook never found out if his hunch was right because McMeekin hurt his knee at 4:35 of the third period in Game One while making a big save to preserve the 2-2 tie. Emile Francis, who hadn't played since March 5th, came to the rescue.

Buffalo had jumped out to a 2-0 lead before goals by Cal Stearns and Jackie Gordon tied things up. It remained that way through regulation, and the game went into overtime.

The Cat was fantastic in goal for Cleveland as he turned in one fine save after another during the first extra period. Buffalo was dominating play, and it seemed just a matter of time before they would end it. And end it they did at 7:30 of the second overtime on a goal by Ken Wharram, his third of the night. Francis was heroic in defeat, but he never had a chance on Wharram's deflection.

The Barons were in dire straits when Buffalo grabbed a 2-0 first-period lead in Game Two at the Arena. The home crowd's jeers turned to cheers when goals by Joe Lund and Eddie Olson tied the score.

The cheers turned to a thunderous ovation when fearless Freddie Glover took the game into his own hands.

On a give-and-go play with Jackie Gordon, Fred put the Barons on top at 5:20 of the second period. He got another on a pass from Olson nearly eight minutes later.

After the teams traded third-period goals, Glover completed his big night by scoring with four minutes left to play. It capped a great evening for Fred and gave him his first career playoff hat trick. More importantly, the playoffs were tied at one game apiece as the series shifted to Buffalo.

The Barons should have stayed home. One thing after another went wrong as the aroused Bisons demoralized Cleveland 8-0 in Game Three. The mistakes seemed to snowball; and the harder they tried, the worse the Barons played. It was one of those games, but it left Cleveland on the brink of elimination.

Coach Cook tried Roy McMeekin in goal for Game Four. While the big puck stopper was game, the Barons still went down to defeat 6-4. But went down fighting.

Down 4-1 as the result of three Buffalo power-play goals, the Barons almost pulled the contest out. Third-period scores by Red Williams, Eric Pogue, and Fred Glover cut the Bison lead to one. But Ken Wharram fired the clincher into an open net to end Cleveland's two-year title reign.

The in and out Barons picked the wrong time to go out. Now they were out for the year. The team faced a serious rebuilding job. But there was light at the end of the tunnel.

What warmed Coach Cook the most while on the road was everyone's concern for Sonmor. "In every rival city we visited on this last trip...Pittsburgh, Springfield, Hershey...players and fans kept coming up to me and asking: 'How's Glen?'...How's Sonmor getting along?'...How's Glen's eye?,'" the great coach said in amazement. "I guess everyone knows him as a great guy." Checks were pouring in from fans and teams in both the NHL and AHL.

Unfortunately, Glen was not released from Mercy Hospital in time to attend the game. Still it was an extremely emotional night. Tears flowed from fans and players alike as Sonmor said a few heartfelt words of thanks via taped recording. His wife, Margaret, talked to the crowd of 7,734 and dropped the puck in a ceremonial faceoff.

The night was a huge success as the game itself raised $8,772 for the Sonmor fund. Much more was added to the till from contributions by fans and other teams.

Sonmor was a unique individual. Throughout the tragedy, he remained in great spirits despite the heartache he felt inside. He never could play the game he loved again.

However, Glen got his degree from the University of Minnesota. He remained in the game as a great college and professional coach. After his coaching career, he became one of the most respected front office executives in hockey. He truly was a credit to the game, and hockey was all the better off because of him.

The only negative aspect of the night was that the Barons lost to Pittsburgh 3-1. This eliminated Cleveland from any chance at first place.

The Barons bounced back and won their final two games of the season. In the final game, Cleveland defeated Buffalo 2-1 in sudden death overtime on a goal by Johnny McLellan. The victory gave Cleveland a 32-29-3 record for 67 points, and a tie with Springfield and Buffalo. Pittsburgh finished first with 70 points.

Springfield had an identical 32-29-3 record, but Cleveland was awarded second place by virtue of scoring more goals, 254 to 251. The Indians finished third by having one more win than fourth place Buffalo.

Despite the great tragedy of Glen Sonmor, the season did have its bright moments. Eddie Olson led the League in scoring for the second time. His 88 points were scored on 41 goals and 47 assists. Fred Glover finished fourth with 75 points. He also established himself as the most respected and feared player in the League. Ready or not, Cleveland prepared to meet Buffalo in the best of five opening round of the playoffs.

FINAL STANDINGS
1954-55

	W	L	T	GF	GA	PTS.
Pittsburgh	31	25	8	187	180	70
Cleveland	32	29	3	254	222	67
Springfield	32	29	3	251	233	67
Buffalo	31	28	5	248	228	67
Hershey	29	28	7	217	225	63
Providence	21	37	6	194	263	48

Top Baron Scorers	G	A	PTS.
Eddie Olson	41	47	88
Fred Glover	33	42	75
Joe Lund	24	44	68
Jackie Gordon	17	50	67
John McLellan	30	31	61
Cal Stearns	18	24	42
Billy Ford	18	22	40
Eddie Reigle	7	30	37
Jim Farelli	14	23	37
Glen Sonmor	11	21	32

Calder Cup Champion – Pittsburgh Hornets

1954-55 CLEVELAND BARONS

Front (L-R): Edward J. Coen, publicity director; Emile (The Cat) Francis; Eric Pogue, Fred (Bun) Cook, Coach; Jack Gordon, Captain; James C. Hendy, General Manager; Fred Glover, Roy McMeekin, Lex Cook, Chief Scout. Seated on floor: Elmo Baumann, Stick Boy. Second: Billy Ford, John McLellan, Ian Cushenan, Gus Karrys, Joe Lund, Ott Heller, Tom Williams, Fred Shero. Third: Charles Homenuk, Trainer; Eddy Reigle, Jimmy Farelli, Steve Kraftcheck, Glen Sonmor, Eddie Olson, Cal Stearns, Floyd Perras, Promotion Director. Larry Smith collection.

1955-56 SEASON

During the off-season, the Barons were sold to a group of local Cleveland businessmen put together by Jim Hendy. Stock was sold to the public as the hockey team became community-owned for the first time. Claire W. Grove was named president, while Hendy retained his role as vice president and general manager.

Hendy had his work cut out for him as the team embarked on a youth movement. In fact, the 1955-56 season was a year of transition for the Barons. With 81 players in the Cleveland system, the time had come to give more than a few of them a chance. Players were brought in and out all season long for a short look-see and then sent out for more seasoning. Many youngsters got their feet wet as the team, for the most part, was committed to youth.

Necessitating the youth movement was the departure of veteran stars Eddie Olson, Eddie Reigle, and Emile Francis. Olson's shoes were the biggest to fill. The two-time scoring champion took a position as player-coach with Vancouver of the Western Hockey League. His leadership and high-spirited play left an indelible mark on the Cleveland sporting scene.

Eddie Reigle retired to coach in the Baron's farm system. The team decided to go with Roy McMeekin in goal and released the Cat, Emile Francis.

Taking their place, among others, were youngsters Gordon Vejprava, Dan Poliziani, Gerry Prince, Gus Karrys, Ed MacQueen, and Ron Morgan.

Early in the season the kids were the talk of the League. With high-spirited play, and a seemingly inexhaustible supply of energy, the young Barons were holding their own against their much more experienced opposition.

But eventually the inexperience of the kids began to manifest itself. Players were beginning to get caught out of position on a regular basis. The helter-skelter play often led to many easy opponent goals. "This team has a lot of courage and is one of the fastest I've ever had," stated Coach Cook. "But we've all made mistakes, including myself, and we must learn by them."

The Barons finished the 1955 portion of their schedule with a respectable 13-12-5 record. They were firmly entrenched in fourth place. Providence and Pittsburgh were proving to be the class of the League, while Hershey and Springfield were far behind Cleveland in the basement. Buffalo found itself in the middle of the pack with the Barons.

Providence truly was the team to beat. The Reds were bolstered by the return of one Johnny Bower. The great Panther Man returned to the AHL by way of New York. After one great season in the Big Apple, the Rangers decided to go with Lorne "Gump" Worsely in goal. They sent Bower to Vancouver for one season and placed Johnny in Providence for the current campaign. One has to wonder about New York's wisdom here.

Bower had a superb 2.45 goals against average in the Ranger nets. Still this was not deemed good enough. His demotion to Providence made the Reds odds-on favorites for the AHL title.

Cal Stearns poured in 35 goals during the 1955-56 season, including a remarkable 13 during the month of February. Bill Hudec collection.

One thing was certain about the Barons. This was the roughest Cleveland hockey club to date. Roughhouse play would characterize Barons' hockey for the next decade, and this team could slug it out with the best of them. "We've got some guys who play rough," understated Jim Hendy. "They don't take any guff from anybody." Players like Fred Glover, Jim Farelli, John McLellan, and Ian Cushenan loved to mix it up. In one back-to-back series with the Pittsburgh Hornets, an amazing total of 63 penalties were called.

Leading the way, of course, was Freddie Glover. By mid-December the rugged winger had piled up 82 penalty minutes on his way to a club record of 187. Ironically, much of Fred's trouble stemmed from his close association with the rule book.

Early in his career, Fred's ambition was to be a referee when his playing days were over. Of course, he never dreamed that his playing days would stretch through the 1967-68 season. He knew the rules inside and out. This, in fact, led to his many misconduct penalties. In the heat of battle, Fred would often argue vehemently with the refs over rule interpretations. More often than not, he would blow his stack and wind up in the penalty box. This made him a marked man in the referee's eyes. As he got older, these infractions lessened. But his notorious aggressive play never abated. When a point was to be made with fisticuffs, nobody made a better point than Fred Glover.

During a heartbreaking 4-3 overtime loss at Providence on Christmas night, Glover got into a wild melee with the Red's George McAvoy. Two Providence players jumped in to aid their teammate. One player, Camille Bedard, swung wildly and accidentally decked Howie Glover, Fred's brother, who was called up for a two-game tryout. Naturally, brother Fred then directed his rage at Bedard. It was always in the best interest of opposing players to not mess with the pugilistic Baron star.

After staying within shouting distance of Providence and Pittsburgh during the first half of the season, the roof caved in during January. The team won only one game during the entire month and saw their record dip to 14-20-7. They were as cold as the winter weather outside.

Injuries to star players such as Jackie Gordon, Gordon Vejprava, and Gus Karrys were contributing factors. But inexperience was the main culprit. The injuries allowed management the opportunity to shuttle in amateurs for brief tryouts. Future stars such as Bob Barlow, Art Stratton, and Bo Elik got their feet wet during these trying times. They would come back in the near future to help lead the Barons during better times.

An important deal was pulled off by Jim Hendy on February 1st, and it sparked a reversal of fortunes in February.

The Barons sent Eric Pogue to Buffalo for veteran forward Ken Hayden. One of the better goal scorers in the League for the past few seasons, Hayden was recovering from a broken ankle. That the injury was healed was evident, as the right winger scored 14 goals for Cleveland during the last 14 games of the season.

During the month of February, the Clevelanders posted a 8-4-0 mark to move within two points of Buffalo for third place. Leading the upsurge in the standings was Cal Stearns.

Until the month began, Cal had been used primarily as a penalty killer. This was in deference to the youth movement. But when Coach Cook called upon the veteran, Stearns responded in a big way. Cal poured in 13 goals in February's 12 games to spark the Cleveland comeback. Stearn's play, coupled with the arrival of Ken Hayden and the steady brilliance of Fred Glover, gave Cleveland fans a lot to cheer about.

The Barons rolled off four straight victories in early March. They finally moved into third place all alone by defeating Pittsburgh 7-4 on March 9th. Joe

Lund, Ken Hayden, and Gordy Vejprava struck for two goals apiece, while Cal Stearns scored a single. The game was a typical Cleveland-Pittsburgh donnybrook with fights and penalties galore. Baron rookie defenseman Ron Morgan was even knocked cold by a tough Jack Bionda check. It took several minutes to revive the rookie, but he showed his mettle by coming back to play the third period.

Fred Glover scored a hat trick to pace Cleveland to a 6-4 win over Hershey on March 14th. The victory improved the club's record to an even 26-26-7. The team had played great hockey for a month and a half and 3rd place looked good.

Unfortunately, the season lasted five games too long as the Barons blew third place by losing their final five games. All their hard work to catch Buffalo went down the drain with the late season slump.

The 26-31-7 record was nothing to write home about. Still, the fans appreciated the Barons' aggressive style of play, and it showed at the box office. Attendance for the 32 home games was 201,000. This averaged out to 6,281 per game. While this did not approach the glory days of the 1940's, it did mark an increase of 35% over the previous year.

The big question was whether or not the Barons were ready for their best-of-five playoff series against the second-place Pittsburgh Hornets.

THE PLAYOFFS

For the first time in years, the Barons were huge underdogs entering the Pittsburgh series. The Hornets finished second behind Providence by a mere two points. Their 90 points was 27 more than Cleveland.

Still, the Barons held their own against the much stronger Hornets during the regular season. The local icers' 5-6-1 record with Pittsburgh showed that they could play inspired hockey when they put their mind to it.

On paper, the Hornets were the far superior club, and they showed it with a 3-1 victory in Game One. Surprisingly, the Barons played a listless game. If not for the great goaltending of Roy McMeekin, the game would have been a rout. The big goalie kicked out 42 shots to keep his club in the game. But except for a goal by Jackie Gordon, the Barons could never mount a serious attack.

Cleveland trailed 3-0 after one period in Game Two at Pittsburgh. Their goose appeared to be cooked. "There isn't much I can say to you boys," Coach Cook told his players between periods. "Let's just go out there and keep plugging." And plug away they did.

The spark was lit when Johnny McLellan scored on a scramble in front of Hornet goalie Gil Mayer. When McLellan lit the red light again seven minutes later, the Barons were back in the game. They played like a team possessed. When Jackie Gordon tied the score at 14:39, the Cleveland bench exploded. But ex-Baron Bob Bailey put the Hornets back on top 4-3 a short time later.

The two teams battled ferociously all during the third period. It looked as if Bailey's goal would hold up. But nobody told Joe Lund. The big winger tied the score at 4-4 with only 20 seconds remaining in regulation time. The Pittsburgh team and crowd was stunned. They thought that they had the game in the bag.

Big Joe Lund wasn't through yet. During a full ten-minute overtime, Lund scored the go-ahead goal. Fred Glover added another, and Cleveland had an unbelievable 6-4 win. The Barons seemed down for the count, but somehow got off the floor to win a remarkable game. With the series tied 1-1, the teams headed back to Cleveland for the pivotal third game.

Game Three was more overtime fun for these two fierce rivals. With the score tied at four apiece, the teams battled through a scoreless ten-minute extra session. This set up a twenty-minute sudden death period.

Both clubs played somewhat cautiously at first, waiting for a break. The break came for Cleveland at the 8:30 mark. Johnny McLellan was parked next to the Hornet cage when he was left momentarily unguarded. From the point at the blueline, Ian Cushenan spotted the wide-open McLellan and fired a bullet pass to the winger. Johnny twirled around and beat Gil Mayer to give the Barons a 5-4 victory. More importantly, Cleveland was now only one game from the finals.

Game Four at the Arena was a classic. The Hornets, fighting for their playoff lives, took a 2-0 first-period lead on a pair of goals by Joe Klukay.

Things looked bad for Cleveland until Jackie Gordon fired a shorthanded goal at 18:16 of the second period. The Baron captain won a faceoff deep in the Pittsburgh end and shot his team back into the game.

Spurred on by the loud and vocal crowd, the local icers tied it up at 11:02 of the third period. Big Joe Lund, always a clutch performer, got the tying goal on a pass from Steve Kraftcheck.

Once again, the teams went into overtime. The tension was electric as the Hornets and Barons battled through a full 10-minute overtime plus a 20-minute sudden death period with still no score.

Both teams were exhausted during the third overtime. The end finally came at 14:02, when Jackie Gordon once again came through when his team needed him most. His game-winning goal came at 17 minutes past midnight and set off a wild celebration. The Barons had pulled off one of the greatest upsets in their history. Their reward was the chance to play the powerful Providence Reds in the finals.

The Reds were loaded. Boasting the League-scoring champion in Zelio Toppazzini (42 goals, 71 assists, for 113 points), and 50-goal scorer Camille Henry, Providence had a great attack. More importantly, they had the great Johnny Bower in goal. Many experts felt Johnny was the top goalie in all of hockey (even if the New York Rangers didn't). Any team with Bower in goal was an excellent threat to win a title.

Providence also had the most boisterous fans in the League. They were like an extra man on the ice. One never knew what to expect from the frenzied Reds fans. Once, when a Red player scored against Cleveland, an exuberant fan took off his wooden leg and tossed it on the ice in celebration. No one was sure how he got home that night, but he hopped around merrily.

The Barons were playing a vastly superior team, and it showed. The first two games in Providence were strictly no contest. The Reds dominated both games and won 6-1 and 7-2 respectively. Johnny Bower was terrific in goal for the home team, especially in Game One. In that one, he turned aside 45 shots to break the Barons' hearts.

In Game Three at Cleveland, Bower once again was the difference. The Barons stayed in the game on goals by Joe Lund and Jim Farelli. If not for the great play of Bower, Cleveland might have scored in double figures. His biggest save came at the eighteen-minute mark of the final period.

With the Reds leading 3-2, Cal Stearns broke free in front of the Providence net and fired what appeared to be the tying goal. But somehow the Panther Man dove from nowhere and made the save. The Reds then scored into an empty net when Coach Cook pulled his netminder in favor of an extra attacker. The 4-2 Providence win put the Reds on the threshold of a championship sweep.

The Reds got out their brooms and completed the sweep in Game Four. The Barons fought hard to the bitter end but succumbed to the better team 6-3.

In essence, this was the tale of the series. Providence simply was the better club, and Cleveland had used all of its magic in defeating Pittsburgh in the opening playoff round.

Still, strides were made. Many young players gained invaluable experience. Soon the light at the end of the tunnel would become a shining beacon of joy.

FINAL STANDINGS
1955-56

	W	L	T	GF	GA	PTS.
Providence	45	17	2	263	193	92
Pittsburgh	43	17	4	271	186	90
Buffalo	29	30	5	239	250	63
Cleveland	26	31	7	225	231	59
Hershey	19	39	6	218	271	44
Springfield	17	45	2	212	297	36

Top Baron Scorers	G	A	PTS.
Fred Glover	31	48	79
Cal Stearns	35	36	71
Jackie Gordon	26	43	69
Joe Lund	30	32	62
Gordon Vejprava	20	16	36
Steve Kraftcheck	5	29	34
Ken Hayden	16	15	31

Calder Cup Champion – Providence Reds

THE 1955-56 CLEVELAND BARONS

Back (L-R) Gordon Vejprava, Ike Hildebrand, Howard Lee, Ken Hayden, Cal Stearns, Gordon Stratton, Jerry Prince, Steve Kraftcheck, Floyd Perras, Promotional Director. Second: Charles Homenuk, Trainer; Jim Farelli, Ronald Morgan, Joe Lund, Gus Karrys, Ian Cushenan, John McLellan, Tom Williams, Edward J. Coen, Publicity Director. Front: Fred (Bun) Cook, Coach; Fred Glover, James C. Hendy, Vice-President and General Manager; Roy McMeekin, Claire Grove, President; Jack Gordon, Captain; Lex Cook, Chief Scout. Seated: Elmo Baumann, Stick Boy. Bill Hudec collection.

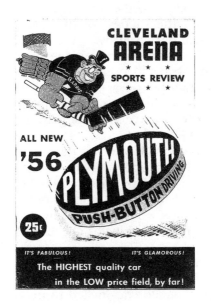

1956-57 SEASON

The end of an era in Cleveland hockey came on June 6, 1956 when Bun Cook resigned as coach of the Barons. In truth, his resignation came at the request of the Barons' executive board.

It was no secret to insiders that there were strained relations between Cook and vice president and general manager Jim Hendy. They didn't see eye to eye on a number of issues. The tempest in the teapot centered around Cook's handling of his players. The coach took a fatherly approach toward his team. Obviously, it worked. Cook won more championships than any other coach in the game.

Still, Hendy thought he should have won more. He, and many of the team's stockholders, thought that Coach Cook was too soft on his players. Hendy actually wanted to make the change years before, but the team was doing so well that he resisted, fearing bad publicity.

So Bun Cook was gone. One of the game's truly great gentlemen, he took with him a legendary coaching record. In a Cleveland career that covered 13 seasons, Cook coached 847 regular season games, winning 488, losing 276, and tying 83. His teams won 5 Calder Cup titles and 7 regular season championships. Before coming to Cleveland, Bun coached 6 years at Providence, winning 2 Calder Cups.

The greatest coach in AHL history would be missed in Cleveland. He was one of sport's most well liked figures, beloved by players and fans alike.

Hired to replace Cook was Baron star center Jackie Gordon. Even the 28-year-old Gordon was surprised when asked to coach the team by Jim Hendy. It was an opportunity Gordon could not pass up. Jack was a highly respected individual who would not be intimidated by anyone. He had his own ideas

Jackie Gordon became Player-Coach of the Barons for the 1956-57 season after Bun Cook stepped down. The star playmaking center was an instant success as he won the Calder Cup during his rookie year behind the bench. Bill Hudec collection.

Left Winger Bo Elik enjoyed a tremendous first season in the American Hockey League during the 1956-57 season. After scoring 23 goals in the team's first 23 games, Bo finished with a total of 40 and was elected Rookie of the Year. Kay Horiba collection.

on coaching and intended to make his own imprint on the team. His contract as player-coach was for one year, with automatic renewal at the end of each season if agreed upon by both parties.

The new coach would operate with many of the veterans from last season's club plus five new and important rookies. The four newcomers from the amateur ranks were Bo Elik, Jimmy Moore, Bill Shvetz, and Pete Goegan. All would play major roles in the team's success this season.

In goal, the Barons released Roy McMeekin. In his place would be another rookie, Marcel Paille. The 23-year-old netminder was obtained for the year from the New York Rangers. His rights would return to New York at season's end.

Except for veterans Glover, Stearns, Kraftcheck, McLellan, Gordon, and Hayden, this was still a very young and inexperienced team – but one loaded with talent. If Coach Gordon could blend the talent, the Barons could surprise a few people. The coach himself felt that his team was capable of finishing first or second.

The League itself remained a six-team circuit with one old team folding and one new team added. The Pittsburgh Hornets were forced to disband when their arena, the venerable old Duquesne Gardens, was torn down. They would return to the League in 1961. Replacing the Hornets were the Rochester Americans.

The Barons got off to a nice 3-1-1 start to surprise many of their critics. Despite the optimism of their new coach, many close to the team, including some stockholders, felt the success of the youth movement was still a year or two away.

This seemed to be borne out when the team went on a six-game road trip and lost five of the contests. But this was only a temporary setback. The Barons began to click in earnest by mid-November. They went on a 6-0-1 run to move into first place by December 1st with a 10-7-2 record.

Leading the Barons up the ladder was the team's new #1 line of Fred Glover, Jimmy Moore, and Bo Elik. All were off to great starts, Elik in particular. After 23 games, the 27-year-old rookie left winger had a sensational 23 goals. Bo was white hot and credited his great start to playing with linemates Glover and Moore.

Cleveland was fortunate to even have Elik on its roster. After playing five years with North Bay in the Ontario Hockey Association, Bo was invited to training camp and was going to be cut on the last day of camp. He was slated to be returned to North Bay. But a knee injury to Calum MacKay created an open roster spot that was filled by Elik. The rest was history.

Glover-Elik-Moore (the "GEM line") clicked right from the start. Rookie Moore proved to be an outstanding playmaker, while Elik and Glover poured in the goals. Not since the Glover-Olson-Gordon line had a trio worked so beautifully together.

Glover himself was enjoying a super year with 16 early-season goals. Fred was also trying to cut down on his misconduct penalties. "I'm captain this year and I'm trying to set an example for the rest of the team. Don't get me wrong though," stated the fiery right winger. "I'm not backing off from anything."

By mid-December, the Barons were down to three defensemen. Pete Goegan was nursing a knee injury; Bert Bourassa was called home upon the death of his father; and Ron Morgan left the team, preferring to play near his home in western Canada.

The crippled defense didn't bother the Barons on a trip to Springfield when they flattened the last place Indians 11-3 behind Dan Poliziani's four goals. But the next night in Providence was another story.

The Reds were a veteran team and knew that the Cleveland defense was hurting. They seized the moment and attacked relentlessly. The result was an 11-4 drubbing absorbed by the Barons.

The loss had a lingering effect on the club. They felt that they were equal in strength with the Reds, and the big loss put a temporary dent in their confidence. Sure, the defense was in a weak state, but eleven goals was a shock to the Barons. It looked as though Providence was just as strong as they were the season before.

Cleveland stumbled through the rest of the month and went into January with four straight losses and an even 15-15-2 record.

Coach Gordon kept preaching defense to his troops. The American League was now so strong a unit that a strong defense was the only way to sure success. When Pete Goegan and Bert Bourassa returned to the lineup after the first of the year, Gordon's defensive strategy finally began to produce results.

The Barons began to play playoff style position hockey. No more of the haram-scaram wild offense. The wingers stayed with their man, and the defensemen began to meet the opposition at the blue line. The new style paid off in victories. Cleveland won five out of their next six games to move into third place, four points behind Providence and three behind Hershey. This set up a big matchup with the Reds on January 19th.

The Barons had something to prove to Providence and themselves. Was their new-found defensive prowess for real? Could they play with the powerful Reds? 9,624 Arena fans came away from the game convinced that their team was for real.

The Clevelanders played a flawless defensive game and shut out the mighty Reds 2-0. Marcel Paille was magnificent in goal, and he had to be. At the other end of the rink, Johnny Bower was having a great night also. The Panther Man was up to his old tricks with 42 saves. Only goals by Jimmy Moore in the second period and Ken Hayden at 14:05 of the third marred Bower's super performance.

But the night belonged to Marcel Paille and the rugged Baron defense. Not just the rearguards, but the forwards checked ferociously as Paille needed to make only 27 saves. The Barons made their point. They could play with anyone.

Defense was not the only reason for Cleveland's rise in the standings. Fred Glover was on a season-long scoring binge. In a 7-0 shutout of Springfield that lifted the team's record to 24-19-3, Glover fired a three-goal hat trick. This gave him 35 goals for the season to go along with his 39 assists. His 74 points led the League. It was important that Fred was so hot because linemate Bo Elik had cooled off. After scoring 23 goals in the first 23 games, Bo slid to 10 goals in the next 23. This was not unexpected since his early pace was impossible to keep up. Thus Glover's steady excellence was a must for the offense.

Cleveland's drive toward first place hit a fever pitch during the middle of February.

A crowd of 8,465 at the Arena saw Hayden fire a hat trick to give the Barons a 7-3 win over Buffalo and keep the team two points behind Providence. Hayden's second goal of the night was the 200th of his career. He became the 18th player in League history to hit the two century mark.

The next afternoon, 10,371 fans saw a fantastic goaltender's battle and one of the wildest donnybrooks ever at the old ice house.

Marcel Paille racked up his fourth shutout as the Barons edged Hershey 1-0. The victory overshadowed a magnificent performance by Bear goalie Gerry McNamara, who kicked out 52 shots. His play had the two teams and the fans shaking their heads in amazement.

Still, all of the great play took a back seat to a wild fight between Cleveland's Ian Cushenan and Hershey's Don Cherry.

After staging a knock-down, drag-out fight near center ice, the two combatants were sent to the penalty box. It was here that things got out of hand. Cushenan and Cherry decided that they hadn't had enough and began a fierce fight in the sin bin. In the savage brawl a portion of the wire screen near the box was torn down and a support bar bent in half.

It was then that Larry Zeidel got in on the act. Larry was a mild-mannered intellectual off the ice, but a wild man on it. He could lose control at any moment. At the height of the Cushenan-Cherry brawl, Zeidel lost his cool and ripped the penalty box door off its hinges and hurled it down the ice. This led to both benches emptying as players paired off all over the ice and went at each other. It took nearly a half hour to restore order.

The Cleveland-Hershey rivalry had now become the fiercest in the League. With Fred Glover and Larry Zeidel on opposite sides, the two teams became bitter enemies for the next decade.

The Barons hit their peak on February 19th when Marcel Paille blanked Providence 2-0 at the Arena for his fifth shutout. The win moved Cleveland into a first-place tie with the Reds and climaxed a season-long struggle to reach the top. Goals by Gordon Vejprava and Freddie Glover gave Paille all the breathing room he needed.

After defeating Buffalo in their next game, the Barons lost three straight and fell seven points behind the Reds with time running out. It was an unfortunate short slump and spurred Jim Hendy to make a trade.

The Cleveland general manager dealt Ian Cushenan to Chicago for bright prospect Ron Ingram. The deal was a gamble since the Baron's defense was playing so well. But Hendy was never a big fan of Cushenan and took the chance.

The Barons went on a four-game road trip and came home with an even 2-2 split. This left them seven points behind Providence with six games to play. The deficit was too much to overcome.

Although the Barons won 4 of their remaining six games, they still finished 3 points behind the Reds. The final nail in their first-place coffin came with a 5-1 loss at Springfield.

Greatly disappointed by not finishing first, Cleveland still had two games remaining, and they were of the utmost importance. After beating Buffalo in the next to last game, the Barons needed to defeat dreaded Hershey in the season finale in order to finish in second place.

The game meant nothing to the Bears, who were settled into fourth place. And they played like it. The Barons belted their hated rival 7-3 and took the runner-up spot. Cleveland's 35-26-3 record actually tied Rochester at 73 points. But the Barons were awarded second place by virtue of having one more win.

The exciting season saw three Cleveland players land on the first all-star team – Bo Elik, who finished with 40 goals; defenseman Steve Kraftcheck, and Fred Glover. Glover won his first scoring title with 42 goals and 57 assists for 99 points. Jackie Gordon was named Coach of the Year.

The individual honors were great. But the Barons had a lot of hard work ahead of them. Their hated rivals, the Hershey Bears, waited in the wings as the best of seven opening playoff round was about to begin.

THE PLAYOFFS

On paper, the Cleveland-Hershey affair appeared to be a toss-up between two extremely rugged teams. During the regular season, Hershey held a 7-4-1 edge over Cleveland, although four of the wins came early in the year. The Barons seemed to have the upper hand later in the season. But none of that mattered as the two combatants started their war at the Cleveland Arena.

Game One was a shock to the Barons and their fans. Hershey totally shut down Cleveland's offense and skated away with a 3-0 win. So complete was their domination, Bear goalie Gerry McNamara was forced to make only 16 saves. "We were on 'em before they could turn around," stated ex-Baron Bob Solinger as he described Hershey's strategy.

"We couldn't play two games in a row like that first one," declared Coach Gordon after the game – and he was right.

Cleveland came out firing in Game Two, determined to prove that the opening game was a fluke. They fired 43 shots at Bear goalie Gerry McNamara, who had to make 39 saves in the Barons' 4-2 victory.

A quick goal by Jimmy Moore after the game was only 54 seconds old got Cleveland off to a flying start, and they never looked back. Fred Glover's goal at 17:59 gave the home team a cushion that they never relinquished.

The Barons took a 2-1 series lead at Hershey with a big 5-2 win in Game Three. With the score tied at 2-2 after one period, Ron Ingram fired in the go-ahead goal at 4:33 of the second period.

The violent contest ended on a sour note as the ill will between the two teams reached a boiling point.

As the game's final seconds ticked off, Bear defenseman Larry Zeidel skated across the ice to Bo Elik and swung his stick into the Baron player's face. Elik, taken by surprise, went down in a heap with a broken nose. Zeidel, standing over the fallen Baron, bellowed, "That'll teach you to laugh at me!" The Hershey "bad man" was handed a five-minute major penalty and sent to the locker room before any more trouble broke out.

The Cleveland players wanted revenge, but Coach Jackie Gordon would have none of that. "We can't afford to lose our heads because of what one man does," said the coach. Gordon was more concerned with winning the series than shedding more blood.

Cleveland gave a good effort in Game Four but came up on the short end of a 3-2 score. Both teams played cautiously in the first period. Bo Elik, playing with a broken nose, put the Barons ahead at 15:38. But three unanswered Hershey goals gave the Bears a lead they never gave up. Cal Stearns' shorthanded tally at 15:25 of the third period gave the Clevelanders hope. But it was a little too late as Hershey held on to tie the series at two games apiece.

Come playoff time, there was no substitute for experience. Coach Gordon was aware of this and called upon an old reliable pro to lift the team in Game Five. And player Gordon responded.

The game was a cliffhanger from the outset, with up-and-down action and hard-hitting galore.

The battle remained scoreless until Hershey veteran Duncan Fisher beat Paille with a wicked slapshot at 9:59 of the second period. Then late in the period Cleveland's old pro's took over.

With Larry Zeidel in the penalty box, the Barons were applying heavy pressure. Gordon had the puck behind the Hershey net and attempted a pass to Fred Glover. The puck ricocheted off of Bear center Arnie Kullman into the net to tie the score. The goal was a fluke, but it ignited the team and the crowd.

Cleveland kept the pressure up, and it paid off with a beautiful score. At 19:13 Jimmy Moore raced into the Hershey zone on the left side. When the Bear defenseman moved over to confront him, Jim flipped the puck over the defender's stick to an onrushing Fred Glover. The Baron captain's aim was true as he fired in the game winner. The Barons weathered a desperate Hershey attack in the third period to preserve a hard-fought 2-1 victory.

Cleveland hoped to wrap up the series in Hershey but came up empty. Game Six went to the Bears as goalie Gerry McNamara rang up his second 3-0 victory of the series. The contest was a carbon copy of Game One as the Hersheys stopped Cleveland's vaunted attack cold once again. The loss set up a climactic seventh game at the Cleveland Arena.

Hershey carried its momentum into Game Seven and led 2-1 after the first period. Two goals by Bear Duncan Fisher and one by Cleveland's Jackie Gordon accounted for the scoring in the hectic frame.

Things looked extremely bleak for the home team when Hershey's Willie Marshall scored on a breakaway early in the second period. At this point the Bears began to taunt and snicker at the Barons. They obviously thought that the game was in the bag.

This was a fatal mistake. Never kick a wounded animal when he is hurt. Incensed by the chortling, the Barons fought back with a vengeance. Taking a pass from Bill Shvetz, Gordy Vejprava streaked in on goalie McNamara and scored at 5:23. Cleveland was now consumed with determination.

They kept up the pressure as the crowd exhorted the home team on. Finally, at 16:15, Johnny MacLellan tied the score after taking a beautiful pass from Ken Hayden, who had circled behind the net.

There was no scoring in the third period. The big game would be settled in a full ten-minute overtime.

Cleveland was all over the Bears in the extra period, and the intense pressure paid off. Taking a perfect feed from Ron Ingram at the blue line, Bo Elik broke free on goalie McNamara and blasted home the tie-breaker at 5:53.

The crowd began celebrating, but four minutes still remained in the overtime. The Bears frantically tried to tie the score but to no avail. They pulled McNamara in favor of an extra attacker, but the move backfired when Fred Glover scored from mid-ice into an empty cage.

The extremely satisfying series victory put Cleveland in the finals for the twelfth time. They would launch their bid for an eighth Calder Cup against the Rochester Americans.

The Amerks were fresh off a huge upset of the Providence Reds in the other semi-final series. Big underdogs at the outset, they blasted the Reds in five games. Rochester goalie Bobby Perreault was a big hero in the startling conquest. He racked up two shutouts while allowing the Reds only seven goals in five games.

The Americans were a troublesome opponent for Cleveland all season. The Barons had a 4-6-2 record against their opponent and failed to win a game on Rochester ice. Due to winning 12 of their last 16 regular season games, and their playoff win over Providence, the Americans were slight favorites entering the finals.

The opener of the best of seven series was a nail-biting thriller at the Arena. The game was fast-paced with good, hard checking by both clubs.

The Amerks drew first blood with a goal by Bronco Horvath at 5:28 of the opening period.

The Barons loosened up in the second stanza and tied the score on a blast by Johnny McLellan. From then on it was close checking and hard hitting, as each team looked for an opening. Rochester appeared to score the go-ahead goal at 18:06. But the score was disallowed because Amerk Ron Hurst was ruled in the goal crease. Rochester coach Billy Reay was incensed.

Thus, the game went into a full 10-minute overtime. The extra period was only 48 seconds old when defenseman Ron Ingram blasted a high-screened shot from the blue line that beat Rochester goalie Bobby Perreault. Cleveland held on for the big 2-1 win.

After the game, American coach Billy Reay had to be restrained by two policemen from entering the referees' private locker room. He was still seething because referee Lou Maschio had disallowed the apparent game-winning Rochester goal late in the third period.

Game Two in Rochester was another nip and tuck affair. After trailing 2-0, Cleveland rallied behind goals by Ron Ingram and Fred Glover to send the game into another 10-minute overtime. But this time, the Barons ran out of gas.

Playing their fourth game in five nights, the Clevelanders were exhausted. After a penalty to Pete Goegan for hooking, the Americans scored three times to skate away with a 5-2 win. "The best thing for us now is a real good rest," understated Coach Jackie Gordon. "This is a tired club."

10,753 fans turned out at the Arena for Game Three, and they saw the Barons at the top of their game.

Johnny McLellan, elevated to the number one line with Jimmy Moore and Fred Glover, scored the three goal hat trick to lead Cleveland to a decisive 5-1 triumph. Glover and Dan Poliziani had the other Baron scores.

The game was a savage contest from start to finish. At one point, even Amerk goalie Bobby Perreault got into the act, fighting with Ken Hayden, who had crashed into him. The penalty box door swung open all night long as each team tried to intimidate the other, with neither club succeeding.

McLellan stayed hot in Game Four at Rochester. Scoring two more goals, he led the Barons to a 6-3 victory. It was Cleveland's first win on Amerk ice all season.

The Barons held a 2-0 first-period lead on goals by Cal Stearns and McLellan. They stretched their lead to 4-1 on tallies by Stearns again and Gordy Vejprava. The Barons appeared home free. But the Americans had other ideas.

Goals by Earl Balfour late in the second period and Bronco Horvath early in the third put Rochester back in the game.

But McLellan was Johnny on the spot when he scored again at 13:02 to give the Barons a 5-3 lead. Bo Elik's tally at 18:14 was icing on the cake. The decisive victory put the Barons in position to clinch the Calder Cup on home ice as the series shifted back to Cleveland.

Game Five at the Arena was simply one of the finest hockey games ever played in Cleveland. It was an emotional rollercoaster that had the 9,505 fans exhausted and drenched with tension. It was also a personal triumph for one man who never gave up.

The Barons jumped out to a 2-0 first-period lead on goals by Cal Stearns and Ken Hayden. But the joy was shortlived as the Amerks bounced back shortly afterward with two goals of their own.

In the second period, Hayden struck again to put Cleveland back on top. However, Rochester would not quit. Goals by Eddie Mazur and Gordon Hannigan gave the Americans the lead as the big crowd groaned and feared for the worst. Their prayers were answered when Danny Poliziani flipped a backhander past Bobby Perreault at 17:09 to tie the score at 4-4.

The tension mounted in the third period as both teams came close to scoring on numerous occasions. Super goaltending by Perreault and Paille kept both teams off the board, and the game went into overtime.

The crowd was on the edge of its seats, but neither team could score in the 10-minute extra session, which was marked by extremely close checking.

Thus the game entered sudden death. The first team to score would be the winner.

The winning play developed when Cal Stearns took a pass from Steve Kraftcheck in his own zone. Cal skated the puck up ice and over the Rochester blue line. Here he dropped a pass back to Ken Hayden, who was trailing behind. Ken wound up for a spectacular slapshot that sailed under the arm of Bobby Perreault at 6:58 of sudden death and gave the Barons a 5-4 victory. Absolute pandemonium broke out as the Barons and their loving fans celebrated the club's eighth Calder Cup championship.

Long after most of his teammates had showered and dressed, Ken Hayden still sat in uniform in front of his locker. He was savoring every moment of his personal triumph.

Hayden had endured a long playoff jinx throughout his career. His goal against Hershey in Game Two of the semi-finals was the first of his long playoff career. He had endured 27 playoff games in six series with three different clubs before bagging that goal.

His hat trick, and Calder Cup winning shot against Rochester, was the crowning moment of his hockey life. Through all his frustrations, he never gave up. And in the end, his perseverance paid off. Ken Hayden was now a Baron hero for the ages.

THE 1956-57 CLEVELAND BARONS

Back (L-R): Gordon Vejprava, Jimmy Moore, Boris Elik, Ronald Ingram, John McLellan, Ken Hayden, Ed MacQueen, Floyd Perras, Promotional Director. Second: Jack Boag, Trainer; Dan Poliziani, Bill Shvetz, Frank Milne, Gordon Hudson, Pete Goegan, Camille Bedard, Steve Kraftcheck. Front: Edward J. Coen, Publicity Director; Marcel Paille, Fred Glover, Captain; James C. Hendy, Vice President and General Manager; Jack Gordon, Coach; Claire Grove, President; Cal Stearns, John Albani, Lex Cook, Chief Scout. Kay Horiba collection.

FINAL STANDINGS
1956-57

West	W	L	T	GF	GA	PTS.
Providence	34	22	8	236	168	76
Cleveland	35	26	3	249	210	73
Rochester	34	25	5	224	199	73
Hershey	32	28	4	223	237	68
Buffalo	25	37	2	209	270	52
Springfield	19	41	4	217	274	42

Top Baron Scorers	G	A	PTS.
Fred Glover	42	57	99
Jimmy Moore	23	66	89
Bo Elik	40	40	80
Gordon Vejprava	24	35	59
Cal Stearns	16	34	50
Dan Poliziani	21	25	46
Bill Shvetz	15	25	40
Steve Kraftcheck	7	33	40
John McLellan	20	13	33
Ken Hayden	20	10	30

Calder Cup Champion – Cleveland Barons

1957-58 SEASON

*Cleveland hockey fans had plenty of reasons to rejoice.
Their team was coming off a championship season,
and during the off season it was announced that
Johnny Bower was returning to Cleveland.*

The great puckstopper was purchased back from New York when the Rangers decided to keep Lorne "Gump" Worsley and Marcel Paille. Worsley started the season in New York, while Paille was sent to Providence to replace Bower. Marcel had been on loan to Cleveland for one year and backstopped the Barons to a championship. The Rangers considered him their goalie of the future with Bower expendable and too old.

One has to wonder at New York's judgement. Johnny Bower was still in his prime, and his greatest years were still ahead of him. The Rangers could not see what a unique talent they had. This was their loss and Cleveland's gain.

And no one was happier than the Panther Man himself. Bower considered Cleveland his second home and loved playing with the Barons. He was all set to finish his career on the shores of Lake Erie.

Besides the return of Bower, the Barons welcomed two rookie defensemen, Bill Needham and Billy Watson, to the team.

Also, veteran defenders George (Butch) Bouchard and Gordon Hudson were added to last season's returnees. They replaced the retired Ken Hayden and defensemen Ron Morgan and Ron Ingram.

Cleveland's hockey followers were somewhat surprised with the team's mediocre 4-7-1 start. With Johnny Bower back in goal, immediate results were expected. The slow getaway was unfortunate because Hershey was threatening to run away and hide from the rest of the division. The Bears' incredible 10-1-1 start put them 12 points up on Cleveland in the season's first month. The Barons would be digging out of this hole for most of the season.

Of immediate concern for the Barons was a grueling eight game road trip while the Ice Capades took over the Arena. The backbreaking journey through the East was moderately successful as the Barons won three while dropping five. Playing near .500 on the road was considered acceptable; but with Hershey now at 13-2-2, Cleveland's 6-9-1 record was a full 15 points behind the Bears. A quick turn-around was needed, and needed fast.

First measure of order for Coach Jackie Gordon was the reuniting of the Glover-Elik-Moore line. The coach had been experimenting with various line combinations during the first month of the season. Unfortunately, none seemed to be working.

Gordon was reluctant to put the "GEM" line together again because there had been some friction between the trio during last season's playoffs. Egos were bruised, but any bad feelings now seemed

Simply put, Johnny Bower was the greatest goaltender in American Hockey League history. His 45 career shutouts and shutout streak of 249:51 consecutive minutes have stood the test of time and still are league records. The three-time MVP hit his American league peak during the 1957-58 season. His 2.19 goals against average and 8 shutouts in 64 games were a career best. Only a late season injury kept the Barons from another title. Bill Hudec collection.

Small in physical stature, but huge in heart, little Gordon Vejprava was a big fan favorite from 1955-56 through 1958-59. "Vegy" produced 83 goals during his stint with the club, but it was his constant hustle and drive that endeared him to his teammates and fans alike. Kay Horiba collection.

to be in the past. The team needed a spark before it fell any further behind Hershey. Gordon kept his fingers crossed that the reunited "GEM" line would be the answer.

The results were instantaneous. The Barons won three in a row and then tied Buffalo to set up a "must-win" game with Hershey on November 30th.

A must-win game that early in the season might seem a bit premature, but the Bears were storming into Cleveland with a phenomenal 17-3-2 record. The Barons' 9-9-2 mark put them 16 points behind the frontrunners. To fall much further behind would make first place virtually unreachable.

The game marked the beginning of the greatest goaltending streak in American Hockey League history.

Behind Johnny Bower's 24 saves, the Barons shut out the mighty Hersheys 1-0 in a tense superthriller. One would have thought that Cleveland had just won the championship the way they celebrated when Gordy Vejprava scored at 6:24 of a 10-minute "sudden death" overtime. The entire team hoisted up the little center, who batted in a rebound of a Pete Goegan shot.

Vegy wasn't the only hero. Every member on the team could take a bow. It had been a long time since a Cleveland team had checked so effectively. Every Hershey player was covered at every step. The effort was outstanding and carried over into the next night's game at Springfield.

Bower recorded his second straight whitewash with a 2-0 shutout over the Indians. Goals by rookie Don Hogan and Jimmy Moore stretched Cleveland's unbeaten streak to seven games. More importantly, Bower's shutout streak reached 141 minutes and 15 seconds. He was now within striking distance of Hershey's Nick Damore's record set during the 1939-40 season. Damore blanked the opposition for 221:02 during his monumental streak. But standing in the way were the mighty Bears. Hershey was returning to the Arena for another slugfest on December 5th.

As incredible as it seemed, Johnny Bower hung another shutout on the Bears. Forechecking and backchecking to perfection, the Barons destroyed the League leaders 9-0. Cleveland was led by Gordy Vejprava, Don Hogan, Fred Glover, and Billy Watson with two goals apiece. Bo Elik had the other.

But the story of the game was Bower. Johnny ran his streak to 201 minutes and 15 seconds. The Bears left the ice shaking their heads. They were stunned that they could be manhandled in such a way.

The shutout was the fifth of the season for the Baron netminder. He got his shot at AHL history on December 7th at the Cleveland Arena against the Buffalo Bisons.

The crowd was in a festive mood, hoping that their beloved hero could shut out the Bisons through the first period. John needed 19 minutes, 14 seconds to be exact.

The minutes seemed to pass like hours as the record-breaking moment neared. The crowd was on its feet as the Barons and Bower desperately tried to keep Buffalo off the board – and they succeeded. A thunderous roar echoed from the fans as Nick Damore's 17-year-old record came tumbling down. Bower's teammates mobbed the great goalie as the period ended, and the fans carried on well into the intermission.

But the great Panther Man was not through yet. He held Buffalo scoreless until Lou Jankowski finally scored at 8:36 of the third period. Once again, the Cleveland fans gave their sensational goaltender a prolonged ovation for this magnificent feat. That the Barons won 6-2, to extend their unbeaten streak to nine games, was an afterthought.

All told, Johnny Bower's shutout streak reached 249 minutes and 51 seconds. It was an accomplishment of superhuman proportions. It also cemented the fact that the greatest goalie in all of hockey, in any league, was right here in Cleveland, Ohio.

Johnny had a lot of help during the streak. The forwards checked like never before. Also, the great defense core needed to take a bow – Steve Kraftcheck, Pete Goegan, Bill Needham, George Bouchard, and Gordon Hudson. The rock-solid defense had allowed only 53 goals in the first 24 games. No Cleveland team ever played better defense than what was played then.

The nine-game unbeaten streak ended when Cleveland lost at Rochester 3-1 the night after Bower set his record. The loss left the Barons 11 points behind Hershey.

The great Cleveland goalie was then the center of attention again. The entire season seemed to revolve around one Johnny Bower.

Gump Worsley, the man the New York Rangers kept over Bower, had recently been sent to Providence. Marcel Paille was given his chance in the NHL. Bower and Worsley were keen rivals, and each looked forward to a two-game series between their respective teams.

Gump had the better of it at the Arena as he put on a clinic in defeating Bower and the Barons 2-1. John was terrific with 26 hard-earned saves, but Worsley would not be denied as he kicked out 31 shots himself.

Bower racked up shutout number six the next night over Springfield 4-0. He then went into Providence and got some revenge as the Barons topped the Reds 5-2. The fans who witnessed Bower during this period were seeing some of the greatest goaltending imaginable, and it was not by accident. John was a great student of the game. When opposing teams would go through off-day workouts the day before a game at the arena, Bower would be there watching them. He studied players' tendencies, techniques, and habits. He watched how players would shoot.

"Many players always shoot at the same spot," said the great goalie. "But the smart ones try to shoot to the opposite side of the catching hand. That's a goalie's weakness. He can't move his right foot as good as his left. The left leg is faster because it's always working with the left hand to block shots." Nothing went unnoticed by Johnny. He knew all the tricks of the trade and worked on them endlessly.

Slowly but surely the Barons whittled away at the Hershey lead. Goalie Bower celebrated the birth of his daughter Cynthia Ann on January 11, 1958 by recording his seventh shutout of the season that night. Fred Glover and Jimmy Moore led the scoring parade with two goals and four assists each as the Barons routed Buffalo 12-0. The lopsided win left Cleveland only five points behind the Hersheys.

Playing without Glover, who banged up his knee in the Buffalo game, for the next two weeks, the good guys were still able to stay close to the Bears. In fact, they had an opportunity to move to within one point of first place when they visited Chocolate Town on January 29th. However, the stubborn Bears refused to wilt and turned back the determined Barons 5-2.

The only good news to come out of Hershey was that Cal Stearns scored in the third period. This marked the end of a season-long drought for Cal, as it was his first goal of the year. Always a steady goal getter in the past, Stearns could not score this season for the life of him. But through it all Cal never stopped working or hustling. If anything, he went about his play with more determination than ever in an effort to break out of the dismal slump. The young players looked up to the veteran as he set quite an example for them.

One youngster having a fine year was Danny Poliziani. In a season when Johnny Bower seemed to snatch most of the headlines, it was easy to overlook the contributions of the 23-year-old sophomore. But Baron management was well aware of their up and coming star.

Poliziani had been scouted by Cleveland since he was 12 years old in midget hockey. After turning pro in 1955, Dan played five games as a Baron before being farmed out to Quebec City. He then scored 21 goals in his rookie year and would record 23 this campaign.

The super quick winger scored the winning goals in back to back wins over Rochester in mid-February. These were important victories, as Hershey was heating up again with six straight wins of their own. The back to back wins put Cleveland at 29-19-3, seven points behind the red hot Bears.

The second game of the Rochester set, a 2-1 Cleveland win, demonstrated the tension that was developing in the Barons' quest to catch Hershey.

Fred Glover and young Amerk defenseman Noel Price had been jostling each other all night, but no fight broke out between the two. Apparently this did not satisfy Price. Acting like a young gun trying to knock off the king of the hill, Price accosted Glover outside of the Rochester dressing room after the game. It was a challenge Fred could not overlook.

As the melee began to build, players from both teams encircled the two combatants. Glover and Price put on a battle royal. Although there was no clear-cut winner, old gunslinger Fred seemed to get the upper hand. Neither team supported such shenanigans, but sometimes boys will be boys.

Cleveland climbed to within four points of Hershey to set up a showdown at the Arena on February

19th. A few days before the big game, the Toronto Maple Leafs of the NHL made a big offer to the Barons for Johnny Bower. Jim Hendy mulled over the offer and felt obligated to let Bower himself decide whether he wanted to remain a Baron or move up to Toronto. Johnny didn't hesitate. He vetoed the deal saying he wanted to remain in Cleveland. He simply loved playing here.

Both management and Bower were relieved and happy. In fact, Johnny went out and celebrated by blanking the vaunted Hersheys 2-0 in the big showdown. It was the eighth shutout of the year for Bower, tying Bill Beveridge's club record set in 1941-42. Gordon Bell of Buffalo held the League record of nine set in 1942-43.

Goals by Jimmy Moore and Gordon Hudson gave Cleveland the win and left them only two points out of first place.

It was a savage contest loaded with hard-hitting fisticuffs. Jack Price of Hershey had three teeth broken, and Gordy Vejprava sustained a large cut over the right eye.

The Bears, totally frustrated in being shut out for the fourth time by Cleveland, blew their corks in the last minute of the game. A savage fight between Bo Elik and Bear Gordon Hollingsworth actually knocked the Hershey net off its pins and against the boards. Both teams joined the fun in a battle royal that featured a tough draw between Freddie Glover and Larry Zeidel. This tussle had the fans buzzing since the two old pros were the toughest hombres in the League.

After the game, news hit that defenseman Pete Goegan had been traded to Detroit of the NHL for backliner Gordon Strate and $15,000. Hendy, sure that Goegan would be taken by an NHL club in the draft after the season, decided to get a quality player while he could. The deal saddened the club, but the players understood and went on with their goal of catching Hershey.

The season-long quest was finally realized on February 23rd. Cleveland's 4-1 win at Rochester, coupled with the Bears' 7-3 loss to Providence, gave the Barons a 34-20-3 record and a share of first place with Hershey.

The victory climaxed a season-long uphill battle. At one point the Bears held a 16-point lead over Cleveland and seemed a sure runaway winner of the regular season title. Now the season began anew with 13 games remaining.

After gaining first place, the Barons let down a little by losing two straight at home before embarking on a backbreaking eight-game road trip that would decide their fate.

The road trip got off to a spectacular start with victories at Buffalo and Hershey. The 3-1 win over the Bears was especially significant, since it boosted the Barons back into a first-place tie with their Chocolate Town rivals. Big man for Cleveland was Gordy Vejprava with two goals. The smallest Baron was having another fine season.

After losing at Rochester and edging Springfield 4-3 on Danny Poliziani's sudden death goal, Cleveland moved on to Providence for a date with destiny on March 9th.

The Reds and Barons were locked in a tense, scoreless battle that featured the spectacular goaltending of Johnny Bower. The Panther Man was making one great save after another as Providence poured on continuous pressure. His last save at 7:44 of the third period changed the Barons' season.

Jim Bartlett of the Reds stormed in on goal and fired a bullet. Bower dove to his right to make the save. At that same instant, Bartlett cut across the goal mouth and accidentally collided with the fallen netminder. His skate rammed into Bower's side. Johnny rolled over in tremendous pain as his teammates held their breath.

After a long delay, the stricken goalie was helped to his feet and taken to Roger Williams General Hospital.

Trainer Jack Boag was rushed into action to finish the game and did a fine job in goal. He allowed only one goal, but it was enough as the Reds blanked Cleveland 1-0.

The Barons fell two points behind Hershey, but no one seemed to care. Everyone was concerned about Bower. When word arrived from the hospital, it was like a pin was stuck in a balloon. The great

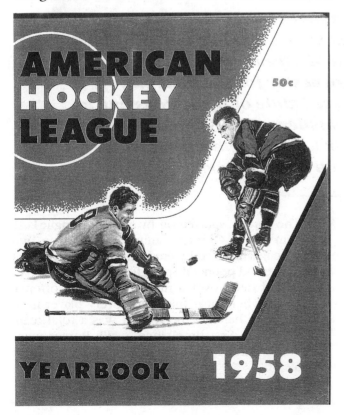

James Peter Hendy collection.

netminder had suffered three cracked ribs and was through for the season.

Nothing could have been more damaging to this club. Although the entire team was playing fine hockey, everything revolved around Johnny Bower. He was the supreme backstop of the team, and now he was gone.

Despite this severe setback, the season still went on. Jim Hendy was forced to scour the country for an available goalie to finish the season. Under League rules, a team could sign a goalie from a lower league in an emergency situation. Cleveland owned Johnny Albani, but he was injured and could not be brought up. No other farm hand was ready for AHL play.

Hendy settled on Lucien (Lou) Dechene of the Western league's Saskatoon club. Dechene's team was in last place and had no chance to make the playoffs. Thus, he was available. Lou was a fine goalie, but he was in an impossible situation replacing the legendary Bower.

Dechene could not arrive in time for Cleveland's showdown at Hershey on March 12th. Floyd Perras, sales promotion director and the team's practice goalie, was forced into action against the Bears.

Perras and the Barons gave it their all, but this obstacle was too much to overcome. Cleveland dropped a 6-3 decision to Hershey to fall four points behind the Bears in a violent contest.

Tempers exploded when Jimmy Moore and ex-Baron Bob Solinger got into a big fight. Fred Glover soon afterward swung his stick at some fans who were constantly harassing him all night. He was given a ten-minute misconduct penalty. While in the penalty box, the fans tried to get at him. After a large commotion, Fred needed a police escort to the dressing room to ensure his safety. The loss just about ended the Barons' hopes for first place.

Cleveland returned home with a 3-4-1 mark on the road trip. Their hopes for first place were officially dashed when they lost a 3-2 overtime decision to Rochester at the Arena in the season's second last game. They bounced back to defeat Hershey in the season finale in a meaningless game to finish in second place with a fine 39-28-3 record.

But second place was sour grapes to this Baron squad. They fought so hard all season long to catch Hershey. If not for the injury to Johnny Bower, they most likely would have accomplished their goal. The disappointment was like a dark cloud hanging over the club as they prepared to face Springfield in the opening round of the playoffs.

THE PLAYOFFS

Although they finished 15 points behind Cleveland with a 29-33-8 record, the Indians were a confident bunch heading into Cleveland for the opening game of the best of seven semi-final series. Springfield had just edged out Rochester for the final playoff berth. They also knew of the depressed state of the Barons due to the loss of Johnny Bower. The Clevelanders went 3-6-0 to close out the season after the injury to their famed goalkeeper, and the Indians planned to jump on them early.

Springfield did just that in Game One, as they defeated the Barons at the Arena 2-1. The home team seemed listless as they let the Indians control the tempo of the game from the outset. The Barons kept dumping the puck into the attacking zone but seldom chased after it with any gusto.

Cal Stearns gave the Barons a 1-0 lead, but it didn't last long. Cal Gardner tied the score at 15:47. Jack Caffery scored the game winner at 2:26 of the third period as the Indians took the home ice advantage away from Cleveland.

The Barons, spurred on by a severe tongue-lashing from Coach Gordon, came back in Game Two with a vengeance. Led by Fred Glover's three-goal hat trick, Cleveland pounded Springfield 9-1 at the Arena.

It had been over a month since the offense looked anywhere near this sharp. Every player from A to Z had a hand in the rout. It was a total team effort. For the first time since goalie Bower went down, the Barons played with the zest they were capable of.

They were at it again the next night in Springfield in Game Three. Behind the super goaltending of Lou Dechene, Cleveland overwhelmed the Indians again 5-1. Every time the defense broke down, Lou came up big. He committed highway robbery on Indians Harry Pidhirny, Cal Gardner, and Gerry Ehman to keep his team ahead when they appeared ready to cave in. Thanks to their fine replacement goalie, the Barons appeared to be in the driver's seat.

Just when the Cleveland icers appeared to turn the corner, they lapsed back into their lazy play. The reversal of form led to a 2-0 loss to the Indians in Game Four. The only good thing about the game was the continued fine play of Lou Dechene. Whatever the team's problem was, it was not in goal. Lou had given up a mere 6 goals in the first four games.

The elusive drive that Coach Gordon strived for reappeared in Game Five as the Barons soundly defeated Springfield 5-2 at the Arena. Fleet Danny Poliziani proved to be the difference as he fired in three goals to lead the home team to the big win. Danny was in high gear as he skated circles around the Indian defense.

The effort definitely was there in Game Six at Springfield as the Barons tried to close out the series. But so was a stone wall in the Indian goal named Claude Evans. The Springfield netminder turned in a masterpiece as his team again shut out Cleveland 3-0. Time and again he turned back "sure" Baron scores. The series was now tied at three games apiece. The grand finale would be played out on Cleveland Arena ice.

The Barons got off to a quick start in Game Seven as Bill Shvetz scored on a rebound of a Danny Poliziani shot at 2:09 of the opening period. Gerry Ehman got that one back at 10:48, while Bill Needham was in the penalty box.

Bob Beckett put the visitors on top late in the second period. But Gordy Vejprava tied the game at 2-2 at 2:31 of the third period on an end to end solo dash. Cleveland had the edge in play for the remainder of the period but could not dent Claude Evans, the hot Springfield goalie. The game then went into a full ten-minute overtime.

Both teams appeared tense as the extra session began, and they played cautiously.

The big break came at 2:44 when Bob Beckett broke between defensemen Gordon Hudson and George Bouchard and beat Baron goalie Dechene. The air went of Cleveland right there. From that point on, the Indians were all over the Barons at every turn as they smelled victory. The icing was put on the cake when Ken Schinkel scored into an open net at 9:23 as the Barons had pulled their goalie for an extra attacker. For the first time, a Cleveland team had lost a seventh game on home ice, 4-2.

If ever there was a season of "could have been", this was it. The Barons could have, should have, and probably would have won the Calder Cup had not Johnny Bower been hurt. His replacement, Lou Dechene, did play outstanding hockey.

THE FAST AND RUGGED GOEGAN IS ONE OF BEST PUCK-CARRYING DEFENSEMEN—

PETE GOEGAN

BARONS' CENTER JIMMIE MOORE, IS THE LEAGUE'S LEADING PLAY-MAKER WITH 52 ASSISTS... ...HE'LL BE SETTING THEM UP TONIGHT AGAINST PROVIDENCE AT THE ARENA. "SO NICE TO HAVE AROUN'"

But when Bower got hurt, something happened to the Cleveland icers. Johnny brought with him an intangible feeling of invincibility that spread throughout the team. When he went down, the team lost that important mystique and never got it back.

The team and its fans were in a depressed state after the playoff failure. But this was nothing compared to the disastrous off-season events that would soon transpire.

FINAL STANDINGS
1957-58

	W	L	T	GF	GA	PTS.
Hershey	39	24	7	241	198	85
Cleveland	39	28	3	232	163	81
Providence	33	32	5	237	220	71
Springfield	29	33	8	231	246	66
Rochester	29	35	6	205	242	64
Buffalo	25	42	3	224	301	53

Top Baron Scorers	G	A	PTS.
Jimmy Moore	25	58	83
Fred Glover	28	48	76
Bo Elik	31	37	68
Gordon Vejprava	22	28	50
Steve Kraftcheck	15	34	49
Don Hogan	21	22	43
Dan Poliziani	23	19	42

Calder Cup Champion – Hershey Bears

THE 1957-58 CLEVELAND BARONS

Front (L-R): Lex Cook, Chief Scout; Lucien Dechene, Claire W. Grove, President; Jack Gordon, Coach; James C. Hendy, Vice President and General Manager; Fred Glover, John Bower; Edward J. Coen, Publicity Director. Second: Jack Boag, Trainer; Elmo Baumann, Stick Boy; Billy Watson, Dan Poliziani, Don Hogan, Bob Barlow, Bo Elik, Jimmy Moore, Gordon Vejprava, Floyd Perras, Promotional Director. Back: Ken Gribbons, Cal Stearns, Bill Shvetz, Gordon Hudson, John McLellan, George Bouchard, Bill Needham, Steve Kraftcheck. Bill Hudec collection.

1958-59 SEASON

The Barons were hit hard by the NHL inter-League draft during the off season. Taken into the National League were Johnny Bower (Toronto), Howie Glover (Chicago), and Danny Poliziani by Boston, who in turn sent him to Providence.

Of course, losing Bower was the biggest blow imaginable. When Cleveland purchased Johnny from New York one year before, they figured he was safe from the draft. After all, the goaltender was entering his 13th season and was 33 years old. No team would spend $15,000 for an aging goaltender; no team, that is, except Toronto.

The Maple Leafs wanted John in the worst way. They were convinced that he had several great years left in him despite his advanced age. In fact, they made an attractive offer for his services late in the 1957-58 season. The deal was turned down by Bower himself, for the goalie wanted to remain in Cleveland.

Jim Hendy was worried. As an inducement for Toronto to let John remain a Baron, Hendy sold all star defenseman Steve Kraftcheck to the Leafs. It was bad enough that Toronto assigned Kraftcheck to rival Rochester, but the Maple Leafs turned around and drafted Bower anyway.

Hendy, the Barons, and their fans were stunned. Suddenly, the guts of their great defense was gone. As a direct result of this raid, and others throughout the League, the AHL abolished the inter-League draft on August 31st. But this was too late to help Cleveland.

Johnny Bower was gone for good. The AHL's greatest goalie, who only wanted to play for Cleveland, found it difficult to adjust to Toronto, at first. But eventually he learned to love the Canadian city. He would go on to play 11 years for the Leafs and backstop the NHL club to 4 Stanley Cup Championships.

Bower was a credit to hockey and the City of Cleveland. Other fine goalies would play for the Barons. But none would ever compare to the great Panther Man. Johnny Bower was in a class all by himself.

James Peter Hendy collection.

Player-Coach Jackie Gordon instructs the troops.
Cleveland State University archives – photo by Fred Bottomer

On the positive side, Hendy engineered two important off season deals that would greatly benefit the club. Left Wing Eddie Mazur was obtained from Rochester in a trade for Bo Elik. At first, fans did not like the deal. But Mazur turned out to be a big fan favorite and enjoyed several fine seasons in Cleveland. On the other hand, Elik would never again approach the success that he achieved during his rookie year.

The other important acquisition was obtaining Bob Bailey from Detroit as part of the Pete Goegan deal. Bailey, in his second tour of duty with Cleveland, would blossom into a big scorer in addition to his roughhouse leadership.

The Barons opened the season with little Johnny Albani in goal and only two experienced defensemen, Bill Needham and Gordon Hollingworth, who was obtained from Hershey. It was no wonder that they gave up 13 goals in their first two games, a loss and a tie to Rochester.

It was obvious to Jim Hendy that Albani was not ready for AHL competition. So he went hunting for a new goalie.

Toronto, perhaps feeling a little guilty for stripping Cleveland of Johnny Bower and Steve Kraftcheck, agreed to sell Gerry McNamara to Cleveland on a year-to-year basis. His rights would then revert back to the Maple Leafs. It wasn't an ideal situation, but it solved the immediate problem – for McNamara was a fine netminder.

The value of their new goalie was not immediately noticeable because the Barons' defense was still in shambles. After defeating Springfield and Providence in Gerry's first two games, Cleveland embarked on a seven-game road trip. Road disaster was the proper term.

The Barons lost all seven games on the trip and fell into the basement with a 2-8-1 record. Worse than the losses was the pitiful brand of hockey they played. The team scored only 15 goals while giving up 41 on the journey East. Lowest point of all came in a 14-5 debacle at Springfield. Defense was only a distant memory. Clearly, the Barons needed help, and Jim Hendy came to the rescue.

The Cleveland general manager obtained Bob Robertson from Providence for Ed MacQueen. One week later he purchased George McAvoy from New Westminster of the Western league. The two hard-hitting defensemen were a back line combination in Providence and knew each other's every move. With George Bouchard returning from the injured list, the Barons suddenly possessed a very formidable defense. McAvoy, Robertson, and Bouchard, along with Gordon Hollingworth and Bill Needham were as good a defense grouping as any in the League.

Hendy had one more trick up his sleeve. He recalled Michel Labadie from Quebec City. The speedy Labadie was pure rookie gold. The high scoring winger was also a tremendous backchecker. His constant hustle seemed to inspire his sluggish teammates as the whole team seemed to pick up his tempo.

The new blood on the team produced instant results as the Barons went on a tear. They served notice to the rest of the League that this was not the same team that opened the season. Springfield, in particular, got the message in spades.

Barons were after. Seven years earlier, Cleveland management actually purchased an entire junior A team in Winnipeg just because Gordon Stratton was a member. This secured his playing rights. Unfortunately, Gordon did not turn out to be the player Cleveland thought he would be. Luckily, the Barons discovered his younger brother, Art, who would turn out to be the star.

Jim Hendy guided young Art through his amateur career with St. Catherines and North Bay. He turned pro with Winnipeg in the Western league in 1957-58 and was Rookie of the Year. He moved up to Cleveland for the current campaign and was an instant sensation. Art placed second on the Barons in scoring and seventh in the League overall.

The entire team was back playing its hard-hitting swashbuckling style. Although the Barons couldn't win them all, they would never go down without a fight.

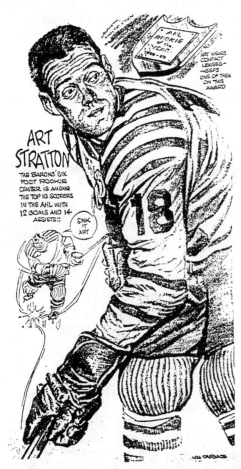

A large sellout crowd of 10,597 saw the Barons completely destroy the Indians 15-4. This avenged the 14-5 defeat at Springfield the month before. Top guns for Cleveland were Bob Bailey with four goals and rookie Art Stratton with six points on two goals and four assists.

Stratton proved to be a real find for Cleveland. Actually, the Barons were rather lucky to have him. Originally, it was Art's brother, Gordon, that the

Fred Glover was always the great equalizer. Whether a teammate needed protection or a measure of revenge had to be extracted, Fred never needed encouragement to drop his gloves. Sometimes he would fight to inspire his team, to give it a needed lift. Whatever the reason, Glover would give everything he had to help the Barons win. Kay Horiba collection.

On December 7th, in what was called the stormiest game in twenty years at Providence, the Barons had a four-game winning streak stopped 5-2.

Fred Glover, as so often was the case, was the center of attention. A fight between Fred and the Red's Jack Bionda precipitated an all-out riot that had players, fans, and even police involved. At the height of the ruckus, Reds' president Lou Pieri charged onto the ice. Glover, at the center of the melee, spotted Pieri trying to make peace. Fearing for the safety of the popular owner, Fred went over to Pieri and placed an arm around him. "Come on Lou...this is no place for you," Fred said to the Reds' owner. He then escorted Pieri off the ice and went back to his brawling. A gentlemen fighter was Fred Glover on this night. Incredible!

By mid-December, the Barons rested in third place with a 15-12-1 record. They had turned their season around by winning 13 of their last 17 games. The team was geared up for a big game with Hershey when violence once again took center stage.

During a big 6-2 Cleveland win that elevated the Barons to within three points of first place Buffalo, the Bears' Larry Zeidel tried to intimidate the Barons. He played the game in a fit of rage; but when he raised his stick at Bob Bailey, all hell broke loose. The two star ruffians engaged in a bloody stick-swinging duel that left both players cut and battered.

Bailey, in particular, lost a lot of blood as his wounds required 11 stitches on the forehead and five on the cheek. The Cleveland-Hershey rivalry was at its peak and League officials feared further violence between the clubs. As a result, Zeidel was banned from the next three games against Cleveland while Bailey would miss the next Hershey contest.

The Barons stayed on the doorstep of first place Buffalo for the next month. But on January 10th, the first and worst of a long string of injuries hit the team.

Near the end of a 4-4 tie with Providence at the Arena, goalie Gerry McNamara went down with torn ligaments in his left knee that would keep him out of the lineup for five weeks.

Cleveland State University archives – photo by Fred Bottomer.

Cleveland State University archives.

Claude Dufour, recently with Three Rivers in the Quebec Amateur League, was signed as a replacement, and he won his first game as a Baron in a big way. With the rookie in goal, Cleveland played an inspired game as they won in Buffalo 5-3.

The Barons came back home to defeat Buffalo 6-3 at the Arena. This pulled them within one single point of the first place Bisons with a 23-16-2 record. As fate would have it, this was as close as Cleveland would come to the lead as injuries and illness began to take their toll on the club.

Joining Gerry McNamara with a banged up knee was Art Stratton. He would miss a month of action, and the inactivity cost him the scoring title. Two Barons were rushed to the hospital for emergency appendectomies – Cal Stearns and Bucky Hollingworth. Bob Bailey was out with bronchitis. Three others were playing with painful nagging injuries – George Bouchard (fractured toe), Bill Shvetz (bruised heel), and Fred Glover (bad back).

The injuries led to an inevitable slump that knocked the team 10 points out of first place. After a five-game losing streak during the first two weeks of February, Coach Jackie Gordon had had it.

"If we don't come out of it tonight, the boom is going to be lowered – and lowered hard," stated the angry coach. "I've gone along so far with this slump, figuring it was a letdown after our January winning streak and lots of injuries. But this has now definitely gone past a letdown. It's still a case of needing to do some skating, checking, and a little hard work."

Cleveland State University archives.

Glover Aims at 300-Goal Record at Arena Tomorrow and Saturday

The scolding by the coach had an effect on the team as they went out and beat Springfield 5-4 in overtime and then blanked Hershey 3-0. It was goalie Claude Dufour's first shutout and brought the team back to within seven points of Buffalo.

Near the end of February, Cleveland still sat in third place. But through all of the ups and downs of this wild season, Fred Glover kept scoring at a steady pace and was now ready to become the second member of the 300-goal club, joining Fred Thurier.

His 100th goal came against Cleveland's Johnny Bower on March 10, 1951 while he was with Indianapolis. Number 200 came against Hershey's John Henderson on February 17, 1956 at the Arena.

Glover's entire philosophy on hockey was centered around his team's success. As any player would be, he was proud of his accomplishments; but the team always came before individual accolades. "I never have set myself a target for any particular number of goals in a season," stated Fred. "All I want to do is win games."

His big night came at the Arena on February 27, 1959 as the Barons blanked Providence 5-0 behind Gerry McNamara, who was back in goal after an 18-game absence. Fred entered the contest with 298 goals. Number 299 came at 7:22 of the second period.

With the crowd of 7,775 loudly cheering his every move, the 31-year-old right winger finally scored his monumental 300th at 15:13 of the third period. The game was stopped, as Cleveland's hero retrieved the puck as a souvenir. The crowd gave Glover an extended ovation. His next milestone would be breaking Fred Thurier's League record of 319; but that would have to wait until the next season.

After Glover's historic night, the Barons had to deal with a make-or-break seven-game road trip. Since losing their first ten road games early in the season, Cleveland had gone 8-10-0. This was very respectable, but a near clean sweep was needed if the team was to catch Buffalo for first place.

A perfect road trip dream went up in smoke after the first game, as Rochester dashed any Cleveland title hopes by defeating the Barons 4-2. The loss left the Clevelanders eight points behind Buffalo with a 31-28-2 record. But instead of throwing in the towel, this Barons club kept right on fighting to the end.

Cleveland won four and tied one of the remaining six games to conclude their most successful road trip in years. The action-packed journey East saw Fred Glover sustain a badly broken nose off of a deflected shot. Some feared that the captain would miss the rest of the year. But Fred would have none of that. He was fitted with a special plastic face shield to protect the nose and was right back in the lineup a week later.

On the trip four Barons were arrested after an altercation with the fans outside of the Cleveland dressing room in Springfield. The fans began throwing drinks and spitting on the Baron players after the Indians' 11-1 victory. An incensed Bob Robertson went after a heckler, and Bill Needham, Gordon Hollingworth, and George Bouchard joined in the ruckus. When fans go beyond the bounds of common decency, they are asking for trouble. In this case, they got it.

The players appeared in Springfield court when the Barons played a second game there a week later. They were fined $10.00 each and released.

Despite the fine trip, Buffalo clinched first place, as they were just as hot as the Barons. Cleveland returned home seven points behind the Bisons with only three games to play.

Cleveland won two of those last three games to finish in second place by three points with a 37-30-3 record. They closed out the season with a 5-1 victory over the fourth place Hershey Bears, their opponent in the playoffs' best of seven opening round.

THE PLAYOFFS

Hershey entered the playoffs in the throes of the worst slump in their history. The defending champions lost nine and tied one of their last ten games. After challenging Buffalo for first place all season long, the Bears fell to fourth place with a 32-32-6 record.

Cleveland, on the other hand, went 7-2-1 in their last ten games to close in fine fashion. The team was completely healthy for the first time in months and looked primed for a strong title bid.

During the regular season, the Barons handled the Bears well, winning 10 of 14 games. Although all the games were extremely hard fought, Cleveland clearly was the favorite to advance to the finals.

Even though the Bears hibernated near the end of the season, the mere sight of the Barons was enough to awake the slumbering Hersheys. They came out all fired up for Game One at the Arena and manhandled the Barons 6-2.

After the Bears jumped out to a 2-0 first period lead, goals by Eddie Mazur and Bob Barlow 91 seconds apart evened the score. But after that, it was all Hershey. The loss made it imperative for Cleveland to win the second game.

The Barons knew what they had to do in Game Two, but it was Hershey's rambunctious defenseman Larry Zeidel who scored first at 5:31 of the second period. The goal seemed to light a fire under the Barons as they then woke up and started to play hockey.

Two lightning-quick goals by Don Hogan at 7:25 and Fred Glover at 7:53 gave Cleveland the lead. Now the Arena crowd was into the game and would not let the home team ease up. Don Hogan scored an insurance goal in the third period as the Barons tied the series with a 3-1 victory.

As the series shifted to Hershey for the next two games, a controversy arose over the plastic face shield Fred Glover was wearing to protect his broken nose. Lloyd Blinco, Hershey general manager, claimed Glover was taking a poke at all of his players knowing that anyone would hurt their hand if they tried to retaliate by throwing a punch. Fred, in turn, would point to black marks on the plastic shield. They were from tape on the sticks that Hershey players were swinging at his face.

The Bears insisted that Glover be made to play without the mask. But in the end, Fred was allowed to keep wearing it, and the series continued.

In Game Three, the Barons came out flying and took an early 1-0 lead on a goal by Bob Bailey at 9:15 of the first period. But once again, Larry Zeidel would haunt the Clevelanders. Usually a low-scoring rearguard, the Wild One scored two power-play goals late in the opening stanza to give the Bears all the scoring they needed. The game became a defensive struggle the rest of the way, and Hershey hung on for a 2-1 win.

In Game Four, the Barons played a defensive gem to even the series with a 2-0 victory. Goals by Bob Bailey in the second period and Fred Glover at 19:01 of the third gave Cleveland its margin of victory.

While the series was extremely rough, and at times quite dirty, it took until the fourth game for a full-scale donnybrook to break out.

At 19:30 of the final period, Cleveland's Bill Shvetz and the Bears' Jack Price engaged in a brief high-sticking episode. Since less than two minutes remained in the game, both players were sent to their dressing rooms. As Shvetz left the ice, words were exchanged with Hershey goalie Bobby Perreault. Suddenly Shvetz and the goaltender were swinging wildly, and both benches emptied and fights broke out all over the ice. The expected bloodbath between the two teams was in full force.

Game Five at the Arena was a brutal affair, as both teams seemed bent on physically punishing the other. As always, Larry Zeidel was at the center of the rough stuff. He wielded his stick like a sword and repeatedly speared Baron players. Fred Glover had a large bruise on his ribs, and Bill Shvetz had bruises on his stomach and chest. All came from Zeidel's stick.

In the hockey part of the game, Hershey edged the Barons 4-3 on Mike Nykoluk's goal at 18:24 of the third period.

In the first period, Eddie Mazur and the Bears' Tom McCarthy traded goals. In the second stanza, Fred Glover and Eddie Stankiewicz did the same.

Cleveland went on top 3-2 early in the third period on a long shot by George Bouchard. But goals by Bob Solinger and Nykoluk proved to be the difference.

Down three games to two, and with their backs firmly planted to the wall, the Barons went to Hershey for Game Six. Their mission was clear. Either win, or their season was over.

Cleveland came out smoking and let Hershey know that they meant business. Hitting anything in sight, the Barons and Bears belted each other with such gusto that one expected the boards to crumble.

Cleveland scored in the first period with a goal by George Bouchard. Hershey's Mike Nykoluk tied it in the second.

Overtime looked likely when Fred Glover worked the puck into the Hershey zone midway in the third period. He spotted Bob Bailey open near the Hershey net and fed him a perfect pass. Bob put the moves on Bobby Perreault and whipped home the tie-breaker at 11:24.

Bill Shvetz scored into an open net at 19:07, and the Barons had tied the series. The 3-1 victory sent the two teams back to Cleveland for the seventh and deciding game.

Sometimes there is so much tension and pressure on the home team in a seventh game that playing at home can be a disadvantage.

The Barons obviously were up tight to open the game and trailed 2-1 after one period and 4-1 after two. Everything seemed to go wrong, and the home crowd was on their backs.

After a fiery pep talk from Jackie Gordon, the Barons came out for the third period determined to make a comeback. And come back they did – almost.

Bob Bailey scored his fourth playoff goal after only 26 seconds of the third chapter. When Art Stratton scored at 13:35, Arena fans went wild hoping for a miracle. But a storybook finish was not to be, as Hershey hung on for a 4-3 victory and a series win.

Everyone in Cleveland was bitterly disappointed. For the second straight year, the Barons had been eliminated from the playoffs in the first round by losing a seventh game on home ice.

This series was as fierce a playoff as ever played in the AHL. A total of 119 minor penalties, six majors, and 12 misconducts were called. This came to a record 368 penalty minutes for the seven games. "That was the roughest series I've ever seen," said player-coach Frank Mathers of Hershey.

Although they failed to win the championship, this Barons' team was one of the most exciting to watch. It gave the fans plenty to cheer about, and the next season was eagerly awaited.

FINAL STANDINGS
1958-59

	W	L	T	GF	GA	PTS.
Buffalo	38	28	4	233	201	80
Cleveland	37	30	3	261	252	77
Rochester	34	31	5	242	209	73
Hershey	32	32	6	200	202	70
Springfield	30	38	2	253	282	62
Providence	28	40	2	222	265	58

Top Baron Scorers	G	A	PTS.
Eddie Mazur	34	44	78
Art Stratton	29	47	76
Bob Bailey	28	41	69
Fred Glover	22	39	61
Michel Labadie	23	35	58
Don Hogan	24	32	56
Bob Barlow	27	27	54
Bill Shvetz	13	26	39
Gordon Vejprava	17	20	37

Calder Cup Champion – Hershey Bears

THE 1958-59 CLEVELAND BARONS

Front (L-R): Eddie Coen, Director of Publicity, Claude Dufour (sub goaltender), Jack Gordon, Coach; James C. Hendy, V.P. and G.M.; Fred Glover, Captain; Gerry McNamara, Floyd Perras, Promotions. Middle: Bill Needham, Michel Labadie, "Bucky" Hollingworth, Bobby Robertson, Ed "Spider" Mazur, Bob Bailey, George McAvoy, Art Stratton. Back: Gordie Vejprava, Cal Stearns, Bill Shvetz, Georges Bouchard, Bill Hogan, Bob Barlow, Jack Boag, Trainer. Kay Horiba collection.

Walt Voysey collection.

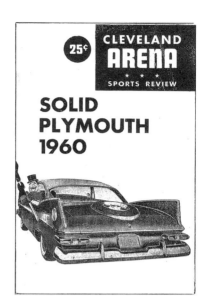

1959-60 SEASON

During the off-season, the AHL added a seventh team to the League in the Quebec Aces. The loop would still operate as one division with the top four teams making the playoffs.

The Barons kept busy on the trading front during the summer months. Unable to work out a deal with Toronto to secure the rights of Gerry McNamara for another season, Cleveland was forced to search for another goaltender. While Claude Dufour did a fine job filling in for McNamara the year before, Jim Hendy wanted a veteran in goal.

The Cleveland GM was able to pry old nemesis Gil Mayer away from Hershey for Dufour and defenseman Bucky Hollingworth.

The local icers also traded up and coming Art Stratton to New York for two top-notch players, center Ed Hoekstra and defenseman Aldo Guidolin. Guidolin, in particular, was a prize addition to the Baron backline.

With high expectations, the Barons hoped for a fast getaway. But it was not in the cards. Opening the season with seven games on the road, Cleveland came home with a 2-4-1 record and was missing a star player.

Bob Bailey, who married a local girl and lived in Cleveland, quit the team. Citing the extreme pressure of playing in front of family and friends, Bailey demanded a trade or he would give up the game. A surprised Jim Hendy was able to give Bailey his wish. The disgruntled icer was sent to Buffalo for center Bill Dineen. Having played four years in Detroit and one in Chicago before going to the Bisons, Bill was a fine acquisition for the Barons. Although Cleveland would miss Bailey's muscle, Dineen was a big-time scorer and a veteran leader.

Things went from bad to worse for Cleveland. After losing their home opener to Springfield, goalie Gil Mayer suffered a broken jaw in an 8-1 win over Quebec. The aging star would miss two months after taking a shot square on the jaw bone.

The Barons lost three straight games with spare goalie Don Rigazio in the nets. With the team now encamped in the League basement with a 3-8-1 record, Jim Hendy went frantically searching for a replacement. He came up with Gilles Boisvert, who had been playing in Sudbury, Ontario with a Detroit Red Wing farm club.

Boisvert was an adequate replacement during his time with the club. But still the team was treading water and going nowhere.

The only bright spot for the team in the early going was the tremendous play of Captain Freddie Glover. He scored 4 goals, including the game winner in overtime, during an 8-7 victory at Rochester. This sent him winging his way to a record-breaking season.

The first of three all-time AHL records that Fred would set this season came on December 12th in an 8-3 victory over Buffalo at the Arena.

Greig Hicks
Gene Kiczek collection.

Cal Stearns
Gene Kiczek collection.

Aldo Guidolin was a hard-hitting force on the Cleveland Blueline for three years. Beginning in 1959-60, Aldo racked up penalty minute totals of 168, 152, and 177 over the next three seasons.
Kay Horiba collection.

Bill Dineen
Three important players for the Barons during the 1959-60 season were Bill Dineen (top), Cal Stearns (middle), and Greig Hicks (bottom).
Gene Kiczek collection.

Glover became the all-time League scoring champion by breaking Fred Thurier's mark of 744 points. His one goal and two assists gave him a total of 745. It was a goal at 16:07 of the third period that put Fred over the top. He retrieved the puck as a souvenir and was warmly congratulated by Thurier himself. The ex-Baron great now served as a linesman during home games and was on the ice when the record-breaking point was scored.

Glover now had 314 goals and 431 assists in 635 games. He was now only five goals away from Thurier's record of 319 and three assists shy of Jackie Gordon's mark of 434. The record book would soon be wiped clean.

While Captain Fred was the center of attention, the team itself was in trouble. The Barons were not scoring with any consistency. So Jim Hendy once again went into action. He acquired the rights to center Earl Ingarfield from the New York Rangers.

Earl played the previous season in New York but was not seeing regular action this year with the Rangers. He asked to be sent to New York's farm club at Springfield so he could stay sharp. But the Indians, who were on top of the AHL, did not want to break up their winning combination. So Earl sat the bench and thus was available.

Coach Gordon put Ingarfield on a line with Fred Glover and Eddie Mazur. His other switch was to put Bill Dineen to work with Mike Labadie and rookie Greig Hicks. With these moves, the team began to make its move.

The Barons began to turn their season around on January 16th in a game against Providence that saw Fred Glover break Fred Thurier's goal-scoring record. The great Cleveland veteran scored two goals and two assists in a 7-4 thrashing of the Reds. This gave him a clean sweep of all the all-time scoring records. He now had 320 goals, 438 assists, and 758 points. The assist mark was set a few games earlier against Quebec. Fred also was the League's most penalized player with 1,113 penalty minutes.

The Barons finally pulled even with a 17-17-6 record when they defeated the Reds at Providence on January 24th. In the game, newly acquired Earl Ingarfield made his presence felt with a three-goal hat trick. His effect on the team was amazing. The once dormant offense was now buzzing with confidence.

The team now had gone 4-1-1 in their last six games to move into 5th place, one point behind Hershey and six in arrear of Buffalo.

Cleveland had a chance to flex its new-found muscles in a big game at Springfield on January 31st. The Indians were now firmly established as the League's new powerhouse. Their new working agreement with the New York Rangers had supplied them with a wealth of talent.

As if the Barons' task was not difficult enough, Springfield had won 16 straight games on home ice. They faced Cleveland gunning for the League record of 17 held by the 1937-38 Barons.

The Indians wanted this game badly and threw everything they had at the Barons. Time and again they bombarded the Cleveland net only to have goalie Gil Mayer come up with one miracle save after another. In all, the little netminder made 58 stops in one of his all-time best games. While Cleveland didn't win, the 4-4 tie preserved the '37-38 team's record. Goals by Mike Labadie and Earl Ingarfield midway through the third period enabled the Barons to come from behind for the tie. But the night belonged to Mayer. If not for his sensational performance, the Indians would have won in a landslide.

The Barons were now playing with a measure of confidence not seen before in this season. Leader of the pack, of course, was Glover. Fred took over the League's scoring lead with three assists in a 4-3 win at Quebec on February 17th. All of the assists came on goals by the red-hot Earl Ingarfield.

While the Baron captain's scoring was the talk of the town, he still remained a player not to be messed with. Buffalo's "bad man" Gus Mortson found out the hard way.

With five minutes left in a 4-2 Baron win at Buffalo on February 7th, the huge 230-pound Bison defenseman decided to take out his frustrations on Glover. Fred had the puck near the boards when Mortson charged him from 15 feet away. In a vicious scene, the big Bison crosschecked Fred from behind. Glover's head bounced off the glass above the boards with a sickening thud, and he lay unconscious for several minutes. Five stitches were needed to close a gash on Fred's head.

Fred and his teammates were enraged at the deliberate intent to injure. Said GM Jim Hendy, "There will be another game with Buffalo. And when there is, I think Glover and the boys will take care of Mr. Mortson."

That game came on February 26th. The Barons were in the midst of an awful evening. Besides losing to Buffalo 7-2 at the Arena, goalie Gil Mayer was injured again. Gil suffered a torn rib cartilege on his right side in the loss and would miss three and a half weeks of action. Once again Gilles Boisvert, who was now playing for Edmonton in the Western league, was summoned to the rescue.

Fred Glover spent the night in a foul mood. When the game was out of hand, he first got into a skirmish with the Bisons' Ivan Irwin early in the third period. After returning from the penalty box, Fred decided it was time to pay Mr. Mortson a visit. The fight was Glover's way of saying "don't ever

Old Rough and Ready
By LOU DARVAS

mess with me again." With knuckle prints all over his face, Mortson got the message. He stayed out of Fred's way from that day forward.

Cleveland started the pivotal month of March with an eight-game road trip. The long journey East started out on the right foot with two victories. The second, a 3-2 overtime win at Hershey, on Don Hogan's goal, finally moved the team into fourth place for the first time in months. But three straight losses followed to put a damper on the team's spirits.

They bounced back with a 6-3 victory at Quebec and tasted third place for a day. Big gun for Cleveland as usual was Captain Fred. Glover's two goals and two assists gave him a total of 94 points and a tight grip on the League scoring lead.

But two losses to end the lengthy trip dropped the team back into fifth place, one point behind both Providence and Buffalo, with a 30-28-7 record.

The Barons played well down the stretch, moved into fourth place, and stayed there. They pulled three points ahead of Buffalo with a 6-1 rout of the Bisons. The game was another record setter for Freddie Glover. Fred assisted on three goals to bring his season point total to 103. This broke Jackie Gordon's team record of 102.

Still the club's goal of clinching a playoff spot was not accomplished. They finally eased a sigh of relief on March 26th when they bombarded Quebec 10-2. Needing only one point to make the playoffs, the Barons poured home five first-period goals to settle the issue early. The big win set up a best-of-seven opening round series against the second-place Rochester Americans.

On an individual note, Fred Glover became the fourth player in League history to win the scoring title twice. The others were Jack Markle of Syracuse, Les Douglas of Indianapolis and Cleveland, and Eddie Olson of the Barons. With 38 goals and 69 assists for 107 points, Glover set a team mark that would never be broken. He was later named the League's Most Valuable Player.

THE PLAYOFFS

The Barons were facing a powerful Rochester club in the playoffs. The Americans finished in second place, seven points behind Springfield with a 40-27-5 record. Cleveland had finished fourth with a 34-30-8 mark. The two teams split their 12 games going 5-5-2. Still, the Amerks were heavily favored to advance to the finals.

Cleveland was bound and determined to make up for their two seven-game playoff losses the last two seasons.

They went into Rochester sky high and hung a 2-0 shutout on the Americans. Goalie Gil Mayer was terrific and got the only goal he needed by Greig Hicks at 10:10 of the second period. Bill Dineen put icing on the cake with an insurance marker at 15:06 of the third period.

The stunned Americans were really shocked when Cleveland won Game Two, 2-1. The Barons ground Rochester's high-powered offense to a halt as they played a near flawless defensive game. While Earl Ingarfield and Fred Glover provided the offense, the big hero of the game was Cal Stearns. The "old man" of the team at 33, perhaps the greatest penalty killer in the history of the League, was simply outstanding. At one point, while the Amerks held a 5-3 manpower advantage, Cal blocked five shots with his body. Every time Rochester had a power play, Stearns was there to stop them.

Coming home with an unexpected two-game lead, the Barons pounced on Rochester in Game Three. Behind two goals each by Freddie Glover and Eddie Mazur, Cleveland beat the Americans 7-5. The Barons were one game from the finals and seemed primed for the kill.

What transpired over the next week was the competitive low point in the history of the team. Although they would miss the playoffs three times during their remaining years in the League, nothing compared to the shocking events that would now occur.

Perhaps a bit tired and overconfident from their three surprising victories, the Barons dropped a 5-3 decision to Rochester at the Arena. Steve Kraftcheck, ex-Baron and now Amerk playing coach, said "We're not thinking about the length of the series. We've just got to keep plugging along, game by game."

And plug along they did. Behind goalie Ed Chadwick, the Americans moved closer to a League first by beating Cleveland 4-1 in Rochester. No team had ever come back from a three-game deficit to win a playoff series, but the Americans now believed that they could become the first to turn the trick.

Playing like a team looking over its shoulder, the Barons dropped the pivotal sixth game 5-3 at the Arena. With the noose tightening around their necks, the seventh game in Rochester was a foregone conclusion.

The gloom following the Barons' 4-1 loss at Rochester in Game Seven sent shock waves through the franchise. They had completed the worst fold-up in League history. The players went home for the longest summer of their lives.

FINAL STANDINGS
1959-60

West	W	L	T	GF	GA	PTS.
Springfield	43	23	6	280	219	92
Rochester	40	27	5	285	211	85
Providence	38	32	2	251	237	78
Cleveland	34	30	8	267	229	76
Buffalo	33	35	4	251	271	70
Hershey	28	37	7	226	238	63
Quebec	19	51	2	178	333	40

Top Baron Scorers	G	A	PTS.
Fred Glover	38	69	107
Earl Ingarfield	25	40	65
Ed Hoekstra	20	38	58
Bill Dineen	26	28	54
Eddie Mazur	29	24	53
Cal Stearns	21	31	52
Greig Hicks	17	34	51
Michel Labadie	24	22	46
Don Hogan	16	28	44

Calder Cup Champion – Springfield Indians

THE 1959-60 CLEVELAND BARONS

Front (L-R): Edward J. Coen, Publicity Director; Gil Mayer, Jack Gordon, Coach; Fred Glover, Captain; James C. Hendy, Vice-President and General Manager; Gil Boisvert, Peter Hendy, Business Manager. Second: Jack Boag, Trainer; Andre Martin, Don Hogan, Michel Labadie, Eddie Mazur, George Gosselin, Georges Bouchard, Bill Shvetz, Lex Cook, Advertising Sales Manager and Chief Scout. Third: Greig Hicks, Bill Needham, Bill Dineen, Aldo Guidolin, Ed Hoekstra, George McAvoy, Earl Ingarfield, Cal Stearns, Dan Blair. James Peter Hendy collection.

1960-61 SEASON

The times were changing, and so were the ways and means of hockey. No longer was it possible for the Barons to sign and develop all of their own talent. There were approximately 600 professional hockey players in North America, and more than 500 of them were owned by NHL teams. Promising players usually signed with National League teams, who in turn sent them out to their own farm clubs for development.

Cleveland now owned only 25 players outright, and not all of them were ready for AHL play. In order to field a competitive team, the Barons were forced to sign limited working agreements with NHL teams in order to fill out their roster. None of these players were subject to recall during their time in Cleveland until the season was over.

The first such agreements were with the New York Rangers and Montreal Canadiens. The Rangers sent Cleveland Aldo Guidolin again, while Montreal loaned Ron Attwell, Moe Mantha, and Billy Sutherland to the Barons.

As a result of the previous year's playoff disaster, 50% of the roster was changed. Earl Ingarfield and Ed Hoekstra were recalled by New York. Michel Labadie was sent to Quebec. Don Hogan, George Bouchard, George McAvoy, Bill Shvetz, and Dan Blair were released. Holdovers were Fred Glover, Gil Mayer, Cal Stearns, Bill Dineen, Ed Mazur, Bill Needham, and Aldo Guidolin.

Many youngsters were brought in to pump new life into the team. On defense were Maurice (Moe) Mantha, and Jim Mikol; center Ron Attwell; wingers John Ferguson, Wayne Larkin, and Bill Sutherland. The lone new veteran was Cal Gardner, who had played twelve seasons in the NHL.

There was a lot of talent among these new youngsters, but it would take a while for it all to mesh together. Coach Gordon had his work cut out.

After splitting their first four games on the road, the Barons came home and were shut out by Springfield 3-0. This was the second of three early season shutouts at the hands of the Indians and their great goalie, ex-Baron Marcel Paille. The other two scores were 6-0 whitewashes. It became obvious early on that Springfield once again was the team to beat in the AHL. If anything, they were stronger than ever.

The Barons played .500 hockey for the first six weeks of the season. The players were getting to know each other and learn each other's moves and tendencies. But it was obvious to Coach Gordon that this team would have trouble scoring goals.

Through their first 18 games, the team had only scored 50 goals. While this average improved somewhat over the course of the season, this team had to win with defense. But Cleveland was not alone in this regard.

Except for Springfield, in a class by itself averaging over five goals per game, scoring was down throughout the League. Aside from the Indians, the other teams were all evenly matched. The goaltending and the defenses were all very strong, and low scoring games were often the result.

Ed "The Spider" Mazur was a solid veteran for the Barons from 1958-59 through 1961-62. The team's good humour man, Ed led the club in scoring in '58-'59.
Kay Horiba collection.

Fred Glover, Ed (Spider) Mazur, and Michel Labadie each score a goal in a 3-0 victory over Hershey.
Cleveland Public Library collection.

Cleveland finally scored against Springfield with a goal by Ron Attwell on November 23rd. His score at 11:35 of the second period broke a scoreless streak of 211 minutes and 35 seconds against the powerful Indians. But it was far from enough, as the Barons were beaten 7-3.

Although they were beaten by Springfield, the mere fact that they scored against the Indians seemed to inspire the Barons. They suddenly found their stride and won seven of their next eight games to improve their record to 17-12-0. Two Barons who played a major role in the upsurge were Gil Mayer and Eddie Mazur.

The 30-year-old Mayer was having a fine season in goal. He finally seemed to be regaining the form that made him one of the League's top goalies at Pittsburgh from 1949-50 through 1955-56. Five times during those years he had the League's top goaltending average. When the Hornets' rink was torn down after the 1956 season, Gil moved on to Hershey. It was here that his luck changed.

Forced to alternate with the Bears' Bobby Perreault, Mayer's effectiveness suffered. He also was hit with the injury bug. Pneumonia and a knee operation kept him sidelined for long periods.

Traded to Cleveland after the 1958-59 season, his luck remained bad. A broken jaw and torn rib cartilage kept him out of actions for over two months.

But this season, he was injury free, and his play showed it. His average was down to 2.97 after 29 games. In the midst of the Baron hot streak, he backstopped his team to a big 4-1 win over Springfield. What made his performance all the more remarkable was that he was battling a case of the flu that saw him lose 10 pounds.

The 6'2", 210-pound Mazur was putting together a fine season himself. Called "The Spider" because he seemed to be all arms and legs when he skated, Eddie was leading the team in scoring.

Besides his scoring exploits, Ed was a great team leader and the club's good humor man. Although a 13-year veteran, the Spider skated and hustled like a rookie. Off the ice he kept his teammates in stitches with his constant joking and tomfoolery. He also played a mean piano and would often lead his teammates in the rock and roll of the times. Since coming to Cleveland from Rochester for Bo Elik, Mazur had a profound influence on the team, both on and off the ice.

After moving into second place, the Barons got the holiday blues and went into a slide. They went 2-4-0 over their next six games and fell further behind Springfield. The Indians were now 16 points ahead of the Barons as they headed into Cleveland on January 6th.

Besides trying to stop Springfield's runaway train, the game was a special night for Fred Glover. The Baron ace was to receive three trophies prior to the game before dignitaries of both the NHL and AHL. He received the John B. Sollenberger Trophy for last season's scoring championship; the Les Cunningham plaque as the League's MVP; and a gold puck for making the first all star team.

Unfortunately, the Indians were not in a giving mood and spoiled Glover's party. If there was any doubt that Springfield was in a class by itself, that doubt was erased during the 4-1 loss. The Indians put on a passing clinic and only Gil Mayer's great work kept the score close. Cleveland actually played well and led 1-0 until 18:05 of the second period. But a goal by Gerry Foley opened the floodgates. To the Barons' credit, they gave it their all, but they were just no match for the East Coast juggernaut.

Cleveland's losing streak reached five games before Bill Sutherland's goal beat Quebec 4-3. The Aces came back to beat the Barons two nights later. The team left Quebec with a 20-20-0 record. Returning to Cleveland for a Saturday night game against Providence, they had no idea that the day would prove to be the end of an era in Cleveland hockey history.

The City of Cleveland, the Barons' hockey club, and all of its fans were shocked and saddened by the news that vice president and general manager Jim Hendy had suddenly died of a heart attack on Saturday, January 14th.

Hendy was the third man to carry the fortunes of Cleveland hockey on his shoulders. Harry (Hap) Holmes was the first through professional hockey's infant years here. Holmes was followed by Al Sutphin, who built the Arena and presided over the Barons' glory years. When Al sold the club in 1949, Hendy left his position as president of the United States Hockey League to take over the Barons.

Hendy's tenure in Cleveland was a highly successful one. His teams won three regular season championships and four Calder Cup titles. Jim was named Hockey Executive the the Year by The Hockey News newspaper in 1949-50 and 1956-57.

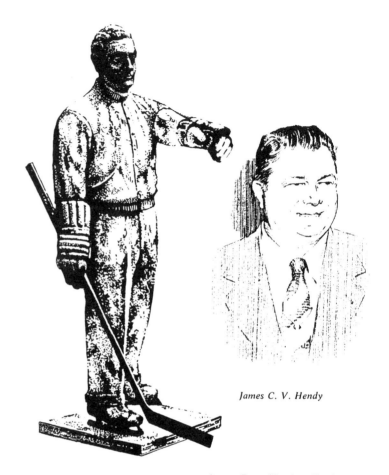

James C. V. Hendy

James Peter Hendy collection.

The loss of Jim Hendy was felt throughout the world of hockey. He was one of the most respected executives to ever grace the ice sport. A two-time winner of the Hockey News "Executive of the Year" award, his greatest honor came posthumously. On March 9, 1970, Jim Hendy was awarded the Lester Patrick Trophy for outstanding service to hockey in the United States.
Cleveland Public Library collection.

Most of all, Hendy won many friends for the Cleveland club. He was accepted into hockey's highest circles, and he was without a peer in judging talent.

Dignitaries from all over the hockey world came to pay their last respects at the Saxton Funeral Home in Lakewood. Among them was ex-Baron great Johnny Bower, now starring for Toronto in the NHL. "Jim gave me my big break," said the peerless netminder. "In 1958, when I was drafted by Toronto, I had decided to quit the game. Jim persuaded me to go ahead and join the Leafs. He said I could make it, so I decided to try. Except for him, I would have retired."

Taking over Hendy's duties as general manager was Coach Jackie Gordon. "Jim was getting to be something like a father to me," stated the Baron coach. "He took me into his complete confidence. He always told me to speak up, and I did, and he always respected my opinion. I can't tell you how much I'll miss him."

The team itself, though greatly saddened by the loss of its leader, banded together and won 7 of its next 10 games. Included in the streak was an emotional 5-3 victory over dreaded Springfield in the first game after Hendy's funeral. Staying all over the Indians, the Barons played one of their best games of the year and did their late boss proud.

Things were proceeding smoothly for the second-place Barons who had a 27-23-0 record as the result of their mini-streak. But a sudden rash of injuries exposed the lack of depth on the team, and a huge slump followed.

A badly bruised hip to Bill Sutherland and Fred Glover's knee woes left center Ron Attwell as the only healthy member of the team's first line. Combined with a leg injury to center Greig Hicks, the thin Cleveland roster was now exposed.

The five rookies on the roster were now expected to take up the slack. This was easier said than done. Injured Sutherland aside, the first-year Cleveland players were defensemen Jim Mikol and Moe Mantha and forwards John Ferguson and Wayne Larkin. They all played fine hockey at times, but the pressure of the playoff fight on this depleted squad was a great burden. The result was a skid where Cleveland lost 12 of its next 15 games. Included in the slump was a winless seven-game road trip from hell. The team fell to fifth place with a 30-35-0 record. Only seven games remained on the schedule, and a playoff spot looked remote – even though all of the games were on Arena ice.

The biggest obstacle confronting the club was the powerful Springfield Indians. The Barons faced the runaway League leaders in the first game after their road disaster.

After two periods, the Indians' led 2-0, and all that was missing from the game was funeral music. The local icers played lethargically and seemed ready to throw in the towel. But Jackie Gordon would have none of that.

The "never say die" coach lit into his team after the second period. The air was filled with words as blue as the team's uniforms. Although the players would not comment on the "pep" talk later, it seemed to be the tonic that was needed.

A different Cleveland team showed up for the final stanza. The rejuvenated local icers completely took away the play from the stunned Indians. They expected Cleveland to roll over dead, but the opposite was true.

Still the Barons didn't score until 14:54 on a goal by Wayne Larkin. With the crowd now in a wild mood, the home team put on a display of pressure hockey not seen all year at the Arena. The constant attack paid off on Ron Attwell's long slapshot at 19:01.

A comeback tie would look great, but Cleveland would not settle for that. The Barons kept firing away, and at 19:51 they hit pay dirt. A long shot by Defenseman Jim Mikol was tipped in by Freddie Glover for the biggest and most improbable win of the season. Sure defeat was turned into a 3-2 win, and the Barons were on their way.

The most interesting angle to the victory was that trainer and practice goalie Les Binkley was in the nets. Coach Gordon decided to rest an exhausted Gil Mayer after the team's ill-fated road trip. But he never dreamed that Binkley would respond in such a grand way.

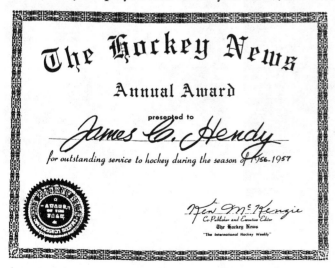

James Peter Hendy collection.

Gil Mayer
Kay Horiba collection.

He stayed with Les in the afternoon of March 18th. Cleveland and Buffalo were to finish a game that was started on February 25th. A power failure at the Arena after the second period caused the game to be halted with the Barons ahead 2-1. The teams battled through a scoreless third period, and the Clevelanders had a valuable win.

The Barons and Bisons went back at it that evening, and Cleveland came away with another 2-1 victory. Once gain, Binkley was the unlikely hero.

A 2-2 tie with Hershey lifted the Barons into fourth place, only one point out of third heading into the season's final weekend. In his three full games plus one period, Les Binkley had given up only five goals and had given the team a much-needed shot in the arm. Coach Gordon had no choice but to stick with him for the final three games of the season.

The Barons' final big weekend of the season started with a Friday night bang. They blasted the Quebec Aces 10-1 to move into third place, one point ahead of Buffalo and two up on Rochester. Still they needed one more victory to clinch a playoff spot. Next up was a showdown with the Americans.

Many Barons with the previous year's club still vividly remembered the team's fold-up to Rochester in the playoffs. They relished the big game with the Amerks for not only would it clinch a Cleveland playoff berth, but it would eliminate Rochester from any hope for post-season play.

Performing like a team possessed, the Barons struck for five first-period goals as they went on to rout Rochester 7-1. The victory was sweet revenge, and the Cleveland icers relished every minute of it. The playoffs were in the bag.

The team concluded its incredible season ending rush by defeating Hershey 3-1 in the regular season finale. Once gain, goalie Les Binkley stood out in the nets. Since taking over for Gil Mayer on March 15th, Les had given up 8 goals. His only other action

Les Binkley
Gil Mayer was one of the top goalies in the American Hockey League during the 1950's while with the Pittsburgh Hornets. He played well for the Barons during the 1959-60 and 1960-61 seasons. But he was near the end of the line when Trainer Les Binkley took over in the nets on March 15, 1961. Binkley was sensational and became a fixture in goal through the 1965-66 season.
Kay Horiba collection.

(Left to Right) Bill Needham, Billy Sutherland, and Cal Gardner were all integral parts in the Barons late season rush to the Playoffs. Gene Kiczek collection.

during the season was in a 3-2 loss at Buffalo last October. He thus finished the season with a remarkable 1.38 goals against average. Everyone on the team knew that they wouldn't be in the playoffs without him.

By defeating Hershey on the season's last day, the Barons finished in third place with a 36-35-1 record. As a reward, they got the dubious distinction of playing the powerhouse Springfield Indians in the playoffs' opening round.

THE PLAYOFFS

Cleveland playing Springfield in the playoffs was like David meeting Goliath. Only David had more luck than the Barons.

The Indians rolled through the regular season in near record-breaking fashion. Their 49-22-1 record for 99 points was only one off the 100-point mark set by the 1949-50 Cleveland team. They blistered the nets for 344 goals. Once again, the 1949-50 Barons held the record of 358. Defensively, the Indians' 206 goals allowed was the lowest in the League.

It was no surprise that Springfield won nine of the twelve games played against Cleveland. This included all six played on Indian ice, where the first two games of the series would be played.

Springfield lived up to its reputation in Game One, as they pounded the Barons 8-1. The game was so one-sided that Indian goalie Marcel Paille only had to make 10 saves on the evening. Besides losing the game, the Barons also lost their best defenseman, Aldo Guidolin. Aldo severely pulled a hip muscle when jammed into the boards early in the game. The defense completely fell apart without him.

Cleveland came up with a much better effort in Game Two but still wound up on the short end of a 3-2 score.

The Barons held a 1-0 first-period lead on a goal by Cal Gardner. The first 20 minutes were highlighted by the renewal of an old feud between Fred Glover and Noel Price. The two combatants, who battled both on and off the ice for the last few years, went at each other savagely.

After Eddie Mazur gave Cleveland a 2-0 lead midway in the second period, the Indians began to take control. Behind 2-1 after two periods, the home team went ahead on goals by Price and Jim Anderson. They then held on to the lead and carried a 2-0 series lead back to Cleveland.

Cleveland fans didn't give their heroes much of a chance in the remaining two games of the series. Only 3,324 showed up to see the Barons drop a 4-1 decision in Game Three. The local icers gave it everything they had and held the powerful Indians to a 1-1 tie late into the second period. But three rapid-fire Springfield goals sewed up the contest. The loss left the plucky Barons one game from elimination.

A slim turnout of 2,576 saw the Barons bow out in game Four, 3-1. Once again, Cleveland would not back down to the mighty Indians. Except for Game One, the Barons made a game fight of it. But Springfield was playing on a level above everyone else in the AHL.

The Cleveland hockey club was facing a major task over the summer months. Not only did management have to strengthen the club, they had to rekindle interest among the general public. The team needed a fast turn-around before it was too late.

FINAL STANDINGS
1960-61

	W	L	T	GF	GA	PTS.
Springfield	49	22	1	344	206	99
Hershey	36	32	4	218	210	76
Cleveland	36	35	1	231	234	73
Buffalo	35	34	3	259	261	73
Rochester	32	36	4	261	244	68
Quebec	30	39	3	217	267	63
Providence	26	46	0	225	333	52

Top Baron Scorers	G	A	PTS.
Fred Glover	23	46	69
Eddie Mazur	30	39	69
Cal Gardner	25	39	64
Bill Dineen	28	31	59
Ron Attwell	23	35	58
Aldo Guidolin	10	35	45
Cal Stearns	16	25	41
Greig Hicks	10	29	39
Jim Mikol	12	23	35
Wayne Larkin	12	23	35
John Ferguson	13	21	34
Bill Sutherland	19	14	33

Calder Cup Champion – Springfield Indians

STRUGGLES OF THE 1960S

1961-62 SEASON

The AHL welcomed back an old friend for the 1961-62 season. The Pittsburgh Hornets returned to the League after a five-year absence with a brand new arena.

The League went back to a two-division setup of four teams each. In the West were Cleveland, Buffalo, Rochester, and Pittsburgh. The Eastern division consisted of Springfield, Hershey, Providence, and Quebec.

Coach Gordon added only three players to the previous year's team. But all three would prove to be major additions during the upcoming campaign.

Gordon swung his first trade since taking on the dual duties of general manager-coach when he sent Bill Dineen to Rochester for center Hank Ciesla. The 6'2" 195lb. power man was the American's leading scorer the year before with 74 points. The Barons desperately needed a high-scoring forward, and Ciesla fit the bill perfectly.

The new GM also plucked one of the Amerk's plums by purchasing up-and-coming Dick Van Impe. The 24-year-old right wing registered 56 points in his first year at Rochester.

Gordon then took defenseman Gary Bergman from Montreal on a lend-lease agreement. The Canadiens gave Cleveland a choice between Bergman and Moe Mantha. Moe performed well with the Barons the year before, but Gordon saw real star potential in the 22-year-old Bergman. His hunch would prove to be a winner.

The Barons sold the aging Gil Mayer to Providence and went with young Les Binkley in goal. This was a gutsy move on Gordon's part because Binkley only played in 12 games the previous season. But Jack liked what he saw in Les, and once again his big gamble would pay off.

The Coach convinced 39-year-old defenseman Tommy Williams to come back to the team on a full-time basis. This was necessitated by the move of Jim Mikol from defense to left wing.

Tommy Williams was a rookie with Cleveland in 1949-50. He would spend the better part of the next 14 years starring on the Baron blueline. Bill Hudec collection.

Les Binkley began the 1960-61 season as the Barons' Trainer and finished it as their #1 goalie. He backstopped the club to a West Division title the next year and won the Harry (Hap) Holmes Memorial Trophy as the American Hockey League's Top Goalie for 1965-66. Dick Dugan collection.

With guarded optimism, the Barons began the new season with a big and strong team that was loaded with question marks.

The question marks became larger when the Clevelanders were massacred 9-1 in the season opener at Providence. Binkley was shaky in goal, and his teammates also had the jitters.

The team returned from the season opening road trip with a 1-3-0 record and promptly dropped a 2-0 decision to Buffalo in the home opener. The bad start made Coach Gordon's worst fears come true. Fan interest was extremely low, and a sharp turnaround was needed.

The shot in the arm that the team needed was a goal by newly acquired Dick Van Impe. Dick's tally came at 1:53 of sudden death overtime in a 5-4 victory at Pittsburgh. The hard-earned victory seemed to inspire the team, and they won 8 of their next 10 games after the 1-4-0 start.

Included in the streak was Les Binkley's first professional shutout, a 3-0 whitewash of Hershey. Les was at the heart of the club's resurgence as he was beginning to make Jackie Gordon's decision to stick with him look good. He was beginning to make a name for himself, as word spread throughout the League that Binkley's performance last last season was no fluke. Cleveland had uncovered a great new goalie.

The Barons and Binkley hit an early season high on November 18th in Springfield. Cleveland had gone 18 straight games in the tiny Eastern city without tasting victory. But on this night the jinx was shattered as Binkley and his playmates came up big with a 3-1 victory. The Barons felt like the weight of the world had been lifted from their shoulders. After Cleveland took a 2-0 second-period lead, the Indians attacked savagely. But time after time Binkley would come up with a miracle save. He literally had the defending champions talking to themselves.

The suddenly surging Barons now felt that they could beat anyone. Perhaps they got a bit overconfident, because the great surge suddenly stopped. Over the course of their next eleven games, Cleveland went 2-7-2 to fall nine points behind Buffalo. Their 12-13-2 record reflected their inconsistency. Most of the blame was put on the offense. Promising plays seemed to go awry at the last moment. This is where hard work and extra practice time pays off. And these players were willing to sacrifice whatever it took to get back on track. They worked steadfastly with Coach Gordon, and eventually the team began to click again.

Cleveland fans were eagerly awaiting a December 30th matchup with the Rochester Americans. Word was out around the League that the Amerks were out to get John Ferguson of the Barons.

Back on December 10th in Rochester, Ferguson and the Amerk's Alex Faulkner began a shoving match. Fergy didn't take kindly to Faulkner and beat up the Rochester player so badly that he was hospitalized with a broken nose and fractured cheekbone. One colossal blow did most of the damage. Faulkner's teammates were incensed and vowed revenge on Ferguson.

Arena fans were surprised when there wasn't the slightest hint of fisticuffs in the Barons' 4-0 win. But word leaked out that the Americans were waiting to exact their revenge on their home ice in Rochester on January 7th.

Ferguson relished the challenge. "Let them try to start something!" fired back Big John. "Guys have tried it before, but that sort of thing just makes me go all the harder." The 6', 185-lb. winger was not a man to be taken lightly.

Coach Gordon had words of advise for Ferguson. He warned the truculent Baron that the crowd would be all over him trying to make him lose his cool. "So just remember to keep your head," said the Coach. "The best thing you can do is score a goal."

Big John was ready for anything. With eyes burning dark as coal, the fearless icer skated out into the lion's den. The crowd called for blood among other unmentionables. This just made Fergy all the more ready for action.

The look on his face said it all. He stared at each Rochester player one by one. They got the message. Not one Amerk player dared to tangle with Big John. Any thoughts of revenge were permanently put on hold. Ferguson won the battle without ever throwing a punch.

To make his night a complete success, John scored Cleveland's second goal in a big 4-1 win. The victory was the Barons' third in a row and put them over the .500 mark at 17-16-2.

The game was a personal triumph for John Ferguson. But Rochester was neither the first nor the last team to get humbled by Big John. During his three years with the Barons, and a long career with Montreal in the NHL, Fergy never lost a fight. He was the ultimate enforcer. Some of his fights were legendary. One decision over Boston's Ted Green turned an entire playoff series in Montreal's favor. And to top it off, John could also come up with a big

John Ferguson was the ultimate enforcer during his three years in Cleveland and later in Montreal. Throughout his violent career, Big John never lost a fight. In addition to his rugged play, Fergy could also score a big goal when needed. During the 1962-63 season, he popped in 40 while racking up 179 minutes in penalties.
Kay Horiba collection.

Al Cullen, the kid from Woodstock, Ontario, dazzled Cleveland fans when he subbed for injured goalie Les Binkley during the 1961-62 season. In true fairy tale fashion, Al racked up three straight shutouts in a row. He wound up the year with an 8-0 record and a 1.80 goals against average. Kay Horiba collection.

goal when needed. He was the type of player every team wished it had.

In the win over Rochester, goalie Les Binkley suffered a severely sprained ankle. In his place the Barons called on the services of an unknown amateur. Thus began one of the most amazing stories in team history.

Al Cullen, goaltender with the Woodstock, Ontario club in the Ontario Senior Amateur League, was thrown into the fire against the Hershey Bears. "I was little nervous at the start," understated the raw 20-year-old. He obviously got over the jitters, for he beat the Bears in Hershey 3-2.

It was quite an accomplishment for the new kid on the block, but he didn't stop there. In his first game at the Cleveland Arena, Cullen blanked the Buffalo Bisons. This was the Barons' first victory over Buffalo all season.

The Barons stretched their winning streak to six games with an 8-3 win at Providence. A red hot Fred Glover fired a three-goal hat trick to lead the rout. But it was the great goaltending of the kid from Woodstock, Ontario that had the players and Cleveland fans buzzing.

Cullen set all of Cleveland on its ears on January 20th and 21st. On Saturday night the amazing rookie shut out Quebec 2-0. He then followed that up with a 5-0 whitewash of Pittsburgh to stretch the Barons' winning streak to eight.

This gave Cullen three straight shutouts on Arena ice. No other Cleveland goaltender, before or since, had chalked up three straight home ice shutouts. During Johnny Bower's great shutout streak of 249 minutes, 51 seconds set in 1957-58, he recorded three consecutive shutouts, but one was in Springfield.

Cullen's fete was a fairytale come true. A kid from nowhere comes to the big city and becomes an instant hero. In his five straight victories, Al gave up only five goals. The eight-game winning streak gave the Barons a 22-16-2 record and put them into first place, one point ahead of Buffalo.

As all streaks must, this one came to an end when Buffalo stopped Cleveland at the Arena 4-2. The Bisons, who also won earlier in the week, now led the Barons by three points. The loss ended the home ice magic of Al Cullen, but the rookie still played a fine game as he kicked out 24 shots. A 4-3 loss at Providence the next night dropped Cleveland five points off the pace.

The Barons bounced back with two wins, to set up a big confrontation with the Springfield Indians. Before 9,153 fans, Cleveland thoroughly dominated the defending champions 5-1 in Al Cullen's regular season farewell. With Les Binkley's ankle all healed, the rookie sensation went back to Woodstock, Ontario a conquering hero. He won eight of his ten games here and departed with a 1.80 goals against average.

The great goaltending of Cullen overshadowed two other reasons for the Barons' rise in the standings. One was the great play of the team's first line of Fred Glover, Ron Attwell, and Jim Mikol. Mikol was put on the line when Dick Van Impe was shelved with a knee injury in early January. From that point

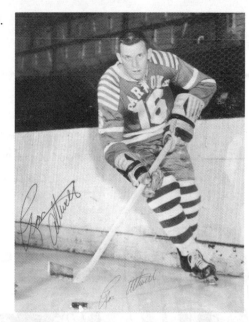

Ron Attwell

Jim Mikol
The line of Fred Glover, Ron Attwell, and Jim Mikol was on fire during the 1961-62 season. The American Hockey League's top trio accounted for an even 100 goals in leading the Barons to the West Division championship. Kay Horiba collection.

on, the trio became the scoring sensation of the League. All three began to score in bunches. Glover, in fact, was closing in on his 400th goal. He bagged his 394th in a 4-1 victory over Pittsburgh on February 11th.

Of equal importance was the inspired play of center iceman Hank Ciesla. The 6'2" center got off to a slow start with his new club, scoring only 5 goals in his first 29 games. But after scoring all four goals in a 4-1 win at Hershey on February 7th, Ceisla was standing tall among his teammates. He now had scored 14 goals in his last 21 games. It was no coincidence that

One of Fred Glover's many milestones occurred on March 25, 1962 when he scored his 400th goal. Six days later, March 31st was declared "Fred Glover Day" in Cleveland. In typical Glover fashion, Fred scored the go-ahead goal in a 6-4 win over Buffalo that gave the Barons the West Division title. Dick Dugan collection.

the Barons won 17 of them. As Coach and GM Jackie Gordon believed from the start, the trade for Ciesla from Rochester was paying off in spades.

The Cleveland pucksters headed into Buffalo for a showdown with the first-place Bisons on February 21st. Trailing Buffalo by three points, the Barons really wanted this game. "It was a good game, and Les Binkley sure played a helluva big game in the nets for us," said Coach Gordon afterwards. But Bink's great game was not enough. Burned by Chico Maki's hat trick, the Barons lost a 5-3 heartbreaker to the Bisons. The loss left Cleveland with a 30-21-2 record, five large points behind Buffalo. On a positive note, Fred Glover notched his 396th goal in the defeat.

The loss was costly because the local icers lost their next game at the Arena to Hershey and then embarked on a make-or-break eight-game road trip.

Cleveland began the trip by blanking Pittsburgh 3-0. The shutout was the third of the season for Les Binkley, and it provided the impetus for a great road journey. Binkley recorded his fourth shutout, a 4-0 whitewash of Hershey, in the trip's final game. This capped off a highly successful road swing that saw Gordon's troops post a 5-2-1 record. Leaving Cleveland five points behind Buffalo, they returned in first place by a single point. "You can only hope for something like this," beamed the Cleveland coach.

The Barons were upset by Quebec 3-0 in their first game back home. But they bounced back the next afternoon by blanking Hershey 6-0. Les Binkley racked up his fifth shutout as the Cleveland defense completely smothered the Bears. The Baron goalie had to make only 17 saves. On the other side of the ice, Hershey's Bobby Perreault was bombarded with 56 shots. The Cleveland attack was in high gear as it kept the club in first place by two points.

Kay Horiba collection.

The season was winding down to a precious few remaining games. Excitement among the players and fans was at a high point not seen in years. Besides the tight battle with Buffalo for first place, Fred Glover was on the verge of scoring his 400th career goal.

The big event occurred on March 25th in the team's fourth last game of the season. The Barons bombarded the Pittsburgh Hornets 13-2 behind hat tricks by John Ferguson and Bill Sutherland. But everything was overshadowed by Glover's historic goal which came at 15:47 of the third period. After his score, Fred received one of the longest and loudest ovations ever heard at the Arena.

The big goal came in Fred's 809th regular season game. He now had 400 goals, 570 assists, for 970 career points. Not bad for a man who had also spent more than 1,500 minutes in the penalty box!

After the game, Fred revealed how close all of his success came to never happening. "The first goal I ever got in the League was what kept me in the League," said the hometown hero. Back in 1948, Fred was scoreless in his first ten games with Indianapolis. The Capitals had seen enough of Glover and were ready to send him back to Omaha, of the United States League. They gave him one last shot against Springfield.

"In that game the puck just came to me and I whirled around without looking. I never saw what happened, but it was my first goal. If I hadn't scored that night, I'd have been sent back to the U. S. League, and all this wouldn't have happened," said Glover.

But Indianapolis did keep Glover, and the rest is history. Fourteen years later he was still going strong and was the AHL's greatest player ever.

The win over Pittsburgh put Cleveland four points ahead of Buffalo. Each team had three games remaining. But when the Barons lost to Springfield and the Bisons defeated Rochester, the first-place lead was down to two points with two games remaining. As fate would have it, these two games were against each other – a home and home series to determine the West division championship.

Buffalo came into Cleveland for the big showdown with a 6-1-1 advantage over the Barons during the season.

March 31, 1962 was declared "Fred Glover Day" by official proclamation by the Mayor of Cleveland. It turned out to be a tremendous day for the team and its long-time hero.

9,218 fans, the largest crowd of the season, turned out to see if their heroes could win the division title.

After the first period, which Cleveland led 1-0 on a goal by Dick Van Impe, Fred Glover was honored with ceremonies at center ice for his 400-goal accomplishment. The gala affair was emceed by WEWS television star Bill Gordon. At center ice with Fred was his wife, Marie, and his mother, Mrs. Jane Glover. The star of the night received an engraved clock from his teammates, a film from the club showing his 400th goal, and a 1962 Oldsmobile from the fans.

When Fred addressed the cheering crowd, the night became highly emotional. Glover's father had passed away three weeks earlier on March 10th. He said that he deeply regretted that his Dad couldn't be there that night. He also stated the same emotional sentiment for Jim Hendy, the late Baron general manager, who gave Fred his chance with the Cleveland team. When all was said and done and all the eyes had dried, the two teams went back to deciding the championship.

Buffalo tied the score early in the second period before Jim Mikol got the lead back for Cleveland at 7:26. But the Bisons tied it up again at 14:18 on a shot by Billy Dea.

The stage was set for the dramatic third period. Who else but the man of the hour rose to the forefront. After only 21 seconds of the third period, Fred Glover flipped in a short shot to give the Barons a 3-2 lead. The shot brought the house down, and the game was delayed as the fans went wild.

The goal by their leader spurred the Barons on. Scores by Ron Attwell at 9:02 and Billy Sutherland at 10:10 upped the lead to 5-2.

The delirious fans were celebrating, but the Bisons were not through yet. Dave Creighton scored two goals at 13:57 and 16:29 to cut the Cleveland lead to one.

The fans were now on the edge of their seats, and with 1:02 to go, the Bisons pulled their goalie. Six Buffalos raged down the ice, and the pressure on goalie Les Binkley was non-stop. A plethora of shots was fired at the Cleveland netminder, who somehow kept them all out.

A faceoff was held at the Baron blue line with 10 seconds to go. Jim Mikol relieved the intense pressure when he fired a puck two-thirds the length of the ice into an empty Buffalo goal. The old Arena shook from the resulting bedlam. The Cleveland Barons were West division champions with the 6-4 victory.

Cleveland's 5-3 victory at Buffalo the next night was icing on the cake. They finished with a 39-28-3 record and would face two-time defending champion and current East division title holder Springfield in the first round of the playoffs.

THE PLAYOFFS

Springfield was not quite the completely dominant outfit that it was the previous year. But they were still a strong and formidable foe. They won the Eastern division crown with a 45-22-3 record for 93 points. The Barons, however, faired rather well against the Indians with a 5-5-0 record. They went to the East Coast confident that they could come up with at least a split of the first two games.

Game One was an old fashioned rock 'em, sock 'em contest with end-to-end action and constant hard-hitting. Neither team gave an inch to the other.

Gary Bergman scored the game's first goal only to have the Indians counter with two of their own. Fred Glover and John Ferguson tallied late in the second period to put Cleveland on top 3-2 after two stanzas. The Indians turned on the power in the third period and tied the game at 12:53 on a score by Bill Sweeney.

Regulation time expired with the game tied 3-3, and the teams went into overtime. The old 10-minute full overtime had been discarded, and 20-minute "sudden death" periods were now used from the start of overtime. The first team to score would win.

Each team had numerous scoring opportunities, but Les Binkley for Cleveland and Marcel Paille of Springfield were magnificent. Neither team could score through a first and then a second overtime.

Two exhausted teams fought on into a third overtime. The goalies stood out until the 10:16 mark. Then the Barons' Wayne Larkin took a pass from Dick Van Impe on the right side and fired a long, hard slapshot that beat Paille. At nearly one o'clock in the morning, the Barons had their upset victory over the defending champs.

The Barons could not capitalize on their momentum in Game Two, as the Springfield defense completely bottled up the Cleveland offense. The Indians won a close checking contest 3-1 behind ex-Baron Pete Goegan's two goals. Only Hank Ciesla could solve Marcel Paille, who was called on to make a mere 22 saves. But the Barons came back to Cleveland with a split of two games in Springfield and were in a confident mood.

That mood was tempered after Cleveland lost a 4-3 overtime heartbreaker in Game Three.

The teams went at each other tooth and nail, and the Barons held a 3-2 lead with 44 seconds left in the game. There was a faceoff in the Cleveland zone, and the Indians had pulled their goalie in favor of a sixth attacker.

The Barons won the important faceoff, and the puck came back to defenseman Aldo Guidolin. Aldo launched a long, rink-length shot that was right on target for the empty Springfield net. But the puck never made it out of the Cleveland zone. As fate would have it, the puck struck the leg of a linesman who was trying to get out of the way. The disc bounced back towards the Cleveland net, and the Indians' Kent Douglas tied the game at 19:23. Talk about a bad bounce!

To make matters worse, Baron goalie Les Binkley hurt his knee while making a save at 7:15 of sudden death overtime. After a 10-minute delay, Bink stayed in the game; but Springfield's Dennis Olson scored nine seconds later to give the Indians a 4-3 win.

The game was Les Binkley's last of the season. While his knee was not severely damaged, he could not bend it for weeks. Al Cullen, Cleveland's mid-season hero, once again took over in goal.

Cullen had another rabbit in his hat, and he pulled it out in Game Four as the Barons evened the series with a big 4-2 victory. "The thing that pleases me most is the spirit of these guys," said Coach Gordon afterward. "The way they bounced back after losing that heartbreaker Sunday night...it's hard to bounce back from those kind."

But bounce back they did behind Cullen's 28 saves. Also instrumental in the victory was Hank Ciesla. After goals by John Ferguson and Ron Attwell had given Cleveland a 2-2 tie after two periods, Ciesla came through in the third. He fired home goals at 1:41 and 7:55 to ice the big win.

This sent the teams back to Springfield for the crucial fifth game.

There were fireworks aplenty in the first period of Game Five. Springfield led 3-2 after one with Cleveland's goals coming off the sticks of Ron Attwell and Hank Ciesla.

The game then settled into a close checking affair as each team seemed to be waiting for the other to make a mistake. But at 3:56 of the third period, Jim Mikol slapped in the tying goal. The checking then became stifling, and the game went into sudden death overtime.

Unfortunately, the third overtime game of the series was not a charm for Cleveland. A Springfield goal in the first minute of the second extra session ended the Barons' upset dreams 4-3.

The two teams went back to Cleveland for Game Six, but the series was actually won in Springfield in Game Five. The Barons just never recovered from that disheartening loss. They dropped Game Six 4-0 and never really were in the contest. They gave it their all, and had their chances, but that special spark was missing.

Naturally, the Barons and their fans were depressed by being knocked out of the playoffs in the first round for the fifth year in a row.

But this team had nothing to be ashamed of and did itself proud. They brought back the Barons' winning tradition by finishing in first place. They then gave Springfield, a dynamic team, all it could handle in a great playoff series.

Les Binkley was named Rookie of the Year, and Fred Glover was the League's Most Valuable Player for the second time. With a few breaks, they could have been Calder Cup champions. Most of all, they renewed interest in the team when it needed it most.

FINAL STANDINGS
1961-62

West	W	L	T	GF	GA	PTS.
Cleveland	39	28	3	255	203	81
Buffalo	36	31	3	247	219	75
Rochester	33	31	6	234	240	72
Pittsburgh	10	58	2	177	367	22
East	**W**	**L**	**T**	**GF**	**GA**	**PTS.**
Springfield	45	22	3	292	194	93
Hershey	37	28	5	236	213	79
Providence	36	32	2	261	267	74
Quebec	30	36	4	208	207	64

Top Baron Scorers	G	A	PTS.
Fred Glover	40	45	85
Ron Attwell	28	55	83
Jim Mikol	32	48	80
Hank Ciesla	25	38	63
Dick Van Impe	10	41	51
Eddie Mazur	24	24	48
Billy Sutherland	20	28	48
Wayne Larkin	19	23	42
Cal Stearns	12	30	42
John Ferguson	20	20	40

Calder Cup Champion – Springfield Indians

THE 1961-62 CLEVELAND BARONS

Front (L-R): Bill Needham, Fred Glover, General Manager and Coach Jack Gordon, Les Binkley, President Thomas H. Roulston, Captain Aldo Guidolin, Cal Stearns. Second: Public Relations Manager Russell J. Schneider, Eddie Mazur, Murray Davison, Jim Mikol, Johnny Ferguson, Hank Ciesla, Ron Attwell, Business Manager Joseph B. Vargo. Third: Billy Sutherland, Wayne Larkin, Gary Bergman, Tommy Williams, Dick Van Impe, Trainer George Polinuk. Dennis Turchek collection.

1962-63 SEASON

For the upcoming season, there were changes both on and off the ice. The most significant was the naming of Fred Glover as player-coach.

Jackie Gordon had found it increasingly difficult to carry on as both general manager and coach. That, plus the fact that the team had been eliminated from the playoffs in the first round for five consecutive years, convinced Gordon that a change was needed. He kept the position of general manager and handed the team over to Glover. Jack finished with a regular season coaching record of 220-177-21.

Fred was Gordon's first and only choice for the coaching job. Now entering his 15th season as a player, there was no telling how much longer he would play. Since his leadership qualities were unquestioned, he was the logical choice to take over as the team's new coach.

There were changes on the ice as well. Most were not of Cleveland's choice. Montreal now had a working agreement with the Quebec Aces as well as the Barons. For the current campaign, they decided to place Ron Attwell, Bill Sutherland, and Gary Bergman with the Aces. This didn't sit well with Cleveland management, as all were top members of last season's team. But since all three were here on lend-lease agreement, they had no say-so in the matter. This was the hazard of taking players on loan.

In their place Montreal sent Cleveland six players: wingers Terry Gray, Wayne Boddy, and Fred Hilts; centers Joe Szura and Bill Masterson; and defenseman Bob Olajos.

The Barons also lost star defenseman Also Guidolin. Aldo, who was property of the New York Rangers on loan to Cleveland, was made the player-coach of the new Baltimore Clippers. Baltimore was now part of the AHL's Eastern division. The Rangers, who broke off their working agreement with the Springfield Indians, were now sending players to the Clippers. This was Springfield's loss and Baltimore's gain. No longer would the Indians be the powerhouse of the last three seasons.

Since most of the new players didn't arrive until just before the season opener, the team was in a state of disarray. New coach Glover must have wondered what he got himself into. The defense was especially weak, and the situation got worse in the team's 3-2 season opening win over Pittsburgh.

Fred Glover was named Player Coach for the 1962-63 season, succeeding Jackie Gordon. He later would add Assistant General Manager to his resume. Bill Hudec collection.

Veteran Tommy Williams suffered a severely gashed right ankle and would miss two weeks of the season. This left Bill Needham as the club's only experienced backliner. The losses began to mount, and drastic action was needed. Help came in the form of two trades made by GM Jackie Gordon.

First off, the Barons sent winger Wayne Larkin and rookie defenseman Murray Davison to Springfield for defenseman Dick Mattiussi. Dick proved to be a solid addition to the club. The big and fast backliner was a tremendous stickhandler and could lead an offensive rush with the best of them. Combined with his hard-hitting, Mattiussi would be a mainstay on defense for the next five years.

Gordon's second deal was made with the consent of the Montreal Canadiens, who owned both players involved. The Barons sent right wing Terry Gray to Quebec in return for defenseman Gary Bergman. Gary was returning to Cleveland where he blossomed on the backline just the year before.

The addition of Mattiussi and Bergman, along with the return to action of Tommy Williams, was just what the doctor ordered. Combined with Bill Needham and Bob Olajos, the Barons now had the makings of a top flight defense corps.

Dick Mattiussi was a bruising defenseman who joined the Barons during the 1962-63 season. During his five years with the club, Dick became the club's top rushing backliner. Dick Dugan collection.

OOPS! Goal or Save? Only Barons' Netminder Les Binkley knows for sure! Cleveland Public Library collection.

Still, bad luck continued to plague the team. In Bergman's first game back with the Barons, he was involved in a play that would knock goalie Les Binkley out of action for nine games.

With Cleveland leading Quebec 4-2, Bergman and Terry Gray – both just traded for the other – crashed into each other next to the Baron net. They smashed into goaltender Binkley, who fell backwards into the goalpost and suffered a concussion.

After a ten-minute delay, Les finished the last few minutes of the game. The next thing Binkley remembered was waking up in the hospital. He had no recollection of finishing the game. In fact, he thought that the Barons won 4-2. The truth was, Quebec scored three late goals on Binkley that he could not even remember! It was a wonder that he finished the game. The loss left the Barons with a 2-9-0 record. But the losing ways were not over yet.

With Al Cullen in the nets, the Barons defeated Pittsburgh 5-1. The game was marred by an ugly incident when Howie Glover, Fred's younger brother now playing with the Hornets, was hit in the head with a chair thrown by a heckling fan. Ten stitches were needed to close the two and one-half inch gash in Howie's head.

Cleveland then lost their next six games to fall to a dismal record of 3-15-0. This certainly was the worst off that any Baron team had ever been. But Coach Glover was not about to throw in the towel.

Even during the latest losing streak, the team began to show signs of breaking out of the doldrums. Fred Glover, the coach, knew better than anyone that he had a team much better than its record indicated. So he worked his men – and worked them hard.

But he worked with them in an encouraging way. He showed them the mistakes they were making and how to go about correcting them. Fred Glover, the rough, tough player-coach was proving to be a fine teacher. And his pupils began to respond.

The result was a three-game winning streak at the end of November. The team actually climbed out of the basement because Pittsburgh and Rochester were also having poor starts.

The main difference in the team as it kept winning in December, January, and February, was its team-oriented, disciplined play. It took a while for Glover's preaching to sink in. But when it did, the results were seen in the victory column.

The local icers no longer were chasing the puck all over the ice. Players were staying in their lanes and picking up their man. When the opposing team had the puck, a winger would always come back to help out. This took pressure off of the defensemen and, in turn, the goaltender.

Along with the improved defensive play was a big breakout by the offense.

The final piece to the puzzle was the return of Jim Mikol. Jim received a tryout with Toronto and stayed with the Maple Leafs for the first 23 games of the season. When he returned to Cleveland, the Barons' offense began to click.

Leading the pack was Hank Ciesla. The big center enjoyed a banner year. During a nine-game splurge in late February and early March, Hank racked up 8 goals and 18 assists for 26 points. His 87 points put him atop the League leaderboard. Although he would eventually be beaten out for the scoring title by Springfield's Bill Sweeney, Ciesla was a model of offensive firepower all season.

Another offensive outburst came from an unexpected source. Big John Ferguson had developed into quite a goal scorer. Absolutely no one expected Fergy to score 40 goals, but that's exactly what he did. His new-found scoring prowess, combined with his 179 penalty minutes, made Ferguson one of the most colorful players in the League. And Cleveland fans loved him.

Coming in first place was out of the question. The Barons had fallen far behind a fine Buffalo team and never had a chance to catch up.

The Bisons enjoyed a 22-point edge on Cleveland when the Barons went to Buffalo on March 10th. Most of that bulge was built up during Cleveland's 3-15-0 start. Losing their first 15 road games didn't help the Barons any either.

But this was now a different Cleveland team. When they handed the Bisons their worst home defeat by the score of 9-3, the Barons served notice to everyone that they were for real.

Two goals each by Fred Glover and rookie Joe Szura led the rout. The victory put Cleveland at 28-29-6, a far cry from their early season miseries.

The Barons went back to Buffalo two weeks later and clinched second place. The Bisons took an early 2-0 lead. Rookie Wayne Boddy got the Barons back in the game before Fred Hilts tied it up at 6:57 of the third period.

When Hank Ciesla fired home the winner at 5:00 of sudden death overtime, one would have thought that the Barons had won the title. But to clinch second place after such a horrible start to the season was quite an accomplishment.

It certainly was a feather in the cap of Fred Glover. When the season looked its darkest, Fred never gave up. He just dug in harder and showed by example what hard work could do.

Les Binkley makes a save.
Cleveland State University archives.

Cal Stearns played twelve outstanding seasons with the Barons. The master of the sweep check was the greatest penalty killer in the history of the American Hockey League.
Bill Hudec collection.

By taking second place, the Barons assured themselves of home-ice advantage in a two-out-of-three mini-series against Rochester. But before the playoffs began, the players and fans were looking forward to the regular season's final game on March 31st against Pittsburgh, which was designated Cal Stearns Day.

The 36-year-old center was retiring after twelve years with the club. The master of the sweep check was also the greatest penalty killer in League history. He came to Cleveland in 1951 after stints with San Diego, Kansas City, Los Angeles, and Seattle. He enjoyed his best scoring year in 1955-56 when he scored 35 goals and 36 assists for 71 points. But Cal would be remembered most for his excellent defensive play.

Stearns had a love affair with the game of hockey. He recalled that the saddest day of his life was when his parents moved from his home town of Edmonton in Canada to San Diego, California.

Cal seemed to live in skates from the time he was four. Hockey was his life. When his parents decided to move to California, he was heartbroken. He thought he would never play his beloved game again.

On moving day, he had a game with his junior college team. Cal played the first two periods of that game and then ran all the way to the railroad station to meet his family. He didn't say a word all the way to California – just sat in his uniform and thought about the game he loved.

Stearns had no idea that San Diego had a hockey team in the Western league. The morning after his arrival, he saw a picture in the paper of a game played the night before. Cal was ecstatic!

His uncle took him to meet the managment of the San Diego team. Manager Lyman McDonald worked Stearns out for two days and liked what he saw. He signed Cal to a contract, and the rest was history.

Cal Stearns celebrated his Day in style. He scored a goal and three assists as the Barons routed Pittsburgh 14-3. Hank Ciesla and Wayne Boddy fired three-goal hat tricks for Cleveland in the final tuneup for the playoffs. Without a doubt, the Barons were ready for Rochester.

THE PLAYOFFS

The Barons, who sported a 5-3-1 record against Rochester during the regular season, were slight favorites entering the best of three mini-series.

Finishing the season with a 31-34-7 mark for 69 points, the Barons were a far cry from the team that began the season 3-15-0.

But the same could be said for Rochester. On February 1st the Amerks had won only three of their last 24 games and were buried in the cellar. However, the additions of star goalie Bobby Perreault and veteran forward Bronco Horvath turned the team around. They finished at 24-39-9 for 57 points. But just like Cleveland, they were hot when the season ended.

The Barons were sky high for Game One. They were determined not to be eliminated in the first round for a sixth straight year.

Jumping all over the Americans right from the start, Cleveland led all the way as they dominated Rochester 6-3. The score really wasn't that close as the Barons held a 6-1 lead with six minutes to go.

First-period tallies by John Ferguson and Cal Stearns got Cleveland off to the races, and they never looked back. The big win gave the Barons all the confidence in the world as they headed to Rochester determined to end the series.

Playing like a team possessed, Cleveland swarmed all over the Amerks in Game Two. Behind rookie Fred Hilt's three-goal hat trick, the Barons once again trimmed Rochester 6-3. Other Barons scorers were Hank Ciesla, Fred Glover, and Dick Mattiussi.

Just as they had in the first game, Cleveland jumped out to a 2-0 first-period lead and was never in danger. The lead was built to 5-1 before the Americans made any noise.

The train ride back to Cleveland was a jubilant one. The first-round jinx had been slain.

The celebrating didn't last long, however, for the Barons immediately began preparing for the Hershey Bears, their second-round opponent. The Bears were a formidable foe. Their 36-28-8 record left them in second place in the East, only one point behind Providence.

Cleveland fared well against Hershey during the regular season, going 5-3-1. But the first two games of the series were in Chocolate Town, giving the Bears a big advantage in the best-of-five series.

Cleveland came out firing in Game One and shocked the Bears by building a 3-0 advantage in the first period. Fred Hilts, Dick Van Impe, and Cal Stearns tallied for the Barons. But in the period's final minute, Hershey's Myron Stankiewicz got one back. This definitely fired up the Bears.

They came out smoking in period two while Cleveland seemed to relax. This was fatal and all Hershey needed. They poured home four goals in slightly more than four minutes to take a 5-3 lead. Fred Hilts cut the margin to 5-4 late in the period, but the damage had been done.

The Hershey defense tightened up in the third period, and they hung on for a large 5-4 victory.

A banged-up bunch of Barons showed up for Game Two. Defenseman Dick Mattiussi was out with a sprained ankle, and fellow backliner Bob Olajos had a severely sprained wrist. Add Jim Mikol's damaged shoulder to the list of the walking wounded.

Cleveland played like they had a hangover from Game One's gut-wrenching defeat, and they entered the third period trailing 1-0. But Gary Bergman supplied the spark that turned into a full-fledged fire. Gary scored at 2:25 and suddenly the Barons went wild.

Fifteen seconds later, John Ferguson tallied. Then it was Dick Van Impe's turn to join the scoring party. Then Fred Glover followed by Fred Hilts. In all, the Barons blasted five shots past a shell-shocked Bobby Perreault for a 5-1 win.

Les Binkley was at his best in Game Three at the Arena as he blanked the Bears 4-0. Time and again he turned back the Hersheys as they swarmed around the Cleveland net all night. Two goals by rookie Bill Masterson and singles by John Ferguson and Fred Glover led the way. The Barons now found themselves only one game away from the finals.

But Fred Glover came up with a bad knee in the game after taking a stiff check. Tommy Williams suffered a back injury, and Dick Van Impe a jammed toe. But the injury to Glover was the most ominous.

Fred could play only two shifts in Game Four, and the rest of the battered Barons let the game get away. After leading 2-0 on goals by Wayne Body and Fred Hilts, Cleveland's 5-3 loss was a bitter pill to swallow. The Barons were operating with a badly-banged lineup, but the defeat hurt all the same. This sent the series back to Hershey for the deciding fifth game.

"It was nothing to be ashamed of," said Fred Glover after Cleveland's 5-2 loss in Game Five.

Glover and Dick Mattiussi were forced to miss the game with knee and ankle injuries respectively. Jim Mikol, Tommy Williams, and Bob Olajos were far from 100%. But still the Barons battled hard to the end. The score was tied at two entering the third period, but the Hersheys were just too much for the outmanned and crippled Barons. Three third-period goals gave the Bears a 5-2 win and ended the Barons' season.

Although they failed to win the title, the Barons had a remarkable year. After their dismal 3-15-0 start, they finished the year with a 28-19-7 rush. They were the League's top team during that time. Only an ill-timed rash of injuries kept them from a possible title.

Still, the fans were greatly disappointed. If only they had a crystal ball. An unbelieveable season was about to unfold.

During the 1962-63 season, Superfan Kay Horiba went on an extended roadtrip with the Barons and brought back the above programs. Kay was a barber in the Belmont Hotel across the street from the Arena and became close friends with many of the players. Kay Horiba collection.

FINAL STANDINGS
1962-63

West	W	L	T	GF	GA	PTS.
Buffalo	41	24	7	237	199	89
Cleveland	31	34	7	270	253	69
Rochester	24	39	9	241	270	57
Pittsburgh	20	48	4	200	317	44
East	W	L	T	GF	GA	PTS.
Providence	38	29	5	239	203	81
Hershey	36	28	8	262	231	80
Baltimore	35	30	7	226	244	77
Quebec	33	28	11	206	210	77
Springfield	33	31	8	282	236	74

Top Baron Scorers	G	A	PTS.
Hank Ciesla	42	56	98
Bill Masterson	27	55	82
Fred Glover	26	54	80
John Ferguson	40	38	78
Fred Hilts	29	41	70
Dick Van Impe	18	35	53
Jim Mikol	20	30	50
Joe Szura	14	30	44
Wayne Boddy	20	21	41

Calder Cup Champion – Buffalo Bisons

THE 1962-63 CLEVELAND BARONS

Front (L to R): Al Cullen, Bill Needham, President Paul L. Bright, Coach Fred Glover, General Manager Jack Gordon, Captain Hank Ciesla, Les Binkley. Second: Business Manager Joseph B. Vargo, Trainer George Polinuk, Pete Shearer, Jim Mikol, Joe Szura, John Ferguson, Gary Bergman, Public Relations Director Shel Fullerton. Third: Wayne Boddy, Bob Olajos, Tommy Williams, Fred Hilts, Bill Masterson, Dick Van Impe, Cal Stearns, Dick Mattiussi. Dennis Turchek collection.

1963-64 SEASON

As the new season approached, the fans were bemoaning the loss of several key players from the previous year's club. Gone were John Ferguson, Hank Ciesla, and Gary Bergman via the NHL draft. Once again the AHL was subject to the National League's player raiding system for the price of $20,000 per player. Ferguson went to Montreal, Bergman and Ciesla to Detroit. Ciesla, in turn, was sent to Pittsburgh of the AHL.

This prompted a revision of the draft rules for next season. If a player did not make the team that drafted him, he would be returned to the club from which he was drafted. This didn't help the Barons in the case of Ciesla this year. But no longer could players be taken away and placed with rival clubs.

Bob Olajos, Wayne Boddy, and Fred Hilts were also dealt away. Bill Masterson retired to finish college, and Dick Van Impe held out for more money and subsequently was suspended and dropped.

While Jackie Gordon hated to part with any of these players, he had no choice.

On defense, Springfield star Ted Harris and Jim Holdaway were brought in to replace Bergman and Olajos. Up front were new players Cecil Hoekstra, Ray Kinasewich, Ray Brunel, Guy Rousseau, Bob Ellet, and ex-Baron Wayne Larkin.

The biggest addition to the offense was the return of Ron Attwell. The Montreal Canadiens, partially in payment for drafting John Ferguson, agreed to transfer Attwell back to Cleveland after a one-year stay in Quebec.

This was great news for the team and its fans. Now the great GAM line of Glover, Attwell, and Mikol could be reunited. Two years earlier, this line was one of the best in the League, racking up 100 goals. Glover scored 40, Attwell 28, and Mikol 32.

They would have to be hot again because this year's team seemed a little short on firepower.

The Barons gave a preview of things to come in their opening two games by beating Hershey 4-2 and shutting out Baltimore 3-0. Cleveland checked its opposition into the ice with a beautiful display of defensive hockey. The five-man Baron defense corps of Ted Harris, Bill Needham, Dick Mattiussi, Tommy Williams, and Jim Holdaway looked to have the makings of a great unit.

The local icers kept up their fine play and held a 7-4-0 record in mid-November. However, they still trailed the first place Pittsburgh Hornets by six points.

The Hornets were a totally rebuilt club and were now considered the class of the League. Their parent Detroit Red Wings pumped new blood into them by drafting many top AHL players and placing them in Pittsburgh. Among these stars were ex-Barons Hank Ciesla, Art Stratton, and Ian Cushenan. Also from Detroit were Floyd Smith and Ted Hampson.

Anchoring all of this talent was rookie goaltender Roger Crozier. The little acrobatic netminder was a real crowd pleaser. He would battle the Baron's Les Binkley for goaltending honors all season.

The Steel City icers showed the Barons just how tough they could be by sweeping back-to-back games in mid-November. This was followed by a 4-1 loss to Quebec, and suddenly Cleveland was at 7-7-0, 12 points behind Pittsburgh. The Barons were digging a hole for themselves once again.

Coach Glover was quick to realize that the only way this club was going to win was by close, hard-hitting checking. He stressed this over and over in practice, and finally his perseverance
The team began a steady rise that put them back into contention.

Over their next eleven games, Cleveland went 7-3-1. There was improved play all through the team, led by Les Binkley and the defense in front of him.

In a 3-0 shutout at Hershey, Binkley only had to make 18 saves in what he called his easiest shutout ever. The defense in front of him was like a stone wall.

Binkley recorded his third shutout with a 2-0 whitewash of Springfield that improved the team to 14-10-1. Led by Ted Harris, the defense once again was magnificent. Ted was proving to be the glue on the backline. He was playing the best hockey of his career, and it was rubbing off on the rest of the defensemen.

But Harris and his defense mates weren't the only reason for the Barons' December rush toward first place.

Fred Glover was having another fine season and was locked in a battle for the League scoring lead. Fred had 12 goals and 17 assists by mid-December, good for second in the AHL.

But by far, the most improved Baron of the young season was Joe Szura. The 6'2" center bulked up over the off-season with 15 pounds of muscle and now weighed a solid 200. The added weight made it extremely difficult to bump Joe off the puck. He was also turning into a fine penalty killer.

Ron Attwell returned to the Barons for the 1963-64 season and led the team with 30 goals. Dick Dugan collection.

Szura credited his improvement to watching and studying the older veterans in the League. He was always alert to pick up the little things that separated the stars from the pretenders.

A pair of two goal games by Szura in victories

Thanks to a Hornet slump and one of their own, the Barons were only two points behind Pittsburgh at Christmas. This was accomplished by virtue of losing only three of their last fifteen starts.

Cleveland finally arrived at the top of the mountain on December 27th when they beat Hershey 4-1 at the Arena. The victory gave the Barons an 18-12-2 record and a tie with Pittsburgh atop the West division. The win climaxed a long haul for the Barons. The team made up a whopping twelve points in the standings since dropping back-to-back games to the Hornets five weeks earlier.

The game with Hershey was a lively affair. Wayne Larkin and the Bears' Barry Ashbee got into two rousing brawls. The first was a draw, but Larkin gave Ashbee a boxing lesson in the second fracas. Even the fans got in on the action as Hershey's Gene Ubriaco went after two heckling fans behind the Bear bench. As for the game itself, Ron Attwell's two third-period goals put the contest away for Cleveland.

The Barons and Pittsburgh stayed even for the next two weeks before the Barons lost their leader. Fred Glover was suspended for three games following an altercation with referee Bill Friday during a 3-3 tie with Buffalo on January 11th.

With 15 seconds left in the second period, and his team trailing, Glover became infuriated by a offside call made by a substitute linesman. A disgusted Glover shot the puck into the boards in the general direction of Referee Friday. Immediately, Friday gave Glover a ten-minute misconduct penalty. This is when Fred really blew his cork.

Claiming that he was only shooting the puck at the boards, not at the referee, Glover followed Friday around the ice protesting the penalty. When Fred would not stop, Friday threw the volatile Glover out of the game. The language then used was not for the feint of heart.

Earlier in the season, also at Buffalo, Fred was thrown out of a game and subsequently was issued a warning by the League office. Any similar disorderly conduct would result in a stiff sentence.

When the three-game suspension came down, Glover was livid. The League said the penalty was for abusive language. The Cleveland Coach denied shooting the puck at the official.

In his sixteen years of hell-raising on ice, this was Fred Glover's first suspension. It cost him the League lead in scoring, with Providence's Willie Marshall regaining the top spot. But the Barons continued their hot play by going 2-1-0 during the Coach's absence.

Cleveland hit the apex of its regular season during the last week of January. They moved eight points ahead of Pittsburgh and thirteen up on Rochester. The big first-place bulge was accomplished by beating both the Hornets and Buffalo twice each before blasting Springfield 7-4.

The back-to-back wins over Pittsburgh were especially satisfying. After winning in the Steel City, the Barons took a 3-2 thriller before 8,114 fans. Wayne Larkin's second-period tally proved to be the game winner. Checking was the key to this team's success. When they stayed with their man, they usually won. But when they didn't check like demons, their general lack of great offensive firepower would put them in trouble.

Cecil Hoekstra was a superb playmaking center who spent six splendid years in Cleveland. His pinpoint passing and fine defensive play made him quite a fan favorite.
Dick Dugan collection.

There was no lack of offense the next night at the Arena as the Barons stretched their home ice unbeaten streak to 14 games with an 8-2 rout of Buffalo.

After capping their successful weekend with a hard-fought 3-2 victory in a return engagement at Buffalo, the Barons came home and routed Springfield. In the 7-4 victory, Cecil Hoekstra fired home three goals. Usually relied upon for his great defensive work, the lanky center surprised everyone with the hat trick. But it should be noted that Cecil would develop into a fine offensive talent over the next few seasons in Cleveland. Although he was now 28 years old, his best scoring years were still to come.

Cleveland's 15th straight game at home without defeat put them at 28-15-3, eight points up on Pittsburgh. The Glover-Attwell-Mikol line was the League's top-scoring trio. Glover had 55 points, Mikol 51, and Attwell 50. Everything seemed too good to be true, and it was.

The unbeaten streak at home was stretched to 17 games before the Baltimore Clippers turned out the lights with a 5-3 triumph.

This loss came in the middle of a 1-4-1 slide for Cleveland. The beginnings of a slump weren't brought on by a few individuals but by the whole team. Coach Glover attributed his team's poor play to a lack of checking.

Glover himself temporarily stopped the team's slide by firing a three-goal hat trick in an 8-1 pasting of Springfield. The win kept the Barons four points ahead of Pittsburgh.

Cleveland split its next four games and then embarked on a tell-tale seven-game road trip.

After losing to Hershey, the Barons showed some life when they defeated the Indians at Springfield 3-2. Goals by Hoekstra, Larkin, and Glover gave Cleveland a 3-0 lead, and they held on behind the clutch goaltending of Les Binkley. The victory upped the Barons' lead over Pittsburgh to six points. Then the roof caved in.

Fred Glover won his third most valuable player award during the 1963-64 season. It was his inspirational play that led the Barons to their 9th Calder Cup victory. Here he is seen shooting against Providence goalie Ed Giacomin.
Cleveland State University archives.

Larry (The Rock) Zeidel was the most hated opponent to ever lace on skates against the Barons. His wild man act on ice was legendary. Thus, Cleveland fans were stunned when Fred Glover signed his most bitter rival late in the 1963-64 season. But the Ex-Hershey bad man curbed his famous temper and became a vital part in the Barons' astonishing sweep to the Calder Cup title.
Dick Dugan collection.

Jean Guy Morissette was a 5'6" 140-pound netminder who took over in goal when regular Les Binkley was injured late in the 1963-64 season. But little Jean Guy stood taller than the Terminal Tower when he backstopped the Barons to the Calder Cup championship. Kay Horiba collection.

Cleveland lost four of the final five games on the trip and dropped out of first place, one point behind Pittsburgh. The last defeat on the road journey was the hardest to take.

The Barons lost a 1-0 heartbreaker at Rochester in a game where everything went wrong except the great goaltending of Binkley. Cleveland just could not get its offense untracked. Their height of frustration came in the second period when they managed only three shots at Amerk goalie Gerry Cheevers.

In the third period a ruckus developed when Fred Glover was sent to the penalty box for high sticking. Fans around the box tried to attack Fred, and the police had to be called to end the altercation. Glover was a hero in Cleveland, but he was the ultimate villain in every other rink around the League.

It was hoped that a return to Cleveland Arena ice would change the fortunes of the club. But that was not to be. Before 9,176 fans, the largest regular season crowd of the year, the Barons laid another egg. Their 4-1 loss to Pittsburgh dropped them three points behind the Hornets with only seven games remaining.

The most distressing point of the game was the ease with which the Hornets disposed of the Barons. The local icers were listless, only a shell of their former selves.

The Barons bounced back to defeat Springfield 4-2 in their next game. But in the victory, winger Wayne Larkin separated his shoulder and was lost for the year. This was the first in a series of developments that would shape the destiny of this club.

The biggest blow to Cleveland's title ambitions came on March 20th in Pittsburgh. The Barons were routed by the Hornets 9-1, falling five points out of first place. Also, the red hot Rochester Americans were now only two points behind Cleveland.

But this was hardly the worst news of the evening. At the 8:09 mark of the first period, the Barons' lost star goalie Les Binkley for the season. The great netminder was hit on top of the head by a shot off the stick of John MacMillan.

It was a scary sight as the stricken goalie lay unconscious in a pool of blood. He was carried off on a stretcher and remained unconscious for over half an hour. He finally came to in Divine Providence Hospital. Les suffered a severe concussion. He had recurring dizzy spells for the next few weeks and did not play again that season. Trainer George Polinuk was forced to play the balance of the game. George doubled as the Barons' practice goalie but was a sitting duck as the Hornets swarmed all over Cleveland the rest of the night.

The Montreal Canadiens sent little Jean Guy Morissette as an emergency replacement for Binkley. The 5'6", 140-pound goalie would remain with Cleveland for the duration of the season.

The most shocking event of the entire season occurred on March 24th. General Manager Jackie Gordon announced that the Barons had signed a replacement for the injured Wayne Larkin. Gordon stunned everyone in Cleveland when he stated that the player was none other than famed "bad man" Larry Zeidel!

Zeidel, of course, was the most hated enemy of the Barons. His wild exploits were legendary, and his run-ins with Fred Glover were equally infamous.

But with his team in trouble, Glover put past animosities behind him. The team always came first. Although Zeidel had been his most bitter foe, Fred always respected the mean hombre from Hershey.

Larry spent eight penalty-filled years with Hershey. The Bears sold him to Seattle before the present campaign. He didn't really fit in out West. The Western League was quite tame with an emphasis on skating, not hitting. Zeidel relished the opportunity to get back into the rough and tumble world of the AHL. But playing on the same team with Fred Glover was mind-boggling.

Pittsburgh took over first place on the second last night of the season. Cleveland beat Quebec that same night and trailed the Hornets by two points and now second place Rochester by one.

Cleveland played at Rochester on the season's final night and lost 4-2. Pittsburgh clinched first place when they defeated Springfield 4-1.

With a 37-30-5 record, the Barons finished in third place, three points behind Rochester and four back of Pittsburgh.

After leading the League from the end of December into March, third place was a bitter pill for Cleveland to swallow. With the first round of the playoffs against Rochester just around the corner, the Barons were written off as also-rans.

THE PLAYOFFS

The Americans were one hot club heading into the playoffs, going 15-4-2 in their last 21 games. Their 40-30-2 record was good for second place, just one point behind Pittsburgh. To make matters worse, the Barons dropped all four games played on Rochester ice.

The series turned into a coming-out party for Joe Szura. The tall center was more than the Americans could handle in Game One. Joe fired a three goal hat trick and assisted on two goals by linemate Ray Kinasewich as Cleveland surprised Rochester 6-3.

After the Amerks opened the scoring, the Barons tied it up on a goal by Fred Glover. They stretched their advantage to 4-1 before the Americans pulled within one midway in the third period. But a goal by Szura gave Cleveland some breathing room at 13:55.

In an unheard of feat, Szura followed up his first game heroics with another hat trick in Game Two at the Arena. Behind their red hot center, the Barons defeated Rochester 4-1 for a two-game sweep of their series.

Szura wasn't the only hero of the night. The entire defense was at the top of its game, especially Jean Guy Morissette in goal. The little netminder turned back 32 shots in the big win.

The series victory matched Cleveland against old nemesis Hershey in second round action. The Bears finished second to Quebec in the East division with a 36-31-5 record. But the Barons fared well against Hershey, winning all five games in Cleveland and two in Chocolate Town.

The Barons were confident heading into the opener of the best-of-five series at the Arena, and they played like it. Thoroughly dominating the Bears in Game One, Cleveland skated off with an easy 7-1 victory. All three forward lines scored at least two goals, including another one by Joe Szura. Joe was now skating with a swagger that made him a standout every time he touched the ice. He simply oozed with confidence.

It was more of the same in Game Two. The line of Szura, Kinasewich, and Ray Brunel struck for four more goals as the Barons humbled the Bears again 5-1.

Two more scores by Szura gave him 9 in the four playoff games to date. This was only two shy of the mark set by Wally Hergesheimer during the 1950-51 playoffs. His mates Brunel and Kinasewich each had one goal, giving them three apiece. This gave the line a whopping 15 goals in the playoffs. They seemed unstoppable.

The hot line was at it again in Game Three in Hershey. Each linemate scored once, as Cleveland built a 3-0 lead early in the second period. But the Bears showed spunk by narrowing the margin to 3-2. Jim Mikol scored a long empty net goal that clinched the 4-2 victory.

Enthusiasm over the sweep of Hershey was tempered a bit because of the continued hindrance of Fred Glover's pulled leg muscle. He injured his leg in the opening game of the Hershey series and had played only sparingly since. He would be needed when the Barons opened the Calder Cup Finals against the high-powered Quebec Aces.

Quebec was the League's top club during the regular season. Their 41-30-1 record led the East division. Loaded with high-powered talent, the Aces routed Pittsburgh four games to one in their first-round series. They were heavy favorites to end Cleveland's party in the Finals.

Fortunately for Cleveland, the Aces, like Rochester and Hershey before them, could not contain Joe Szura. The amazing center iceman scored two more goals in Game One at Quebec as the Barons shocked the Frenchmen 4-2. The two scores were the 11th and 12th of the playoffs for Joe, breaking Wally Hergesheimer's record of eleven. Incredibly, he did the trick in only six games!

The entire team was skating like never before. The Aces were expected to have a wide edge in team speed, but the Barons' checking slowed them to a crawl.

Joe Szura reached, until then, unheard of heights during the 1963-64 Playoffs. His 13 goals in 9 games broke Wally Hergesheimer's record of 11 set in 1950-51 and established Joe as a big-time American Hockey League star.
Dick Dugan collection.

Somewhat overlooked by Joe Szura's scoring feats was the play of Larry Zeidel. Being paired with Bill Needham on defense was one of the keys to Cleveland's playoff success. The former "bad man" was keeping a cool head and was playing the best hockey of his career. Picking him up on loan from Seattle was a coup for GM Jackie Gordon.

Game Two was crucial to Quebec, and they came out flying. After building a 3-0 lead by early in the second period, the Aces appeared ready to blast the Barons out of the building. Cleveland was also handicapped by starting the second period without Fred Glover and Bill Needham. Fred was given a 10-minute misconduct penalty for jawing with Referee Vern Buffey at 18:51 of the first stanza. As the teams headed to their dressing rooms at period's end, Needham blasted Buffey verbally and was thumbed out of the game.

With everything going against them, the Barons sucked it up and started to take the play away from the Aces. This time it was a goal by Bob Ellet at the 6:00 mark that lit the fire. 53 seconds later, Guy Rousseau hit for Cleveland's second goal. The tide had turned, and who else but Joe Szura tied the score at 14:54. It was Joe's unbelievable 13th goal of the playoffs.

The third period was all Cleveland after Cleland Mortson put Quebec on top 4-3 at 9:16 of the final frame. Thereafter Cleveland attacked relentlessly and tied it with a goal by Cecil Hoekstra at 11:21.

The Aces managed only five shots at goalie Morissette during the entire third period. The Barons' intense pressure paid off when Dick Mattiusi fired a dramatic game-winning goal at 18:50. The 5-4 victory gave Cleveland a commanding two-game series edge.

Quebec was in serious trouble and played a great Game Three in Cleveland. But the Barons played an even greater one.

Once again the Aces struck first with a goal by ex-Baron Ed Hoekstra. But brother Cecil, of the Barons, was not to be denied. He put a beautiful pass on the stick of Guy Rousseau at 19:02 of the second period, and Guy's shot was true.

The Barons wasted no time in the third period. With the Aces' Cleland Mortson in the penalty box, Ted Harris wound up at the point for an apparent shot. Everyone, including goalie Gump Worsley, thought a shot was coming. But Harris spotted an open Ray Kinasewich next to the Ace's cage and slapped a long pass to him. Ray deflected the pass past Worsley for the go-ahead score. The goal held up, and Cleveland had a big 2-1 win.

The entire City of Cleveland was now caught up with Baron fever. Lines formed early the next morning at the Arena as fans all wanted to be part of the expected victory celebration. The largest crowd in years would see Game Four at the old Arena, 10,016 to be exact.

During the glory years of the 1940's, huge crowds of 11-12,000 were common. But this was no longer possible in the 1960's. Al Sutphin took care of the fire marshalls, so they would let the overflow throngs in. Present-day marshalls would have none of that. If the Arena was twice as large, it could have been filled on this historic day. Hundreds of fans were turned away when the "Sold Out" signs went up.

No team in the history of the American Hockey League had ever won nine straight playoff games. The massive Arena crowd longed for the record book to be rewritten, and they were not disappointed. Playing with a burning fire seldom seen in any team, the Barons became a team of destiny by defeating Quebec 5-2.

After the Aces led 1-0 for half the game, Len Ronson tied it up for Cleveland at 10:49. Then the Barons' magnificent player-coach Fred Glover gave his team the lead for good at 18:07. The goal gave Fred 98 career playoff points, one more than Providence's Willie Marshall. The old Ice House on Euclid Avenue was really rocking now.

Little Guy Rousseau scored his sixth playoff goal for Cleveland at 1:35 of the third period. Jim Morrison then brought the Aces back to within one at 12:57. Suddenly there were thousands of sweaty palms at the Arena.

But this team would not be denied. Cecil Hoekstra scored an insurance goal at 17:31. Before the jubilant fans had a chance to sit down, Bob Ellet scored just eight seconds later.

How the roof stayed on the Arena is still a mystery. The huge crowd never bothered to sit back down. They cheered and hollered on their feet for the balance of the game. When the final gong sounded, the Barons had a 5-2 victory and their ninth Calder Cup.

This great victory seemed to symbolize the city. Cleveland was, and is, a blue-collar town. It prides itself in its hard-working citizenry.

Hard work was the essence of this Barons' team. No where near the most talented Cleveland team, this squad had the heart of a lion. No mountain was too big for it to climb. It truly was a team of destiny.

Individually, the stories were many. Fred Glover was named the League's MVP for the third time. Jackie Gordon was named hockey's Executive of the Year. Ted Harris was the League's top defenseman. Late addition Larry Zeidel curbed his famous temper and proved invaluable on the back line. Jean Guy Morissette came from nowhere to fashion a Cinderella story in goal. Big Joe Szura put on a playoff surge never seen before.

But most of all, this unique collection of athletes epitomized the word TEAM. They made our City proud and should never be forgotten.

FINAL STANDINGS
1963-64

West	W	L	T	GF	GA	PTS.
Pittsburgh	40	29	3	242	196	83
Rochester	40	30	2	256	223	82
Cleveland	37	30	5	239	207	79
Buffalo	25	40	7	194	260	57
East	**W**	**L**	**T**	**GF**	**GA**	**PTS.**
Quebec	41	30	1	258	225	83
Hershey	36	31	5	236	249	77
Providence	32	35	5	248	239	69
Baltimore	32	37	3	200	220	67
Springfield	23	44	5	238	292	51

Top Baron Scorers	G	A	PTS.
Fred Glover	26	50	76
Ron Attwell	30	38	68
Jim Mikol	24	44	68
Joe Szura	23	44	67
Ray Kinasewich	28	30	58
Cecil Hoekstra	23	28	51
Wayne Larkin	18	22	40
Ray Brunel	12	25	37
Guy Rousseau	18	16	34
Bob Ellet	18	14	32

Calder Cup Champion – Cleveland Barons

THE 1963-64 CLEVELAND BARONS

Front (L-R): Jean-Guy Morissette, Bob Ellett, General Manager Jack Gordon, Coach Fred Glover, President Paul L. Bright, Captain Bill Needham, Les Binkley. Second: Trainer George Polinuk, Public Relations Director Shel Fullerton, Jim Holdaway, Cecil Hoekstra, Ron Attwell, Ted Harris, Joe Szura, Pete Shearer, Promotion Director Dino Lucarelli, Business Manager Joseph B. Vargo. Third: Tommy Williams, Ray Brunel, Ray Kinasewich, Jim Mikol, Larry Zeidel, Dick Mattiussi, Wayne Larkin, Guy Rousseau. James Peter Hendy collection.

1964-65 SEASON

From the word "go", this new edition of the Barons was a team in trouble. Many important veterans from the previous year's Calder Cup champions were gone. Jim Mikol was re-purchased by Toronto. Ted Harris was up with Montreal. Larry Zeidel was back in Seattle. Ray Kinasewich retired. Guy Rousseau and Ray Brunel were placed elsewhere in the Montreal organization.

Asked to take their places were a group of inexperienced youngsters. Some of these kids had genuine promise, but they were still too wet behind the ears for tough AHL competition. Doug Senior, Gordon Wilke, and Wayne Freitag were new forwards. Bill Speer and Ted Lanyon were brought in on defense. Two solid veterans also made their debuts in Cleveland. Defenseman Frank Martin, who played against Cleveland with Quebec the year before, was a solid edition to the backline. He previously played six years for the NHL Chicago Blackhawks.

Up front, big things were expected from Bob Courcy. The 28-year-old right wing led the Central League in scoring the year before with 82 points. He had previous AHL experience with Buffalo and Quebec.

A portent of things to come were early season injuries to defenseman Dick Mattiussi and goalie Les Binkley. Dick broke his ankle early in training camp. He missed the season's first five games but took much longer to regain his effectiveness.

Binkley severely pulled a groin muscle in the first period of the season opening 3-3 tie with Baltimore. He would be slow to recover and missed the season's first month. In his place was 21-year-old Andre Gagnon, technically still an amateur from the Canadian Junior Leagues.

Gagnon won his first start, a 4-2 victory over Springfield. He made 29 saves and was a pleasant surprise. But soon his inexperience began to show, and the team began to sag.

It wasn't all Gagnon's fault. In fact, he played rather well. In all, he played 12 games and posted a 3.38 average. Injuries were the main culprit. Bob Courcy, who led the local icers in scoring, was checked into the hospital after taking a solid check in a 4-3 loss at Springfield. He would miss six games and became part of the walking wounded.

Along with the injuries was a woeful lack of scoring. In fact, the Barons were the lowest scoring team in the League early in the year. All this added up to a 3-10-3 start. Things couldn't get any worse, or could they?

In late November, Les Binkley, who had just returned to action, was frowned upon by Lady Luck again. This time he suffered a broken bone in his foot during practice. Nothing was going right for Binkley or the team. Last year's Calder Cup hero, Jean Guy Morissette, was called up to fill in.

The losses kept mounting, and the team's fortunes kept sinking. Incredibly, the injury jinx struck the Barons once again in mid-December.

Cecil Hoekstra, the team's third-line center, had been playing with severe back pain all season long.

Bob Courcy was a lightning quick right winger with a deadly shot and great playmaking ability. He led the team in scoring during the 1964-65 and 1965-66 seasons. Dick Dugan collection

When the pain became acute in early December, Cecil was placed in traction at Huron Road Hospital. Two slipped discs were discovered, and surgery was required. This finished Hoekstra for the season.

GM Jackie Gordon was now desperate. His defending champions were only a crippled shell of their former selves. So for the first time in the team's history, Gordon took a player on loan from a National League team on 24-hour recall.

Montreal sent veteran winger Bill Hicke to Cleveland, and his impact was immediately felt. But as luck would have it, Hicke's stay was very brief – a week and a half to be exact.

When Montreal's Gilles Tremblay suffered a broken leg, the Canadiens traded Hicke and Jean Guy Morissette of the Barons to New York for Les Duff and Dave McComb. Montreal, of course, kept Duff, and the Barons were left holding an empty bag.

Montreal sent McComb and goalie Ernie Wakely to Cleveland, but the damage was already done. The embarrassing incident only sent the team's spirit lower. But such was life in the AHL when a team was dependent upon the NHL for players. The big league now owned the majority of all players. Only a few clubs, like Cleveland, operated on a semi-independent basis. Most teams were now solely dependent upon the National League.

By year's end, the Barons were buried in last place with a 9-17-4 record, eleven points behind third-place Pittsburgh. Rochester was out of sight with 46 points.

The local icers finally received a lift near the end of January. Howie Glover, Fred's younger brother, joined the club. Howie had been purchased from New York during the off season. But the younger Glover

235

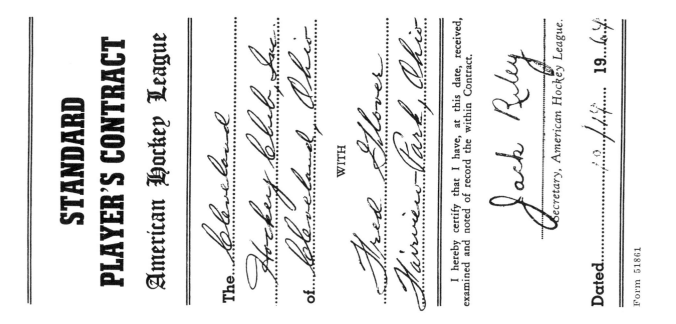

IMPORTANT NOTICE TO PLAYER

Before signing this contract you should carefully examine it to be sure that all terms and conditions agreed upon have been incorporated herein, and if any has been omitted, you should insist upon having it inserted in the contract before you sign.

AMERICAN HOCKEY LEAGUE
STANDARD PLAYER'S CONTRACT

This Agreement

BETWEEN: CLEVELAND HOCKEY CLUB, INC.

hereinafter called the "Club,"

A member of the American Hockey League, hereinafter called the "League"

— AND — Fred Glover

hereinafter called the "Player"

of Fairview Park in { Province / State } of Ohio

Witnesseth:

THAT in consideration of the respective obligations herein and hereby assumed, the Parties to this Contract severally agree as follows:—

1. The Club hereby employs the Player as a skilled Hockey Player for the term of one year commencing October 1st, 19 64 and agrees, subject to the terms and conditions hereof, to pay the Player a salary of

TWELVE-THOUSAND Dollars ($12000.00).

Larry Smith collection.

Fred Glover (L) and Howie Glover (R) – A big night for the Glover brothers on February 3, 1965. Fred played in his 1,000th game and Howie scored a three-goal hat trick.
Cleveland State University archives.

The Barons lost 15 of their next 19 games as the team was eliminated from the playoffs for the first time in 25 years. The sad event became official on March 7th. Cleveland had defeated Quebec 3-2. But Pittsburgh's 1-1 tie with Buffalo clinched third place for the Hornets. Actually, the playoff race had been over for weeks.

Coach Glover warned the team to give its best in the last five games. The threat must have worked because Cleveland did win its last five. Included in the streak was a four-goal game by Howie Glover in an 8-5 victory over Baltimore.

Unfortunately for Cleveland and its fans, it was far too little, too late. The Barons finished with a dismal 24-43-5 record. This was 12 points behind Pittsburgh and a whopping 46 behind first-place Rochester. Official attendance hit rock bottom at 134,003, an average of 3,722 per game. In the Barons' worst season ever, there was one gleam of hope. Next season could only be better, and it definitely was.

reported to training camp with a pinched nerve in his shoulder and had been disabled ever since.

In a season destroyed by injuries, Howie became the team's shining light. Although he would only play the final 25 games of the campaign, Glover would score a remarkable 21 goals. This would be third highest on the team. From the moment Howie laced on his skates, he played like a man possessed. Obviously, playing with brother Fred revived his career.

The Glover brothers had a night to remember on February 3rd. Fred played in his 1,000th game and rewarded his fans with two goals. Howie added three scores of his own. But most of all, the Barons had their biggest night of the year as they humbled Springfield 13-4. Joe Szura, Bob Ellet, and Dick Mattiussi also scored twice each.

The laugher over Springfield turned out to be the highlight of the year. It raised the team's record to 15-28-5. But the night's joy was shortlived as Cleveland's losing ways returned, in a big way.

FINAL STANDINGS
1964-65

West	W	L	T	GF	GA	PTS.
Rochester	48	21	3	310	199	99
Buffalo	40	26	6	261	218	86
Pittsburgh	29	36	7	268	256	65
Cleveland	24	43	5	228	285	53
East	**W**	**L**	**T**	**GF**	**GA**	**PTS.**
Quebec	44	26	2	280	223	90
Hershey	36	32	4	246	243	76
Baltimore	35	32	5	275	249	75
Springfield	29	39	4	237	273	62
Providence	20	50	2	193	312	42

Top Baron Scorers	G	A	PTS.
Bob Courcy	33	34	67
Ron Attwell	14	49	63
Joe Szura	32	30	62
Fred Glover	20	42	62
Wayne Larkin	17	33	50
Bob Ellet	9	37	46
Gordon Wilke	16	25	41
Doug Senior	18	16	34
Howie Glover	21	7	28

Calder Cup Champion – Rochester Americans

Bob Ellett

Dick Dugan collection.

THE 1964-65 CLEVELAND BARONS

Front (L-R): Andre Gagnon, General Manager Jack Gordon, Coach Fred Glover, President Paul L. Bright, Captain Bill Needham, Business Manager Joseph B. Vargo, Les Binkley. Second: Publicity & Promotion Director Dino Lucarelli, Howie Glover, Gordon Wilkie, Dave McComb, Ron Attwell, Joe Szura, Frank Martin, Bill Speer, Trainer George Polinuk. Third: Doug Senior, Bob Courcy, Ted Lanyon, Dick Mattiussi, Wayne Larkin, Bob Ellett. Dennis Turchek collection.

1965-66 SEASON

Mrs. Lewis Darvas collection.

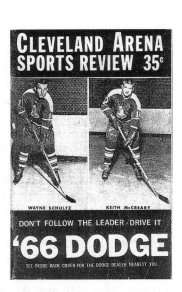

It was a busy off season for the Barons. Jackie Gordon left the team to become assistant general manager of the New York Rangers of the NHL. Jack hated to leave, but this was an opportunity he could not refuse.

Barons' president Paul Bright added the vacant general manager's title to his list of duties. To help Bright in matters of player personnel, player-coach Fred Glover took on the added responsibility of assistant general manager.

During his years with the team, Fred Glover was always the heart and soul of the Barons. This was never more evident than during the 1965-66 season. With his team going nowhere while he was injured, Fred came back early from knee surgery and almost singlehandedly led the Barons to second place and the Calder Cup finals. Here, his eyes say it all, burning with fire, he scores agnist Hershey's Andre Gill. Cleveland State University archives.

Glover and Bright went back to the tried and true method of adding veterans to bolster the club. First off was the reacquisition of defenseman Larry Zeidel from the Seattle Totems. Larry was overjoyed at being reunited with Fred Glover and the Barons. His boyish enthusiasm and fierce determination would rub off on the club and make the ex-villain a big fan favorite.

Up front, the additions of Tom McCarthy and Keith McCreary were a welcome sight for the offense. McCarthy scored 53 goals for Tulsa in the Central League the year before. McCreary was a top goalgetter with the Hershey Bears. Both would make big contributions to the team.

Cleveland was extremely optimistic heading into the season opener against the Los Angeles Blades. The AHL and Western Hockey League were playing an interlocking schedule for the first time. Each AHL team would play a home and home set against each Western league club.

Tom McCarthy lived up to his advance billing as he scored three goals to lead the Barons to a 5-2 win over Los Angeles. It was a rousing debut, but a costly one also.

Howie Glover was checked hard into the boards and suffered a broken jaw as a result. The injury was serious enough that Howie had to have the jaw wired shut. It would be mid-December before he could play again. During that time, Howie was on a liquid diet and lost 25 pounds. It would be months before he regained his full strength and effectiveness.

Brother Fred was not in the best of health either. His often injured right knee was giving him trouble, and he was only playing sparingly. Without the two Glovers in the lineup, the team went out of sync.

When the hoped for good start didn't happen, the club began to press. Everyone in the organization wanted to redeem themselves for last season's failure so much that they were tight as a drum. The result was a 5-7-0 record at Thanksgiving.

Finally, the team began to show signs of life as they won three straight games. Then the roof caved in.

Player-coach Fred Glover's knee was not responding to treatment. On December 6th he underwent surgery to repair a torn cartilage in the ailing right knee. At first it was feared that his career could be over. After all, Fred was 37 years old, 38 on January 5th, and was now in his 18th season of play. He could not go on forever. But Fred would play again after a six-week recovery period.

Shorn of their leader, the Barons went into a terrible tailspin. They played lethargically and ran a distant third in the standings.

Keith McCreary
Dick Dugan collection.

Tom McCarthy was born to score goals. Although he sometimes seemed to play in slow motion, Tom would plant himself in from of the enemy net where his stick would become a magic wand. Dick Dugan collection.

Bill Speer
Dick Dugan collection.

Ted Lanyon
Dick Dugan collection.

A new start with the New Year failed to improve the team's fortunes. In fact, the Barons lost six in a row to fall to a dreadful 13-21-1. All of the great early season expectations were going up in smoke. It seemed as if only a miracle could save the Barons now. Well, they didn't get a miracle, but they did get Fred Glover. And that was even better.

With his team on a slow ride to oblivion, 18 points behind second-place Pittsburgh, Coach Glover decided it was time to take matters into his own hands. Telling no one his plans, Fred walked into the locker room on January 16th and began suiting up for the afternoon's game against Baltimore.

Fred had missed 18 games since his knee operation on December 6th. Although he had resumed skating, his knee really wasn't ready for action. But Glover had played with pain before. His team needed him, and he was ready to give it his all.

The sight of their leader dressing for the game was all the incentive the Barons needed. From the moment they hit the ice, this was a changed club. The local icers played with a verve not seen all season long. Larry Zeidel in particular played with the zip of a kid again. Being reunited with his old ex-rival seemed to light a fire under Larry, and he played with the zest of days gone by.

Glover inserted himself at right wing on a line with Ron Attwell and brother Howie. The results were dramatic. Attwell and Howie each scored a goal, and Fred assisted on both. Howie's score was his first of the year. He was just now beginning to regain his strength after losing 25 pounds after breaking his jaw.

The eventual game winner was scored by Bill Needham. The 3-2 victory was no indication of the way Cleveland outplayed the Clippers. Had it not been for Baltimore goalie Ed Giacomin's 51 saves, the Barons would have been in double figures.

Cleveland knocked another game off of Pittsburgh's big lead by knocking off the Hornets 4-2 in their very next game. The team was finally beginning to play like it could.

In fact, the Barons were like a runaway train for the next five weeks. And it all began with the return of Fred Glover to the lineup. His presence on the ice cannot be overestimated.

In a game against Hershey on January 28th, both Glover brothers scored two goals as the Barons defeated the Bears 5-3. The Glover-Attwell-Glover line so dominated play that the Hersheys left the ice shaking their heads. Could this be the same team that was so listless the first half of the year?

The next night at the Arena, Cleveland served notice to the rest of the League that they were now a force to be reckoned with. Behind the fantastic goaltending of Les Binkley, the Barons upset mighty Rochester 3-1.

The Amerks, along with Quebec, were the class of the League. They led Cleveland by 26 points. But on this night, the Barons clearly were the better team. Binkley was outstanding with 46 saves. Goals were scored by Dick Mattiussi, Keith McCreary, and Joe Szura. The score by Szura, who was on his way to a big year, was his 21st of the season.

The Barons got a big scare on February 6th. In winning their sixth straight game, 4-0 over Baltimore, goalie Binkley was injured. Les was struck above the right knee by a hard shot from Clipper Ray Cullen and was removed from the game.

His injury was diagnosed as a bruised cartilage, and it kept him out of action for 6 games. Jean Guy Morissette took over in goal.

Jean Guy's first full game in the nets resulted in a 6-4 victory over Baltimore. The win was the team's seventh straight and put them over the .500 mark at 23-22-1. They also had reduced Pittsburgh's second-place margin to eight points.

Hershey temporarily cooled off Cleveland by winning back-to-back games. But the Barons came back to win three more in a row with Morissette in goal.

Cleveland pulled to within four points of Pittsburgh when they rolled over Providence 9-1. The local icers tied a club record for most goals in a period by scoring seven in the second period. Leading the way were Joe Szura and Bob Courcy, with three goals each. Szura's hat trick gave him 33 lamplighters for the season.

In all, Szura's line accounted for 18 points on the night. Joe had 3 goals, 2 assists; Courcy 3 goals and 4 assists; and Bob Ellett 1 goal and 5 assists. The trio had been on fire for weeks and had accounted for nearly half of the team's goal total.

The big win over Providence set up a showdown with Pittsburgh at the Arena. Even though their once seemingly insurmountable second-place lead had dwindled to four points, the Hornets were still a cocky bunch. Pittsburgh Coach Eddie Bush was popping off as to how the Hornets were going to stick it to the Barons. He also called the Cleveland defense the weakest part of the club. Bush should have stayed quiet.

Stung by the Hornet coach's criticism, the Barons clobbered Pittsburgh 8-1. Hornet goalie George Gardner called it a nightmare. But actually, it was pay-back time. After rolling up a 4-0 first period lead, the game was never in doubt. Particularly fired up was the Cleveland defense. The backliners hit everything that moved and made Hornet Coach Bush eat his words, and then some.

The Barons vaulted into a second-place tie the very next night when they defeated Quebec 3-1 before 8,597 at the Arena. Cleveland's meteoric rise to second place was astounding. Only five weeks

242

High scoring Joe Szura popped in a whopping 46 goals during the 1965-66 season and further established himself as one of the American Hockey League's top snipers. Kay Horiba collection.

earlier, the Barons trailed Pittsburgh by 18 points. But after Fred Glover returned to the lineup, the team won 16 of its next 19 games. With a 29-24-1 record, the sky now seemed the limit.

Unfortunately, a six-game road trip brought the team back to earth in a big way. The local pucksters lost all six games on the road and returned to Cleveland eight points behind Pittsburgh.

Particularly embarrassing were back-to-back routs suffered in Quebec. The Aces humiliated the Barons twice, 11-2 and 10-1. All of the great work in the recent hot streak had been stripped away. The slump was hard to explain since the Clevelanders were red hot before this road trip. Coach Glover expressed hope that a return to home cooking would cure the team's ills. He proved to be a prophet.

A return to home ice was not the only cure. Getting back to the basics of hard work and dedication were the real keys to success. Coach Glover drilled his troops hard, and it paid off in their return to the Arena against Providence.

The Coach mixed up his lines in an effort to get some offense, but the new combinations failed to click. Behind 3-2 entering the third period, Fred went back to his old combinations, and suddenly the team woke up. Goals by McCarthy, Attwell, Mattiussi, Hoekstra, and Szura turned a close game into a 7-2 rout.

The Barons stretched their latest winning streak to four games when they defeated Springfield 4-1 at the Arena. The hot streak erased the eight-point deficit to Pittsburgh. Cleveland once again shared second place with the slumping Hornets. As if written by a script writer, the two clubs then faced off against each other in back-to-back games. To no one's surprise, the two rivals split the games, each winning on home ice. The Hornets drilled Cleveland 6-2 in Pittsburgh, while the Barons came back at the Arena 4-1.

The game in Cleveland featured two penalty shots awarded to the Hornets. On each, Les Binkley came up with a remarkable save to keep his team in the game. On offense, Joe Szura led the way with two goals, numbers 41 and 42 of the season.

Defenseman Dick Mattiussi loved to rush the puck. Here he almost scores against Springfield Goalie Jacques Caron. Dick Dugan collection.

The two clubs fought tooth and nail for the rest of the season. Cleveland won four of its next five games and carried a 38-31-1 record into the last game of the season at Toronto against Rochester. The Amerks were forced out of their Arena by a huge bowling tournament that had been previously booked.

The Barons held a slim two-point lead over Pittsburgh entering the final game. They needed at least a tie to clinch the number two spot.

Howie Glover opened the scoring in the first period taking a pass from brother Fred. But Rochester came roaring back with three goals of their own to lead 3-1 after one period.

Defenseman Bill Speer got one back at 11:07 of the second period. When the teams retired to the dressing room, word came that Pittsburgh had defeated Baltimore 5-4. The Barons had to come back, or finish in third place.

With the pressure firmly on their backs, the Barons came out charging. At the 4:40 mark Tom McCarthy tied the score with a neat flip over goalie Gary Smith. From that point on, it was a battle of goaltenders as each team pressed for the winning goal. Neither team scored, and the game went into a 10-minute sudden death overtime.

The Barons had the better of play in the extra session but were continually denied by goalie Smith. The Amerk puckstopper came up with two especially outstanding saves off the stick of Cecil Hoekstra. Finally, time ran out with the teams deadlocked 3-3.

The single point in the standings was enough to give the Barons second place. Everyone in the organization was ecstatic over the team's accomplishment. From 18 points back, the Barons had charged to overtake Pittsburgh. But their work had just begun. Right around the corner was the first round of the playoffs. Their opponent? The Pittsburgh Hornets.

Les Binkley was at his best during the 1965-66 season when he led the league with a 2.93 goals against average. Here he stops Buffalo's Gerry Melnyk, while Bill Speer dives to help out.
Cleveland State University archives.

THE PLAYOFFS

The Baron squad that met the Hornets in the best-of-five series was an extremely confident group. Besides overtaking Pittsburgh in the standings, Cleveland fared extremely well against the Steel City crew during the regular season. In winning five of the eight games between the clubs, the Clevelanders were poison to Hornet goaltender George Gardner.

Although Gardner sported a fine 2.98 goals against average, he gave up 30 goals in the seven games he played against Cleveland. It was no secret that the Barons were his jinx team.

Whether it was just psychological or Cleveland's great play, the jinx continued during the playoffs.

Gardner could do nothing right in the two games in Cleveland, while the Barons' Les Binkley was at the top of his game. The Hornets were continually frustrated by the scintillating saves of the great Cleveland netminder.

Coming to the forefront of the Barons' attack was Bob Courcy. Bob scored two goals in Game One, as the Barons skated off with a 5-2 victory. Game Two was a much closer affair with Cleveland holding a slim 3-2 lead after two periods. But Courcy put the game out of reach with a pair of lamplighters 22 seconds apart midway through the last frame. When Joe Szura scored as the game was winding down, the Barons had a 6-2 win that was much closer than the final score indicated.

Cleveland was looking for a sweep as the series shifted to Pittsburgh, but the Hornets had other ideas. Fighting for their playoff lives, the Pittsburghers held a 2-1 edge heading into the third period. However, the Barons struck for two quick goals by Howie Glover and Cecil Hoekstra to take the lead.

After that, the Cleveland defense threw up a brick wall in front of Binkley. When the Hornets did get off a shot, Les was ready to hold the fort. His stop on a wide open Bob Cunningham with four minutes to go took the wind out of Pittsburgh's sails.

Hornet goalie Gardner was pulled in the game's last two minutes, but Cleveland's Tom McCarthy spoiled the strategy by scoring an empty net goal. The 4-2 victory gave the Barons a sweep of the series. It also was Cleveland's fifth series win over Pittsburgh without a loss. The Hornets were truly the Barons' playoff cousins.

Cleveland moved on to the playoffs' second round against Springfield. The Indians had just upset the Hershey Bears in three straight games. The Barons had beaten Springfield six of eight games during the regular season, but the Indians were dangerous despite their 30-39-3 record.

Still run by the old taskmaster Eddie Shore, the Indians were a strange team. No longer the explosive powerhouse of a few years past, they tried to lull their opponents to sleep. Using a slowdown style with long stretches of short passes, Springfield could slow a game to a waltz.

Game One was a yawner with Les Binkley having to make only 15 saves and Springfield's Jacque Caron 20. The Indians slowed the game to a crawl with Bob Courcy's fifth playoff goal, the game's only excitement for two periods.

When Indian Howie Menard tied the score early in the third period, the strategy seemed to be paying off. But the goal woke the Barons up. Fred Glover once again came to the rescue when he set up Gordon Wilkie with a beautiful pass. Wilkie gave Cleveland a 2-1 lead with his first playoff goal ever. In contrast, the assist was Glover's 100th playoff point.

Tom McCarthy's insurance goal at 13:08 was all the Barons needed for a 3-1 win.

Game Two at the Arena was a true defensive thriller. With Les Binkley flawless in goal, the Barons edged Springfield 1-0. Cleveland picked up the pace in this one, not letting the Indians lull them to sleep. Still, goalie Jacques Caron kept them off the scoreboard until the 14:12 mark of the second period.

Howie Glover chased after a pass from Bill Speer in the Springfield zone, and Caron came out of his net in a race with Howie to the puck. Glover tripped and fell face first on the ice. While sliding on his stomach, he somehow swiped at the puck and directed it past the also sliding Caron. The weird goal proved to be the game winner.

Howie was the hero again in Game Three at Springfield as the Barons swept the Indians out of the playoffs.

Down 2-0 after two periods, Cleveland mounted a great comeback. Bob Ellett scored after only 36 seconds of the final frame, and Keith McCreary tied it at 3:20. From then on, the goaltenders took over making one great save after another.

The game appeared headed for overtime when Howie shocked the Indians at 19:12. Scoring the game winner in two straight games seemed to ease the pain of a frustrating season for Glover. After breaking his jaw in the season's opener, he missed 17 games. Then it took him most of the season to regain his strength after losing 25 pounds. But now Howie was back playing with the dash and flair of which he was capable.

Barons' Bob Courcy scores against Springfield in Game 1 of the 1965-55 semi-finals.
Dick Dugan collection.

The big series win vaulted the Barons into the Calder Cup finals. But as hot as they were, Cleveland was still a big underdog against the powerful Rochester Americans.

Led by League-scoring champion Dick Gamble, Garry Ehman, Jim Pappin, Mike Walton, and Bronco Horvath, the Amerks were loaded once again. Although the Barons were hot and playing their best hockey of the year, it would take a Herculean effort to upset the defending champions.

The Americans, fresh off their first-round play-off victory over East Division champion Quebec, thoroughly dominated Game One. Behind the expert goaltending of pudgy Bobby Perreault, the Amerks shut out Cleveland 4-0 in Toronto. The Rochester War Memorial Auditorium was booked by a national bowling tournament, and the hockey team had to use arenas in Toronto and Buffalo for "home" games. The Barons were outclassed in the opener but hoped for better results in the second and third games back in Cleveland.

As he had done all season long, Coach Fred Glover picked up his team in Game Two. This time he did it with his iron fists. After taking on Red Armstrong in the first period, Fred traded punches with Mike Walton in the second stanza. In all, Fred spent 29 minutes in the sin bin. While this didn't give him much time on the ice, he inspired his team not to back down to their powerful foe. Brother Howie, Bill Speer, and Bill Needham also were involved in altercations during the bloody game.

Howie Glover (11), Tom McCarthy (16), and Ron Attwell (8), surround Rochester goalie Bobby Perreault during the 1965-66 Calder Cup finals. Dick Dugan collection.

As for the game itself, the Barons beat the Amerks on the scoreboard as well. Tom McCarthy and Rochester's Jim Pappin traded second-period goals. As the game was heading for overtime, Cleveland's Dick Mattiussi was called for holding at the 18:00 mark of the third period.

Rochester sent its big guns on the ice for its power play, but the Barons pulled a rabbit out of their top hat.

Tom McCarthy picked up a loose puck at center ice and broke in on Bobby Perreault. The Amerk goalie made the save, but Cleveland's Cecil Hoekstra pounced on the rebound and fired home the game winner at 18:56. The 2-1 victory gave the team a huge boost, and the euphoria carried over into the next game.

Picking up where they left off, the Barons romped over Rochester 5-1 in Game Three before 8,045 Arena fans. Ron Attwell, playing his first game since breaking his thumb on April 1st, got the local icers off to a flying start at 3:49 of the first period. After that goal, the Barons never looked back and skated the Americans right off the ice. Bill Speer and Keith McCreary also scored before Tom McCarthy's two third-period goals sewed up the contest.

Game Four, played in Buffalo, was too much Jim Pappin. The big winger scored all of Rochester's goals in the Amerks' 3-1 victory. Pappin's hat trick more than matched Cleveland's singleton by Keith McCreary. The Amerk victory tied the series at two games each, with the pivotal fifth game scheduled in Toronto.

Game Five was no contest. Rochester stormed all over Cleveland and blew the Barons out of Maple Leaf Gardens 7-0. Sparked by Mike Walton's hat trick, the Americans were in control from the opening faceoff.

Needing only one victory to clinch their second straight Calder Cup, Rochester jumped all over the Barons in the first period of Game Six at the Arena. Striking for three quick goals, the Amerks appeared on the verge of another blowout.

But as they had done all season long, the Barons came fighting back. Second-period goals by Howie Glover and Keith McCreary brought Cleveland to within one entering the third period.

Unfortunately, try as they might, Cleveland could not get the tying goal past Rochester's Bobby Perreault. The Amerk goalie was outstanding in turning back the fired-up Clevelanders. When all was said and done, the Barons had come close. But Rochester had the Cup.

The Barons had nothing to be ashamed of. In fact, their season was quite remarkable. Mired in third place, 18 points behind Pittsburgh on January 16th, the local icers thrilled their fans with their stirring second-place drive.

Most of all, the value of Fred Glover to this team was never more evident. The team's second-half comeback was directly related to the coach's return to the lineup after knee surgery. His mere presence on the ice gave the team all the lift it needed. More than ever, Fred Glover was the heart and soul of the Cleveland Barons.

Cleveland's 2-1 victory over Rochester in Game #2 of the 1965-66 Finals was an all-out war. Fred Glover led the way with 29 minutes in penalties. In this brawl, Barons in white left to right are Bill Speer (falling), Bill Needham, Fred Glover, and Howie Glover. Cleveland State University archives.

FINAL STANDINGS
1965-66

West	W	L	T	GF	GA	PTS.
Rochester	46	21	5	288	221	97
Cleveland	38	32	2	243	217	78
Pittsburgh	38	33	1	236	218	77
Buffalo	29	40	3	215	243	61

East	W	L	T	GF	GA	PTS.
Quebec	47	21	4	337	226	98
Hershey	37	30	5	268	232	79
Springfield	31	38	3	203	239	65
Baltimore	27	43	2	212	254	56
Providence	20	49	3	188	306	43

Top Baron Scorers	G	A	PTS.
Bob Courcy	26	60	86
Joe Szura	46	30	76
Tom McCarthy	33	34	67
Bob Ellett	24	36	60
Ron Attwell	23	25	48
Cecil Hoekstra	21	26	47
Dick Mattiussi	8	35	43
Keith McCreary	18	24	42
Fred Glover	8	28	36

Calder Cup Champion – Rochester Americans

THE 1965-66 CLEVELAND BARONS

Front (L-R): Business Manager Joseph B. Vargo, Jean-Guy Morissette, Captain Bill Needham, President & General Manager Paul L. Bright, Coach Fred Glover, Les Binkley, Publicity and Promotion Director Dino A. Lucarelli. Second: Larry Zeidel, Gordon Wilkie, Wayne Schultz, Ron Attwell, Cecil Hoekstra, Joe Szura, Tom McCarthy. Third: Ted Lanyon, Howie Glover, Bill Speer, Keith McCreary, Dick Mattiussi, Bob Courcy, Bob Ellett, Trainer Barry Keast. Kay Horiba collection.

1966-67 SEASON

Once again, the Barons approached the new season with high expectations. The core of the team was kept intact with one large exception. Ernie Wakely would start the season in goal instead of Les Binkley.

During the off-season, the National Hockey League announced its plans for expansion. New franchises were granted to Pittsburgh, St. Louis, Minnesota, Philadelphia, Los Angeles, and Oakland. Cleveland was left out because the Arena was deemed too small.

The new teams would begin play during the 1967-68 season. Except for players protected by existing NHL clubs, all players in hockey would be subject to an expansion draft to stock the new clubs after the current season. In the meantime, the new clubs could purchase contracts of minor leaguers owned my minor league clubs.

Cleveland owned Binkley and knew they would lose him in the expansion draft. They also were fully aware that Montreal wanted to place Wakely here. So the Barons sold Binkley to Pittsburgh a year before the expansion draft. They crossed their fingers, hoping that Wakely would prove to be an adequate replacement.

In other moves, defensemen Bill Speer and Ted Lanyon were sold to Buffalo, and Gordon Wilkie was placed in San Diego. In their place were three new rookies – forwards Gary Butler and Gary Schall, and defenseman Jacques Lemieux.

The big hope entering the new season was to avoid the slow start that the club experienced the year before. But it was not meant to be. In fact, the '66-67 season became close to a mirror image of the previous campaign.

The AHL eliminated overtimes for the upcoming regular season; and sure enough, the Barons opened with a 2-2 tie at the Arena. Then things took a turn for the worse. The club went on their annual early season road trip as the circus took over the Arena. Once again, the seven-game journey put the team into a big hole. Long road trips are always hard. But having one so early in the year, before players have had a chance to jell together, is murder.

The Barons blasted Rochester, 7-1, behind Tom McCarthy's hat trick to get the trip off to a good start. But they then dropped five of the next six games to sink into last place. When the club dropped its first game back at the Arena to Springfield, Coach Glover lit into his team. He called them just plain lazy and said changes were forthcoming. The team simply had too much talent to play so poorly.

Of particular consternation was the Barons' total lack of offense. Most frustrated of all the Clevelanders was Howie Glover. Howie was hoping for a big year but only had two assists and no goals after 10 games. Then, on November 19th against Buffalo, the younger Glover hurt his knee and would miss more than a month of action. The entire first half of the season turned into a washout for Howie.

Glover's misfortune opened the door for a rookie to step forward. Gary Butler, two years out of the University of Michigan, supplied the offensive spark that lifted the Barons back to the .500 mark and into third place. By Christmas Gary had scored 11 goals in

the 15 games since Glover hurt his knee. Howie was ready to play again, but Butler was too hot to remove from the lineup. Playing on a line with Fred Glover and Ron Attwell, Butler sparked the team to nine straight undefeated games at home. The streak lifted the Barons to 14-12-3 as the New Year rolled around.

Coach Freddie Glover celebrated the eve of his 39th birthday in a big way as Cleveland leveled Springfield 10-2. The victory was the Barons' 11th in their last 13 games and solidified their hold on third place behind Rochester.

Ernie Wakely took over for Les Binkley in the Barons' nets for the 1966-67 season and upheld a Cleveland tradition of great goaltending. Lost in the expansion draft a year later, he returned in 1968-69 and had another outstanding season. Dick Dugan collection.

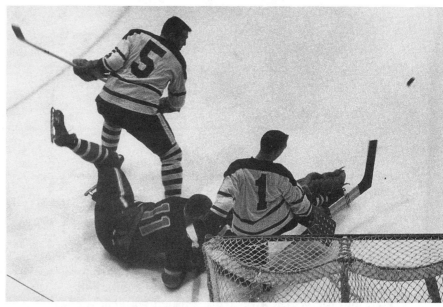

Ernie Wakely makes the save as Dick Mattiussi (5) defends during Cleveland's 10-2 victory over Springfield. Dick Dugan collection – photo by Robert J. Quinlan.

Gary Butler (18) was a big spark to the Barons during the first half of the 1966-67 season. Here he tries to score against Pittsburgh goalie George Gardner. Dick Dugan collection – photo by Robert J. Quinlan.

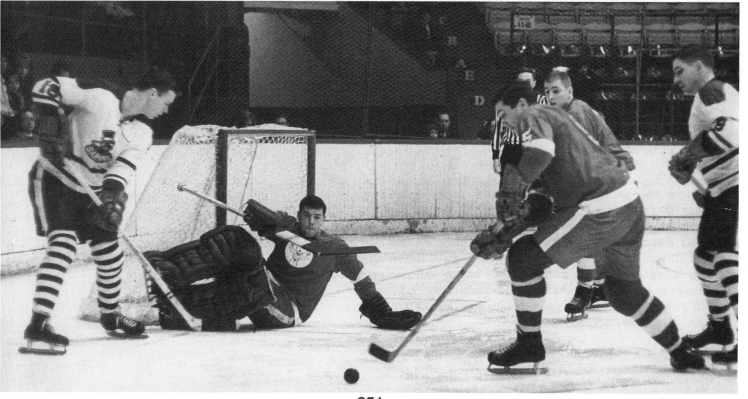

Glover scored two goals in the rout, giving him a career total of 489. Fred wasn't satisfied with the two goals, however. He took on the Indians with his bare knuckles also. In the season's best rhubarb, Glover took on not one, but two Indians at the same time.

Midway through the third period, Fred bowled over Jacque Caron when the goalie strayed from his net. Indian defenseman Barclay Plager took offense to Glover's treatment of his netminder and knocked Fred into the goal. A lively battle ensued with Glover showing the younger player that the old man could still punch it out with the best of them.

After Glover took care of Plager, Goalie Caron then charged after the Cleveland player-coach. A huge brawl followed with the top Baron once again gaining a bloody victory. Come one, come all. It didn't matter. Fred Glover was still the League's fiercest competitor.

Glover stayed in the limelight a few nights later in Buffalo. On January 8th, Fred led the Barons to a 7-3 rout of the Bisons as he scored three goals in less than two minutes. His scores came at 17:24, 18:46, and 19:13 of the second period. The remarkable feat by the 39-year-old legend gave him 492 goals. It also was the 14th career hat trick in his stellar career.

After the Buffalo victory, the team seemed to become caught up in their leader's quest for his 500th goal. While Fred Glover seemed to have found the fountain of youth, his teammates began standing around, watching his exploits. Cleveland went 1-3-2 in its next six games as the offense once again went into hibernation.

True to form, Cleveland's player-coach picked up his team once again on January 21st at the Arena. With the local icers trailing Quebec 3-1 entering the third period, Glover struck for two quick goals around one by Keith McCreary to lead his team to a 4-3 win. He now had 496 goals and counting.

The moment everyone was waiting for occurred on February 11th at the Arena against Buffalo. With 499 goals in his pocket, Cleveland's great hockey hero didn't keep the fans waiting long. During Fred's first turn on the ice, the historic goal was scored at 3:23 of the opening period.

Bill Needham took a shot from about 20 feet directly in front of Bison goalie Ed Chadwick. Buffalo's netminder made the save. The puck dropped down to Glover, who was camped next to the Buffalo goal. In the blink of an eye, Fred backhanded the puck past Chadwick for his crowning moment of glory.

Glover retrieved the puck and was rewarded with a roaring two-minute standing ovation by the fans. To cap his great night, Fred scored number 501 late in the third period as Cleveland walloped Buffalo 9-1.

Larry Smith collection.

Fred Glover's crowning moment of individual glory occurred on February 11, 1966 when he scored his 500th goal against Buffalo goalie Ed Chadwick: Dick Dugan collection.

True to his nature, Glover shrugged off his accomplishment after the game. He said he was happiest about the two points that his team got with the victory. To some people this might seem like false humility. But not with Fred Glover. The team always came first before individual accomplishments. He truly was one of a kind.

The victory raised Cleveland's record to 24-22-7. It moved them six points behind Rochester, and a spirited battle for second place had begun. First-place Pittsburgh was the class of the League and too far in front to worry about.

The Barons moved to within one point of Rochester at the end of February. During their top weekend of the season, Cleveland defeated first-place Pittsburgh for the first time that year, 5-1. Ernie Wakely was sensational with 35 saves, and Bob Courcy fired his 30th goal in the big win.

Cleveland followed this up with back-to-back wins over Rochester, 4-3 and 6-3. The great weekend was needed because the Ice Follies would chase the Barons out of the Arena for 4 games.

Cleveland lost 3 of the 4 games on the trip; but even worse was the loss of three top players.

Ron Attwell suffered a painful groin injury that would slow him down for the next two weeks. Far more serious were the injuries to Bob Courcy and Cecil Hoekstra. Courcy tore ligaments in his knee during a loss at Hershey and would miss the rest of the season. One of the League's most feared right wingers, Bob's loss was a severe blow.

Hoekstra, enjoying his greatest year ever, suffered a pinched nerve in his leg and also was done

A familiar sight during his long career of mayhem on ice was Fred Glover battling both opponents and referees alike. His fierce determination was a constant inspiration to anyone who was lucky enough to be on his side.
Cleveland State University archives – photo by Paul Tepley.

Cleveland State University archives – photo by Paul Tepley.

for the season. Cecil did try to play in the playoffs but had to quit after two shifts on the ice as his leg would fail him again.

As bad as the injury situation was, it got worse in mid-March when Joe Szura also hurt his knee. Big Joe continued to play, since the team was so crippled; but he was only a shadow of his healthy self.

All of the injuries would have devastated a lesser-spirited club. But these Barons fought on in their drive toward second place.

Cleveland closed to within one point of Rochester again when they defeated the Hornets in Pittsburgh 5-1 on March 29th. The game saw Fred Glover score his 25th goal of the season, a remarkable achievement for the 39-year-old player-coach.

During the last weekend of the season, the Barons needed a Baltimore victory over Rochester to set up a season-ending battle with the Amerks for second place. But it was not meant to be. The Americans routed the Clippers 9-1 to take the second spot. The Barons went to Rochester knowing that their thrilling bid for second place had failed.

Their 4-2 loss left them four points behind Rochester in third place. They had gone 12-5-2 after Fred Glover scored his 500th goal in February and almost achieved their goal. All this with a badly crippled squad was a feat to be proud of. But the Barons had a chance for revenge. They opened the first round of the playoffs against Rochester.

Cleveland State University archives.

THE PLAYOFFS

The Barons traveled to Rochester without Bob Courcy, Joe Szura, and Cecil Hoekstra. Without these big guns, the series figured to be short but not sweet for Cleveland.

But this was a "never say die" bunch of Barons. They shocked the Amerks in Game One. Behind the sensational goaltending of Ernie Wakely, Cleveland won the first game 4-1.

Wakely had 29 saves that included three clear breakaways. The game was tied 1-1 after two periods as Rochester's Wayne Carleton and the Barons' Keith McCreary traded goals. Cleveland then put the game away with three third-period scores. The go-ahead goal was scored by Tom McCarthy. Rochester goalie Bobby Perreault had made a save of a Howie Glover shot and attempted to smother the puck under his leg. But McCarthy kept poking at it until it went in.

Wayne Schultz and Howie Glover scored later in the period to sew up the game.

The Barons' momentum carried over into Game Two at Rochester. Once again Wakely was the difference, as Cleveland beat the Amerks again 4-1.

The Barons didn't even have a shot on goal for the game's first 12:52, but they hit pay dirt when Fred Glover canned a power play tally at 13:18. Less than a minute later, Tom McCarthy got another when he fired one in off of Bobby Perreault's leg.

Wayne Carleton brought Rochester to within one, but goals by Wayne Schultz and Bob Ellett 12 seconds apart early in the second period did the Amerks in. The Barons now held an improbable two-game lead as the teams headed to Cleveland.

Game Three in Cleveland was a heartbreaker of giant proportions.

The Barons were outplayed for better than two periods and entered the third frame trailing 2-0.

Ron Attwell put Cleveland back in the game with a beautiful goal at 8:39. Taking a pass from Bill Needham, Ron skated around the American defense and fired a shot from 20 feet away that sailed over Bobby Perreault's shoulder for the score.

From that point on, Cleveland attacked furiously. However, the Amerks looked as if they would hold on for the victory. But Coach Glover pulled Ernie Wakely with one minute to go in favor of an extra attacker. At the 19:22 mark, brother Howie made Fred look like a genius. Taking a pass from Tom McCarthy, Howie let fly from 15 feet and tied the score as the old Arena went wild.

Time ran out, and a twenty-minute sudden death period ensued. 39 seconds later, Cleveland's season took a 360 degree turn into oblivion.

Dick Gamble, Rochester's ace left wing, took a pass from Gerry Ehman and broke free through the Baron defense. He sailed in alone on Ernie Wakely and let fly a vicious slapshot from 20 feet that cleanly beat the Cleveland netminder.

In that one moment, the momentum in the series clearly shifted over to Rochester. To make matters worse, Howie Glover injured his shoulder in Game Three and could barely move his arm. He did manage his great tying goal in the last minute of play, but the sprained shoulder turned much worse after the game. But the gutsy Glover kept playing, although he basically was now a one-armed hockey player.

The Barons played in a fog in Game Four and lost 2-0. It was obvious that the crushing overtime defeat in Game Three still hung over the team. The Barons' spirit seemed broken.

The Barons fought hard in the deciding fifth game at Rochester but came up short 3-1.

After Dick Mattiussi opened the scoring at 1:52 of the first period, the Amerks threw up a brick wall around goalie Bobby Perreault. First-period goals by Eddie Joyal and Kent Douglas gave the home team the lead for good. Douglas's second goal of the game midway through the final period put the game on ice for Rochester.

The playoff loss was a tough pill for the Barons to swallow. They never made excuses, but injuries tore this team apart late in the year and in the playoffs. Bob Courcy, Cecil Hoekstra, Joe Szura, Howie Glover – all were struck down. It was a testimony to the team's true grit that they accomplished as much as they did. Still, when a true professional does not attain his ultimate goal – the championship- only disappointment remains.

To a man, this Baron team knew that if it had stayed healthy, it could have won it all.

FINAL STANDINGS
1966-67

West	W	L	T	GF	GA	PTS.
Pittsburgh	41	21	10	282	209	92
Rochester	38	25	9	300	223	85
Cleveland	36	27	9	284	230	81
Buffalo	14	51	7	207	386	35
East	**W**	**L**	**T**	**GF**	**GA**	**PTS.**
Hershey	38	24	10	273	216	86
Baltimore	35	27	10	252	247	80
Quebec	35	30	7	275	249	77
Springfield	32	31	9	267	261	73
Providence	13	46	13	210	329	39

Top Baron Scorers	G	A	PTS.
Tom McCarthy	36	38	74
Joe Szura	27	42	69
Ron Attwell	24	37	61
Fred Glover	25	35	60
Bob Courcy	32	28	60
Keith McCreary	28	29	57
Cecil Hoekstra	20	34	54
Howie Glover	18	16	34
Gary Butler	18	14	32
Bob Ellett	12	20	32

Calder Cup Champion – Pittsburgh Hornets

THE 1966-67 CLEVELAND BARONS

Front (L-R): Business Manager Joseph B. Vargo, Chuck Goddard, Coach Fred Glover, President & General Manager Paul L. Bright, Captain Bill Needham, Ernie Wakely, Publicity & Promotion Director Dino A. Lucarelli. Second: Ron Attwell, Jacques Lemieux, Larry Zeidel, Joe Szura, Cecil Hoekstra, Tom McCarthy, Wayne Schultz, Gary Butler. Third: Howie Glover, Bob Courcy, Keith McCreary, Dick Mattiussi, Bob Ellett, Stan Fuller, Gary Schall, Trainer Barry Keast. Kay Horiba collection.

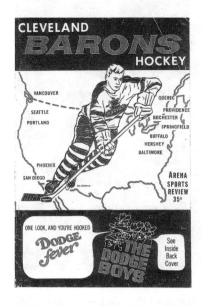

1967-68 SEASON

The new season was one of change and controversy.

The six new teams in the National Hockey League were ready to begin play. During the off season, an expansion draft was held to stock the upstart clubs. All teams in the AHL lost important players but, unfortunately, Cleveland was one of the hardest hit.

Taken by the various new teams were Joe Szura, Bob Courcy, Ron Attwell, Tom McCarthy, Keith McCreary, Jacques Lemieux, Dick Mattiussi, and Larry Zeidel, plus goaltender Ernie Wakely. The guts of the Cleveland team had been taken away. But fortunately, Montreal sent a group of young players that were able to surprise a lot of people.

The loss of Zeidel was unique in the fact that Larry actually sold himself to the Philadelphia Flyers.

The 39-year-old defenseman longed for one last shot at the big time. He spent two seasons in the NHL early in his career. Then came 13 wild years with Hershey, Seattle, and Cleveland.

Larry actually put together a brochure that included a resume, photograph, press clippings, and references. He sent it out to all of the NHL clubs, and Philadelphia decided to give the reformed "bad man" one last chance.

Zeidel made the most of it. He became the top defenseman on the Flyers and continually outplayed players nearly half his age. Larry loved every minute in the big league.

New players who would play a prominent role with the 1967-68 Barons were goalie Gerry Desjardins, defensemen Bob (Butch) Barber and Doug Piper; and forwards Jim Paterson and Norm Ferguson.

Far and away the most exciting addition to the team was Bryan Watson, the famed Superpest of hockey. The 5'10", 170 pound defenseman was one of the fiercest competitors in all of hockey. Absolutely no one played the game with more enthusiasm.

Bryan obtained the Superpest moniker during the 1966 playoffs while a member of the NHL's Detroit Red Wings. The Wings were playing the Chicago Black Hawks, who were led by the great Golden Jet, Bobby Hull. Detroit felt that the only way to beat Chicago was to stop Hull. Wing coach Sid Abel assigned Watson the task of being Hull's "Shadow."

It was Bryan's personal responsibility to stop the great Black Hawk star. Although outweighed by nearly 25 pounds, Watson drove Hull mad. Harrassing, clawing, grabbing, hitting – the Shadow's antics completely distracted the Golden Jet. Hull had a poor series, and Detroit eliminated Chicago from the playoffs. Bryan became an instant hero in Detroit and was given full credit for the Wings' victory. The legend of Superpest was born.

The next season, the two went at it again in the playoffs. This time Bobby was better prepared for his Shadow and gave the smaller Watson a rough going over. But Bryan never gave an inch and gained even more respect the second time around. This kid would not back down from anybody. One of their

Cleveland's Doug Piper (21) and Norm Dennis (10) storm the Vancouver Canuck goal in a 5-2 Baron victory. Dick Dugan collection.

scraps erupted into one of the biggest brawls in the NHL in years.

Bryan was taken by Minnesota in the expansion draft and traded to Montreal. The Canadiens, who were loaded on defense, sent Watson to Cleveland when Larry Zeidel left the team. The Barons were obviously elated. Superpest turned out to be everything he was expected to be, and more.

In the Barons' opening night 2-0 victory over Baltimore, Watson was tremendous. Hitting with a ferocity not seen here in a long time, Bryan quickly became the darling of the fans. Even his smooth, gliding skating style captivated the audience. By mid-game Bryan was receiving a standing ovation every time he left the ice. Never had one player made such an immediate positive impression at the Arena. Bryan Watson was an instant hero.

After the opening night victory, the Barons went on their annual early-season road trip for seven games. But this time the team was ready. Behind the enthusiasm created by the Superpest, Cleveland marched through this road journey in grand style, winning five of seven games.

Watson's spirit was insidious. Not only did he inspire the team's new young players, but he lit a flame under the older members as well.

With the AHL once again playing an interlocking schedule with the Western League, the Barons came home to play Vancouver. Behind 5'9" Norm Ferguson's hat trick, Cleveland smashed the Canucks 5-2. Rookie Ferguson could hardly contain himself after the game. "It was great, wonderful," Fergy bubbled. "Mr. Glover is the greatest; this club's spirit is unbelievable. Me? I was lucky."

New goalie Gerry Desjardins racked up his second shutout in the Barons' next outing. The 1-0 win over Quebec, however, really belonged to Bryan Watson.

Besides scoring the game's only goal, the Superpest dominated the contest from start to finish. The Arena boards took as bad a beating as did the Aces, for Watson's bodychecking was simply ferocious. The rest of his teammates fed off his fire and played with remarkable wreckless abandon. The fans loved every bit of it. Bryan Watson was Cleveland's new sporting hero, and the Barons were back on top again with an 8-2-0 record. What an impact this Superpest had made!

Bryan "Superpest" Watson – Bryan was the focal point of the entire 1967-68 season. Loaned to Cleveland from Montreal, Watson soon became a huge fan favorite. But the adulation was shortlived, as the Canadiens recalled the fiery defenseman and then sent him to Houston. He returned to Cleveland late in the season and immediately became the center of controversy. Never had one individual played so few games yet meant so much to a team as Superpest did to the Barons.

Howie Glover finally beat the injury bug and had a really big year in 1967-68 with 41 goals.
Dick Dugan collection.

GOALIE JERRY DESJARDINS

Cleveland State University archives – photo by Bill Nehez

The Barons skated off the ice after the Quebec game on cloud nine, but they came back to earth the very next day. Bryan Watson was recalled to Montreal. The Canadiens had been hit by injuries and called up the fiery defenseman to fill in during the emergency. The loss of the new team leader was a hard blow, but it was thought to be only temporary. Before leaving, Watson talked to his teammates and told them to hold the fort until he got back.

Bryan's pep talk seemed to work, because the team went right out and whipped Baltimore 6-3 in their next game. Cleveland was paced by Howie Glover's hat trick. Howie was finally healthy after a two-year bout with injuries and was on his way to a really big year. His three goals gave him eight in the first eleven games.

After a loss and a tie, goalie Gerry Desjardins racked up his third early-season shutout when the Barons blanked the tough Bears at Hershey 2-0. Gerry was a pleasant surprise for Cleveland. The off-season forest ranger had a tough act to follow replacing Ernie Wakely. But he was proving to be the find of the year.

The Barons had been eagerly waiting for the return of Bryan Watson since the Montreal injury situation had brightened considerably. But on December 7th, the team was jolted when it was learned that Watson had been sent by Montreal to its other farm team, the Houston Apollos.

The Barons and their fans were stunned. It had been generally accepted that the Canadiens would return Superpest to Cleveland. However, the Apollos were a team in trouble and without a leader. The Houston club was mired in last place, 13 points out of third. On the surface it appeared to be a waste of talent to send Bryan to this floundering team.

Jerry DesJardins gave the Barons outstanding goaltending during the 1967-68 season. Named to the first All Star team, he also claimed Rookie of the Year honors.

Barons' Wilf Martin breaks in on goal against the Quebec Aces.
Dick Dugan collection.

Montreal General Manager Sam Pollack thought otherwise. He felt Watson was just what the young Apollos needed. After all, Cleveland was in first place, he reasoned.

Of course President-General Manager Paul Bright argued long and hard with Pollack. He stressed that Watson was the main man on the Barons team and the key to a resurrection in fan interest. But Bright's protests fell on deaf ears. Superpest was gone.

The Barons were still playing good hockey despite the loss of Watson. Player-Coach Fred Glover picked up some of the slack.

In a game against Springfield on December 26th, Fred was slapped with three minor penalties, a five-minute major for fighting, and two 10-minute misconduct penalties. This gave him a total of 31 minutes in penalties for the game.

After the 3-3 tie, the Coach explained that he would not let anyone take advantage of his club. Bryan Watson was gone; but he expected everyone, including himself, to pick up the slack.

The Coach was apprehensive because his team was falling into some bad habits. His fears were borne out on New Year's Day when Cleveland was destroyed in Hershey 11-2. The Barons just did not check and were continually out-hustled by the Bears. Coach Glover warned the players after the game that just because they were in first place with a 17-10-5 record didn't mean that they were home free. There was no way that they could cruise home to the title.

Jerry DesJardins in action during the 1967-68 season.
Cleveland State University archives – photo by Paul Tepley.

Glover had something else to worry about. Rochester, who had been in last place for most of the season's first half, swung a trade that had far-reaching ramifications. The Amerks sent star winger Jean Paul Parise to Minnesota of the NHL for a group of solid veterans. Duke Harris, Murray Hall, Ted Taylor, and defenseman Don Johns had all been through the ice wars for years and gave the Amerks tremendous depth. The aging veterans didn't have much time left, but they made Rochester a powerful force for the rest of this season.

Cleveland went 4-2-1 in their next seven games to maintain a five-point first place lead. Howie Glover's third hat trick of the season paced the team to a 4-2 victory over Portland; but still the Barons did not look sharp. Coach Glover was worried.

The bottom began to drop out after a 2-1 loss to Buffalo on January 20th. The next afternoon, Cleveland was nipped by Hershey 2-1 when Bear Roger DeJordy beat Gerry Desjardins with only 20 seconds remaining for the winning goal. This was the beginning of a seven-game winless streak for the Barons – four losses and three ties.

They were knocked out of first place for the first time all season on January 26th. Ex-Baron Aldo Guidolin broke Cleveland's heart with a 55-foot slapshot at 19:13 of the third period that beat the Barons 4-3.

Fred Glover put Cleveland back on top of the division on February 4th when he called on some of his old-time magic in a 4-1 barn burner at Buffalo.

It was a game the Barons desperately needed, since the Bisons were closing in on them. Glover, however, took matters into his own hands. Hated with a passion in Buffalo, Fred had Bison fans in a tizzy with his rough play. The coup de grace came when the 40-year-old player-coach scored two goals 57 seconds apart late in the second period that gave his team its 4-1 lead.

The Barons held on in a frantic third period as the crowd called for Glover's scalp.

After the game, hundreds of fans stormed the Cleveland dressing room trying to get at the great Baron star. Riot police were called to disperse the crowd. Finally, after more than a half hour, the disturbance was quelled.

After 20 years in the game, Cleveland's hockey legend still had it. Fred Glover could still score a big goal and arouse a crowd like no other player ever.

The Barons managed to cling to first place by the skin of their teeth for the next month, even though they were not playing well. They went 4-7-3 over that span. The problem was that Quebec and Buffalo had closed in on Cleveland while the Barons were battling Rochester for first place. Suddenly, the basement was perilously close.

Cleveland smelled the sweet scent of first place for the last time on March 8th. A 3-0 loss at Providence dropped them to second behind Rochester with a 27-23-13 record. The team was reeling with no relief in sight.

The Barons dropped to third behind Quebec when they were drubbed 8-3 by Buffalo on March 15th. The loss also left Cleveland only four points in front of the charging Bisons. All of Coach Glover's worst fears two months earlier were coming true. He warned his team that their bad habits could catch up with them. Now the cold reality of a total collapse was staring the Barons in the face.

Coach Glover ripped his team after a 6-3 loss to Quebec at the Arena.

"This is not a great hockey club. It never was," barked the disgusted Coach, "but they worked. That's how they got in first place and stayed there so long. Now they don't want to work. Some of them are downright lazy."

To make matters worse, all five of Cleveland's remaining games were on the road.

The Barons won the first game on the crucial season-ending trip. But after defeating Springfield 2-1, they dropped a 7-5 decision at Quebec. The loss put Cleveland all alone in last place – three points behind the Aces and two back of Buffalo. The now-loaded Rochester Americans had locked up first place. Only a gift from above could save the Barons now.

That gift came in the form of Bryan Watson. The Houston Apollos season had ended, and Superpest was sent by Montreal to fill in for injured defenseman Don Fedon. Don hurt his left hand in the Quebec loss.

Coach Glover and the rest of the Barons welcomed Watson with open arms. Immediately the spirit of the team rose out of the gloom and doom. Bryan had that kind of effect on this team.

Before the Quebec rematch on March 26th, Ace's Coach Vic Stasiuk claimed that the Barons were faking the injury to Don Fedon. In fact, two Quebec doctors took a quick look at Fedon's hand and stated he could play. But Fedon's hand was so swollen he could not grip a hockey stick!

Cleveland's management knew Fedon was injured and had x-rays to prove it. They allowed Bryan Watson to play in the must-win game against the Aces.

Superpest was magnificent. He wreaked havoc all over the ice and led the Barons to a great 3-2 victory. Howie Glover scored his 40th goal, and Cecil Hoekstra nailed two others, including the game winner at 12:43 of the third period.

But it was Watson who made it happen. Bryan belted every enemy icer he came near. Just the sight of Bryan inspired his teammates to hustle like they did early in the season. The hero had arrived in the nick of time, or had he?

After the victory, the Barons learned that Quebec had protested the game. They claimed that Bryan

Watson was an illegal player and therefore Cleveland should forfeit its victory. The Barons claimed that Watson's playing in the game was a legal emergency move since Don Fedon could not play. Fedon was x-rayed in Cleveland the day after the Quebec game by Dr. Ivan Lust and Dr. John Clough. Both ruled that Fedon could not have played, thus substantiating the Barons' use of Watson.

After a March 29th hearing, AHL President Jack Butterfield upheld the protest of the Aces. Butterfield stated that Cleveland needed to have a written doctor's report *prior* to the Quebec game as he had ordered. The Barons failed to do so. Cleveland GM Paul Bright was told that if he had supplied such a report prior to the game, there would have been no protest.

The Barons were stunned and angry. They felt that they deserved the victory, but the two points were taken away. The most confusing aspect to Jack Butterfield's ruling was that he did not award the game to Quebec. He erased the game from the League records. It was as if the contest never happened. It would be replayed at season's end if it had any bearing on the standings.

Talk about waffling. If Cleveland did indeed use an ineligible player, Quebec should have been rewarded a victory.

If Watson was a legal player, the Barons deserved the two points. Butterfield seemed to be trying to pacify both parties by ordering the game replayed. Instead, he pleased no one.

This all became a moot point from the Ace's standpoint when they gained the playoffs by defeating Buffalo 5-3.

By losing the Quebec protest, the Barons now had to defeat Rochester, Buffalo, and the replay in Quebec in order to make the playoffs. But it wasn't in the cards.

Cleveland lost to Rochester 6-4, even though Bryan Watson was now ruled eligible to play. They were eliminated from the playoffs when Buffalo blanked Baltimore 5-0 the next night. This made the season finales against the Bisons and Quebec meaningless.

Cleveland State University archives – photo by Paul Tepley.

The Barons were warned by Coach Glover more than two months earlier that they were becoming lax in their fundamentals. But the message did not sink in. Missing the playoffs after leading the League for most of the year was very hard to take.

Still, it was not a season without excitement. For two-thirds of the year, the Barons thrilled their fans. Gerry Desjardins was marvelous in goal, especially when the team collapsed around him. Rookie Norm Ferguson parlayed total hustle and intense determination into a team-high 42 goals. Howie Glover fired home a career high 41.

However, from the day he arrived, Bryan Watson was the key to this team. He was the catalyst that got the team off to a great start. After he was recalled to Montreal, his great spirit spurred the team on. Even while at Houston, his name was always mentioned as to what the team needed to shake its slump. Bryan came back, but he was a little too late.

Oh, what might have been. Had Superpest remained a Baron all year. …He was a Baron for only 12 games. But those who saw him play will never forget Bryan Watson, Superpest…Super Baron.

FINAL STANDINGS
1967-68

West	W	L	T	GF	GA	PTS.
Rochester	38	25	9	273	233	85
Quebec	33	28	11	277	240	77
Buffalo	32	28	12	238	224	76
Cleveland	28	30	14	236	255	70
East	**W**	**L**	**T**	**GF**	**GA**	**PTS.**
Hershey	34	30	8	276	248	76
Springfield	31	33	8	247	276	70
Providence	30	33	9	235	272	69
Baltimore	28	34	10	235	255	66

Top Baron Scorers	G	A	PTS.
Jim Paterson	27	54	81
Norm Ferguson	42	33	75
Howie Glover	41	22	63
Cecil Hoekstra	24	35	59
Bob Ellett	15	35	50
Fred Glover	13	30	43

Calder Cup Champion – Rochester Americans

THE 1967-68 CLEVELAND BARONS

Front (L-R): Business Manager Joseph Vargo, Lyle Carter, Coach Fred Glover, President & General Manager Paul L. Bright, Captain Bill Needham, Jerry Desjardins, Publicity Director Gail Egan. Second: Wayne Schultz, Norm Dennis, Jim Paterson, Howie Glover, Doug Piper, Dale Blomquist, Cecil Hoekstra, Steve Hunt. Third: Trainer Barry Keast, Bob Barber, Wilf Martin, Stan Fuller, Bob Ellett, Don Fedun, Norm Ferguson, Doug Senior. Dennis Turchek collection.

The Nick Mileti Era: ROCKY ROAD and REVIVAL

They're (Gulp) Off!

By Lou Darvas

THE COACH-LESS BARONS, STILL TRYING TO GET EVERTHING INTO PLACE SINCE CHANGING OWNERS, OPEN THE SEASON TONIGHT AT BALTIMORE.

1968-69 SEASON

During the off season, the Barons said goodbye to a very familiar face and said hello to an important new one.

Saying farewell was the pride and joy of Cleveland hockey, Fred Glover. Fred agreed to take over the coaching reins of the Oakland Seals of the NHL. The opportunity to coach in the big leagues was too good to pass up. After all, Fred could not go on playing forever.

Hockey in Cleveland would never be the same.

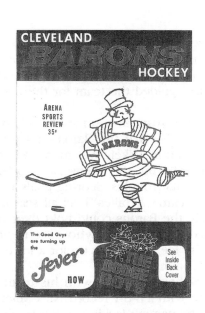

The statistics tell everything: 522 goals, 815 assists, 1,337 career points; 2,402 penalty minutes. Fred Glover truly was the greatest of them all.
Bill Hudec collection.

Fred Glover epitomized the word "competitor." His fierce desire to win and excel made up for a lack of God-given physical talents – only 5'9" and 165 pounds, and a step too slow for the NHL. But inside, Fred had the heart of a lion and a burning fire to be the best he could be.

During his AHL career, Fearless Freddie played 1,201 games, scored 522 goals, 815 assists, for 1,337 points. He also was far and away the League's most penalized player with 2,402 penalty minutes.

Fred was appointed player-coach for the 1962-63 season. Whether scoring a big goal or engaging the ice enemy in fisticuffs, Glover was always an inspiration to his teammates. When it came to The American Hockey League, Fred Glover was the greatest of them all.

Mrs. Lewis Darvas collection.

Saying hello was the Barons' new owner, Nick Mileti. Nick and his group of investors purchased both the team and the Arena for $2,000,000. Mileti was a Cleveland man all the way. A graduate of John Adams High School in 1949, and Bowling Green University in 1953, Nick received his law degree from Ohio State in 1956. After spending two years in the Army, Nick became a practicing attorney and settled in Fairview Park.

Nick Mileti proved to be a great visionary of big dreams. He dreamed of big league hockey and basketball in Cleveland. Before long, his sports empire would include the Barons, Crusaders, Cavaliers, Indians, the Coliseum, and radio station WWWE. The sky was the limit for Cleveland's greatest promoter since Al Sutphin and Bill Veeck. But in 1968, Nick's yellow brick road began with a bumpy ride.

The Barons lost many of the previous year's players in the NHL draft, including Norm Ferguson, Jim Paterson, and goalie Gerry Desjardins.

Returning to the team were Jim Mikol and goaltender Ernie Wakely. Mikol had spent the previous three winters in Providence, while Wakely starred in Cleveland two years earlier. Both veterans were welcome additions because the Barons had only four other experience players – Howie Glover, Cecil Hoekstra, Bill Needham, and Wayne Schultz.

Montreal sent several promising but green kids in defensemen Pierre Bouchard and Marshall Johnston, plus forwards Bob Berry, Garry Monahan and Rey Comeau.

Cleveland was also operating with an interim coach while Nick Mileti searched for a permanent bench boss. Montreal assistant general manager Floyd Curry guided the team for the first month of the season.

With the team in a somewhat chaotic state, it was no surprise that the Barons got off to a lukewarm start. Ernie Wakely was more than holding up his end in goal, but the offense, as had been feared, was having its troubles. Scoring goals would prove to be this team's Achilles' heel all season long. But defensively, the Barons could hold their own. These were hard-working kids who gave their all every shift on the ice. This made up for a lot of the offensive shortcomings.

On November 20th, with his team resting in third place with a 6-8-1 record, Nick Mileti surprised everyone by naming Jackie Gordon as his new head coach and general manager.

This was a coup for Mileti. The extremely popular Gordon returned to Cleveland after a three-year stint as assistant general manager of the NHL's New York Rangers. The move came as a surprise, since Jackie was well set in the NHL. Many thought he was also hoping Mileti could bring big league hockey to Cleveland. He would then be the team's #1 man.

But first things first. Gordon had his work cut out for him with this Barons' team. After losing his first two games as the new coach, Gordon finally was rewarded with a 4-1 victory over Springfield. Then a game of "who's the goalie" made his new job really tough.

For one magical weekend, Rocky Farr made Cleveland fans gasp with his acrobatic saves.
Cleveland State University archives – photo by Paul Tepley.

Montreal called up Ernie Wakely on December 3rd when they suddenly found themselves without a goaltender. Starter Gump Worsley had a case of the jitters and was ordered to rest for a month. Backup Rogatien Vachon broke his right hand. Wakely would be gone until December 29th, and Coach Gordon didn't know from one week to the next who his goalie would be.

The first substitute for Wakely was Norman (Rocky) Farr. Rocky had been tending goal for Denver in the Western league and turned out to be a super sub.

His first game at the Arena was one to remember. Rocky shut out the Rochester Americans 1-0 with an acrobatic display that dazzled both players and fans alike. Farr was a total scrambler who often came far out of the net to cut down the shooter's angle. He would dive and sprawl all over the ice in order to stop a goal. He got the only goal he needed when Howie Glover scored in the second period. The victory evened the Barons' record at 10-10-2 and increased their second-place lead to 10 points over Quebec.

First-place Buffalo was the next team to test Farr in a home-and-home series. The Bisons had not been beaten in fifteen games and were in the process of running away with the Western division.

Once again Rocky Farr was equal to the test. After holding the powerful Bisons to a 2-2 tie at the Arena, the Barons went up to Buffalo and ended the Bison streak at sixteen with a thrilling 2-1 victory. Once again Rocky was the difference, with 33 mostly spectacular saves.

The little netminder then went back to Denver, but he left a lasting impression. The Barons were now in the midst of an undefeated streak of their own, and Rocky Farr had a lot to do with it.

The unbeaten streak reached eight when another sub goalie racked up a shutout in his debut. Carl Wetzel, on loan from the Memphis South Stars, blanked Quebec 4-0. But as luck would have it, Carl twisted his right knee in the win. Twice the game had to be held up as Wetzel required medical aid. But in a courageous performance, Carl finished the contest, his only game as a Baron.

The eight-game unbeaten streak came to a crashing halt at the hands of Rochester 9-1. This was the first of three straight losses with Michel Plasse in the nets. Michel then defeated Buffalo 3-2 before Ernie Wakely returned with a 4-1 win over Rochester.

The Barons went a fine 5-3-2 with their three substitute goalies. This was far better than they could have hoped for. They closed out 1968 with a 15-13-4 record and seemed to be in fine shape for the season's second half.

However, the Barons went 0-5-1 in their next six games to drop back into third place. It seemed as if Ernie Wakely was the only Baron playing up to par. The defense was like swiss cheese, and the forwards were guilty of not getting back to help out. One would have thought that the departed Fred Glover had taken all of the hard bodychecks with him to Oakland.

Cleveland needed someone to step forward, and Ernie Wakely did just that. The Barons defeated Hershey 3-1 to break out of their slump. The defense was tremendous as the players finally began to check like they were capable.

The next night Wakely got his first shutout in two seasons as a Baron. The hard-working netminder blanked Quebec 1-0 on Rick Sentes' goal to put his team back in second place. Ernie was tremendous in making 35 saves, several while lying flat on his back. This was only a so-so Barons squad; but when Wakely was hot, they could beat anyone.

Cleveland was hot and cold for the rest of the season – win a couple, lose a couple. More often than not, play was lackadaisical. With no high scorers, and a team without any big hitters, fans stayed away in droves. Miniscule crowds were the norm rather than the exception.

But the fans came back on March 15th as the Barons honored their greatest hero with Fred Glover Night. 7,282 fans, the season's largest crowd, saw Fred inducted into the new Barons Hall of Fame. All fans attending the game received a commemorative puck with Glover's picture on it.

After the first period of the game against Rochester, Fred was honored by having his famous #9 uniform retired. True to his nature, Glover thanked his teammates and the fans for his success. He said that without the fans, there would be no game.

The evening became a complete success when the Barons held off Rochester for a 4-3 victory. The win gave Cleveland a 27-27-10 record. They were comfortably in second place, 10 points ahead of Rochester, eleven up on Quebec. However, they were 19 points behind Buffalo.

This put the Barons somewhat in limbo. They were virtually sure of the playoffs but had no prayer for the top spot. With nothing to shoot for, the team went flat. They finished the season with a 30-32-12 record, good for second place.

No one was sure what to expect in the playoffs. If the team skated hard, and Ernie Wakely stayed hot, they could go far. But could they turn on the jets? The Quebec Aces, as well as the Barons, would soon find out in a best-of-five opening round series.

Carolyn Chukayne collection.

Mrs. Lewis Darvas collection.

Bob Berry
Larry Smith collection.

Wayne Schultz
Larry Smith collection.

Ray Comeau
Larry Smith collection.

THE PLAYOFFS

Cleveland and Quebec met 14 times during the regular season, with the Barons holding a 7-4-3 edge. But the Aces closed out the season on a high note. They lost only two of their last eight games to finish at 26-34-14, six points behind Cleveland.

The Aces could be tough. With center Rene Drolet, and wingers Simon Nolet and Rosie Paiement, Quebec could really turn it on if all cylinders clicked.

Game One at the Arena was a tight, close-checking game. Pierre Bouchard gave Cleveland an early 1-0 lead with a 50-foot slapshot at the 1:54 mark of the first period. Then the teams settled into a conservative skate and check game.

Howie Glover gave the Barons a 2-0 lead early in the third chapter. It was then that the Aces opened up with a barrage at goalie Ernie Wakely. But Ernie was on top of his game. He did give up a goal to Jean Lapoint at 7:39; but then he closed the door, and Cleveland hung on for a 2-1 win.

Wakely was brilliant again in Game Two. Time after time he thwarted Quebec as the Aces generally dominated play. It was a scary sight as the Baron defense constantly broke down but was always saved by the superb efforts of the Baron netminder. It wasn't until Wayne Schultz' goal at 1:19 of sudden death overtime that the fans and the team could stop holding their breath. The 2-1 victory was won strictly because of Ernie Wakely.

The next two encounters in Quebec were two games that the Barons would like to forget.

Game Three was a total massacre as the Aces bombed Cleveland 9-2. It was a pathetic performance on the Barons' part. They found out the hard way that only hard work wins hockey games. If a team doesn't skate, a game like this is the result.

Unfortunately, the team didn't get the message. They were out-skated and out-hustled in Game Four and lost again 5-1. Cleveland seemed completely disorganized much to the consternation of Coach Jackie Gordon. The poor performance evened the series at two games apiece. The deciding game was played the following night in Cleveland.

Simply put, Game Five at the Arena was one great sporting event. Only 1,862 turned out on a weekday night to see the game. But not one fan who was there will ever forget it.

A picture is worth a thousand words. The Quebec Aces celebrate their 3-2 overtime victory while the Barons console a dejected Ernie Wakely. But Ernie had nothing to be ashamed of. He played his greatest game in one of the most dramatic contests in Barons' history.
Cleveland State University archives – photo by Paul Tepley.

Cleveland and Quebec went at each other with everything they had. Every player on each team played as if his life was at stake, especially Ernie Wakely. The Barons' goaltender played one of the finest games ever at the old Arena.

Cleveland's Rick Sentes and Ace Lyle Bradley traded first-period goals. From then on, the game featured tremendous saves by Quebec's Dunc Wilson and Wakely. Time and again "sure" goals were denied with incredible saves that left the crowd breathless.

The game appeared to be won by Cleveland when little Rey Comeau scored with only 3 minutes and 44 seconds to play. But the Aces kept pressing, and Wakely kept making saves.

As the clock was clicking off its final precious seconds, the Barons had possession of the puck in their own zone. The Aces had pulled their goalie and sent six attackers into Cleveland's end in a desperate effort to tie the score.

The Aces stole the puck, and Darryl Edestrand passed the puck back to defenseman Terry Ball at the point. The game was almost over as Ball let fly with a bullet through a mass of players in front of the net. Somehow the puck found its way home past a stunned Wakely. Incredibly, only one second remained on the clock!

The Aces went wild and the Barons could not believe it. One could have heard a pin drop in the crowd. It all seemed so unreal. But real it was. Quebec tied the game with only one second left in the contest.

The cruel end to Cleveland's season came when Rosie Paiement broke behind the Barons' defense and poked home the game winner at 2:37 of sudden death overtime. But Paiement's goal was an anti-climax to Terry Ball's last-second heroics.

In the end, one man stood tall even in defeat. Ernie Wakely played his heart out and almost single-handedly kept the Barons in the game. Try as they might, the Clevelanders could not keep up with the much quicker Aces, who repeatedly broke in free on the Barons' goal. But every time, Ernie Wakely somehow kept the puck out of the net. Sadly, his luck ran out with one second left in the game. Despite losing, Ernie Wakely was a hero.

The defeat was taken hard by owner Nick Mileti. Aside from the heartbreaking loss, his team was in serious trouble. Attendance had hit an all-time low of 126,338 for 37 games, an average of 3,415 per game. This was hardly what Mileti had envisioned when he purchased the struggling franchise.

FINAL STANDINGS
1968-69

West	W	L	T	GF	GA	PTS.
Buffalo	41	18	15	282	192	97
Cleveland	30	32	12	213	245	72
Quebec	26	34	14	235	258	66
Rochester	25	38	11	237	295	61

East	W	L	T	GF	GA	PTS.
Hershey	41	27	6	307	234	88
Baltimore	33	34	7	266	257	73
Providence	32	36	6	242	284	70
Springfield	27	36	11	257	274	65

Top Baron Scorers	G	A	PTS.
Howie Glover	24	35	59
Jim Mikol	20	35	55
Bob Berry	24	28	52
Garry Monahan	18	26	44
Wayne Schultz	22	20	42
Cecil Hoekstra	15	27	42
Rey Comeau	17	23	40

Calder Cup Champion – Hershey Bears

1969-70 SEASON

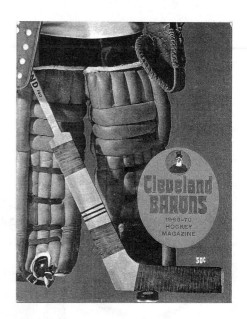

The AHL added a new team and restructured its divisions for the upcoming season. The Montreal Voyageurs would play in the East division along with Quebec, Springfield, and Providence. Competing in the West with Cleveland was Buffalo, Hershey, Baltimore, and Rochester.

With the Voyageurs now the top farm club of the Montreal Canadiens, the Barons were forced to sign a working agreement with the Detroit Red Wings.

This would have been fine except that the Wings already had a development club in Fort Worth of the Central Hockey League. Most of their top minor league talent was already committed to the Texas team. This left Cleveland with only marginal talent.

New players coming to Cleveland from Detroit were goalies Gary Kurt and Gerry Gray; defensemen Jim Watson, Jim Niekamp, Hap Myers, and Bob Falkenberg; and forwards Ken Kelly, Craig Reichmuth, Rene LeClerc, John Cunniff, and Dick Mortenson.

Nick Mileti purchased two players to help out the attack. High-scoring Norm Beaudin came to Cleveland from Buffalo, and popular Rey Comeau was secured from Montreal. Beaudin was to become the new ace scorer for the Barons.

Back for another go around were veterans Bill Needham, Howie Glover, Cecil Hoekstra, Jim Mikol, Bob Ellett, and Wayne Schultz.

Cleveland won its first two games of the season over Quebec and Buffalo. Who could have known that this was to be the high point of the first four months of the season? The local icers went into a disastrous skid that saw them lose nine games in a row. Their record dipped to 3-11-1 before they finally ended the streak with a 3-1 victory over Hershey.

But the losses kept piling up, and the team was dead last at Christmas with a 6-17-5 record. It seemed as if all of the veterans got old at the same time. By losing a step or two, the older players had trouble keeping up with the multitude of young speedsters now in the League. Also, the kids from Detroit were having a rough time adjusting to the tough competition in the AHL. Cleveland now appeared to be a weak sister in the League.

As bad as things were, they got even worse in January. The Barons' 3-0 loss to Baltimore on February 1st was the team's eighth in a row and dropped them to a terrible 9-28-8. Many of the players had stopped putting out. The chorus of boo's at the Arena, however, let them know that the loafing would not be tolerated. Coach Jackie Gordon expressed his displeasure by benching the players not putting out. But he couldn't bench the whole team and hoped that the club would start playing with some pride.

One player who always gave his all was Cecil Hoekstra. The 34-year-old center was winding down his career and was now taking a back seat to the younger players. But whenever called upon by Coach Gordon, Cecil always gave his best effort.

It was Hoekstra's great penalty killing in a 2-0 win over Providence that started the team on a different kind of streak. After losing eight straight games, the Barons put together a nine-game unbeaten streak of four wins and five ties. This included a 6-0 triumph

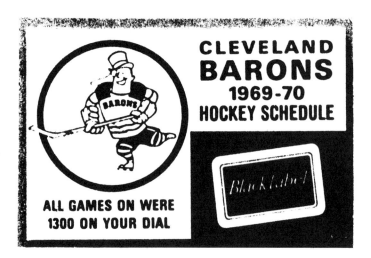

Walt Voysey collection.

over Hershey that brought Cleveland to within seven points of the Bears. Suddenly, the Barons were thinking playoffs.

While the whole team was playing better, the biggest revival was seen in the play of Norm Beaudin. The right winger was counted upon heavily by his new team. But early in the year he badly injured his shoulder. A pinched nerve and deep muscle bruise greatly affected Beaudin's play. The injury lingered for three months, but Norm kept playing in pain. Through it all, he never complained. He just kept working, but the zip was gone from his shots.

In early February, the arm began to come around, and with it came a flock of goals. During Cleveland's undefeated streak, Norm fired in seven scores and assisted on four others. This brought his total up to 21, and he kept on scoring through the rest of the year. His 37 goals and 44 assists would be far and away tops on the team.

Unfortunately, the Barons went sour again at the wrong time. They went 1-5-2 over their next eight games and stood in last place with a 14-33-13 record, 12 points out of third.

Twelve games remained in the season, and a funny thing happened. The Barons went undefeated the rest of the way, nine victories and three ties.

While the Barons defeated Rochester 6-1, Baltimore beat Quebec 7-2, to eliminate Cleveland from the playoffs. But to their credit, the Barons went down fighting.

While disappointed in missing the playoffs, Jackie Gordon was proud of the way his team finished the year. They didn't quit at the end and showed a lot of class during the season's last month.

Attendance again was dismal. Only 139,961 fans turned out for 36 home games, a 3,888 per game average. The team was in serious trouble and now stood at the crossroads. But one last revival, both on the ice and at the turnstiles, was right around the corner.

FINAL STANDINGS
1969-70

West	W	L	T	GF	GA	PTS.
Buffalo	40	17	15	280	193	95
Hershey	28	28	16	247	249	72
Baltimore	25	30	17	230	252	67
Cleveland	23	33	16	222	255	62
Rochester	18	38	16	253	315	52
East	**W**	**L**	**T**	**GF**	**GA**	**PTS.**
Montreal	43	15	14	327	195	100
Springfield	38	29	5	287	287	81
Quebec	27	39	6	221	272	60
Providence	23	36	13	218	267	59

Top Baron Scorers	G	A	PTS.
Norm Beaudin	37	44	81
Rey Comeau	27	38	65
John Cunniff	26	17	43
Bob Ellett	20	17	37
Hap Myers	9	28	37
Rene LeClerc	16	20	36

Calder Cup Champion – Buffalo Bisons

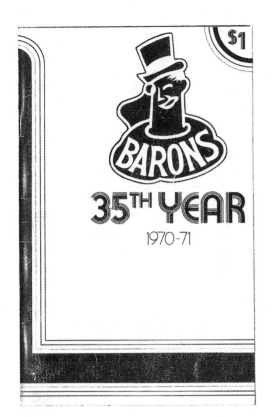
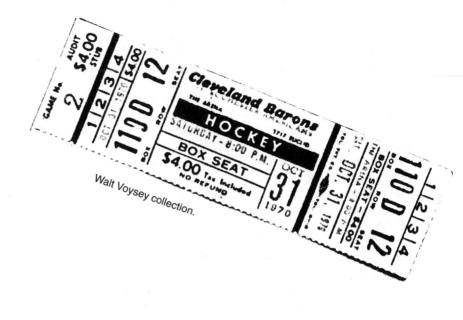

Walt Voysey collection.

1970-71 SEASON

The winds of change blew through Cleveland, and the entire complexion of the hockey team was changed.

During the Summer of 1970, Jackie Gordon moved up to the National Hockey League as coach of the Minnesota North Stars. Owner Nick Mileti hated to part with Gordon, but he knew this was a dream come true for Jackie. Mileti also knew that Gordon was a Cleveland man at heart. So Nick worked a deal whereby the Barons would become the new development club of the North Stars.

Mileti had been leaning in this direction. It had become almost impossible to operate a successful semi or totally independent minor league club by 1970. With Gordon moving to Minnesota, his decision became an easy one. The Cleveland owner knew that Jackie would take care of the Barons.

Parker MacDonald became the new head coach of the local icers, while John Muckler took over as general manager. The new tandem brought with them a highly touted group of kids that would prove to be the most exciting act on the Arena ice in years.

Only five members from the previous year's fourth place team would return. Defenseman Bill Needham; forwards Norm Beaudin, Rey Comeau, and Wayne Schultz; along with goalie Gary Kurt. Their contracts were purchased by Minnesota from Nick Mileti.

Most of the new blood from Minnesota had played together the year before with Waterloo, Iowa – the North Star's Central League farm club. They moved en masse upward to Cleveland. The lone exception was defenseman Gary Geldart, who played junior in London, Ontario. The newcomers were goalie Fern Rivard; defensemen Dennis (Obie) O'Brien, Marshall Johnston (an ex-Baron), Tom Polonic, and Geldart; forwards Billy Heindl, Mike Chernoff, Barrie Meissner, Ron Williams, Bobby Whitlock, Billy Orban, Joey Johnston, Rick Dudley, and Grant Erickson. Erickson broke his ankle in training camp and missed the first month of the season.

Captain Bill Needham, entering his 13th season as a Baron, led the Cleveland squad into the 1970-71 season. No Baron team in years had such high expectations.

Area fans got their first look at their new team in an exhibition game against Minnesota. The game was part of a unique hockey-basketball doubleheader put together by Nick Mileti. The hockey game was played in the late afternoon. That evening Mileti's second sports child, the Cavaliers, took on Lew Alcindor's Milwaukee Bucks in an NBA exhibition.

While the Barons were edged by the North Stars 3-2, Cleveland hockey fans came away delighted. This group of wild, reckless, rough and tough kids actually outplayed their NHL opposition. Any resemblance to the previous year's Barons was in name only.

The kids were dubbed the Mod Squad. They wore the long, flowing hair and sideburns that were fashionable with the kids of the late sixties and early seventies. They were as hard-hitting and flamboyant as their looks conveyed. And the young people of Cleveland responded.

A fine opening night crowd of 5,224 came to see if all the hype given to the new Barons was justified. They came away breathless as the Mod Squad held on to defeat the tough Montreal Voyageurs 4-3. But it wasn't just the score that was satisfying. The crowd really was captivated by this new band of Barons. They were on their feet for the entire final two minutes of the game shouting encouragement to their new heroes. Excitement was definitely back at the old Arena.

Unfortunately, the Barons immediately went on their annual early-season death march out East as the Ice Capades took over the Arena. New team or not, these early-season road trips were murder. Cleveland went a so-so 3-4-0 on the journey before coming home to blank Rochester 4-0.

Although victorious, the game against the Amerks was tough on Cleveland. Three players were injured, two seriously. Bill Needham jammed his shoulder and would miss a week. Wayne Schultz broke his collarbone and would be out ten weeks. Billy Orban damaged his knee and would be in and out of the lineup for the next two months. With Grant Erickson and Barrie Meissner already out of the lineup, the Barons faced a manpower shortage. Fortunately, parent club Minnesota was talent rich.

The North Stars sent offensive-minded defenseman Dick Redmond and forward John Gofton to help out the Barons.

Cleveland's main weakness early in the season was a bad tendency by their defensemen to get caught too far up the ice. It seemed like the backliners were more concerned with scoring goals than stopping the other team. Coach McDonald put a stop to this the only way he knew how. After a sloppy five-game stretch, where the Barons gave up 25 goals in five games, the new Coach worked his team overtime in practice. This was too good a club to be 6-6-2.

The hard work paid off as the Barons streaked to four straight victories. With Gary Kurt replacing the injured Fern Rivard in goal, the Blue and White of Cleveland finally began clicking on all cylinders.

The Barons became the talk of the town on December 5th after a 2-2 standoff with the Montreal Voyageurs at the Arena. It wasn't the score that had the 6,120 fans buzzing, but a riotous first period that saw the wildest donnybrook in years.

Cleveland State University archives – photo by Paul Tepley

Bobby Whitlock attempts to score against Baltimore's Andy Brown.
Cleveland State University archives – photo by Paul Tepley

Walt McKechnie's midseason arrival was a big boost to the mod squad. His expert playmaking down the stretch run helped boost the Barons to a second place finish. Dick Dugan collection.

Billy Orban scores against Rochester. He would return in the Playoffs as a Springfield King and haunt the Barons.
Cleveland State University archives – photo by Paul Tepley.

The trouble started when Billy Orban and the Vee's Mike Hyndman began scrapping near the Montreal net. Suddenly the Barons' Dick Redmond began shoving Montreal's Murray Anderson. Before this fight really got going, the Voyageurs' Ron Busniuk jumped in for Anderson and squared off with Redmond. The ensuing fight was a classic. The two players slugged it out all over the ice.

When the two combatants moved near the Montreal bench, Voyageur player-coach Terry Gray jumped from his bench into the fight. That was it. At that instant, both benches emptied, and a full riot ensued. The battle raged for 15 minutes, as fights broke out all over the ice.

The fans loved every minute of it. Dick Redmond was an instant hero, and the Mod Squad reigned. They were the new darlings in town.

Near the end of December, the Barons were knocking on Baltimore's first-place door after a 6-4 road victory in Rochester. The victory put Cleveland at 16-10-4, one point behind the Clippers.

However, a 4-3 setback at Baltimore thwarted Cleveland's first-place ambitions. It would prove to be only one in a series of frustrating losses to the Clippers.

Barons' fans were geared up for a rematch in Cleveland between the AHL's two top clubs on January 8th. Baltimore, led by free-spirited goalie Andy Brown, was the exact opposite of the Barons. While Cleveland was a young, flashy team, the Clippers were an experienced group of old-timers. Only three players were under 24 years old.

Baltimore may have been an aging team, but they stuck it to the Barons 4-3. The loss really hurt because it dropped Cleveland 6 points behind the Clippers.

After losing to Providence, also at home, the local heroes fell 10 points behind their first-place dream. And to make matters worse, they had a six-game road trip staring them in the face.

The trip East that could have ruined Cleveland's season turned out to be a blessing in disguise. After pressing in front of their home fans, the Mod Squad put the time away from the Arena to good use. Behind the play of two new players from Minnesota, Walt McKechnie and Danny Lawson, the Barons roared to four straight victories.

The last of these four big wins was an 8-3 triumph in Baltimore. Racing to a 6-2 first-period lead, Cleveland was led by first-year pro Billy Heindl. Billy knocked in three goals to boost his team lead to 18. Flashy center Joey Johnston chipped in with one goal and four assists as he took over the team scoring lead from Norm Beaudin, who had been called up to Minnesota.

While being a development club for Minnesota stocked the Barons with valuable talent, the arrangement also had its drawbacks. Players came and went depending upon the fortunes of the big club. This was never more evident than on January 26th.

Norm Beaudin was returned to Cleveland, but Billy Heindl and Danny Lawson were called up to Minnesota. But the North Stars were not done dealing. In search of an experienced center, they traded young Rey Comeau from the Barons to the Montreal Canadiens for veteran Gordon Labossiere. Minnesota kept Labossiere, and the Barons ended up with nothing. To make matters worse, Montreal sent Comeau to their hometown farm team, the Voyageurs. The end result of all these dizzy maneuvers was that the Barons lost Heindl, Lawson, and Comeau and received Beaudin in return. The fans didn't like all of the wheeling and dealing, but fortunately they understood. In the days of expansion hockey, these arrangements were the only way a minor league team could survive. Fortunately, more help would arrive.

After the dust had cleared from the Rey Comeau deal, the Barons came home and blasted Springfield 12-0. Instead of hanging their heads, they came out fighting. This made their fans admire them even more.

8,479 fans showed up for a very special night at the Arena on February 6th. Moe Roberts, Bobby Carse, and Eddie Olson were inducted into the Barons Hall of Fame. They joined Fred Glover, Al Sutphin, Les Cunningham, Danny Sprout, Jackie Gordon, Johnny Bower, Fred Thurier, and Bun Cook in Cleveland's hallowed Hall. As fate would have it, Nick Mileti couldn't have picked a better night for the induction ceremonies.

The Barons dominated the game against Rochester, but the superb goaltending of Amerk Lynn Zimmerman kept the score tied at two each. A tie game seemed inevitable. But with four seconds left to play, the Barons forced a faceoff in the Rochester zone. Center Joey Johnston won the draw for Cleveland and shot as the puck was dropped. Zimmerman made the save. When the puck dropped in front of him the Barons' Barrie Meissner jumped on the rebound and fired home the game winner with only one second left in the game! The big Arena crowd went wild for several minutes after the game had ended. The huge roaring audience certainly brought back memories of the glory days of Roberts, Carse, and Olson.

Cleveland State University archives – photo by Paul Tepley.

The large crowds were becoming just as big a story as the Barons themselves. When 8,511 fans turned out to see Cleveland bop Hershey 8-5 on February 13th, fond memories of the great bygone years of the 1940's were recalled. The Barons were now playing before their largest crowds in over fifteen years, and no one was smiling wider than Nick Mileti. The great promoter was basking in his team's success.

The big win over Hershey behind Joey Johnston's hat trick left the Barons with a 26-18-5 record. They were now eight points behind Baltimore setting up a showdown with the Clippers on February 20th.

Behind 9,681 roaring fans, the Barons jumped out to a 2-0 lead over Baltimore and appeared on the verge of running their first-place rivals out of the Arena. But the Clippers were on top for good reason. Their veterans had poise, and they settled down to business in the second stanza. In fact, by the end of the period, it was Cleveland who was on the verge of being run out of their own building. Baltimore scored four times in the middle frame to practically put the game on ice.

The final period was scoreless as the Clippers played great defensive hockey. The Barons rarely got off a good shot. The 4-2 loss left Cleveland eleven points out of first place. The worst aspect of the game was how the Mod Squad folded in front of the season's largest crowd. But more than ever, the big sellout proved that hockey was back in Cleveland.

Baltimore stretched its lead over Cleveland to 16 points by early March, and the race appeared over. It was then that GM John Muckler swung into action in an effort to shake up the team.

First off, he traded Wayne Schultz to Springfield for defensive-oriented winger Terry Holbrook. A few days later, Muckler hooked up with Springfield again in a big deal. Center Billy Orban was sent to the Kings for rugged defenseman Roger Cote. Muckler had been trying to obtain Cote for almost two months. The former "bad man" was one tough customer, and the young Barons needed another wise veteran to look up to.

On March 10th, for the fourth time in so many tries, Baltimore swaggered into Cleveland and beat the Barons. The latest mugging was an embarrassing 3-0 shutout. This loss all but sewed up the division title for the Clippers. Cleveland now trailed their rivals by 14 points with only 13 games remaining.

Cleveland State University archives – photo by Paul Tepley.

The Barons could have coasted into the playoffs, and nobody would have complained. But the Mod Squad would have none of that. In their hearts they all felt that they were the best team in the League, and they set out to prove it.

Cleveland won five of its next six games, while Baltimore went into a slump. Suddenly the Barons found themselves only five points from the top. This team had been given up for dead on numerous occasions, but it refused to die. Included in the streak were two big wins over the Clippers.

The Barons won 3-1 at Baltimore and then dumped the Clippers in Cleveland 4-0. Gary Kurt's third shutout of the season was the sweetest of his career. He and his teammates now firmly believed they could overtake Baltimore. But it was not meant to be.

Cleveland won five of its next seven games to keep the heat on the Clippers. But the grizzled veterans of Baltimore pulled themselves together down the stretch. They refused to fold and held off the charging Barons, winning the West division by four points.

Cleveland did themselves proud. They won 10 of their last 13 games to finish 39-26-7 for 85 points. This was their highest point total since the 1952-53 season.

However, the Barons' mission was not complete. Their goal was to win the Calder Cup.

Cleveland State University archives – photo by Paul Tepley.

THE PLAYOFFS

The Barons took on the Hershey Bears in a best-of-five first-round series. The boys from Chocolate Town finished with an even 31-31-10 record. But this was a dangerous crew with several members of the Calder Cup title team of two years' past still around. Led by veteran goaltender Andre Gill, the Barons figured to have their hands full.

Gill was the difference in Game One at the Arena. The contest was a knock-down, drag-out affair with both teams throwing their weight around. Stan Gilbertson stunned the Barons with a goal after only 32 seconds, but Cleveland tied it on a goal by Joey Johnston. In the second period, Billy Heindl was able to beat Gill for the frame's only score.

Cleveland gave it everything they had in the third stanza as they tried to apply the knock-out punch. But Andre Gill came up with 15 saves to keep the Barons stymied at two. The Bears seized the momentum generated by their goalie and tied the game at 9:17 on Gilbertson's second goal of the game. The 2-2 tie held up as regulation time ended.

During a hectic sudden death overtime, Hershey's Michel Harvey picked up a loose puck at center ice and broke in free on Gary Kurt. Goalie Kurt went down at Harvey's fake, and the Hershey veteran broke Cleveland's heart at 5:58. With the 3-2 overtime loss, the Barons headed to Hershey for the second game.

In Game Two, the Bears came out flying, trying to drive a stake through the Barons' hearts. But Cleveland goalie Gary Kurt put on a marvelous display of clutch goaltending that thwarted the Bears at every turn. He was especially brilliant during a two-minute span when his team was two men short. In all, Gary kicked out 13 first-period shots, most of them difficult.

The great goaltending demoralized Hershey. They weren't the same team in the second period, and the Barons sensed it. Roger Cote scored for Cleveland at 10:22 to make the score 2-0. In the third period, Joey Johnston's second goal of the game put the game on ice. Grant Erickson and Hershey's Bud DeBrody traded goals to close out the scoring. The 4-1 victory was sweet revenge for the Barons as they headed back to Cleveland for Game Three the next night.

The Barons turned on their jets in the third game as they romped over Hershey 7-1 before 7,186 wild-eyed fans. The Clevelanders thoroughly dominated play as they poured 44 shots at Bear netminder Andre Gill. On the defensive side, Cleveland's backliners were superb. They allowed only 22 shots at Gary Kurt. Time after time, Baron blueliners blocked Hershey shots before they got to Kurt. The Barons sewed things up by scoring three goals within 55 seconds midway through the third period. Billy Heindl, Barrie Meissner, and Grant Erickson turned the trick.

Over all, this was Cleveland's best game of the year, and the momentum carried over into the next game at Hershey.

Game Four turned out to be the Gary Kurt Show. The 6'3" Cleveland netminder was Houdini on ice, as he escaped one Hershey barrage after another in Cleveland's 3-2 series-clinching win.

In all, Kurt made 44 wonderful saves as the Bears desperately tried to stave off elimination. Gary was especially tough in the second period when he stopped 17 shots, many of them "sure" goals.

The Barons built up a 3-0 lead on goals by Joey Johnston, Mike Chernoff, and Norm Beaudin. They appeared in complete control until Hershey scored two quick third-period goals. Then it was nail-biting time. But in the end, Gary Kurt was the difference.

The series victory over Hershey put the Barons into the League semi-finals against the Springfield Kings. These were the former Indians who changed their nickname when they signed on as the development club of the NHL's Los Angeles Kings.

Whatever their name, this team was as hot as the Barons. Despite their 29-35-8 regular-season record, the Kings had won six straight games. This included a three-game sweep of the Montreal Voyageurs in their first-round series.

During the regular season, the Barons and Kings split their 10-game series, each team winning five games. So something had to give in Game One.

The opener at the Arena was a close, tight-checking affair. The teams were deadlocked at 1-1 late in the third period when Cleveland defenseman

Gary Kurt sparkled in the nets against Hershey during the 1970-71 Playoffs. Cleveland State University archives – photo by Paul Tepley.

Dennis Patterson was called for tripping at 17:39. The Barons would be a man short for two minutes and were in deep trouble.

However, while killing off the penalty, Cleveland center Walt McKechnie scooped up a loose puck at his own blue line and skated down the ice with Grant Erickson on a 2-on-1 breakaway. Using Erickson as a decoy, McKechnie blasted a 25-foot slapshot past King goalie Billy Smith to give the Barons a 2-1 victory. The big win put Cleveland in the driver's seat as the two teams headed to Springfield for the next game.

The Barons had every opportunity to win Game Two, but were not able to take advantage of Springfield's charity. During the course of their 6-3 loss, Cleveland was given seven power-play opportunities and was able to capitalize on only one. Even more embarrassing was the fact that the Kings scored two shorthanded goals themselves. Springfield was much more aggressive in Game Two and seemed to intimidate the suddenly tight Barons.

Game Three at the Arena was a night for revenge for one Billy Orban. Billy had been traded late in the year for Roger Cote, and the deal made him bitter. "I think they traded me because they thought I was faking those injuries," said the new Springfield hero.

All Orban did was score four goals in Springfield's 6-5 win over the Barons. His last score came at 7:04 of the third period and was the game winner. Billy's pride was hurt by the trade, and the best way to prove his old team was wrong about him was to beat them. And beat them he did.

Orban had help from his ex-teammates. The Barons skated around in a confused state and seldom even touched the Kings. One would have thought bodychecking had been outlawed. The Barons let Springfield skate free all over the ice and then paid the price.

Game Four in Springfield was a disaster. The Barons played an awful game and were beaten badly 6-0. All of the aggressiveness that they showed all season long went out the window.

It seemed as if the intense pressure of the playoffs got to this team. Inexperience also did them in. Each Baron seemed to look to someone else to do the job. No one stepped forward. The better team did not win this series, but the team that wanted it most did.

No matter how disappointed the team and its fans were, one fact remained. Hockey interest in Cleveland was on the upswing again. People of all ages responded to this young and exciting team. In 36 home games, 184,400 people swung through the Arena turnstiles, an average of 5,122 per game. For the first time in years, the future of the team appeared bright.

FINAL STANDINGS
1970-71

West	W	L	T	GF	GA	PTS.
Baltimore	40	23	9	263	224	89
Cleveland	39	26	7	272	208	85
Hershey	31	31	10	238	212	72
Rochester	25	36	11	222	248	61
East	**W**	**L**	**T**	**GF**	**GA**	**PTS.**
Providence	28	31	13	257	270	69
Montreal	27	31	14	215	239	68
Springfield	29	35	8	244	281	66
Quebec	25	31	16	211	240	66

Top Baron Scorers	G	A	PTS.
Norm Beaudin	27	48	75
Joey Johnston	27	47	74
Marshall Johnston	11	45	56
Mike Chernoff	31	23	54
Walt McKechnie	16	32	48
Grant Erickson	18	25	43
Barrie Meissner	22	16	38
Billy Heindl	25	11	36
Bobby Whitlock	19	15	34
John Gofton	18	13	31

Calder Cup Champion – Springfield Kings

Larry Smith collection.

THE 1970-71 CLEVELAND BARONS

Back (L-R): Grant Erickson, Gary Geldart, Bobby Whitlock, Trainer Joey Maxwell, Ron Williams, Rick Dudley, Bill Heindl, Barrie Meissner. Middle: Norm Beaudin, Dick Redmond, Marshall Johnston, Tom Polonic, John Gofton, Fern Rivard, Mike Chernoff. Front: Rey Comeau, Bill Needham, General Manager John Muckler, Owner Nick Mileti (with son Jim on his lap), Coach Parker MacDonald, Joey Johnston, Dennis (Obie) O'Brien. Jim Mileti collection.

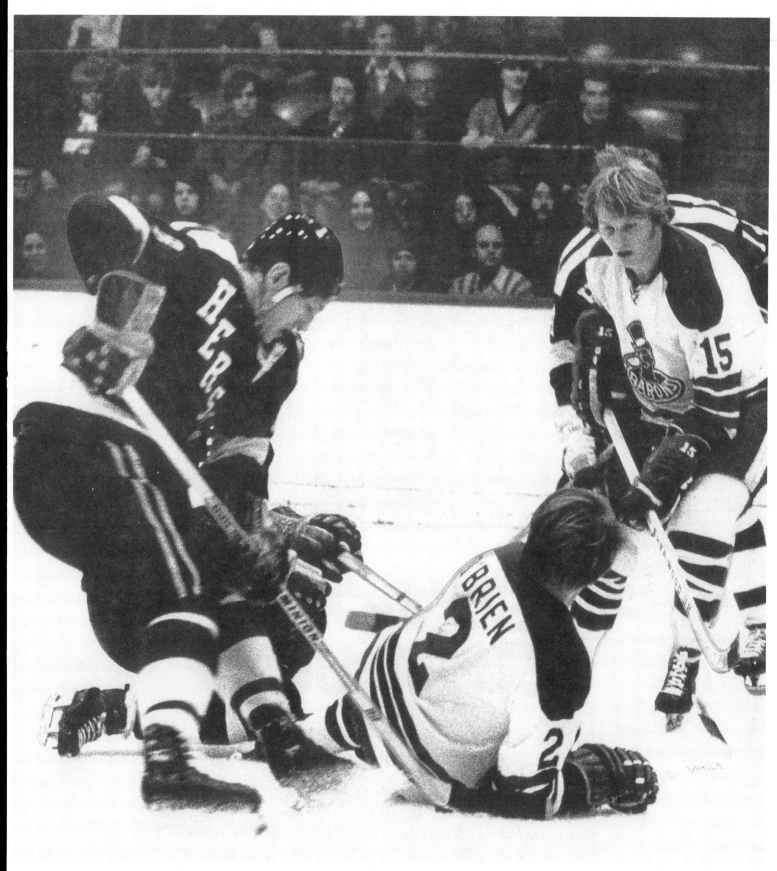

Ron Williams (15) in action against Hershey.
Cleveland State University archives – photo by Paul Tepley.

1971-72 SEASON

The American Hockey League and the Barons both took on a new look for the 1971-72 season.

The League had been operating as an eight-team loop, since Buffalo had moved up to the NHL the previous year. But with the National League expanding, the need for more development clubs became a necessity. Thus, the AHL expanded and shifted two franchises to new markets.

The Arena as it appeared during the Summer of 1971.
Cleveland State University archives – photo by Bill Nehez.

Joining the League were the Boston Braves, Tidewater Wings, and the Cincinnati Swords. The Montreal Voyageurs relocated to Nova Scotia, while the Quebec Aces moved to Richmond, Virginia, and became the Robins.

The League was now set up as follows: West Division – Cleveland, Baltimore, Hershey, Cincinnati, Richmond, and Tidewater. East Division – Boston, Nova Scotia, Springfield, Providence, and Rochester.

On the home front, the Barons were once again hit hard by the NHL draft. Gone from the previous year's strong club were Joey Johnston, Marshall Johnston, Walt McKechnie, Bobby Whitlock, Tom Polinic, and goalie Gary Kurt.

One large hole was caused by the retirement of defenseman Bill Needham. Bill got his first taste of AHL action with the Barons during the 1956-57 championship season. For the past fifteen years, he spent his entire career in Cleveland and played 981 regular season games, second only to Fred Glover's team record of 1,201. One of the greatest backliners the League had ever seen, Needham was a true workhorse. During one stretch, Silent Sam, as he was known, played in 525 consecutive games, a record since broken by Buffalo's Billy Dea's 548.

While never a big scorer, Needham was the quintessential defensive defenseman. A true leader on and off the ice, Bill Needham was a credit to his team and his adopted City of Cleveland.

During the off season, general manager John Muckler added the duties of coach to his resume after the departure of Parker MacDonald. Together with Minnesota GM Wren Blair, Muckler began shaping the team for the upcoming season.

Four key additions to the club came from the North Stars. Centers Gordon Labossiere, Terry Caffery, and winger Dennis Giannini would become key cogs in the attack. Wayne Muloin, the master of the hip check, was brought over from Providence and was named the team's new captain, succeeding Bill Needham.

Still, the roster was not set as the Barons opened the season. Playing with only thirteen men, the Clevelanders went 0-4-1 in the season's first five games.

The local icers got their Christmas presents early when the parent North Stars played Santa Claus and sent the Barons three key players. Coming to Cleveland were defenseman Fred Barrett, right wing Buster Harvey, and goalie Gilles Gilbert. All three had played with Minnesota in the NHL the year before. They were considered the crown jewels of the North Star's system. But after deciding to go with a veteran team for one more year, the Stars decided to send their top trio of youngsters to Cleveland for

Bill Needham was a true iron man during his 15 years with the Barons. Only Fred Glover played more games. A brick wall on the backline, "Silent Sam" was one of the greatest defensemen in the history of the American Hockey League.
Dick Dugan collection.

Gordon Labossiere was the Barons' leader on and off the ice during the 1971-72 season. Here he tries to score against Hershey's Cam Newton as ex-Baron Butch Barber defends.
Cleveland State University archives – photo by Paul Tepley.

one more year of seasoning. Barons' GM Coach John Muckler had a grin from ear to ear.

In Gilbert's first game in goal, Cleveland beat Rochester 4-3 for their first victory of the year. Naturally, Muckler figured his team would take off. But the club took longer to jell than the new coach figured. They went 5-3-4 after their 0-4-1 start but were shaky much of the time. It wasn't until a six-game home stand that the team hit its stride.

A hat trick by Gordon Labossiere in a 7-4 win over Cincinnati started the local icers on to a six-game victory streak. Labossiere, who led the League in scoring while with Quebec in 1966-67, was becoming the offensive key to the team. Considered a step too slow for the NHL, Gordon had as much savvy as any player in the American League. A deft stickhandler and expert playmaker, he made any linemate a better player.

The final game of the streak was a 3-0 blanking of powerful Boston. It was only the third loss in 22 games for the Braves and Gilles Gilbert's first shutout as a Baron. Gilbert had been inconsistent since his arrival in Cleveland and had been sharing the netminding duties with Fern Rivard. However, a mild chastising from Coach Muckler seemed to straighten him out.

The Barons, who were now 11-3-4 in their last 18 games, moved into second place behind Hershey in the West Division. They seemed ready to make their move toward the top. But an unfortunate event occurred. The Barons went on the road.

Cleveland lost three straight games away from the Arena, and it had become apparent that this edition of the Barons was a poor road outfit. Certain members of the team played like tigers at home but became pussycats away from the Arena.

It didn't take long for word to spread around the League that Cleveland could be intimidated on the road. Hit them, and they would not retaliate. They were now 9-1-3 at home, but only 2-9-2 as a visitor. This would be a source of consternation for Coach Muckler all season long. To make matters worse, Gordon Labossiere, the team's leading scorer with 20 goals and 16 assists, was recalled to Minnesota for a month due to injuries on the big club.

The Jekyll-Hyde routine occurred again as soon as the Barons returned home. In a remarkable game, they defeated Cincinnati 6-5. Trailing the Swords 5-3 with less than two minutes to play, Barons' fans headed to the exits. But the Clevelanders shocked everyone, including themselves, by rallying to victory.

The local Blue and White scored three goals in 53 seconds to bring the house down. Gary Geldart scored at 18:22 while Cincinnati was two men short. When Coach Muckler pulled goalie Gilles Gilbert,

Buster Harvey blasted home a shot from the point at 18:44. With the crowd now going crazy, Terry Caffery dug out a puck next to the Barons' net and passed to Dennis Patterson. Dennis didn't hesitate when he spotted a streaking Billy Heindl near the blue line. He fed Heindl a perfect pass, and Billy broke in alone on Sword goalie Rocky Farr. Heindl's shot was true at 19:15, and the Barons had an improbable victory.

The Barons finished out December with a game against Boston at the Arena on the 29th. Playing without Fred Barrett, who broke a rib the game before against Cincinnati, Cleveland and its fans were treated to one of the greatest displays of goaltending ever seen at the Arena.

Gilles Gilbert, who like his teammates was having his troubles on the road, played the game of a lifetime in defeating the Braves 4-1. Gilles seemed to be everywhere as he made an unbelievable 55 saves on his great night. Quick as a cat, the Cleveland netminder continually frustrated the Braves, who constantly broke through a porous Cleveland defense.

Twenty times he stopped Boston shots in the first period. Gilles followed that with 19 second-period saves and 16 in the third. Through it all, the crowd of 5,453 roared its approval. Few, if any, had ever seen an exhibition like that, and they responded with standing ovation after standing ovation. It seemed as if the fans were on their feet more than in their seats.

Gilbert was so busy that he even got into a fight with the Braves' Fred O'Donnell. In the end, Gilles showed why he was considered the best young goalie in hockey.

Cleveland dropped a rare home game on New Years Day to Cincinnati 4-3. The loss was the first at the Arena since the home opener and broke a streak of 17 straight undefeated games on home ice. The team now stood in third place with a 15-14-6 record.

The Barons' spirits were given a boost by the return of Gordon Labossiere from Minnesota. The great center played well for the North Stars but was returned when the Stars' injured players returned.

Labossiere's return came none too soon, since Cleveland then faced a long seven-game road trip. Starting the journey with a pitiful 2-13-2 road record, the Barons played surprisingly well away from home, going 3-4-0 on the trip. They came back to the Arena, where they would play nine of their next ten games, in fourth place with a 19-20-6 record. Fortunately, the West Division was tightly packed; and though they were in fourth place, the Barons stood only six points out of first.

Cleveland was given a boost when it was announced that they had acquired the services of Fred Speck. Fred led the AHL in scoring the previous year with Baltimore on 31 goals and 61 assists for 92 points. Along with the scoring title, the 5'9", 160

pound center was voted "Rookie of the Year" and the League's Most Valuable Player.

After his great season, Speck was drafted by the NHL's Vancouver Canucks. He failed to crack the Canuck's lineup and sat idle on the bench until traded to Minnesota. Fred was nursing a groin injury when the North Stars decided to get him some ice time in Cleveland. Covered with rust from lack of playing time, Fred never did regain his form of the year before. But his arrival coincided with the high point of the Barons' season.

Cleveland went on a tremendous 10-game unbeaten streak. Starting with their 3-2 victory at Richmond on the just-completed road trip, the Barons won eight and tied two games. When they defeated Tidewater 7-1 on February 11th, the local icers moved into a first-place tie with Baltimore.

The Cleveland fans responded in big numbers to the streak. 9,511 turned out for a 6-3 victory over Hershey on February 12th. That game saw Cleveland play as well as they had all season long. They threw their weight around with reckless abandon and checked like a team on a mission. This had been a weakness in the club all year long, getting the players to check all the time. They now seemed to be seriously bearing down, and the recent string of victories was the result.

A super weekday crowd of 8,183 saw the Barons extend their undefeated streak to ten with a 6-1 thrashing of Springfield. Dennis Giannini, benefiting from playing on a line with Gordon Labossiere, scored three goals in the rout. Cleveland was now in first place by one point over Baltimore with a 26-20-8 record.

Unfortunately, stellar defenseman Fred Barrett suffered a shoulder separation in the first period of the Springfield game and would be lost for six weeks. This was the beginning of a near disastrous slide for Cleveland. Starting with a 4-1 loss to Boston that ended their 10-game unbeaten streak, the Barons went 1-4-1 over their next six games. Along the way they lost Terry Caffery for three weeks with a broken cheekbone. The loss of the team's third leading scorer (28 goals, 46 assists, 74 points) couldn't have come at a worse time. Although they were only one point out of first place, the Barons were stumbling, and then faced a long eight-game road trip.

The trip East turned out to be a disaster. Cleveland won only one of the eight games. They slipped to fourth place, although the team was only four points out of first. However, the club was playing terrible hockey. Added to the poor play was the recall of Gilles Gilbert to Minnesota for two weeks. Also, Norm Beaudin suffered a torn rib cartilage in Cincinnati and played in severe pain for the duration of the season. Cleveland was now 2-11-1 in their 14 games since the end of their 10-game unbeaten streak. How the mighty had fallen! Only eight games remained in the season, and the Barons were now in danger of missing the playoffs.

Cleveland came around a bit, winning two of their next three games. When they pounded Baltimore 7-1 behind Buster Harvey's hat trick, the Barons sat in second place. They were four points behind the Clippers; but of most importance, the team was only three points ahead of fifth-place Richmond. The top four teams in each division would make the playoffs.

The Barons were their own worst enemies. They dropped two in a row before tying Richmond 3-3. Cleveland then stood at 30-34-10. They entered the last two games of the season only one point ahead of the Robins in the battle for the last playoff spot. Their backs were against the wall, and they needed two victories at the Arena to assure themselves a spot in the post-season tournament.

Keyed by the return of defenseman Fred Barrett after a six-week layoff, the Barons took care of business against Hershey in a big way. The Bears had a good chance at first place and wanted this game also. But Cleveland was at the top of their game and blasted the Hersheys 8-3. First-period breakaway goals by Buster Harvey and Gordon Labossiere ignited the Barons to their most emotional victory of the season.

And what a big win it was. Richmond also won that evening to prolong the suspense of who would take the last playoff spot. Cleveland played Tidewater the next night at the Arena, while Richmond tangled with Hershey. A Cleveland win or a Robin loss would put the Barons into post-season play.

Fortunately, Cleveland was at home; and at the Arena, the Barons were a powerful force. They were ready to play for all the marbles and dominated play throughout the rough contest.

First-period goals by the Big Two – Gordon Labossiere and Buster Harvey – were sandwiched around a Wing tally by Rick Sentes. Cleveland then increased its lead to 4-1 on second-period scores by Harvey and Billy Heindl.

The Barons were now in complete control and played marvelous defensive hockey in the final frame. Near the end of the game, the Arena scoreboard delivered the message that everyone was waiting to hear: "Final score: Hershey 3 – Richmond 1." The crowd erupted in a joyous celebration as it became official – the Barons were in the playoffs.

Cleveland defeated Tidewater 4-1, but the Barons still finished a disappointing fourth with a 32-34-10 record. From top to bottom, every player on this team knew that they were much better than their record showed. Their road record was a source of embarrassment. The team was determined to atone for its sins against Baltimore in the first round of the playoffs.

Goalie Gilles Gilbert makes a save while Fred Barrett (24) defends. Cleveland State University archives – photo by Paul Tepley.

THE PLAYOFFS

All series in the playoffs were now best-of-seven affairs, and Cleveland appeared to match up well against Baltimore. Although the Clippers did come in first place in the West Division, the Barons held a decisive 5-2-1 advantage during the regular season. Cleveland also had the younger legs, as Baltimore was an aging team. But the Clippers' grizzled veterans, many of them ex-NHL'ers, were a smart bunch. They knew that in the playoffs, the tortoise often beat the hare.

In Game One at Baltimore, the Clippers came out smoking and tried to intimidate the Barons right from the start. Although the roughhouse tactics seemed to be working, it was Cleveland's Dennis Giannini who scored first. But the Clippers kept on hitting every Baron that moved and eventually took a 2-1 first-period lead. It looked like the same old road blues for Cleveland.

However, Baltimore did not count upon the pure magic of Baron netminder Gilles Gilbert. When the Frenchman was hot, no one was better. He repeatedly kept his teammates in the game when the defense broke down. Four times Gilles stopped clear Clipper breakaways. Finally, his teammates got the message that they could win this game and kicked into gear. Second-period goals by Gordon Labossiere and Terry Holbrook put Cleveland on top 3-2 after two frames.

Baltimore really poured on the pressure in the third period and eventually tied the game at 3-3. With the pressure on, Gilbert kept up his magic act, and it paid off. With 7:03 remaining in the game, Labossiere took a beautiful pass from Terry Caffery on a power play and beat goalie Jim Shaw for the game winner.

The Clippers pulled their goalie with 1:23 left in the game and came oh so close to scoring. But Gilbert managed to keep the door shut. Norm Beaudin put the icing on the cake with an empty net goal with 10 seconds left. However, the victory was costly in that tough-luck defenseman Fred Barrett suffered a severe charley horse and then wrenched his knee. He would miss the remainder of the series.

Game Two in Baltimore was really no game at all. It was over almost as soon as it started.

Trailing 1-0 early in the game, the Barons got a break when the Clippers were hit with a five-minute major penalty. Unfortunately, Cleveland managed only two shots on goal for the entire power play and scored no goals. Baltimore could sense that the Barons were flat and skated away with an easy 6-0 win.

Once again, the injury bug hit Cleveland. Roger Cote, who was playing with a partially-slipped disc in his back, took a jarring hit that made him practically immobile. He played only a few shifts the rest of the series.

Hard-working winger Dennis Giannini suffered stretched ligaments in his right knee. While the gritty kid continued to play, he limped noticeably and was severely hampered.

Baltimore played exceptional defensive hockey in Game Three at the Arena and defeated Cleveland 3-1 before 7,848 disappointed fans. The veteran Clippers slowed the game down to a crawl and continually frustrated the usually speedy Barons with their fine positional play.

However, the biggest blow suffered by Cleveland was the loss of captain Wayne Muloin. The veteran rearguard injured his hip while throwing one of his patented hip checks. He also was lost for the remainder of the series. This put Cleveland's top three defensemen on the shelf – Muloin, Roger Cote, and Fred Barrett.

Playing with only three inexperienced backliners – Gary Geldart, Jim McElmury, and Dennis Patterson – the Barons came up with a gutsy performance in Game Four.

4,259 Arena fans saw the Blue and White dig deep down for an inspirational 5-3 victory. The fans saw Norm Beaudin go down for the count when accidentally poked in the eye with a stick. When all appeared lost, it was one of the walking wounded who carried his team.

Dennis Giannini, who could barely skate with his damaged knee, played his heart out. He worked, and he hit, and he scored two goals. The second turned out to be the game winner. The crowd loudly appreciated the courageous effort of their heroes, as the series was then deadlocked at two games apiece.

All of the injuries caught up to the Barons in Game Five at Baltimore. The Clippers jumped all over the undermanned Clevelanders and romped to

Norm Beaudin was a powerful force during the Nick Mileti era.
Cleveland State University archives – photo by Paul Tepley.

a 10-1 victory. It was inevitable that this would happen, since the Barons were simply exhausted.

In Game Six at the Arena, the Barons gave it the old college try, but they were now no match for Baltimore. They gave an all-out effort, but finally succumbed 4-1.

The team had nothing to be ashamed of. With the club wrecked by injuries, it was amazing that the Barons only lost four games to two to the veteran Clippers.

Still, this was a strange squad. Almost unbeatable at the Arena all year long, the Barons were a bitter disappointment on the road. With a little more effort on foreign ice, they could have run away with the West Division. They had no one to blame but themselves for their fourth-place finish.

All in all, it was an exciting year at the old Arena. However, unknown to anyone except the powers that be, negotiations were underway that would make the just-completed hockey campaign the last full season ever played by the Barons in Cleveland, Ohio.

FINAL STANDINGS
1971-72

West	W	L	T	GF	GA	PTS.
Baltimore	34	31	11	240	249	79
Hershey	33	30	13	266	253	79
Cincinnati	30	28	18	252	258	78
Cleveland	32	34	10	269	263	74
Richmond	29	34	13	237	218	71
Tidewater	22	45	9	197	275	53
East	**W**	**L**	**T**	**GF**	**GA**	**PTS.**
Boston	41	21	14	260	191	96
Nova Scotia	41	21	14	274	202	96
Springfield	31	30	15	273	266	77
Providence	28	37	11	250	274	67
Rochester	28	38	10	242	311	66

Top Baron Scorers	G	A	PTS.
Buster Harvey	41	54	95
Terry Caffery	29	59	88
Gordon Labossiere	40	45	85
Norm Beaudin	33	33	66
Grant Erickson	26	34	50
Billy Heindl	22	25	47
Dennis Giannini	28	16	44

Calder Cup Champion – Nova Scotia Voyageurs

1972-73 SEASON

When Nick Mileti purchased the Barons and the Arena just before the start of the 1968-69 season, his fondest dream was to bring big league hockey to Cleveland. When his final bid for an NHL franchise was turned down in June of 1972, Mileti turned his back on the National League.

Soon after this latest disappointment, Nick announced that he had obtained a franchise in the brand new World Hockey Association. The new twelve-team loop was now set to challenge the long established National Hockey League.

An all-out bidding war for players soon developed. WHA owners offered huge sums of money to NHL players whose contracts had expired. The NHL scoffed. They felt that none of their stars would jump to the new league. They soon stopped laughing when superstars such as The Golden Jet Bobby Hull, Derek Sanderson, and Johnny McKenzie bolted to the upstart league. The two leagues soon became bitter rivals.

Although Mileti's Crusaders, as his new team was called, were the last team to join the WHA, they soon made a major impact. Nick pulled out a plum when he signed Boston Bruins' goalie Gerry Cheevers. Cheesy was the NHL's number one goaltender and had just led his Bruin team to the Stanley Cup championship.

Cleveland hockey fans were stunned. They really were getting a major league team, even if it wasn't the NHL. Soon other NHL veterans followed in Cheevers' footsteps: Paul Shmyr, Gerry Pinder, and Garry Jarrett. Veteran minor league stars such as Ron Buchanan, John Hanna, Paul Andrea, and Joe Hardy signed on with the Crusaders. Cleveland fans were even more pleased when ex-Barons Wayne Muloin, Grant Erickson, and Billy Heindl jumped to the new team. Cleveland clearly had a winner.

Nick Mileti boldly declared that Cleveland now would have two hockey teams – the Crusaders and the Barons. He publicly stated his belief that there was enough interest in hockey to support both clubs. But privately, he knew different.

There were only so many sports entertainment dollars to go around. Cleveland now had three winter sports teams. Two were major league – the NBA Cavaliers and the Crusaders. It soon became obvious that the minor league Barons would be lost in the shuffle.

The Crusaders took over all of the choice dates and times originally scheduled for the Barons. 24 Baron games were moved to Saturday and Sunday afternoons. On many occasions, the Crusaders would play the very same evening.

The writing was on the wall for the Barons as soon as the season opened. Crowds were miniscule. On October 15th, a Saturday afternoon, only 240 fans turned out to see the Barons lose to Cincinnati. Even a Saturday night game against Nova Scotia on October 28th drew only 873.

Empty seats say it all during the 1972-73 season. The Barons would soon be heading to Jacksonville Florida.
Cleveland State University archives – photo by Paul Tepley.

The team was doomed. The fans had switched their allegiance to the Crusaders. And who could blame them? The WHA team was "major league," and the AHL, in fact all of the minor leagues had been depleted. The expanded NHL and the WHA had garnered most of the top talent available. The caliber of play in the AHL was at its lowest level ever.

Nick Mileti was in a quandary. It pained his heart to see what had happened to his beloved Barons. As a kid growing up in Cleveland, Nick had been part of the standing room only crowds at the Arena during the 1940's. He bled Blue and White and began negotiating a deal that would put an end to the Barons' misery.

Mileti's dissolution of the Barons would not be easy. He had signed a three-year deal with the Minnesota North Stars to be their development club. Now that the season had started, he could not just disband the team. The players and coach's livlihoods were at stake. He would also face certain legal action if he broke up the team.

All the while, Nick was losing a ton of money operating a hockey club that no one came to watch. The only solution was to move the team as soon as possible to minimize his losses.

Mileti shopped the team around, and on November 6th it was announced that the Barons would move to Lewiston, Maine pending AHL approval. The end to the Barons' nightmare was over. Or was it?

An emergency meeting of the AHL's Board of Governors on November 15th was called to settle the situation. But instead of granting Mileti permission to move his beleaguered franchise, a four-man committee was formed to review the situation. Behind the scenes, the National Hockey League had become involved.

Nick Mileti made a lot of enemies in the NHL when he joined forces with the WHA. In fact, all WHA owners were on the NHL's black list. Boston and New York, in particular, loved seeing Mileti in a financial bind. Nick had lured Gerry Cheevers away from the Bruins. This left a huge hole in the Boston club. He also offered Ranger stars Vic Hadfield, Rod Gilbert, and Brad Park vast sums of money to jump to the Crusaders. This caused New York to pay much more to keep their stars than they originally intended. The NHL wanted to see Mileti bleed.

Using its influence over the AHL, the NHL persuaded the American League Board of Governors to turn down Mileti's bid to move the club to Lewiston. Thus, the Barons continued to swim in red ink in Cleveland.

It was a sad situation. The one time aristocrats of hockey had been reduced to rubble. The once proud and mighty Barons were now the joke of hockey, through no fault of their own. Morale on the team was non-existent, as everyone connected to the club grieved.

Nick Mileti was determined to end the suffering. He finally found a taker for his team in Jacksonville, Florida. Through long and tough negotiations, and many nights of knashing teeth, Nick finally convinced the NHL to let the AHL Board of Governors approve the transfer of the Barons to Jacksonville. One great sigh of relief was heard by all concerned.

The team had come full circle. From the early struggles of the great Harry "Hap" Holmes...through the giddy, glory years under Al Sutphin...the great championship teams of Jim Hendy...the struggles of the 1960's...to a wonderful revival under Nick Mileti. Now the hockey torch in Cleveland had been passed to the Crusaders.

Auld Lang's Syne came for the Barons on February 4, 1973, when they played their last game ever at the Arena, a 5-1 loss to the Richmond Robins. There was no great, fond farewell. Only 435 mourners came to see the passing of a legend, the greatest minor league team in the history of hockey...The Cleveland Barons were no more.

10 Divisional Championships

9 AHL Caulder Cup Champions

EPILOGUE

...How long I sat in the remains of the Cleveland Arena, I don't remember. It may have been minutes; it may have been hours. When I finally got up to leave, I stood and cheered. One final standing ovation for the Cleveland Barons...Thanks for the memories. Then I turned and walked away, for the last time.

The End

Cleveland State University archives –
photo by Timothy Culer.

Cleveland State University archives – photo by Herman Seid.

The following quotes have been taken from the Cleveland Plain Dealer and the Cleveland Press.

CLEVELAND PLAIN DEALER

11-12-37 JOHN DIETRICH – 8,000 Visit Arena for Gala Opener – "fighting heart of Al Sutphin." (Quote by Mayor of Cleveland.)

3-17-42 JOHN DIETRICH – Locking Scores in First Fifteen Seconds – "I am delighted...this undeniably is the greatest thing that ever happened in the game." (Quote by Al Sutphin.)

4-23-51 JOHN DIETRICH – Playoff Title Melon Carved Into 20 Slices: Icers Head Home After Victory Over Hornets – "Thank you from the bottom of my heart and God bless you all." (Quote by Bun Cook.)

7-3-52 JOHN DIETRICH – National League Rejects Barons' Bid For Franchise – "Well, they slapped us down. All I can hope now is that the people of Cleveland will get behind us to prove to the National Hockey League that we are a major league city in every respect." (Quote by Jim Hendy.)

12-19-52 JOHN DIETRICH – Bower Rated by Cook as Greatest Goalie Today – "I've said it before and I'll say it again, that Bower is the best of them all. Bower is every bit as good as Terry Sawchuk of Detroit, and I would pick Bower over Sawchuk." (Quote by Bun Cook.)

4-16-53 CHUCK HEATON – Chrystal Shot "To Gain Time" – "It was the kind of series that almost had to be decided by something like that. So close, and the teams so evenly matched that it took a break to do it." (Quote by Fun Cook.)

3-1-54 JOHN DIETRICH – Barons Loafing? Hendy Isn't Sure – "I don't know what's wrong, but I'm going to try to find out." (Quote by Bun Cook.)

4-11-54 JOHN DIETRICH – Barons Invade Hershey Tomorrow Night – "I believe Francis played his greatest game for us. Several times I was just waiting for the goal light to flash." (Quote by Bun Cook.)

2-25-59 JOHN DIETRICH – Glover Aims at 300-Goal Record at Arena Tomorrow and Saturday – "I never have set myself a target for any particular number of goals in a season. All I want to do is win games." (Quote by Fred Glover.)

1-18-61 JOHN DIETRICH – Ice Chiefs At Hendy Services – "Jim gave me my big break. In 1958, when I was drafted by Toronto, I had decided to quit the game. Jim persuaded me to go ahead and join the Leafs. He said I could make it, so I decided to try. Except for him, I would have retired." (Quote by Johnny Bower.)

1-18-61 JOHN DIETRICH – Ice Chiefs at Hendy Services – "Jim was getting to be something like a father to me. He took me into his complete confidence. He always told me to speak up, and I did, and he always respected my opinion. I can't tell you how much I'll miss him. (Quote by Jackie Gordon.)

CLEVELAND PRESS

1-26-42 CARL SHATTO – Cook Ponders Goalie Shift Wednesday – "The situation requires a lot of thought. I do not propose to make a hasty decision, and there will be nothing definite for another day or so." (Quote by Bill Cook.)

12-16-42 CARL SHATTO – Hergesheimer to Skate With Barons Tonight – "To me there is no place in all hockey quite like Cleveland. To me it will always seem like home. I would be quite content to wind up my career right here. No where else have I received such fine treatment – and often, when things weren't going just right, I thought of my days with the Barons." (Quote by Phil Hergesheimer.)

12-30-42 CARL SHATTO – Hockey Crowd Hits New High – in Arena Lobby – "I should have had at least three goals before I got the first one. I seem to have lost something." (Quote by Phil Hergesheimer.)

1-14-44 FRANKLIN LEWIS – Saga of Man With One Eye in Ice Business – "I used to think about my eye, I'll admit it. But I went to the Eastern Amateur League in the U.S., I began to think differently. Then I got married, and my wife helps me get over any worry I might have about it. Now I just figure that I've had about all the tough luck I'm entitled to...my mind is on other things than my own troubles." (Quote by Tommy Burlington.)

1-14-44 FRANKLIN LEWIS – Saga of Man With One Eye in Ice Business – "I never would have come back for the third period except for Bun. I was in tough shape, but I knew that Bun really wanted to win this game. And with the score tied 2-2, I thought if I could help out any, I should be back on the ice. Believe me, I don't know of anyone else I would have gone back for." (Quote by Tommy Burlington.)

12-1-44 ISI NEWBORN – Failure of Barons to Lead League Now May Be Good Sign – "Cleveland won't win a single game from us. The Cleveland club was at its peak all winter, but is past it now while my team has been coming around gradually and is at its peak form for the playoffs." (Quote by Eddie Shore.)

1-17-45 ISI NEWBORN – Cunningham, the Reformed Firebrand, Gets Hockey Honors at Arena Tonight – "I wouldn't take anything from anybody. If I got a bodycheck, I'd retaliate – and get a penalty." (Quote by Les Cunningham.)

10-9-45 ISI NEWBORN – Abundance of Star Talent Posing Problem for Barons – "We'll be the goingest team in the League, but I don't know how we'll be in the matter of coming back" (Quote by Bun Cook.)

12-22-45 ISI NEWBORN – Defense Star Receives Award for 8-Year Service – "I've slowed up so much this year – I can tell. A defenseman has to skate around a lot these days in hockey. It's not like the earlier years when you must had to stand on the blue line and bop 'em when they came in." (Quote by Dick Adolph.)

3-26-47 ISI NEWBORN – Cook Orders Changes After Barons Sink From Playoffs – "We were beaten by a Hershey team that's coached tough, plays tough, and is tough. Next year...we'll have to get some heavier men – aggressive men." (Quote by Bun Cook.)

4-27-49 FRANKLIN LEWIS – Big League Hockey a Little Closer Now but Not At Hand – "If it weren't for them, I might make a break for the National League. But I think Cleveland's withdrawal would collapse the American League, and I can't let my fellow owners down." (Quote by Al Sutphin.)

11-28-49 ISI NEWBORN – Barons – Are They Good, Lucky or Great? – "I think our present team is almost as good as the other one. Our team of two years ago had more finesse...more experience. There's one thing we haven't found out yet. That club of two years ago was awful tough when the chips were down. There were lots of games in which we had to rally from two or three goals behind. This club hasn't been tested too much in this way...But we'll find out before too long." (Quote by Bobby Carse.)

4-9-50 ISI NEWBORN – Barons Stale, Tired – "Somewhere along the way we lost that finesse." (Quote by Bobby Carse.)

3-7-51 ISI NEWBORN – Barons Coach Aiming at 'Grand Slam' – "You know, I couldn't ever hope to have a better bunch of boys than this team. The morale is wonderful...I can honestly say that I've never heard one word of discord all season." (Quote by Bun Cook.)

4-20-51 ISI NEWBORN – Barons Foiled by Hornets, Get Last Title Shot Tomorrow – "It's impossible to play any worse." (Quote by Fred Thurier.)

7-3-52 FRANKLIN LEWIS – Barons Lose Out on "Strange" Money in NHL Rebuff – "It was moved by Mr. Conn Smythe, Toronto, and seconded by Mr. James Norris Sr., Detroit, and passed unanimously, that Cleveland Arena Inc. be admitted to membership in the National Hockey League upon fulfillment of the following conditions..." (Quote by National Hockey League.)

4-16-53 ISI NEWBORN – "Unseen" Shot Nails Sixth Calder Trophy – "I didn't see it go in." (Quote by Bob Chrystal.)

2-7-55 ISI NEWBORN – Improved Defense Features Barons' Comeback Drive – "We decided that we'd just have to tighten up our defense and play the game closer to the vest...we would have to concentrate a little more on keeping the other fellows from scoring." (Quote by Bun Cook.)

2-17-55 ISI NEWBORN – Barons Get "Mad" and End Slump – "That's all it takes...we just have to get mad at somebody." (Quote by Glen Sonmor.)

3-15-55 ISI NEWBORN – All Pro Hockey Pulling For Glen – "In every rival city we visited on this last trip...Pittsburgh, Springfield, Hershey...players and fans kept coming up to me and asking: 'How's Glen's eye?' I guess everyone knows him as a great guy." (Quote by Bun Cook.)

11-30-55 ISI NEWBORN – Cook Urges Barons to "Settle Down" On Ice – "This team has a lot of courage and is one of the fastest I've ever had. But we've all made mistakes, including myself, and we must learn by them." (Quote by Bun Cook.)

11-1-55 ISI NEWBORN – Barons on Way to Repeat at AHL "Roughhouse" Champs – "We've got some guys who play rough. They don't take any guff from anybody." (Quote by Jim Hendy.)

4-5-56 ISI NEWBORN – 'Twas a Tiny Spark in Pittsburgh That Set the Barons Afire – "There isn't much I can say to you boys. Let's just go out there and keep plugging." (Quote by Bun Cook.)

12-12-56 ISI NEWBORN - Glover Turns "Good Guy" for Barons - "I'm captain this year and I'm trying to set an example for the rest of the team. Don't get me wrong though, I'm not backing off from anything." (Quote by Fred Glover.)

3-26-57 ISI NEWBORN - Bears outclass Barons in Opener - "We were on 'em before they could turn around." (Quote by Bob Solinger.)

3-26-57 ISI NEWBORN - Bears outclass Barons in Opener - "We couldn't play two games in a row like that first one." (Quote by Jackie Gordon.)

3-30-57 ISI NEWBORN - Barons Quote Zeidel: "That'll Teach You" - "That'll teach you to laugh at me." (Quote by Larry Zeidel.)

3-30-57 ISI NEWBORN - Barons Quote Zeidel: "That'll Teach You" "We can't afford to lose our heads because of what one man does." (Quote by Jackie Gordon.)

4-9-57 ISI NEWBORN - Bushed Barons Welcome Rest - "The best thing for us now is a real good rest. This is a tired club." (Quote by Jackie Gordon.)

1-6-58 BILL SCHOLL - Bower Never Too Busy to Learn - "Many players always shoot at the same spot. But the smart ones try to shoot to the opposite side of the catching hand. That's a goalie's weakness. He can't move his right foot as good as his left. The left leg is faster because its always working with the left hand to block shots." (Quote by Johnny Bower.)

12-9-58 ISI NEWBORN - Cops Will Be Ready for Barons and Reds - "Come on Lou...this is no place for you." (Quote by Fred Glover.)

2-11-59 ISI NEWBORN - Gordon Hot Over Slump - "If we don't come out of it tonight, the boom is going to be lowered - and lowered hard. I've gone along so far with this lump, figuring it was a letdown after our January winning streak and lots of injuries. But this has now definitely gone past a letdown. It's still a case of needing to do some skating, checking, and a little hard work." (Quote by Jackie Gordon.)

4-13-59 ISI NEWBORN - Barons Bow in Record Roughhouse - "That was the roughest series I've ever seen." (Quote by Frank Mathers.)

2-8-60 SPECIAL TO THE PRESS FROM BUFFALO - Barons "out to Get" Buffalo Defenseman - "There will be another game with Buffalo. And when there is, I think Glover and the boys will take care of Mr. Mortson." (Quote by Jim Hendy.)

4-4-60 ISI NEWBORN - Barons Hit First Bump Along Playoff Path - "We're not thinking about the length of the series. We've just got to keep plugging along, game by game." (Quote by Steve Kraftcheck.)

1-6-62 ISI NEWBORN - Who's Afraid? Not Barons' Big John! - "Let them try to start something! Guys have tried it before, but that sort of thing just makes me go all the harder." (Quote by John Ferguson.)

1-8-62 SPECIAL TO THE PRESS - Barons' Ferguson Gets Last Laugh - "So just remember to keep your head. The best thing you can do is score a goal." (Quote by Jackie Gordon.)

1-12-62 ISI NEWBORN - Sub Goalie is Key Man in Barons Bid for Top - "I was a little nervous at the start." (Quote by Al Cullen.)

2-22-62 ISI NEWBORN - Barons Go Fishing - Big One Slips Away - "It was a good game, and Les Binkley sure played a helluva big game in the nets for us." (Quote by Jackie Gordon.)

3-15-62 SPECIAL TO THE PRESS - No Place Like Home? Barons Soar on Road - "You can only hope for something like this." (Quote by Jackie Gordon.)

3-26-62 ISI NEWBORN - Biggest Glover Goals - His First and 400th - "The first goal I ever got in the league was what kept me in the league. In that game the puck just came to me and I whirled around without looking. I never saw what happened, but it was my first goal. If I hadn't scored that night, I'd have been sent back to the U.S. League, and all this wouldn't have happened." (Quote by Fred Glover.)

4-8-62 ISI NEWBORN - Barons Hot on Ice: Singing in Showers - "The thing that pleases me most is the spirit of these guys. The way they bounced back after losing that heartbreaker Sunday night...it's hard to bounce back from those kind." (Quote by Jackie Gordon.)

4-19-63 ISI NEWBORN - Barons Bow Out - "It was nothing to be ashamed of." (Quote by Fred Glover.)

11-2-67 BOB SUDYK - Little Fergey Big Enough - Hat Trick Proves It - "It was great, wonderful...Mr. Glover is the greatest; this club's spirit is unbelievable. Me? I was lucky." (Quote by Norm Ferguson.)

3-18-68 JIM BRAHAM - Angry Glover Rips Barons' "Laziness" - "This is not a great hockey club. It never was," Glover said, "but they worked. That's how they got in first place and stayed there so long. Now they don't want to work...Some of them are downright lazy."

4-22-71 DOUG CLARKE - Billy the Kid Brings Down Barons With 4 Goals - "I think they traded me because they thought I was faking those injuries." (Quote by Billy Orban.)

Gulp!
By Lou Darvas

The Cleveland Arena was a complete entertainment facility. Besides Barons hockey, a plethora of events kept the turnstiles clicking. Ice shows, the circus, and Rodeos were always fan favorites.

James Peter Hendy collection.

(top) Opening night at the Arena November 11, 1937. the Ice Follies.
Cleveland State University archives – photo by Herman Seid.

(bottom) The Moondog Coronation Ball.
Cleveland State University archives – photo by Herman Seid.

(top) High school, college, amateur, and professional basketball.
Cleveland State University archives – photo by Tony Tomsic.

(bottom) The Cleveland Cavaliers
Cleveland State University archives – photo by Paul Tepley.

Boxing was always a huge draw.
Cleveland State University archives – top photo by Glen Zahn.

(top) Public Skating
Cleveland State University archives – photo by James Meli.

(bottom) Interior view of the Elysium
Dudley Humphrey Jr. and Marge Kekic collections.

Edward Chvkayne collection.

Larry Smith collection.

Memories

Those warm but fumey bus rides
Thru deep, crisp wintry nights.
The white glow of readied ice
Beneath the dangling lights.

Fans filling seats; tier by tier,
Anticipation grows.
The big moment's near at hand –
Here comes our show of shows!

Then skate 'em in, our pucksters…
Our rock 'em - sock 'em boys;
Big-time lads who deliver
Such goal-bustin' joys.

There's Johnny!, Steve, Fred and Ed –
O'here comes Tommy, too;
Eddie, Bo, Freddie, Jackie…
Then Glen and Ray in blue.

In glides Ike, Gordie, Gus, Jack
And those Bobs we all cheer.
Last but not least, here's our Cal!,
His nineteen bold and clear.

Now we're ready, here we go! –
Coach Cook sends 'em out.
Chills and thrills, they're facing-off
To one roof-lifting shout.

Those were the days, "way back when,"
Down Euclid Avenue.
Arena rafters echoed,
While Calder fever grew.

So, forever in reverie
Of moments long ago,
Our Blastin' Barons charge and score
In memories…cherished so.

William James Hudec

Cleveland State University archives – photo by Paul Tepley.

Promotion banners of events at the Elysium of the 20's and 30's. The Duluth banner was the Western group of the U.S. Amateur Hockey Association. See the 1924-25 Schedule on page 13.
Ed Chukayne collection.

Zamboni preparing the surface ice for the 1953 production of "Holiday on Ice".
Courtesy of Bill Switaj, Jr.
Kent State Ice Arena collection.

Carrie Kirbish collection.

Left to right: Bill Needham, Former Barons Defenseman, with Author Gene Kiczek and James Peter Hendy, Son of former Barons executive, Jim Hendy

Special thanks to Sam Chiancone and Jim Rajcan of Keener Printing, and also to Carmen Loparo, for their last minute help in meeting our deadline.

The Late 40's and Early 50's